PRAISE FOR JESSE FINK'S INTERNATIONAL BESTSELLER
THE YOUNGS: THE BROTHERS WHO BUILT AC/DC

"The best book I've ever read about AC/DC."

— Mark Evans, bass player of AC/DC

"Fabulous. An awesome book."

— Paul Chapman, guitarist of UFO

"I loved *The Youngs*. From the moment I opened it, I could not put it down. I read it straight through . . . it held me hostage. Just an amazing read. I respected the honesty. I also liked the fact that Fink did not take sides and left the recollection and/or interpretation of events open to discussion. Seriously well done."

— Georg Dolivo, lead singer and guitarist of Rhino Bucket

"A fascinating, insightful look at the brothers who changed the face of rock 'n' roll and the politics and business that goes hand in hand with the music we all know and love."

— Jimmy Stafford, guitarist of Train

"I enjoyed *The Youngs* very much. I realised while reading it that I didn't know as much about AC/DC as I thought I did. Fascinating stuff."

— Charlie Starr, lead singer and guitarist of Blackberry Smoke

"*The Youngs* is incredible in that it brings to the table many elements, not only 'the good, positive elements' about our heroes. It also speaks plainly about the alleged and real negatives of individuals and events. In this, for someone like me who adores truth although when potentially painful, it is almost like a thriller. A very intense book."

— Filippo Olivieri, manufacturer of the Schaffer Replica by SoloDallas.com

"A brilliant and fascinating book. From 'inside the van' to saving the world. There's a saying: 'You couldn't write this.' But Fink certainly did."

— Terry Slesser, lead singer of Back Street Crawler

"I loved it."

— Jerry Greenberg, former president of Atlantic Records

"It's extraordinarily well written and presents a fascinating view of the band and the people that helped make it happen . . . a great piece of research and magnificently presented."

— Phil Carson, former senior vice-president of Atlantic Records

"I loved it. Fink did an amazing job."

— Doug Thaler, booking agent of AC/DC's North American tours, 1977–79

"A great job."

— Tony Platt, engineer of *Highway To Hell* and *Back In Black*

"An essential read for fans of the band. Most important, *The Youngs* gives a full portrait of just how significant a role George Young, Malcolm and Angus's older brother, played in AC/DC's development."

— *New Yorker*

"Fink's ability to overcome the Youngs' code of Scottish-Australian omertà is impressive . . . a cut above other AC/DC tomes, and Fink knows it."

— *Classic Rock*

"A largely untold, much more controversial story . . . anything but a hagiography. A fresh, incisive take on the band."

— *MOJO*

"A great narrative . . . a must read. Well written, thoroughly researched and not fawning at all."

— Public Radio International's *The World*

"A fantastic new AC/DC book . . . Fink did a great job. Essential for an AC/DC fan to read."

— Carter Alan, 100.7 WZLX, Massachusetts

"I think Fink accomplished something pretty great here . . . for AC/DC fans this is a must read."

— Rick Deyulio, TK99, New York

"The latest, greatest 'rock read' . . . an awesome book."

— Buck McWilliams, Gater 98.7 FM, Florida

"An astounding — *astounding* — book."

— Bill Meyer, KMED, Oregon

"The best book on AC/DC ever written."

— Dan Rivers, WKBN, Ohio

"Recent books [about AC/DC] . . . didn't offer much to change our perception of the band. Jesse Fink's study of the Young brothers takes a different approach . . . giving us a different version of many stories, especially when it comes to the wheeling and dealing behind the rock. Fink is clearly in love with AC/DC, but he knows the old bird has some warts under her makeup, and doesn't shy away from revelations that cast the Youngs in a less than flattering light."

— *Rolling Stone* (Australia)

"*The Youngs* is a book that peers into the mist, and sees a little more of a story that its principals don't want told. Given its brief, Fink is to be commended on an outstanding effort to help fill the gaps of knowledge . . . [AC/DC] have had a dozen books written on them. This one just may be the best."

— *Music Trust* (Australia)

"Excellent . . . a fresh take on AC/DC filtered through the Scottish clan's lens. Jesse Fink has delivered a fascinating, highly readable, sometimes critical account of the Young brothers and AC/DC that all fans of the band should read. If you want blood . . . you got it."

— AllMusicBooks.com

"This thought-provoking book definitely breaks some new ground. Arrangement by chapters dedicated to specific songs is a satisfying way of telling the AC/DC story while providing music criticism. Scholarly fans will appreciate the bibliography. This one's a must-read for fans."

— *Library Journal*

"Entertaining . . . Fink doesn't pursue biographical detail; instead he provides an appreciation of the brothers' music. Fans of the band will want to get their hands on this. Pronto."

— *Booklist*

"A savvy new book . . . Fink, quite properly, can't stand the kind of music critic who feels pleasing a crowd is a suspect achievement, somehow antithetical to the spirit of rock. In the end, [he] seems to be in two minds about AC/DC. That seems the right number of minds for an adult to be in about them, especially an adult who encountered their best albums during the sweet spot of his youth . . . like all great popular art, [AC/DC's music] slips past the higher faculties. It makes you forget, for three minutes or so, that there's anything else you'd rather hear."

— *Australian*

"An incredible amount of background . . . really a scholarly approach within a genre that is traditionally hagiography."

— Anthony O'Grady, former editor of *Rock Australia Magazine*

"Insightful, original and fascinating."

— *La Prensa* (Argentina)

"Fink's book is a breakthrough."

— UOL.com.br (Brazil)

"Essential reading for fans of AC/DC and rock in general."

— *El Observador* (Uruguay)

"Jesse Fink sets his book apart from countless other AC/DC biographies out there. The work brings together a pile of great stories and testimonials about the band."
— *Folha de S. Paulo* (Brazil)

"I thought Mark Evans's autobiography *Dirty Deeds* couldn't be beaten regarding my favourite band's history. But now — out of the blue — Jesse Fink's *The Youngs* hits the rock biography scene like a massive meteorite."
— *RockTimes* (Germany)

"The best book on AC/DC. Period. I enjoyed the hell out of it."
— Greg Renoff, author of *Van Halen Rising*

"Jesse Fink is an Australian abroad and he writes like one — with wonderful Aussie terms and flavour . . . [a] remarkable achievement of the book, something quite ambitious, is Fink's attempt to intellectually frame the unframeable; the adolescent, primal beauty of AC/DC's music; its origins, its recording, its live presentations, all of it fluffed off by the critics and even the band as something innately incapable of deconstruction or analysing. Yet, he does it. And you are better for the experience, and so are the music and the band."
— *Aquarian Weekly* (USA)

"Fink's look at the band addresses the question that he believes most mainstream rock critics have never been able to answer about AC/DC: 'Why have they endured and resonated with hundreds of millions of people and inculcated such fierce loyalty and outright fanaticism?' The answer is the unrelenting tenacity of the Young brothers . . . fascinating."
— *Publishers Weekly*

"A rich commentary from more than 75 important figures, many of whom give their stories for the first time about the making of AC/DC and the Glasgow-born brothers, Angus, Malcolm and George Young, who built it. An exceptionally well-researched biography, *The Youngs* is a must read for any true AC/DC fan."
— *Press & Journal* (UK)

"Engrossing, refreshing . . . highly recommended for not just AC/DC fans, but any follower of rock music history."
— *Midwest Book Review* (USA)

"This is a book written about the difficult history of a celebrated band that isn't scared to say that certain songs, and albums, are well below par; to debunk certain myths surrounding the band and its members. For that alone it may well be the best book out there about AC/DC. Maybe Mark Evans is right . . . until a band member puts pen to paper in a proper tell-all exposé — they won't — Jesse Fink's work here is the number one go-to book on the subject, warts 'n' all."
— *Uber Rock* (UK)

BON
THE LAST HIGHWAY

The Untold Story of
BON
SCOTT
and
AC/DC's
Back In Black

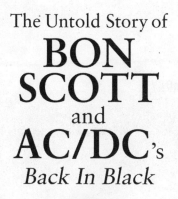

THE LAST HIGHWAY

JESSE FINK

ALSO BY JESSE FINK

SPORT
15 Days in June

AUTOBIOGRAPHY
Laid Bare

MUSIC
The Youngs

MIX
Paper from
responsible sources
FSC® C103567
www.fsc.org

Copyright © Jesse Fink, 2017

Published by ECW Press
665 Gerrard Street East
Toronto, Ontario, Canada, M4M 1Y2
416-694-3348 / info@ecwpress.com

Editor for the press: Michael Holmes
Cover design: Luke Causby/Blue Cork
Cover images: Robert Alford
Author photo: Amy Janowski

LIBRARY AND ARCHIVES CANADA
CATALOGUING IN PUBLICATION

Fink, Jesse, author
Bon : the last highway : the untold
story of Bon Scott and AC/DC's
Back in black / Jesse Fink.

ISBN 978-1-77041-409-9 (softcover)
also issued as: 978-1-77305-112-3 (PDF);
978-1-77305-113-0 (ePUB)

1. Scott, Bon. 2. Rock musicians—
Australia—Biography. 3. AC/DC

(Musical group). 1. Title.

ML420.S424F49 2017   782.42166092
C2017-902395-0

PRINTED AND BOUND IN CANADA

PRINTING: MARQUIS   5   4   3   2   1

For Flavia,
who took a chance while she still had the choice

"If you want to find the secrets of the universe, think in terms of energy, frequency and vibration."

— NIKOLA TESLA

"And do not get drunk with wine, for that is dissipation."

— EPHESIANS 5:18, NEW AMERICAN STANDARD BIBLE

"Rock and roll is not an occupation. It is a disease."

— RICHARD BARRY WOOD, ROAD MANAGER FOR TOMMY BOLIN

"Well you got a choice, alright. Take it!"

— BON SCOTT, VETERANS MEMORIAL AUDITORIUM,
COLUMBUS, OHIO, 10 SEPTEMBER 1978

OPENER

SHOT DOWN
IN FLAMES

It was a hot summer's afternoon, three days before Christmas 2014 in Kings Cross, Sydney, Australia. I'd just left a café with my father, Fred, and a friend of his visiting from Perth, David, whom I'd gifted a copy of my first book about AC/DC, *The Youngs*. As we walked back to our car, David was flicking through the pages of the book. He'd watched a DVD of AC/DC's *Live At River Plate*, the concert film of the band's sold-out 2009 concerts in Buenos Aires, Argentina.

"I've never seen a crowd *move* like that in my life," he said, not realising that we were no more than a couple of hundred metres from the Hampton Court Hotel in Bayswater Road, where in early 1974 AC/DC, only together a few months, had played a short residency to a room of drunks and hookers. Forty years later, there was very little of the original building left, having been turned into residential apartments. AC/DC had come a very long way to be able to fill out football stadiums in South America.

Fred, David and I got in the car and were about to drive off when I noticed a small man

3

approaching. He had brown-grey hair to his shoulders under a Panama hat and was wearing a black T-shirt, black jeans and black sneakers. What was unusual about him was that he was walking arm in arm with a much younger male Pacific Islander, and he seemed to be relatively youthful, not old enough to appear so frail.

I had no doubts at all who was in front of me. I'd finally come face to face with Malcolm Young, the creator of AC/DC. The undisputed hardman of the world's most popular rock 'n' roll band, reduced to walking with a carer. A man who for months hadn't been publicly seen or photographed since an official announcement had been made that he had dementia and wouldn't be coming back. AC/DC had gone on and released their first album in 40 years without him, *Rock Or Bust*. They'd embarked on a world tour that was expected to be their last.

I'd spent years of my life researching and writing about the man known to rock fans around the world by just one name: "Mal." I couldn't get anywhere near him through AC/DC's management or other official and unofficial channels, even though I'd been told by a member of his family that he and his wife, Linda, had read *The Youngs*, and now here I was, buckled up in a Mazda3 with the world's greatest living rhythm guitarist just metres away. Biographer meets subject. A one-in-a-million chance encounter. My mind was racing, and by now Fred and David had twigged who was heading towards us. I simply could have chosen to get out of the car and walk straight up to Malcolm and introduce myself, ambush him, but it didn't feel right. The man was sick. Would he even know who I was or what I was talking about? It was a no-go. So, silently, the three of us just sat in our seats and watched him disappear in the rear-view mirror. It was the closest I ever came to meeting him.

I have been hesitant to write another book featuring AC/DC in which one of the main characters in the story, Malcolm, now has a degenerative condition. I'm cognisant of that, just as I'm cognisant of dredging up things from the past when the man himself can't respond. But had he been in good health, there's no reason to think Malcolm would have cooperated anyway. The Youngs are one of the most private and secretive families in the music business. They have a long history of not telling their stories to biographers, perhaps with good reason.

This, above all else, is a book for a man I've long admired, Bon Scott — not for AC/DC. It's also for people who bought *Back In Black* or heard Bon's apogee "Highway To Hell" over the closing credits of the Hollywood blockbuster *Iron Man 2* and want to know the story of a man whose weaknesses and addictions finally destroyed him. The history of AC/DC, the very existence of the band itself, is anchored in the story of one exceptional but ultimately wasteful man: Bon. Malcolm's dementia doesn't prohibit the writing of that history. As he said himself in Sheffield to a *New Musical Express* reporter in 1978 (a quote even used in the *Bonfire* box set released by AC/DC in honour of Bon), "I'm sick of reading shit. You will print the truth."

Okay, then, Mal. If you want blood, you've got it.

$$\mathbf{\large \textit{f}}$$

The world's collective memory of Bon deserves the restoration of some honesty and truth, not more mythologising. "Official" accounts of AC/DC's history, such as Australian ABC Television's *Blood + Thunder: The Sound of Alberts* (aired on the BBC as *The Easybeats to AC/DC: The Story of Aussie Rock*) or VH1's *Behind the Music: AC/DC*, are designed only to reinforce prevailing myths about him and the band. How can these myths seriously go on being unchallenged when David Krebs, a man whose management company, Leber-Krebs, oversaw AC/DC between 1979 and 1981, the period when they released their most commercially successful albums, doesn't think Brian Johnson wrote the lyrics for *Back In Black*?

As he told me from his home in Malibu, California: "I was really amazed because when I read *The Youngs* I went and looked up the AC/DC discography and, yeah, *Back In Black* is written by the brothers and Brian Johnson. I don't believe that."

There was also an element of personal whimsy involved. I

wanted to take readers back to a time when AC/DC was the most exciting rock 'n' roll band on earth, not what it is today: a corporate brand with only one original member — Angus Young — left standing from the lineup Bon himself knew in the 1970s. I wanted to recreate — in words — a small part of what I regard as the greatest era of rock music: the late '70s, a time that gave rise to the genre we now know as "classic rock." Record stores sold vinyl. MTV didn't exist yet. The internet with its services that would change popular music — YouTube, Pandora, Spotify and iTunes — was decades away. So many of the great bands of the 1970s have either stopped playing music altogether or perform without their original lineups in casinos, wineries or on passenger liners. A special time for music has been lost forever.

To do all this with any effectiveness I had to immerse myself in everything that was available to me. But when it comes to AC/DC, impenetrable to outsiders, a band that strikes fear into the hearts of former members and employees because the Young family remains so rich, intimidating and powerful, information is not easy to come by. A friend of Brian Johnson warned me, "They are all way, *way* past any possible human tolerance on having their words or actions distorted just to sell a story." Another insider told me that the secrecy around the band is "worse than the CIA, worse than the Church of Scientology."

He wasn't kidding.

Says Grahame "Yogi" Harrison, a legendary Australian roadie who worked with AC/DC in Sydney in 1977 and knew Bon socially: "It's not a bad thing you didn't have access to them because you wouldn't know what they were telling was the truth. They cover their arse all the way into the ground."

⚡

Biographers don't have "access" to the band, as I see it, because the truth is uncomfortable for some people. Talking to biographers, people whose job it is to look under the surface of stories to obtain something closely approximating the truth, in effect legitimises whatever they uncover. It's easy to reject a book's conclusions when you can say you didn't cooperate with the author, just as it's easy to predict AC/DC's fans will rally around their heroes when a halo or two has been knocked off.

Inescapably, there are also commercial reasons not to talk. The tell-all autobiographies or "official" biographies of major stars can be sold for millions of dollars to publishing houses in London and New York. Never before have these stories been so in demand, as we have seen with recent multimillion-dollar advances to Phil Collins, Elton John and Bruce Springsteen. Nearly as much money is spent again in marketing. The value of these book projects is diminished, can even be rendered worthless, if these celebrities have already told their story or expounded in detail on a controversial topic elsewhere.

So musicians and their agents are increasingly aware of the value of their words. They are not about to help a stranger — a biographer — when they can profit directly from their reminiscences by releasing a book themselves. Phil Rudd, AC/DC's former drummer, is one band member with plans to write his own book. Provided they aren't bound by non-disclosure agreements (a distinct possibility), Brian Johnson and former bass player Cliff Williams are also prime candidates to release their autobiographies now that they've left the band and its future is uncertain.

Perhaps as a portent of things to come, AC/DC released its first official "photo book" in 2017. Collectors with deeper pockets had the option of buying a leather-and-metal version with a "light up" slipcase. While ghostwriters, hagiographers and vanity publishers thrive, traditional biographers are becoming an endangered species in music writing.

But in any event this book was never intended to come from the point of view of the band or Bon's two brothers and their families. AC/DC has spoken about Bon in the press before. So has Bon's family. We have those views on the record and they aren't about to change.

If anything, *Bon: The Last Highway* benefited from not being beholden to their involvement, oversight and approval. That's because the real story — not the preferred, sanitised, legacy-friendly story — lies somewhere else, well away from the proprietorship of the band, the Scott family and its lawyers. It's a story some people don't want told.

There's a clear reason why so many mooted AC/DC feature films have never seen the light of day. Unless the band can control the narrative, they will never license their music. Nor will you ever read the truth about AC/DC in a magazine or hear it in a radio or TV interview when the band has an album to promote. Specially vetted print journalists, radio announcers and TV presenters play by the rules of the media game, both spoken and unspoken. Angus mumbles his way through another tour interview, giving away very little of substance, and fans, starved of genuine insights, lap it up.

It is actually quite remarkable that the real story of Bon's final years has been concealed for so long. My wish all along with *Bon: The Last Highway* was to write his story without any prejudice or confirmation bias, without pandering to vested interests, and above all else to keep an open mind.

Bon is one of the most adored rock musicians of all time, especially outside Australia where he's arguably more recognised than any other Australian entertainer, living or dead. In 2004, most notably, he placed #1 on *Classic Rock* magazine's "100 Greatest Frontmen of All Time" list, ahead of Queen's Freddie Mercury, The Doors' Jim Morrison and Led Zeppelin's Robert Plant.

But he was not the rock 'n' roll Danny Kaye he's made out to be from the tin figurines and commemorative memorabilia peddled on eBay.

Sydney Morning Herald TV critic Doug Anderson once described him as "a dangerous individual who gave the impression he didn't know who he was or where he belonged," and as early as 1984 the same writer alluded to more than alcohol being involved in his demise: "Bon Scott succumbed to recreational substances."

Anderson was closer to the mark than even he knows. Bon could be unpredictable and destructive. He used drugs, including cocaine, Quaaludes and heroin. If that upsets AC/DC or its management, the band's fans or the Bon Scott Estate, it's unfortunate, but there is compelling evidence for it. It is not treasonous to tell the truth; it is a privilege and responsibility. Writing biography can be unkind to our popular heroes.

Among Bon's friends and acquaintances in Australia, it has also become a kind of bragging right to say that they "knew him best." Yet it is mostly empty rhetoric. *Live Wire: Bon Scott, a Memoir by Three of the People Who Knew Him Best*, Mary Renshaw's book about Bon, is one example. Renshaw met Bon in 1968 and remained friends with him until his death. She claims that her book (published in Australia in 2015 and co-written with Bon's friends John and Gabby D'Arcy) is "a way of remembering the real Bon by the people who knew him best and to clear up a lot of the rubbish out there." Mary may have known Bon but in my view it didn't even come close to either presenting the "real Bon" or debunking the myths of Bon and AC/DC that simply won't go away.

Live Wire glossed over the grubby circumstances of Bon's death. It didn't attempt to answer the perennial question of who really wrote the lyrics for *Back In Black*; in fact it went out of its way to avoid it.[1] In a Scottish media interview, Mary said Bon's missing lyric notebook "may" have been returned to his family but there's no evidence of that happening. Mary has been cast as Bon's lover, soulmate or "ex" in book publicity and even writes that a friend of hers was informed by Bon just before he died, "There were three women in his life that he truly loved: his mother, [his ex-wife] Irene [Thornton] and me."

With all due respect to Mary, I don't believe this is true. Who were the women who really lit a fire under Bon, romantically and sexually? Who inspired the songs he wrote? If, as many suspect, he did contribute lyrics to *Back In Black* then it stands to reason he was writing about real people and real events. If some of the lyrics to "You Shook Me All Night Long" were not Brian's but actually Bon's, which I firmly believe they were, they had to have a backstory.

Who knocked him out with those American thighs?

⚡

In the course of writing *Bon: The Last Highway* I'd meet two of Bon's most significant lovers, both American, both previously unknown: hairdresser Pattee Bishop and photographer/model Holly X (she requested a pseudonym and changes in her personal details for privacy and professional reasons). Bon also had a string of other girlfriends in the United States, some of whose stories have been lost and will likely remain that way. But perhaps most importantly of all, there was his torturous, on-off relationship with Australian woman Margaret "Silver" Smith, a spectral figure in the Bon saga who was to feature prominently in the last 24 hours of his life. Silver died on 12 December 2016. The interviews she granted for this book were her last.

This is the first time the story of all three women has been told. They shared his bed. They knew his secrets. They knew the man as he really was away from the stage and the pressures of the road. There's evidence that Bon even wrote some of his best songs about them.

Silver, who was living an almost hermitic life with her adult son and dogs in Jamestown, South Australia, readily admitted she dealt and used heroin, "but not in today's context . . . the label means something so totally different to what it meant back then.

"I liked [heroin]. I'm not sorry that I took it . . . so long as you're sensible and moderate there's not much harm in doing any of the drugs that were popular back in the day. It's a different story now. I don't know enough about it. Don't want to know about it."

She got arrested by London police a year before Bon died. Her friend Phil Lynott of Thin Lizzy was raided the same day. Silver was charged with possession of and intent to supply heroin, cocaine and hashish (the amounts, however, were small: "Two grams of coke, one of smack and less than a half ounce of hashish"). She pleaded guilty to possession but fought the supply charge all the way to the Crown Court, where she was cleared. This "colourful" background, however, doesn't mean she was responsible for his death. The biggest danger to Bon was Bon himself.

"Bon was not called 'Ronnie Roadtest' because of motorcy-cles," she told me, referring to a recent book that had made this laughable claim. "If someone had broken into a vet or something and didn't know what they had, Bon would find out for them the hard way. I'm just so sick of being portrayed as a junkie who gave Bon smack. It really pisses me off and a lot of other people off. I definitely never gave him heroin at any time, *ever*."

Bon's legend only becomes bigger with each passing year. He has transcended music to become a totem for *living*. In 2016, his 70th birthday was celebrated in Australia as if it were some sort of national event. Yet in 1980 newspapers from Australia to the United Kingdom to Europe to North America didn't deem him significant enough to mention by name in their headlines. "ROCK SINGER FOUND DEAD" in Australia's *Canberra Times* was a typical treatment, away from the front page, just six lines of copy under a story about the United States boycotting the Moscow Olympics. It simply wasn't that big a deal, unlike John Lennon's murder in New York that December.

But Bon's music of that period is as good as anything the decade produced, so why wasn't he recognised at the time for his artistry? The truth is very few critics have ever taken AC/DC that seriously. It took 28 years from Bon's death for the world's most prestigious music magazine, *Rolling Stone*, to put AC/DC on its cover. When *Black Ice* came out in 2008, the magazine's executive editor, Jason Fine, did some digging in their archives and was stunned: "Literally the last story that we did on AC/DC that was of any size was in 1980. We had literally not covered the band at all. We did very few short news stories, and *Rolling Stone* was not the only one. AC/DC was never a band that was really covered a lot by the critics; they were always kind of looked down on."

Which is very true, chiefly by *Rolling Stone* itself. When they were originally released, Bon's best records — *Let There Be Rock*, *Powerage*, *If You Want Blood You've Got It* and *Highway To Hell* — weren't even reviewed in the magazine.[2]

AC/DC's eventual embrace by the mainstream American music

press came far too late for Bon, all of which greatly amused Angus Young: "It's weird, because when he was alive, all people would say about Bon was that he was this creature straight from the gutter; no one would take him seriously. Then after he died all of a sudden he was a great poet. Even he himself would have been laughing at that."[3]

The truth of the matter is that the glory years of 1977–79 forged the legend of Bon and created the platform for AC/DC's breakout success with 1980's *Back In Black*. There could scarcely have been a harder working group in rock, AC/DC playing nearly 450 shows during that time, most of them in the United States.

It was a punishing schedule that would have broken lesser bands. Bon's last two North American tours, running almost consecutively from May to October 1979, were a blur of airport lounges and roadside diners. By the end of that critical year, AC/DC had played three dozen American states and three Canadian provinces. They were so good, so relentless, so full of momentum, other major bands didn't want to play with them. Molly Hatchet was one. Their album *Flirtin' With Disaster* had just been released.

"There were 10 shows lined up for us and AC/DC," said late lead singer Danny Joe Brown. "They had more albums out, but we were selling hotter at the time. We were trying to decide who would open and close the show. We decided that we would open one night, and they would open the other. We were playing in Knoxville, Tennessee [sic],[4] and AC/DC got out there, and *damn*, people were ripping their shirts off. The show was half over and you could see everybody was singing every damn word to every song they sang onstage. And I said, 'Goddamn, we're going to sing "Gator Country" to these mothers.' It was unreal. I went to the telephone and I called our manager, and said, 'Never put these fuckin' *dogs* on us again.' Needless to say, we opened the rest of the tour. That was the only band that ever kicked Hatchet in the ass, and they sure did."

Those three years touring North America also provided ample material for Bon's songwriting. It was during this time that the band got crucial traction on American and Canadian radio and became a headline band in their own right on the U.S. touring circuit. They played huge arena concerts with bands that were already or would go on to be some of the biggest acts in the world: Aerosmith, Journey, Van Halen, Kiss. But Bon wanted more from his life, personally and musically. He was creatively frustrated. He became depressed. He struggled with alcohol dependency and drug use. He was in serious conflict with Malcolm Young. He suffered from back pain, his liver was in a poor state and he was asthmatic, though Pattee Bishop says today, "I never saw him use an inhaler." Silver said he occasionally used one after smoking.

Bon described his daily routine with AC/DC as "day-in, day-out, fly, drive, hotel-in, hotel-out," but for all its challenges, he was altogether happy with the path he'd chosen.

"It's sometimes a drag, being in a different hotel every night but it's not as bad as being stuck in front of a lathe every day of your life for 50 years. I am here and I am free and I'm seeing new faces every night and touching new bodies or whatever. It's great; there's nothing like it."

Effectively, though, he'd only swap one lathe for another: rock 'n' roll. Bon cut through a lot of the attendant boredom of travelling with writing and called the precious notebook he carried with him a "book of words, all my poetry."

He told Australian TV personality Ian "Molly" Meldrum: "I've got pages of stuff, and out of it might come, you know, three or four good ideas for songs."

What happened to Bon's notebook or notebooks after his death? Were any of the contents — titles, lines, verses, choruses — used on *Back In Black*? As much as Angus, Malcolm and their bandmates have tried to bat away these questions, what answers they deign to provide have been contradictory and unconvincing. Some of the songs on *Back In Black* sound so much like Bon had written or part-written them ("You Shook Me All Night Long," "Back In Black," "Hells Bells," "Have A Drink On Me," "Rock And Roll Ain't Noise Pollution" prime among them) that the conspiracy theory — that Bon did in fact contribute lyrics to the album only to go completely uncredited — actually isn't far-fetched at all.

Bon had mentioned to the band's former bass player Mark Evans during a visit to Australia just before he died that he wanted to record a solo album of Southern rock–style music. Southern rock, a unique musical hybrid of guitar-based rock, blues and country, was very popular when Bon first arrived in North America and a number of Southern rock bands spent time on the road with AC/DC.

His fondness for the genre and the American South was obvious from the Confederate Battle Flag belt buckle he wore virtually everywhere during 1979, the letters LYNYRD SKYNYRD in place of the 13 stars representing the states of the Confederacy. But as far as we know, Bon didn't even get to raise the issue of his mooted Southern rock album with Malcolm, let alone actually go ahead and make preparations for it.

I spoke to several musicians from or individuals connected to the most famous Southern rock bands of the 1970s — Lynyrd Skynyrd, .38 Special, Outlaws, Blackfoot and more — but conflicting evidence emerged, indicating Bon had not gone ahead and made any concrete plans to record the album.[5]

Silver confirmed that he'd talked to her about a solo project, though only in vague terms, and nothing specifically about Southern rock. Making it with AC/DC was his true priority.

"He knew [AC/DC] was his last shot; it was either he did this or it was never going to happen. He would have liked to have done [a solo record], because he had a really good voice. He loved singers. We both had a passion for really good singers . . . we both liked the same sort of stuff.

"It was one of his hopes that at some stage, he knew it wouldn't be any time soon, not with [AC/DC's] schedule, he would be able to do a solo album. The Southern rock thing, I think that's someone else's idea of what he liked but I think it would have been quite varied: the styles, the type of songs. He liked everyone from Hank Williams to Sam Cooke and a lot of women singers that aren't particularly famous."

But Holly X says otherwise: "Bon loved all things Southern and Western: cowboys, the Wild West. My mom was a real Southern belle from Georgia and he seemed to enjoy this fact. I remember making him laugh by talking to him once in a while with a heavy Southern drawl. Given the obvious tension between Bon and Malcolm, I wouldn't be surprised if this were his Plan B in case Malcolm fired him from the band due to his excessive alcohol use."

⚡

Bon's immortal words in "Rock 'N' Roll Damnation" — *Take a chance while you still got the choice* — are a prescription for living to millions of people. Yet the manner of his demise wasn't heroic or tragic, the cliché of all clichés. It was *telegraphed*. His death had been coming for years, as those tours in North America made obvious to anyone who was around him. Why didn't his bandmates and the band's management help him? Why wasn't he stopped from destroying himself? Was alcohol an antidote to the pressures of life on the road, or was it more? Was it AC/DC itself, and the personalities inside it, that were wrecking him?

Back In Black, the biggest selling hard-rock album of all time, was much more than a "tribute" to Bon. It couldn't have existed without Bon, irrespective of whether his lyrics appeared on the album. Statements made by members of the band that they were contemplating throwing in the towel when Bon died should also be treated as highly questionable. It's a narrative that has benefited AC/DC greatly and is so pervasive, so embedded in the psyche of the music media and the band's fans, no one dares think otherwise.

When Bon's successor, Brian Johnson, was sensationally "kicked to the kerb" by AC/DC in 2016 after 36 years of service, the band issuing a press release thanking Brian "for his contributions and dedication to the band throughout the years" like he'd just been made redundant at a motor plant, the near-universal reaction of fans was sheer amazement and contemptuous disapproval. How could anyone be so callous? Malcolm's brothers — Angus and older brother George, who has always played a key role behind the scenes — had lost their minds.

Brian's explanation that his hearing was so damaged that he couldn't continue playing live still didn't explain why he was shunted aside so quickly: the same day he was given the prognosis by his doctor, AC/DC issued a press release saying that a "guest vocalist" would be replacing Johnson. The Youngs weren't going to wait around for him to get better and cancel the remainder of the world tour.[6] Before he died, Bon too had been in their cross-hairs. What really mattered to the Young family was making it, and making money, with or without Bon.

For all his undoubted talent, Bon blew it. Yet despite his abundant character flaws, it was his basic decency — demonstrated in the gestures he made to people (letters, postcards, gifts), the connection he had with fans, the memories they have of his surprising gentleness — that was the hallmark of his humanity and why his story is so resonant, even today. What makes it all the more heart-breaking is that he went far too early and in circumstances that have never been properly explained.

Says Larry Van Kriedt, AC/DC's first bass player and a childhood friend of the Youngs: "The old 'rock star choking on his own vomit' thing just defaults him into a category that he maybe didn't deserve."

$$\frac{\displaystyle\unicode{x21af}}{}$$

The late Vince Lovegrove told Australian writer Clinton Walker for his 1994 biography, *Highway to Hell*, that Bon, his old friend and bandmate in 1960s bubblegum pop band The Valentines, "always seemed troubled by something, whether it was his creative desire as opposed to feelings of inadequacy due to his working-class origins, or lack of education, I don't know. But there was some sort of conflict there, where he was unsure of himself. He had a lot of bravado, but really he was a softie underneath."

Years later, Lovegrove was asked by AC/DC fan Dr. Volker Janssen: "What is your opinion of Clinton Walker's book?"

"I think it is an honest attempt by a fan to capture in words the real Bon Scott by portraying his personality as opined by his friends," he answered. "I think [Walker] captures the essence of a part of Bon, the good part which attracted everyone to him, but fails on the darker side."

It's this darker side that I was interested in. While I am an admirer of what Walker attempted in his book about Bon — written well before the age of Google, when every fact could be rigorously checked; valiantly put together in the face of stiff resistance from AC/DC and its longtime Australian record label, Albert Productions or Alberts — I came to realise through my own investigation that many of his statements and conclusions about the man were wrong.

Silver Smith told me she regarded her involvement in Walker's book as a "mistake . . . I have read a lot of crap and after Clinton Walker's first effort I realised that people are more interested in mythology than truth."

Mary Renshaw has claimed Bon's brother Graeme Scott "threw it in the rubbish bin." Which, to be fair to Walker, could be either a good or bad thing. Pleasing a subject's family is not a prerequisite for writing a good biography. In any case, Walker's book was far superior to Renshaw's. He deserves great credit for producing the first true biography of Bon.

So *Highway to Hell* is not the definitive story of the man by any means, nor are any of the other books written about Bon and AC/DC. I make no claim that *Bon: The Last Highway* is definitive either; but I believe it tells a brand new story that is closer to the truth than anything previously published.

⚡

Certainly not nearly enough has been written about the final three years of Bon's life, when he was fronting what would become the mightiest rock band in the world. Most of that time was spent in North America.

There have also been plenty of people who knew Bon personally who have written books and abundantly told their Bon stories, from bandmates to managers to ex-wives and friends. Then there are those individuals who have been interviewed substantially in books by other biographers or appeared in documentaries. These existing stories have been told and recycled so many times that they have contributed to the elaborate construction of the anointed Bon narrative — the myth — most of us are already well familiar with.

Where I have felt the need to quote these sources, I have done so largely from existing books or press interviews. I have also drawn on my own interview archives for unpublished comments about Bon and unearthed previously unknown audio interviews with the man himself, as well as conducted hundreds of new interviews. Many of the interviewees were musicians who went on the road in North America with AC/DC between 1977 and 1979.

This book focuses only on the last 32 months of Bon's life, principally his experiences in America and his last hours in London. This is a book about giving those who haven't told their stories a platform to tell the world, and much of it is built around the reminiscences of a group of people who lived in Miami, Florida, in the late 1970s, as well as an alcoholic cowboy from Austin, Texas, who befriended Bon on the eve of AC/DC's first gig in the United States.

Importantly, it is also based on the accounts of members of AC/DC, past and present. Although, just like every serious AC/DC biographer before me, I was denied personal access to the current lineup of the band, and with the subject of this book — Bon — dead for nearly 40 years, I was able to piece together a mosaic of Bon from deep within long-forgotten books, newspapers, magazines, TV shows and radio programs. This hidden story has been under our noses all along. As much as they might be potentially embarrassed by what comes out on these pages, the members of AC/DC cannot back away from words they uttered themselves.

Over the years I have also been privileged to speak with or have contact with a number of former members of AC/DC. I am very grateful to them and people currently within the

AC/DC camp who have communicated with me on or off the record. I fully appreciate that it is not a simple thing to "break ranks" with this band, even when you're no longer in it. They have been brave to do so.

The band member most likely to open up in a meaningful way for this book, Phil Rudd, initially agreed to an interview then at the last minute withdrew without explanation. I could sense his anxiety.

"I don't like to tell tales about Bon," he told me from his home in New Zealand. "He was a great guy. I've been advised not to make any comment on anything. Good luck with your book and hopefully I'll read it. Cheers, mate. Thanks for your call. You alright? You all good?"

"Sorry, you've been advised not to talk to me?"

"Yeah, yeah, that's right, *yeah*."

But even his own legal counsel didn't know who was advising Phil, then in the midst of well-publicised personal and legal troubles, not to speak. Was he panicking about saying something out of line that would affect his chances of ever returning? AC/DC's *omertà* was still in effect, even when the man in question had been ruthlessly cast aside.

As some consolation, though, he'd heard about my work: "Send me a copy of *The Youngs* book that you wrote. That looks quite interesting. I'll give it a read."

But what I came to learn about Bon is that away from the stage even his own band was peripheral to his story.

"Bon wasn't close to the rest of AC/DC," says Pattee Bishop. "He didn't hang with them. He always just wanted to leave after the show. I knew it was because of how much he drank. They didn't like it. He would tell me they had meetings about him. They cut him out of rehearsals when they were pissed. Their roadie would fill Bon's drink and put water in it. He felt left out. It hurt him."

Silver Smith agreed: "They were just quite happy to have him off their hands when he was with me."

Angus Young, of course, saw it differently: "We were on the road for 10 or 11 months every year, and the rest of the time we were in the studio recording the next album. We were all close to Bon."

He also gave an intriguing insight into how AC/DC regards biographers: with contempt and suspicion bordering on paranoia.

"Over the years, there have been numerous people asking us to write things but, the thing is, they go in and they are not looking for an impartial story. They're looking for a bit of dirt to dig up. It's the *Sun* angle. The last one I heard was that Bon Scott was poisoned, there was a conspiracy, and the government was involved. I take them with a pinch of salt. There's a lot of books out there — people had the opportunity to find out stuff and they never bothered. They just talked to people that weren't even there. Instead of going to the horse they would go to the stable, and would talk to the person who made a cup of tea or something.

"I'll sit and talk to any fan that asks me a question. I'll talk to them, but when somebody comes and says, 'I've been paid X number of dollars, I don't know you, I don't even like you, and I'm here to do a story!' — I just don't wanna know it. I've had the same with journalists who come from newspapers like that. All they want to hear me do is trip up, or Brian or any of the guys, they just wanna trip you up on what you say. If they can edit it and make an even uglier thing out of it, you know they will."

But this is both a convenient get-out card and a falsehood. Writing a biography and having a sense of decency or a conscience aren't mutually exclusive. In fact, I was told things about some members of AC/DC that I simply could not bring myself to publish. I knew this book would have an impact on some individuals, living and dead. And what's there to trip up on? A story the band hasn't got straight, like how *Back In Black* came to be?

Plenty of biographers, like myself, have gone to the horse: the Young family. But they have been turned away. Just like I was by AC/DC's record company, Sony. AC/DC's personal publicist at their management firm didn't respond to my request for an interview. Brian's and Cliff's attorney George Fearon similarly did not reply. A number of other former employees associated with AC/DC predictably closed ranks, one citing Malcolm Young's dementia as reason not to talk. Many who did eventually speak said very little and wouldn't agree to follow-up interviews. It is an almost total cone of silence.

"I will always remember that you were the one that uncovered the real truth," said an individual who was filmed for Alberts' vomitous documentary about the rise of AC/DC, *Blood + Thunder*. "I felt as though Alberts was blocking your access to certain members of AC/DC; just a feeling . . . one of them stated that you would never get an interview with the band. I don't remember the exact phrase but that was the general gist of the conversation. They seemed to be proud of that."

But such aversion to scrutiny only encourages a biographer to work harder. I knew the story the Youngs didn't want told about Bon was out there, waiting to be found.

The focus of *Bon: The Last Highway* is unapologetically on Bon's North American experience because this is the blank part of his biography. It's the most difficult part to tell but the most significant of all. The road to Bon's death began in the United States and to this day so many questions remain unanswered. I cannot answer them all but this is my best attempt to do so in the face of some formidable obstacles.

"You'd need several volumes just to chronicle what Bon got up to in one day," Angus once said. "As for my story, well, if it's going to be told, give *me* the money and I'll write it."

He's more than welcome to do it. In the meantime, I'm going to do my best to tell Bon's. This book took three years to write. The real story of his final years and death is revealed here and speaks for itself.

— *Jesse Fink*

PART ONE
1977

CHAPTER I

GO DOWN

Four days before AC/DC arrived in Texas, Barry Manilow had a #1 hit with the dreary ballad "Looks Like We Made It." How this must have irked Bon Scott, who'd only just touched down for the first time in the United States, a place he'd dreamt about since his early teens. Two years later, on *Highway To Hell*, his final album with AC/DC, he wryly referenced Manilow in the song "Get It Hot" as if it were some kind of blessed relief.

Nobody's playing Manilow.

There was no escaping disco, either. The hottest track in New York and Los Angeles was "I Found Love (Now That I Found You)" by Love And Kisses. Andy Gibb was about to supplant Manilow for three consecutive weeks with "I Just Want To Be Your Everything." In rock, "Barracuda" by Heart, Ram Jam's "Black Betty" and Steve Miller Band's cover of Paul Pena's "Jet Airliner" were fighting a losing battle against a relentless glitter-ball onslaught.

The challenge facing AC/DC (including their new English bass player, Cliff Williams) was not insignificant; it was the challenge facing any new rock 'n' roll band in North America. To make money, the name of the game was touring — and Kiss and Led Zeppelin were the unassailable market leaders. The latter had played to 80,000 people at the Pontiac Silverdome in Michigan in April. Zeppelin's 24 July performance at the Day On The Green in Oakland, California, would be their last North American concert.

But Bon was no Robert Plant in front of tens of thousands of screaming girls in a stadium. He and his band were about to commence what would become a remarkable North American journey in front of 1500 stoned university students and cowboys at an armoury turned hothouse music barn called the Armadillo World Headquarters in Austin.

They were there because a couple of San Antonio disc jockeys, Lou Roney and the late Joe "The Godfather" Anthony, hated Manilow as much as AC/DC did. Their station, KMAC/KISS, was one of the first album-oriented rock (AOR) radio stations in the United States. KMAC/KISS played everything from Ted Nugent, Rush and Bob Dylan to Southern rock, Taj Mahal and BB King. Anthony and Roney would tell local promoters which rock acts to bring to San Antonio and would eventually end up being promoters themselves. One of the acts they suggested to local promoter Jack Orbin was AC/DC.

The Australian band needed the help. Their first North American album, *High Voltage*, a compilation of tracks from their first two home releases, had tanked, getting significant airplay only on regional stations in Florida and California. In the press, AC/DC was getting panned everywhere from *Rolling Stone* in New York to Kansas newspaper *Lawrence Journal-World*, which chose *High Voltage* as its "Worst Album" of the year: "These ugly punk Aussies make Johnny Rotten look like Perry Como."[7] In Texas, though, they didn't care what the rest of the country thought about AC/DC.

"In the beginning we never got much attention from the national record companies in the States," says Roney. "We were just a broken down old funky radio station, so we never got any music from 'em. We started doing imports. Joe or myself would go and buy imports from all over the world. He happened to pick up *High Voltage* and he brought it in, and we all looked at it and listened to it, and I said, 'Joe, this music is *really* a killer, man.' Of course, nobody had ever heard of AC/DC at that time. Joe did not want to play it too much. But I did. I put it on. And all of a sudden calls started coming in."

KMAC/KISS "started word of mouth," according to Malcolm Young: "When we came to the States in '77, they told us the timing was wrong for our style of music. It was the time of soul, disco, John Travolta, that type of stuff. There were, I think, five radio stations in the country that were playing rock at the time without the noise and smell about it. When we went down [to the Armadillo] for a soundcheck in the afternoon, there was a bunch of guys in there just sweeping up the building, they were all singing 'TNT,' and we thought, 'How do those guys know this song?'"

They knew it because Roney, enthusiastically, and Anthony, somewhat begrudgingly, were playing AC/DC's albums.

⚡

In 1977, Roy Leonard Allen Jr. was a thickset, long-haired, pot-smoking 21-year-old student at Austin Community College. He'd grown up in Rockdale, Milam County, northeast of Austin, where his father, World War II veteran Roy Leonard Allen Sr., worked as an attorney and a judge in the Justice of the Peace Court. His great-grandfather, Robert, was a soldier in the Texas Cavalry of the Confederate States in the Civil War. His background was respectably middle class but Roy's behaviour was not. He was always in trouble.

"In order to tell this story, I have to tell some of *my* story," he tells me in a thick Central Texas drawl. Roy has a friendly, open, lined face — not dissimilar to Tommy Lee Jones — and a courteous manner that belies his hellraising past. Today he lives in Leander, a suburb north of Austin, where he works as a real-estate broker. "I've forgotten more than I remember, but this is what I do remember."

It was 26 July 1977 and Roy was out of school for the summer, hanging out at a bar called The Back Room on East Riverside Drive. The Back Room was just two miles from the Armadillo World Headquarters, not far from the Colorado River that runs through the middle of Austin. It opened in 1973 and shut down in 2006. It was *the* rock bar in town.

"No windows. Pool tables, foosball, full bar, good jukebox. It always seemed to be dark in there and it had a really good air conditioner. I was alone, just a handful of people in the bar, when about the middle of the afternoon, these three guys walked in; I could tell they were not from anywhere in Texas from the way they talked. They were kind of joking around, laughing. Looked like some pretty cool guys; they really stuck out.

"When they ordered their drinks I hollered at the bartender to put their drinks on my tab — my dad's credit card for school — and they were like, 'Thanks man, we just got to town.' They said they were from Australia and had a rock 'n' roll band and were the opening show at Armadillo World Headquarters the next night. It was Malcolm and Angus Young and another guy, maybe the drummer, Phil. One thing led to another and we ended up going to their hotel room. I had a little weed and everybody got high back then."

Angus was drinking alcohol and smoking pot?

"Yes, I'm sure they all ordered a beer or a drink. I think I would have remembered if one of them didn't. Drinking was the norm. We all got high; really, it was no big deal. Angus was more of a pot smoker than drinker, if I remember right; he liked to get high before a show. Next thing I remember is sitting in the hotel room; it was Bon's room. That's when I first met him. He looked like a regular-type guy of the times except he had a lot of tattoos. I asked them how they came up with the name AC/DC. I told Malcolm, 'Around here we used that term to mean someone who swings both ways. I'm not sure how people might take it.' They all kind of laughed it off. They had to tell me what 'the jack' was.

"I was there for a decent amount of time. I was trying to get them to go with me to Pedernales River before the show the next night; it was not far out of town. I wanted to show off a little of Texas and hang out with these guys more; they were really different. Everybody was getting along very well and really having fun; there was a genuine friendship for each other that showed. Anyway, they couldn't go because they had something they had to do or didn't feel like going, but Bon told them he wanted to go with me. I promised I could have him back at whatever time they said."

Pedernales River was about an hour and a half out of town.

"So I picked up Bon the next day before noon. I knocked on his door and he let me in. He told me to call down and order us a couple of gin and tonics. I picked up the phone and ordered four double G&Ts. I looked back at him to see if he was okay and he had this giant smile. I believe it was at that moment we each knew we had found a new friend.

"Soon, I came to realise that Bon drank like me. I didn't know many people like that. It was like some kind of weird bond we shared and is probably one of the main reasons we became friends. We eventually rode out there and met some friends. We all had a fun day drinking beer and diving off the cliffs. We made it to the Armadillo with about 15 minutes to spare but Bon was not late."[8]

⚡

A refuge for Texas's rock-loving hippies, the Armadillo World Headquarters had had its heyday in the early 1970s playing host to Willie Nelson, Waylon Jennings, Freddie King, Van Morrison, The Grateful Dead, Sir Douglas Quintet, Roy Orbison, Augie Meyers and Doug Sahm, among hundreds of other acts. But it had hit hard times. Its financial difficulties were considerable; in fact there were bankruptcy fears, which was why it was making money in other ways than live music alone. The venue boasted, according to its advertising, a "Concert Hall, Game Room, Beer Garden, T-Shirt Store" and "The Armadillo Kitchen: Home of the World Famous Nachos, Giant Cookies and Armadillo Daily Bread."

Headlining over AC/DC was Canada's Moxy, a Joe Anthony

favourite that had come up through the ranks opening for Nazareth, Styx, Santana, Ritchie Blackmore and Leslie West. They were also big in Texas: in 1976, Moxy was the most requested band on KMAC/KISS. According to American music magazine *Circus*, "When they played Texas they broke previous attendance records set by such heavies as Rush, Thin Lizzy and Foreigner."

So the crowd was there to see Moxy, *not* AC/DC. Anthony had made the 80-mile drive from San Antonio, while a stoned 18-year-old Moxy fan called Wade Smith had come from Rockdale with friends Alan Juergens, Bill Martin and Bubba Greensage. Their ride home was Roy Allen, the younger brother of Waylon, Wade's best friend. But at the venue Wade couldn't find Roy. Instead, in the beer garden, he got talking with his hero, Moxy's lead singer, Buzz Shearman, who was milling about waiting for the Australian support act to start.

"There I was, starstruck, staring at *the* lead singer of Moxy," says Wade. "Out of my mouth came the absolute worst thing you could ever say to a frontman of a hard-rock band: 'So, who is your back-up band tonight?'"

Initially, the question was met with dead silence. Wade was expecting Buzz to walk off.

"They're called AC/DC. This is our first gig with them on this tour. I don't really know much about 'em."

"What do they play?"

"I don't really know. I heard they're good, but I also heard they are a little punk."

"Oh, *no*. Not *punk*."

Earl Johnson, Moxy's guitarist, had been at the soundcheck watching AC/DC.

"I swear to God it was about 98 degrees in that place that night. It was an oven. We were pitching full pails of water on people in the front row; it was that hot that you had salt burning in your eyes from the sweat — it was crazy, *crazy* hot."

Wade, Alan, Bill and Bubba, meanwhile, had planted their elbows on the right side of the stage to get the best possible viewing position.

"I'll never forget seeing AC/DC walk out when getting announced onstage," says Wade. "All anyone saw was this little, short, skinny guitar player, who not only had his guitar around his neck, but had a little satchel. He had a blue suede schoolboy uniform on, with white socks, a little silly-looking cap, and a thin striped tie.[9] We had never seen anything like it; lead guitarists were always macho.

"The stagehand kept coming out onstage to pull up Angus's shorts. Whenever Angus would do a guitar solo his shorts would start falling down. But whatever we were hearing, this new sound worked. It sounded great. I turned to Alan, and yelled, 'I LIKE PUNK ROCK!'"

But it was Bon who impressed Wade the most.

"He exuded confidence and had control of the audience. His jeans were so tight, along with the navy-blue muscle shirt he was wearing; it looked as if he were poured into them. The more songs they played, the louder the crowd got, and the more everyone was into this new sound. I just remember thinking, 'How do they make the guitars sound so good?' I didn't want them to stop playing. I had come all the way to see Moxy, but I didn't want Moxy to come onstage yet. I couldn't get enough of this new band. Neither could the crowd."

Malcolm recalled feeling the positive energy, too.

"We played our first gig in front of a bunch of cowboys, but they really dug it. They saw Angus in his suit, and I think, after they saw him play like he does, it gave us an edge."

It was then that Wade spotted the missing Roy, who was sitting at the back of the stage on a five-gallon bucket.

"He was my ride home, and I hadn't seen him all night, and now he was *backstage*? I tried to get his attention, and finally did. We were pointing to him, motioning that we wanted to come backstage. He kept flipping us off, mouthing to us, 'Fuck no, you little bastards.'"

When AC/DC finished their set, Roy came out the front to talk. Wade didn't hesitate.

"How can we get backstage?"

"I don't know if I can pull that off. You're going to have to find your own ride home tonight."

"But you're our ride. Why can't you take us?"

"I can't. Bon and I are going to an after-concert party at the hotel."

Roy had already begun walking to the backstage area when Wade yelled after him.

"Hey! Who's *Bon*?"

⚡

The mood backstage was triumphant. Even Joe Anthony was hanging out with the band, smoking a joint and swigging beers.

"AC/DC nailed it and the crowd was wild," says Roy. "Very few bands I'd seen play at the Armadillo produced such energy. Springsteen comes to mind or Skynyrd maybe; the same type of electricity in the air. Everybody was like, 'Who the hell were those guys?' I remember thinking along with everybody else that I sure would hate to be the band to have followed AC/DC. The band was on a natural high."

In the beer garden, by the main entrance, Bon was being mobbed.

"It was so cool, all these people coming up to Bon for an autograph. He would sign it and then some of them would give me the eye, like, 'Who *is* this guy? If he's with *him*, he's got to be somebody,' so I got to sign a few autographs too."

Eventually Bon and Roy left the Armadillo and walked out to Roy's car, a silver 1968 Oldsmobile Toronado.

"Bon insisted on driving. I was cool with that as I already had two DWIs and we were not that drunk but neither of us would have done well on a sobriety test."

Bon turned to Roy as they were pulling out from the parking lot.

"You got to give us one thing, Roy," he said, flashing him a big smile. "We know how to rock and roll."

Bon started driving to the Holiday Inn, where the band was staying, but his driving was making Roy anxious: "It took a few blocks for me to realise something was wrong; nobody could drive that bad."

When the pair got to the I-35, they had to cross the interstate bridge and turn left.

"Bon, you've got to stay *right* till you turn left."

"I got it, Roy. Not to worry. I always wanted to drive like this."

They burst out laughing. The West Australian and Texan would go on to become the unlikeliest of friends.

"Lenn and Bon had a long-lasting friendship," says Wade, who calls Roy by his middle name. "Whenever AC/DC would come anywhere close to Texas, Bon would always call Lenn and invite him to come join them wherever they were. Lenn actually ended up making a lasting close friendship with Bon, as whenever Bon got down, he would always find time to call Lenn and talk. Lenn took it very hard when Bon died."

Roy spoke to Bon on the phone just before his death and was told something extraordinary. The Armadillo World Headquarters, meanwhile, would shut down on New Year's Eve, 1980, and never reopen.

⚡

Having lost their ride because of Bon, Wade and his pals got back to Rockdale by hitching a lift. So impressed by what he'd seen at the Armadillo, Wade returned to Austin the next day to search for AC/DC albums, finding only one: an import of *Dirty Deeds Done Dirt Cheap*.

"My first AC/DC album," he says. "I bought every album they made with Bon as singer. Honestly I haven't bought a single AC/DC album after Bon died. I like the music better in the Bon days. I like the guitar sound of the band better in the old days. All my favourite AC/DC songs are from this era. And I think Malcolm is actually the sound of the band. Such a unique guitar sound."

Two days later, he was playing golf with Waylon Allen. Wade noticed Waylon was wearing something he'd found in his brother's Toronado: a navy blue T-shirt.

"Hey, that's the shirt the lead singer of AC/DC was wearing a few nights ago."

Waylon looked at him for a moment, like he had no idea who or what he was talking about, then teed off.

CHAPTER 2

BAD BOY
BOOGIE

On 28 July 1977, as he would many times until getting sober, Roy Allen woke up with a cracking hangover. Only this day was different: he woke up in the hotel room of the lead singer of AC/DC.

"I left with Bon still sleeping. He and I were both alcoholics. It's a sickness, a progressive sickness, somewhat predictable. Therefore, I can make certain assumptions about how Bon was doing when he got so bad off with the drinking. Neither of us were full-blown alcoholics in '77 but we both became that way before the end. Bon just a little sooner than me. Looking back, we were both in a downward spiral but could not see it, or more likely, didn't care. It was just how we lived: for the day, the moment."

Don't worry about tomorrow. This, AC/DC fans are told, was how Bon had lived every day of his short life and it is the emotional fuel behind the cult of the man and the foundation for the outlaw spirit that he has come to embody after his death. It's also a sentiment found in the lyrics to a song reputedly about Bon on *Back In Black*, "Have A Drink On Me," but the credit goes to Young/Young/Johnson. In Roy, a true Texas tearaway, Bon had found a kindred spirit whose history of offending more than matched his own.

"We shared parts of our past," says Roy. "Bon and I had an almost immediate connection on a level that's hard to describe."

⚡

Roy's adolescence had been one long struggle with alcohol that started even before his bipolar 41-year-old mother, Ella Joyce Allen, suicided in June 1971. At 14, he'd begun sneaking sips from a bottle of whisky that was kept above the Allens' refrigerator. When Joyce, as she was known, drew a line on the bottle to mark the level, Roy cut the liquor with iced tea to disguise how much he was drinking. The following year she took her own life at the intersection of Wilcox and Murray Avenue in Rockdale.

"She went and got her hair done, then drove to the gun store, went in and told the owner that it was my birthday — it wasn't — and she wanted to buy me a .38 special for my birthday present. She drove a few blocks and shot herself in the right temple while sitting at a stop sign."

The official cause of death — "gunshot wound" — was ruled accidental on her death certificate. Roy's eldest brother, Carl, a diagnosed schizophrenic, also killed himself a year later, walking in front of a car at 31st and Texas Avenue in Bryan, east of Rockdale. He was 22. This time it was called suicide, Carl succumbing to "multiple trauma about [the] cranial area due to being struck by a moving vehicle."

Two violent deaths in the Allen family within the space of a year — both by their own hand — turned Roy into a wayward, unbalanced and rebellious teenager. Soon, the serious alcohol abuse began, causing him "to get arrested on a regular basis." He became a fixture in the *Rockdale Reporter*'s "Police Report" column. He began shooting methamphetamine. Then, just after midnight on 12 May 1976, Roy got into a drag race on southside Route 79 outside Milano, a town nine miles east of Rockdale.

"I was leaving a beer joint called Nat's Place with my best friend, James Lightsey. I had been drinking beer but I was not really drunk. We were in my 1965 Mustang and as we pulled out of the parking lot to go home, I saw another Mustang that had just pulled onto the highway ahead of us. If it had been any other make of car I probably would not have done what I did.

"On that highway was a long straight stretch of maybe a couple of miles. We raced there, passing each other a few times, then the road went up a hill and made a curve to the right. I was ahead when we got to the curve and I pulled over to the shoulder to let the driver go by. I figured I had won and was done racing since we were getting to a curvy part of the highway and I had slowed down. But the other driver had not.

"I remember him pulling up beside me, flying by, when all of a sudden his car went airborne and started to flip over and over. The car flipped on the uphill part of the road. I turned around and went to where the car had landed on the embankment of the railroad right-of-way, lying upside down, headlights on, pointing up in the air with the wheels still spinning."

A Texas Highway Patrolman, tailing the two speeding vehicles, had watched it all unfold and arrived immediately at the crash scene about two and a half miles east of Rockdale.

"As I pulled up to the wreck the patrolman pulled in at the same time. James and I got out and we were standing by the wrecked car. The patrolman ran up to me and poked my chest and told me the best thing I ever did was to come back to the scene and not try to run away. That thought had never crossed my mind. He told us to start looking for bodies as the car was empty."

Roy spotted the bodies of the driver and his passenger. They'd been flung clear of the wreck. The driver was lying on the embankment near the railroad tracks, the passenger nearby. When Roy got to the driver, he recognised him instantly: it was his 18-year-old friend from Rockdale, Lynn Lankford.

"The very first cigarette I ever smoked was with Lynn when I was 15 and I had known him my whole life. He was lying with his head upwards on the bank. He looked beat up and I could hear gurgling sounds coming out of his chest. I told the patrolman we needed to turn him the other way so his lungs could clear and not fill up due to the way he was lying. He told me very firmly not to touch him."

Lankford was announced dead on arrival at 12:45 a.m. at Richards Memorial Hospital, Rockdale. The official cause of death was "multiple injuries from car wreck." Roy's father signed the death certificate. Roy and James didn't blow over the legal limit and weren't blamed for the crash but because there was a fatality, Roy spent the night in the county lock-up. He was bailed the next morning and no charges were laid. Lankford's passenger, badly injured in the crash, survived. To this day Roy is still haunted by the face of his dying friend.

"I have always felt that if I hadn't started the race, the tragic event would have never happened. In that regard I am responsible and have to live with knowing that."

One of the problems, then, with living your life by the *Don't worry about tomorrow* creed is that by then you can find yourself gurgling blood and dying on the side of a highway, like Lynn Lankford. Bon worried about tomorrow as much as anyone else. He worried about his place in AC/DC, his finances, his relationships, how other people saw him. He'd finalised his divorce from his first wife, Irene, after a separation that lasted nearly as long as their marriage, only a few months before he met Roy. These are the concerns and struggles we all experience and Bon was not unique. What remains a mystery is why he found the idea of being sober so intolerable that he needed to be regularly out of it to get through the night. His new friend Roy clearly had his reasons. What were Bon's?

Silver Smith said he never told her why he drank so heavily.

"He started very early on. He'd go for stretches without drinking at all. He knew it was killing him. Even when he was touring in those late '70s years there were a couple of quite long stretches where Bon went without drinking; a couple of months here and there. But when I first caught up with him in '76, he was drinking a bottle of Scotch a day."

It was a masochistic streak that defied rational explanation and drinking was always at the centre of his troubles. Silver described it as his "destructive side, whereby he would do something absolutely inexplicable, and could really cause major and sometimes long-term problems for whomever he was with. I would say, 'But why the *fuck* did you do that? Why would *anyone* do that?' and he would say he didn't know. I still to this day can't decide whether he knew what he was doing, or whether he was a mystery unto himself."

⚡

By the time AC/DC arrived in San Antonio for the second concert of the band's first American tour, "the people were crazy, I don't know what else to tell you," laughs Lou Roney. Over 6000 people turned up to the Municipal Auditorium and there were plenty of groupies waiting for both bands backstage.

Earl Johnson was impressed by Moxy's opening act: "I sat there and watched the whole set. I just remember saying, 'These guys are going to fucking be big,' because they were like a machine. Everybody just locked into the groove between band and the audience." It was, he says, like the "best of" the Stones and Zeppelin. "You've got this very steady basic Stones kinda beat with all these Zeppelinish kind of riffs on top."

Only in Dallas did he get to acquaint himself more intimately with Bon. Moxy and AC/DC were booked into the same hotel for the first time, and after the show Bon was worse for wear on booze and pills.

"The room that I was in became party room that night, and I was not a real big drinker. Everybody got a little crazy in those days. I wanted to go to bed at about two o'clock in the morning and Bon was asleep on my bed. I just remember trying to wake him up. He wouldn't wake up. I picked him up and put him over my shoulder and I took him down the hall and I knocked on the door and I gave him to either Angus or Malcolm. When I was taking Bon down the hall he was trying to take a swing at me, it was pretty funny, and he could hardly move. He wouldn't have been able to hit a giraffe, he was so out of it. We were dropping everything, man. Quaaludes, some white stuff that was around. The Colombians used to fly low-level planes into Texas and drop the shit in bales. They'd come in at about 8000 feet underneath radar. Now they send submarines up the coast [*laughs*]."

Quaaludes, known on the street as "downers" or "soapers," were the drug of choice in the 1970s rock scene in the United States. Martin Scorsese vividly depicts just how incredible they were in an extended sequence in his film *The Wolf of Wall Street*. Bon mentions them himself in a morose 1978 letter from the road to his ex-wife Irene, two days from the end of AC/DC's tour: "I've dropped a Quaalude."

That he was doing them with alcohol — a highly dangerous combination — so early in AC/DC's tour of America was a sign of how cavalier Bon was with his own health and a portent of the trouble to come.

But the band had reason to celebrate. Within three days of their Austin debut, AC/DC had been added to a clutch of stations around the country: WCOL Columbus, KJSW Seattle, KADI St. Louis, WQDR Raleigh, KZEW Dallas, WNOE New Orleans, KTIM San Rafael, KLBJ Austin, WENE Binghamton, KPRI San Diego, WYDD Pittsburgh, WROQ Charlotte, KDF 103 Nashville, WIYY Baltimore, WNEW New York and WLIR Long Island. *Let There Be Rock* was a *Billboard* "Breakouts" album in the Southwest and Midwest.

On 31 July *Let There Be Rock* got a stellar review in the *Los Angeles Times*, saying it was a marked improvement on *High Voltage*, praising its "Slade/Nazareth-like frenzied power" and marking it as "one of this year's best manic-energy entries."

It had been a successful few days' work.

⚡

From Texas the band went to Florida for three dates in Jacksonville, West Palm Beach and Hollywood. In Jacksonville, near the state line with Georgia, the locals had already switched on to AC/DC thanks to the pioneering airplay of Bill Bartlett at WPDQ/WAIV and the backing of one of rock's most notorious hustlers, Sidney Drashin, whose Jet Set Enterprises dominated the Florida concert scene in the 1970s like the Medellin cartel did the Florida coke trade.

"Bon Scott was probably one of the top-five lead singers in the world for what he did for his genre," he says from his condo at Ponte Vedra Beach outside Jacksonville. "He really *moved* them. Also AC/DC's stage show was something no one had ever seen. They ran around that stadium like firefly ants. They lit it all up. AC/DC invoked *craziness* into the audience. They were magic."

North of Miami at the Sportatorium on West Hollywood Boulevard in Hollywood, AC/DC was second on the bill for a WSHE 103.5 benefit show called "Day for the Kids." The opening act was a local rock band, Tight Squeeze, most notable for its bass player being the late Teddy Rooney, the son of actor Mickey Rooney and actress Martha Vickers. Michael Fazzolare, the 250-pound Italian-American lead singer of a Miami punk-rock four-piece called Critical Mass, was in the audience and awestruck at seeing his favourite band for the first time. He wasn't to know then how close he'd soon become to his hero, Bon.

"It was packed — a typical Sportatorium crowd. We went because we wanted to see AC/DC. We loved their stuff. They were playing 'The Jack' and Bon goes, 'What do you call VD over here?' So someone told him, 'the clap,' and he's singing 'The Clap' instead but he's clapping his hands, and everybody is like, 'She's got the [*claps his hands*].' This band, they were from Mars. And they kicked ass, that's the funny thing about it. It just went nuts."

After the show, the band returned to their hotel where Bon was introduced to Pattee Bishop, a striking Irish-Jewish hairdresser who in her prime would have given nothing away to stars of the day Alana Hamilton, Loni Anderson or Farrah Fawcett-Majors. She was long-legged with fine features and a bright smile, tanned, big haired, big boobed and *blonde*. Bon drew a bead on hot women — and he loved blondes with money.

Today Pattee lives in Venice, California, where she's married to a "Malibu rich dude — they only care about the next wave" — and manages a portfolio of seaside rental properties. She's well aware of the power she held over men.

"It was Cliff [Williams] I went out with first. I thought he was the cute one. But he smoked pot and I couldn't stand the smell. We had our time together. He went on and was with my Chicago best friend Candy Pedroza."

Bon would become Pattee's lover, on and off, until the end of 1979. She knew not all was right with him, even from the beginning.

"Bon was a lonely guy. His hands were so rough, like a worker's hands. He was an old man before his time. It broke my heart when he died alone."

In Manhattan's Upper East Side, in his luxury apartment right by Central Park, Foreigner's lead guitarist and main songwriter, Mick Jones, greets me in a dressing gown à la The Dude. His personal assistant brings me water. We're sitting on his sofa and the French Open tennis is muted on the TV. Various awards and photographs of a well-lived life decorate the room. What looks like a Les Paul Custom electric guitar lies on its stand in a corner.

Jones is one of the legendary figures of the music business, having worked with Eric Clapton, Van Halen and George Harrison outside his own music projects, but I'm here to get a handle on what it's like to be an alcoholic playing in a rock 'n' roll band. There are a lot of similarities and synchronicities between Mick Jones and Bon Scott, despite the obvious differences in what they did onstage and the kind of music they played.

Both Jones and Bon had served time in other bands well before they hit the big time with Foreigner and AC/DC, respectively. Both were alcoholics and drug users. Both were signed to

CHAPTER 3

WHOLE LOTTA ROSIE

the same record company — Atlantic Records — and the biggest albums of their careers, Foreigner's 4 and AC/DC's *Highway To Hell*, were produced by Robert John "Mutt" Lange. Jones is managed by the man who signed AC/DC, Phil Carson. He's also a friend of Brian Johnson. And the week of our meeting, at a glitzy gala in Manhattan, he'd received an honorary award from Caron, a nonprofit addiction treatment centre.

But unlike Bon, Jones is still around to enjoy the fruits of his career. The two men met in Kansas City, Missouri, on 10 August 1977, when UFO and AC/DC supported Foreigner at Memorial Hall. AC/DC had just come from a fairly disastrous gig at Mississippi Nights in St. Louis, where the band and Carson, who's a big man, had got into a brawl with bouncers.

So AC/DC weren't in the friendliest frame of mind when they arrived in Kansas City, especially so because Foreigner was achieving everything AC/DC was not. They'd had an instant smash with their debut self-titled LP and the single "Feels Like The First Time." A print ad put out by Atlantic for the album contained press quotes that were so good they could have been written by Atlantic's PR department: "They have the makings of the next supergroup," their music was a "compelling language" and "leaves the audience screaming for more."

"We got [support] pretty much nationwide, really," says Jones. "It was just an unbelievably magical time: just the timing, maybe it was Atlantic Records. We started to sell records like nobody had ever done before at Atlantic. Where did it say that this new band out of basically *nowhere* was going to end up that year selling four million albums? The only other artist that had done that on Atlantic was Iron Butterfly. *Nobody*, including the Stones, Zeppelin, Genesis, Yes. We had the whole company supporting us. The only other bands [doing well] were Boston, Eagles, Fleetwood Mac. Aerosmith weren't selling in the '70s so much."

AC/DC's hostility to Foreigner was palpable.

"It was a pretty full-on attack. But I guess I'd had experience over the years before and I was really busy trying to teach the rest of the guys in the band how to handle it. At the end of the day it gave us more resolve to play harder and more intense and get up for it."

So the competition was good for the music?

"Yeah, and I think it was probably good for AC/DC too. They were pushing; we were sort of on the defensive a bit, but I don't think you would have gotten that [motivation] necessarily from the crowd. Plus Klenfner and Kalodner pushing everybody in the company."

Michael Klenfner, who headed up Atlantic's marketing and promotion, had gone down to AC/DC's first few gigs in Florida with his right-hand man, Perry Cooper. In April 1977 both had defected from Arista Records to Atlantic, where Klenfner had been head of FM radio promotion. John Kalodner was an A&R executive at Atlantic.

"AC/DC had a great rapport with Klenfner and Cooper. They had just joined Atlantic. They kind of took aim at [Foreigner] a bit. We were different bands. We were sort of a fairly hard-rock band but not as heavy and maybe as hard as AC/DC. We had perhaps more of a varied audience, although a lot of it was rock at the beginning. I think what happened was Kalodner on our side and Klenfner [on AC/DC's] got into this sort of 'Who's gonna do best?' competition, almost."

Jones remembers it as a period when the "social and musical influences were huge" and the music itself had real emotional resonance.

"We fought very hard in those days how to tell a story in 10 lines of six words a line, how to basically deliver a message over that short writing space," he says. "People were still doing that. People are doing it now, of course, but I think there was just a little more concentration on melody back then too, and things that would stay with you."

Bon's drinking was obvious to everyone around him, even in 1977. You're an alcoholic, what do you think motivated it?

"I think there's that feeling that you don't want to be *apart*; you wanna be doing what your peers are kind of doing. 'Is that the reason they come up with these fucking great ideas, 'cause they get blasted on grass?' And to me at that time it was pretty much grass and liquor. It covered up a lot of inhibitions. It made me instantly the heart and soul of the party. It's a slippery kinda slope, as they call it. I was able to cope with it for a number of years and then there came a point when it overtook me, as it has done to a tremendous amount of people in this business. The only saving grace was that I survived through it."

Do you think Bon had a chance of doing anything differently or it was the path he was on?

"At the time, probably not. Because there was no admitting you were a junkie or a drug addict or a drunk. Those weren't things you admitted publicly or openly in those days. The openness about it didn't start until later on in the '80s. I mean pretty much everybody knew that Kurt Cobain had some problems. The social stigma [meant that] it was not cool for a rock musician to admit [you have a problem]. You're supposed to be able to cope with that shit and that's supposed to fuel your music, all the way going back to the blues. Admitting stuff like that was a sign of weakness more than anything.

"I have to admit that I'm still, although I don't like to necessarily call myself that, an alcoholic and I'm still a drug addict. I'm one drink away from destruction. One drug away. If I had a drink tonight by the end of next week I'd be swigging litre bottles of fucking vodka, you know, I'd be in a mess and I'd be in a bar telling a fucking barman all about my life and achievements [*laughs*], you know what I mean? And then somebody would have to fucking carry me home. Then, little by little, I'd lose everything that I'd gained from putting 15 years into my recovery.[10]

"So it's a daily challenge. You don't have to sort of promise or make any plan to be doing this for the rest of your life, because that's too scary, so you take it that famous one day at a time. Which is a daily commitment, a re-upping of your desire and your choice to remain sober and drug free and in recovery. There's only recovery; there's not a cure yet. These places that claim to cure people of drinking; it's bullshit, absolute bullshit. The alcoholic is always just at the mercy of that one drink."

At the time of AC/DC's gigs with Foreigner, UFO was having its own issues with alcohol and drug abuse. Lead guitarist Michael Schenker, who was battling chronic alcoholism, had been replaced by Paul Chapman. But Bon's drinking was on a whole other level to Schenker.

"Bon was a law unto himself," says UFO guitarist and keyboardist Paul Raymond. "Angus would refer jokingly to Bon's exploits: 'Yeah, Bon's been drunk three times today. He was drunk when he woke up, he was drunk again on the plane, had a lie down and now he's drunk again in the dressing room.' It was all said in fun, to make us laugh. UFO were pretty heavy drinkers ourselves, but we thought Bon was young enough to take it.

"We didn't think of it as a problem, and Bon always sang really great. He did his own thing and, as far as I am aware, nobody was trying to manage him or saw it as a particular problem. But with the benefit of hindsight his drinking was very heavy and bourbon was his drink of preference. He once told me he used the drum riser to support the back of his legs to help him stand up. Bon was a really friendly guy — but it always revolved around drink. 'Coming to the bar, *mate?*' The drinks would just keep coming."

Chapman says he can remember "Bon actually doing coke in America" and that no amount of alcohol could put him down.

"Bon had a huge tolerance and a massive propensity for alcohol. Bon could drink a lot. I have the nickname 'Tonka' and I can drink a lot but Bon would walk all over me. He was always up and ready. A lot of times on tour, [Bon would say] 'C'mon, Tonk, let's *go!*' And I'd be like, '*What?* You're out of your mind. It's four o'clock in the morning.'"

On 13 August 1977, the same day the band played The Agora in Columbus, *Let There Be Rock* entered the *Billboard* charts at

#154, three weeks after its release on Atlantic's ATCO Records label. But after shows in Madison and Milwaukee, along with a Foreigner reunion in Dayton and Indianapolis (where AC/DC was paid a paltry $250), it dropped to #183. The album briefly recovered, getting as high as #161 in early September, but by mid October had dropped off the charts altogether. They'd hardly made a dent. To put *Let There Be Rock*'s failure in some perspective, Fleetwood Mac's *Rumours* had sold six million copies by the same month, having only been released that February. It took 13 years for *Let There Be Rock* to sell a million.

After starting its maiden U.S. tour so positively, AC/DC's American mission had faltered.

CHAPTER 4

PROBLEM CHILD

The most important man at Atlantic Records, if not "the most important figure in the record industry of the 20th century," as London's *Independent* would put it in his obituary in 2006, turned up in New York's Bowery district to see AC/DC. But Ahmet Ertegun wasn't so taken with the band: "I'm not sure I would have signed them when I first heard them. They were very modern; they were pushing the envelope."

The evening's entertainment, however, was more significant for another reason: Angus Young's maiden use of a wireless transmitter called the Schaffer-Vega Diversity System (SVDS), an invention that would change what AC/DC could do in concert and open up all kinds of new possibilities for the band's staging. Its inventor was another livewire eccentric, Ken Schaffer, who had been approached by Angus through WEA, Atlantic's parent company, and arranged to meet AC/DC's lead guitarist in his dressing room at The Palladium, the first of AC/DC's two shows that night. At the old Academy of Music movie theatre on East 14th Street, AC/DC would get up onstage for its first New York concert on a shared bill with Michael Stanley Band and The Dictators.

Having the wireless (a radio-like device sending signals to the amplifier) on the guitar strap didn't cut it for AC/DC's lead guitarist.

"I remember Angus's guitar wound up at my shop with a note or a phone call, I don't remember, a *plea*, 'Can you put the wireless *in* it?'" says Schaffer. "I'd thought about it a lot of times but I'd never done it. I was afraid of cutting holes in the back of a guy's guitar [*laughs*]. I had a couple of guys working for me who were more proficient as luthiers, so we cut a hole or we took off a plate, I don't even freaking remember, and we fit the transmitter into it and closed it up and I think the way we closed it up wasn't exactly professional; it was maybe [*laughs*] gaffer tape or something."

British rock journalist Phil Sutcliffe painted quite the picture of what transpired: "Leaving the rest of the band with the amp back at the theatre, Angus set off down the street and walked eight blocks before he turned round. The band said the [wireless transmitter] signal hadn't deteriorated at all despite the concrete towers and the taxi and public service radios in the area."

"It was amazing to see," said Bon. "Angus had this Cheshire cat grin all over his face, and evil thoughts seemed to be going through his brain as to what havoc he could wreak with this evil little invention."

Meanwhile, a seemingly innocuous photo opportunity at The Palladium with two promo girls that evening would be anything but for Bon. Holly X, a full-figured 17-year-old blonde, and her friend Gigi Fredy, both from Miami, turned up in T-shirts with "AC" on one (Holly in black) and "DC" on the other (Gigi in white). Angus and Bon posed with them for photographer Chuck Pulin. In the very first photograph taken of the future couple, Bon was smitten with Holly, goofing off.

"Bon was never one to hide his emotions," she says. "I had no idea who AC/DC was back then and had never even heard one of their songs. I just remember thinking how little Bon was. I was about six feet tall in my high-heeled shoes so I literally towered over him. We started laughing. And we just laughed a lot together. That was our relationship."

⚡

The Dictators would end up touring over half a dozen cities in America with AC/DC, from Tennessee in the Southeast to Nebraska in the Midwest. Rhythm guitarist Scott Kempner got to see the extent of Bon's drinking up close.

"AC/DC were much bigger drinkers than we were. I was never much of a drinker at all, and they liked to partake. One day, I was sitting in a hospitality room, and I hear this commotion outside the door. Some banging, some groaning, and then the door swings open and it's Bon. He looked *bad*. Like a failed attempt at resurrection. I was alarmed. I had seen him drunk but not like this. And this was *before* the show. Turned out he wasn't drunk. Turned out he had been drunk the night before. I asked him, 'Jesus, Bon, are you alright?' He replied: 'Oh, *mate*, I am not feeling me best. I woke up this morning at the bottom of a flight of stairs.'

"In real life, he was, at least in my experience, a real sweetheart of a guy: quiet, even a bit shy, and gracious. He loved his fun, but he seemed to me to be someone who was brought up knowing what really matters, and what is bullshit. Bon was polite, courteous. He would ask around the room to see if anyone else needed anything if he was going to the hospitality room for a beer or something for himself. It was like the wildness, the rowdiness, was something he saved for the stage and the show.

"Not that he was faking anything; just that he left it all on the stage, and offstage he was not a lunatic, but rather a sweet, smart person who was good company, had good manners. That is something you usually get from your parents and home life. Of course, he also had a bad drinking problem, which I am sure brought out that wilder side."

Angus Young once argued that Bon "kept a balance. He could go somewhere and a demon would surface and he would be away, and then he'd be there and he'd be working. He never missed a show. There were a lot of times where people would be on tenter-hooks, going, 'Is this guy going to show?' And a couple of minutes before we were supposed to go on, the door would fly open and in he would walk and hit the stage. He was always dependable getting on the stage."

Or was he? Angus would concede in another interview: "I think in his whole career there's maybe only three shows [Bon] ever missed and that was 'cause his voice wasn't there and we really didn't want him to sing."

It was a rare slip-up from the Youngs in an otherwise water-tight story and an insight into the difficulties they were soon to have with Bon.

CHAPTER 5

DOG EAT DOG

Record sales might have been sluggish, but four weeks after playing live in Austin, AC/DC was going strong on radio in its regional strongholds of Columbus, Jacksonville and Fort Lauderdale. Along with new music from Crosby Stills & Nash, James Taylor and The Alan Parsons Project, *Let There Be Rock* was a "Top Request/ Airplay" in the Southeast.

John Rockwell in the *New York Times*, however, didn't think Bon was up to the task: "The band is tight but the singer is undistinguished."

Bon must have been rattled by the very public slight from one of America's most powerful newspapers, but he wasn't showing it. At 8401 Sunset Boulevard in Los Angeles he took a room at the Continental Hyatt House, aka the "Riot House," with Pattee Bishop. Hyatt House is now the Andaz West Hollywood. In the 1970s it was a notorious hangout for The Who and Led Zeppelin. The Whisky a Go Go, where AC/DC was booked to play three shows from 29 to 31 August 1977, two sets a night, was a mile away along Sunset.

Rock journalist Sylvie Simmons, who was at the hotel, has written of Bon walking around with a "Page Three–type blonde" and "his arm wrapped around a buxom blonde. A bottle of bourbon in one hand, his companion's large breast in the other." It was Pattee, who had two rooms at the hotel, one for her and Bon, the other for her friend Candy, Cliff's squeeze. Ken Schaffer had also flown in from New York with a microphone version of the Schaffer-Vega Diversity System for Bon. Mick Jagger had a unit, and Bon wanted one too.

Yet like the critics in New York, the *Los Angeles Times'* Richard Cromelin wasn't swayed by the lead singer: "Bon Scott has a sturdy, steel-wool voice, but he wavers between effective stylings reminiscent of Streetwalker's renowned Roger Chapman and utterly unlistenable wailing that unfortunately brings Slade's Noddy Holder to mind. If AC-DC had a couple of songs of the calibre of Slade's best pop-rock, the show would take off, but its original material is mired in trite, basic rock patterns, tired macho attitudes and lack of instrumental virtuosity."

The indifference, sometimes disdain, of FM radio and major metropolitan press to AC/DC and specifically Bon in New York and Los Angeles meant it was becoming a serious concern, culminating in Atlantic formulating plans to record the band live and send out promo LPs to radio stations.

AC/DC also needed some new songs if they were to stand any hope of being invited to tour the United States again. They must have read the L.A. reviews because at their second show at San Francisco's Old Waldorf at 444 Battery Street the band performed two songs that would appear on the 1978 album *Powerage*, "Up To My Neck In You" and "Kicked In The Teeth." The tour was proving a boon to Bon's songwriting, going by what ended up on that landmark album. He would never write anything better.

But it was the final show of the *Let There Be Rock* summer tour that would be most critical. It was in front of AC/DC's toughest audience yet, the sort of people who had the power to make or break their entire career: hundreds of record executives who'd flown down to Miami for the 1977 Warner-Elektra-Atlantic National Sales Meeting.

The WEA convention was the first national sales powwow of its kind and held at the Diplomat Hotel in Hollywood, Florida, from 5 to 11 September 1977. It had been a very good year for WEA labels and Atlantic's Ahmet and Nesuhi Ertegun were in attendance, as were Atlantic president Jerry Greenberg and Atlantic general manager David Glew, along with stars of the day Leo Sayer and Steve Martin. Ahmet Ertegun presented Foreigner with its first gold record. Queen played a set.

"In 1977, just six years after its birth, WEA felt flush," wrote the late Stan Cornyn, executive vice-president of Warner Bros Records. "Rather than its usual save-a-buck regional meetings, WEA decided to convene all its infantry, over seven hundred of them, in one major convention. There, in a darkened auditorium, in the Diplomat Hotel near Miami, for the first time, the seven hundred looked up onstage where a banner proclaimed (who knows what this thing meant?) THE FUTURE IS NOW."

WEA's sales had been the fastest rising in the American industry for six years straight, their labels bagging more gold and platinum albums than any other record company. Fleetwood Mac's *Rumours* and Eagles' *Hotel California* were both multiple-platinum sellers. In 1977, according to Cornyn, "more than 70 Warner artists had sold in excess of one million units in the U.S. alone," and WEA "had sold one of every four albums sold in America, a 24 per cent share." CBS's Columbia Records accounted for 17 per cent. In fact, a week after the Diplomat Hotel meeting WEA had four of the top five biggest albums in the United States: Mac's *Rumours*, Linda Ronstadt's *Simple Dreams*, Foreigner's *Foreigner* and The Rolling Stones' *Love You Live*.

"We had a lot of artists," says Barry Freeman, former West Coast regional promotion director for Atlantic Records. "We had The Rolling Stones, Led Zeppelin, Bad Company, Foreigner, Crosby Stills & Nash; the list just went on and on."

So where the hell did AC/DC, a band whose music was difficult to categorise, whose lead singer riled newspaper critics

on both coasts, fit into Atlantic's plans? The truth was they fit ·
in the proverbial middle of nowhere, at the 4 O'Clock Club, a
mobbed-up nightclub in the boondocks of Fort Lauderdale, a
place grandly called "The Venice of America" in postcards, but
in reality, according to Sidney Drashin, "a little baby city; it was
tiny." Tickets were sold for the show on the beach the day before,
raising $4000 for a muscular dystrophy charity.

"These tickets were so valuable, South Florida loves this band
so damn much, that's how much they paid to be here!" late WSHE
disc jockey Tom Judge said to drunken cheers and whistles. "And
here come our friends. You join me in a typical South Florida welcome. Our friends from Australia, AC/DC!"

Rick Tucker, an 18-year-old from Coral Springs, was among a
small group of fans in the audience. Now a semi-retired illustrator,
he lives in Pembroke Pines. "We approached Bon before the show
started and he was very glad to see actual *fans*. He went backstage
to get the band's autographs for us. It was a great concert because
they had nothing to lose with that venue and its near-ignorant
crowd and a handful of crazy young men near the stage cheering
on every tune.

"The stage ran north and south and we sat at long tables right
in front of the stage, running east and west, with smaller tables
behind us seating four to six. They played for just over an hour
but it was an intense set. They paid us a lot of attention during
the concert because we appeared to be about the only people who
knew who they were at the time."

For all of AC/DC's renewed efforts, reviews of their live show,
once again, were worryingly underwhelming. The *Miami News*
reported: "Australian punk-whackos AC/DC played at the 4 ·
O'Clock Club in Fort Lauderdale on Tuesday night; with reports
filtering back that the band was way too loud."

The next night, rather tellingly, given their respective posi-
tions in the American record industry and Atlantic's affections,
Foreigner played at the Diplomat Hotel's Café Cristal.

⚡

The *Let There Be Rock* tour went to Europe and England, giving the band time to reflect on what they had achieved and what they needed to improve. It had been a mixed six months professionally for AC/DC — strong in the regions, not so hot in the big cities — and also personally for Bon. His drinking was off the scale and he was firmly in the habit of mixing alcohol with drugs, despite making a pledge to the band that he wouldn't touch them after a heroin overdose in Melbourne, Australia, in 1975 that had seen him nearly sacked.[11]

"Bon knew that he was on borrowed time after that incident in Melbourne," said Silver Smith. "He told me about that fairly early on that he'd got into serious shit . . . he'd made a commitment to the band that he would only use alcohol."

However, she conceded "it is possible that he hid some behaviours from me, because I had gotten really hurt and angry that he had secretly eaten hash and got shitfaced on alcohol, leaving me to cope with the consequences more than once."

He'd had good, clean, casual fun with various women on the road in America, including Pattee and Holly, but was still besotted with Silver, who'd made time to come see him in the States and in whose company in London the previous year he'd reputedly had a second OD. As one interviewee described Bon's strange fascination with the woman: "After he'd slay a bunch of groupies, he'd say, 'I'm going home to marry my girl, Silver.' *Huh?* Wow."

Silver insisted the story of the second OD — what the band's former manager Michael Browning in his autobiography, *Dog Eat Dog*, calls "a cocktail of heroin and booze . . . this time snorted rather than injected" — is untrue and that Bon's only hospital stay came after a fight in a pub.

"The only hospital visit I know of was when he broke his jaw just after arrival in Britain . . . I'd say there are a couple of other stories that have got confused in there. People can do that. It's bullshit."

But, curiously, she didn't discount the possibility that Bon ODed a second time.

"Whether or not somewhere on the road that happened and

he never told me about [it], I think it quite likely that he would keep that from me, because he already knew that I thought he was careless."

Silver said she never saw Bon smoke or snort heroin, but if he did "it would have been very, very occasional and everyone in my scene was aware that Bon could do really stupid things and that you had to sort of keep an eye on him, because of things that had already happened that they knew about . . . you just couldn't trust him to be sensible about things. It's bad form. You didn't get shitfaced before an important dinner party or meeting. You chose your moments. He wouldn't care about the consequences and how it might affect other people."

She thought this unpredictable behaviour affected Irene Thornton as much as it did her, and ultimately wrecked Bon's only marriage. It also put paid to Bon's plans to marry Silver, which he verbally expressed to her "all the time."

She flatly turned him down the first time, on the way to Heathrow before Bon's flight home to Australia in late 1976: "I knew fairly early on that I would never feel safe about any aspect of my life if I stayed with him."

While she described her late lover as "generous," he was "too reckless" and "also very, *very* selfish and destructive" and "I think Bon would be stunned by the way his myth just keeps growing . . . he put me in some terrible situations with being irresponsible.

"The problem is you didn't know when it was going to happen. It would happen at the most unlikely moments . . . I always thought that's probably why Irene had had enough in the end. I understood Irene I think a lot better than she understands me. Yeah, I could understand why she'd just had enough . . . [I was] so tired of being his babysitter, not his partner."

It's important to note that none of the current members of AC/DC have ever conceded that Bon used heroin; they have only issued denials. Similarly his family has categorically rejected any suggestion he was a user. Graeme Scott, Bon's youngest brother and a merchant seaman, said to Vince Lovegrove in 2006: "I don't like the way people keep saying he died from drugs or heroin.

There's no way Bon would have been on heroin and, if he had, I would have known. We were close."

But not close enough. While Silver acknowledged what Graeme says is "pretty much true," she also had another story. According to her, a member of the Scott family habitually smoked heroin, and made no secret of it from Bon. This person "hugely" consumed heroin.

"[Heroin] was his life," she said. "It was the *only* interest in his life. And that was a long time ago and he'd been like it for a while by the time I met him. So there you go [*laughs*]. Why does he get to keep his sleazy secrets and [*laughs*] the rest of us get slagged?"

He smoked heroin?

"Nonstop."

We're not talking cannabis, we're talking heroin?

"No, we're talking heroin . . . Bon may have had a few toots [of heroin] with [this person] when [he] was visiting. I would have had one too, I'm not saying I wasn't part of it, but that's a possibility. This idea of [Bon] doing heroin in London, the only time that *might* have happened is if he had a few days off, which was rare, he was home, and [this other person] was staying with us. He'd arrived from [undisclosed location]. And was flying straight back to [undisclosed location]. In other words, he came for a reason."

If Bon was using heroin, it was an infrequent habit.

"The thing about heroin is, if you really are a full-on heroin junkie, you can't work, you can't hold down a job, you can't tour unless you're at the top and even then they get sprung because of bad performances and so on . . . you have to be *moderate*. Because it's impossible. I mean, how many full-on junkies do you know that can hold down a job? It's just not doable."

CHAPTER 6

OVERDOSE

In February 2016, I was introduced to Silver Smith through a mutual friend, the young West Australian writer J.P. Quinton, author of a novel about Bon, *Bad Boy Boogie*. Finding any trace of her was extremely difficult because she was off the grid completely.

"I have been a recluse for a long time," she admitted, straight up. She was also very sick with what she described as "genetic heavy metal poisoning," but could easily have been another ailment. I had no idea at the time she had only months to live. After her death her son revealed she'd been diagnosed with terminal cancer.

"I have a genetic illness, chronic exhaustion being a major symptom. I have a lot of downtime because the area I live in has a fairly extreme climate which knocks me around, but I can't afford to move, so I look after myself, my dogs and keep my garden alive when I'm well, and things fall in a heap when I'm not."

My immediate impression of Silver was that she was a far more cheerful, worldly and intelligent woman than the heartless, toothless, heroin-addicted witch she's made out to be online by AC/DC fans who have decided she's to blame for Bon's death and have variously described her, shamefully, as a "fucking skanky vile smackhead lowlife piece of shit," "drug-dealing, stealing skankhead," "fucking junkie mutt," "nasty evil bitch," "waste of human space," "nasty slutbag," "skanky thieving slag" and more. Bon Scott biographer Clinton Walker once called her a "hooker" in Australian *Rolling Stone*. She was uncommonly polite to me, even endearingly sweet, and liked talking about books. Retired, she had worked for many years "as a civil servant and for NGOs and unions in health and education," as well as completing a stint in tertiary teaching.

"I have read some really crazy things about myself online. It is a great consolation to me that the friends I still have who have not passed on have known me well for nearly 50 years, and therefore don't believe any of the nonsense that's out there, and are very protective of me."

Adding to Silver's mystique, up until this book only one photograph of her had ever been widely circulated, taken by Graeme Scott inside Silver's flat in Kensington, London, when Silver was not looking her best. It was published in Walker's biography.

"The photo was taken at about six o'clock in the morning. Bon was up and ready to go because he had to go on tour . . . Graeme was staying with us. And Bon wanted it for his mum. I didn't want Graeme to take it. I'd just got out of bed, didn't have any clothes on, I had a dressing gown on — you feel vulnerable. No makeup. Hadn't even brushed my hair, cleaned my teeth, *nothing*. I *really* didn't want this photo taken. Anyway, Graeme sent it to Bon's mother and she must have given it to Clinton, which is a real bummer, because of all the photos that I've ever had taken in my life, it must be one of the ones that I hate the most. You're the first person I've owned up to that it's actually me. But yeah, it is."

⚡

Silver grew up not knowing her parents. Contrary to popular rumour, she wasn't the daughter of the editor of London's *Times* newspaper.

"I don't know who my biological father was and knew nothing about my biological mother until about 15 years ago . . . I think of my family as the people who raised me. My dad was a white-collar railway worker and I grew up as a strict Catholic in small country towns."

Petite in an approachable, non-intimidating way and fiercely intelligent, with black hair, blue eyes, a slim body and, above all, emanating an uncommon worldliness, it's little wonder Bon was smitten with Silver.

"I was never beautiful, as a child really plain . . . in fact my face had about half a dozen scars that you could see up close. I was small, but I had a style of my own and by the time I left my teens behind I had a really good classic sense of what suited me. Bon said it was my eyes, and that I sang and danced like a white Tina Turner, but I think it was the inside of my head that did it, really. That explains also the number of special people who liked me as a friend and confidante."

She'd won the Miss Beach Girl South Australia title in the late 1960s and for a period, outside her day job for the taxation department, did some modelling and worked part-time as an exotic dancer at the Trocadero nightclub in Hindley Street, Adelaide.

"Not stripping. Just dancing in filmy veils with a very tame carpet snake, and wearing a body stocking and being psychedelically body painted à la Veruschka. Adelaide was very, *very* tame back then, except for the hippies. The modelling was just photographic ads for a department store."

She got her surname from the late Graeme Smith, an audiologist and psychologist — but the marriage, in 1970, wasn't a romantic union. They divorced in 1975.

"We got married because he was called up, and it meant he wouldn't have to go to Vietnam. My high-school love of my life had already been conscripted and was in Vietnam, and the gentlest, smartest boy from my school was in jail for conscientiously objecting. What a fucking waste."

When Silver first met Bon in the early 1970s she was working in the philosophy department at Flinders University.

"It was one of the best jobs I ever had because I was able to learn so much. In the years before equal pay I worked in government offices during the day, and did breakfast or evening waitressing for a couple of years at the Travelodge, saving hard in order to travel. I did stenography and waitressing in order to have tiny but self-contained flats while living in London and San Francisco, being averse to bedsits and sharing a filthy bathroom with strangers."

Silver is widely believed to have had an affair with Bon back in Adelaide while he was married to Irene Thornton, though there's no evidence of it happening. Irene admits as much in her book, *My Bon Scott*: "I don't know if this was going on when Bon and I were together." Talking to me, Silver strenuously denied that Bon committed adultery, even if she herself did, being married to Graeme Smith at the time.

"It was very short. They weren't called 'affairs' in the hippie crowd. Everyone had little flings if they felt so inclined. Everyone in Adelaide knew everyone . . . the thing [Bon and I] had in Adelaide was really, really brief and I for the first time saw him do something which I don't want to discuss but I just thought, '*Whooah*. There's something not quite right with this guy.'" She said Bon's behaviour "certainly affected my family's relationships [with him] and stuff, and Bon made a bad faux pas there that really put the kybosh on anything formal happening."

But there was something special about him.

"The reason Bon was such a hit with women despite his dubious fashion style was that he really *liked* them. This was unusual back in the day. I had four good male friends through high school, but most boys or men fell into two categories: those who saw women as the enemy, and those who were terrified of them. Bon was always comfortable with women, and treated them with respect and affection."

She hooked up again with Bon when AC/DC played their first London gig at the Red Cow in Hammersmith in 1976. The glowering, insular, comic-reading Youngs didn't take kindly to her presence. Silver told me she was made to feel decidedly uncomfortable the first time she met them in the tour van and only saw the band in concert less than a dozen times — so she and Bon were more than happy to escape to her apartment, where they'd read books and listen to records.

"When Bon started visiting in London I didn't have a 'luxury' flat in Kensington. It was one room and a bathroom on Gloucester Road near the Tube in South Kensington, and I had no furniture other than a fridge and a mattress because I'd only recently moved in."

Silver cared for Bon's education, which had been rudimentary. (One former girlfriend of his described him to me as "a rather simple sort from the boondocks in Australia.") She bought him books to read, highbrow ones, while he was on the road: Doris Lessing, Anaïs Nin, Colette, Anthony Trollope, Samuel Pepys, Joseph Conrad. Among his favourite reads were Colette's *Chéri* and *Claudine* books, as well as Lessing's science fiction novels *The Memoirs of a Survivor* and *The Marriages Between Zones Three, Four and Five*. Far from the culturally atrophied atmosphere of AC/DC, Flat 9 at 96 Gloucester Road, and the interesting company Silver kept, was a haven for Bon.

Silver was friends with a young stockbroker called Kenneth Moss, a self-made millionaire who ran a discount air-travel club called Freelandia on his own Douglas DC-8 and Convair 880, a kind of hippie progenitor of Richard Branson's Virgin. Plagued by problems, it operated for all of one year between 1973 and '74. At one of Moss's lavish parties in September 1974, Average White Band drummer Robbie McIntosh snorted what he thought was cocaine. It was heroin. He died later in the Howard Johnson Motel in North Hollywood. The band's bassist, Alan Gorrie, who had also accidentally snorted the same smack, was saved by the intervention of Cher. Alleged to have supplied the drug, Moss was charged with murder. He pleaded guilty to involuntary manslaughter and was sentenced to 120 days in a county jail and four years' probation.

"I stayed with Kenneth in Los Angeles and with his friends in Sausalito in 1974," said Silver. "It was a traumatic and dangerous time for him, and he lost contact with almost everyone. My knowledge of and passion for music opened many doors in California and England, some of them rich, some of them humble."

These included fellow heroin user Phil Lynott (Silver got a credit for a speaking part in the song "Girls" on his 1980 solo album *Solo In Soho*); banker and antiquarian bookseller Milo Cripps, aka Lord Parmoor; and, most famously of all, The Rolling Stones. Silver met Keith Richards at his hotel in Adelaide when the Stones toured Australia. It has long been rumoured that Bon hung out with the Stones in Paris during the making of the *Some Girls* album in '78, but Silver said this is not true.

"Keith Richards never met Bon in my company. Ron Wood and Bon met briefly in the foyer of a sound studio in Paris, just 'hello' before a French band called Trust spotted Bon and carried him off to an adjacent studio where they were recording one of his songs. I went into the Stones' studio with Ron and [Stones personal assistant] Frank Foy, where the Stones were listening to a playback with the engineers . . . I never actually 'partied' with Keith Richards; that was Bon's bullshit . . . we did have a couple of long one-on-one conversations about stuff and a couple of meals."

Were the Stones buying heroin from you?

"No. I knew Ron [Wood] really well over a period of a few years. And I was an acquaintance of Keith. Keith was actually only smoking grass during the time that I knew him in London in the late '70s . . . I didn't know him back when he was using massive amounts of heroin."

Silver believed it was these passing associations with the rich and famous that earned her an unfair reputation from Walker's book. She is quoted in it as saying, "There [were] a few rich men hovering, I wasn't short of rich men," which Walker interprets to mean "she was supported by sugar daddies." In her memoir, too, Irene Thornton erroneously repeats the claim. Silver was of the view that Irene must have got this impression from reading Walker.

And while she readily confessed to her own heroin use and the possibility Bon may have used heroin himself, she maintained up to her death that any suggestion he succumbed to smack and not alcohol poisoning that fateful day in February 1980 is simply wrong.

"Surely that myth has been thoroughly debunked already? Are people still suggesting that the doctors at the hospital — who didn't know Bon was anyone special — and the Coroner's Court, the press and the Alberts/Young mafia were involved in some high conspiracy? I was there at the hospital and the inquest and it's the plain simple truth."

Is it?

⚡

Grahame "Yogi" Harrison spent four years with Rose Tattoo as their sound engineer and, before that, five years with Buffalo, Australia's version of Black Sabbath, including a 1974 tour down under with Geordie, fronted by Brian Johnson. Today, in his 60s, he still works on the road as a sound engineer and tour manager. In 1977, he worked in the engineering crew for AC/DC's farewell show in Sydney.

He got to know Bon, a "massive party animal, an extremely friendly individual," when they'd bump into each other at the Bondi Lifesaver, a live venue in Sydney's eastern suburbs that shut down permanently in 1980. Harrison lived not far away, "so it wasn't far to roll down the hill to get home." He says Bon was cut from the same mould as late Rose Tattoo drummer and heroin user Dallas "Digger" Royall; indeed they were so alike, "they could have been brothers, mate." Royall died in 1991.

"The Bondi Lifesaver was a second home for a lot of us for a long time during a stretch of the '70s. We worked there quite a lot, most of the crew, and bands, and also it was our social centre. Bon was great. He was really the most amenable member of AC/DC by a long shot. He didn't have a malicious bone; if he did he hid it very well."

But he had problems that were obvious even then.

"Bon was a massive consumer of everything that was available. He would get in some serious drinking situations. With Bon personally I'd probably say he got a lot of his courage from alcohol. Guys like Bon Scott and [late Dragon lead singer] Marc Hunter, to me, they appear to carry some rubbish with them when they come out of school, whether it's being bullied or laughed at or whatever it is; they don't have the confidence to get up and do what they do but they have got the ability to do it and they find what my generation calls 'Dutch courage.' It becomes a lifetime habit because without it you don't feel like you can be what you think you've gotta be, as such. Bon used [alcohol] as a crutch and I'd say he probably used drugs obviously as a crutch as well. Because the more out of it he got the more in control he probably felt. Whatever was gnawing at him from inside, both he and Marc Hunter and a few others got over that by the wrong means, really. It killed them both."

Were you aware of Bon using heroin?

"Oh yeah, we knew about that. There were a few individuals in the business doing that. I've seen a lot of people, too many, that have died from it over the years and gone off the rails. In Bon's case, I think whatever you threw at Bon he'd have a crack at it to see where it was gonna take him. I don't think Bon was the kind of person that went looking for heroin by choice. The rock 'n' roll business being what it is, I'd say that it perhaps became *available* to him. Bon being the kind of individual he was probably went [*impersonating Bon*], 'I'll have a crack at *that*. See what's going *on*.' As though he was some kind of human personal experiment. Like, 'I wonder what this will do to me.'

"Heroin has destroyed large chunks of the rock 'n' roll business, large chunks, including Bon, Marc Hunter. You can have great conjecture over all of it. I think Bon died as a result of the accumulated effect of Bon's *life*, to be honest with you. That's the way I'd look at it. Whatever he was still trying to find solace with or enthusiasm from or whatever he was trying to identify in his personality with a need to be out of it all the time, what might have got him in the end was the fact it became an overwhelming thing with him; where he couldn't shake [off] that part of his personality any more. He had to have massive indulgences because anything less than that just wasn't going to work to the degree he needed it to work. I would not be surprised if Bon died of a heroin overdose but I would be surprised if that was the only thing involved."

⚡

Angus and Malcolm Young have never said a word about Bon's alleged ODs in 1975 and 1976, but the vexed issue of his job security would become a major conversation point inside the AC/DC camp, as well as a deep concern for Bon himself. This tumour of doubt was compounded by the caning Bon was getting from critics, Atlantic's rejection of their 1976 album *Dirty Deeds Done Dirt Cheap* for a North American release,[12] record-company chatter about dropping the band, and the summer *Let There Be Rock* tour failing to convert into adequate record sales. Bon was also drinking much more heavily than ever before, bringing him into direct conflict with Malcolm.

It's not hard to imagine how the creative limitations the Youngs placed on the band — straight-up rock 'n' roll or bawdy ditties, nothing but — would have started to frustrate him. Silver Smith said the Youngs didn't like Bon listening to anything but AC/DC. But privately, when they weren't puffing out their chests for the media, the Youngs listened to very different music. Malcolm admitted in an unguarded moment that he and the band listened to The Beatles: "When we want to hear something we put on The Beatles, one of their albums where they got more adventurous." The terms of their lead singer's employment, however, at least publicly, required that he be a musical dolt.

Bon wanted to be taken seriously — or, at the very least, respected — as an artist and all he was getting from the press, even when AC/DC was ripping it up in concert, was scorn. He liked to read. He'd visit bookshops and art galleries while on tour in Europe. But as witty as he was with his lyrics, Bon was no Peter Ustinov or Stephen Fry: letters to friends were frequently peppered with coarse language and he didn't help himself with inarticulate interviews. His answers to questions from journalists — on his own or with other members — were often muddled, sometimes incoherent, with almost every answer ending in "you know."

"Dunno what I'd do without this band, y'know? I live for it. We're a real down 'n' dirty lot. The songs reflect just what we are: booze, women, sex, rock 'n' roll. That's what life's all about."

Except for Bon, deep down, it wasn't. He was merely assuming a role. The boasting about girls he'd slept with or smutty locker room banter about stroke mags was just press padding for the image he'd constructed for himself. The more he fulfilled the role the Young brothers required of him in AC/DC, the more Bon was leaving behind the essence of who he really was. Is it any wonder he drank to the brink of oblivion?

Irene Thornton wrote in her memoir that Bon was "always playing up to this rock star image, trying to be controversial and provoke a reaction. He didn't mean half the shit he said."

She recounts an incident early in Bon's AC/DC career, unexplained, involving Bon, the late Australian roadie Pat Pickett and two groupies. Pickett, she says, did "something really gross . . . a real low point" and Bon "was clearly pretty amused by what happened." She writes that he could get "darker and darker with every beer." There was an ugly side to him that sometimes came out — a meanness. What else other than spite would possess Bon to be "practically bragging" about his sexual involvement with Silver to the only woman he ever married? "He wanted me to know about Silver and for some reason I think he wanted it to hurt." She remarks that "the thing that strikes me" about "Ride On," Bon's signature song off *Dirty Deeds Done Dirt Cheap*, "is how early in his career Bon started to feel unhappy."

"He'd had a bit of success and all of a sudden he thought he was entitled to do anything to anyone. The band was so popular and so many girls were throwing themselves at him that it had totally messed up his idea of reality. I was really disgusted with him."

Silver did not remember this side of Bon fondly, either.

"Perhaps I should not say this, but Bon was a bit of a braggart, and it took me a while to realise that this included me, and it caused me a lot of grief down the line. Discretion was my middle name, but definitely not Bon's. He was really indiscreet with his stories and exaggerated a lot to impress. I found out the hard way when I discovered he'd been doing it about me. It could be embarrassing and damaging. But then he was so winning and charming when he was caught out."

She also agreed that Bon had become trapped in a persona that wasn't his true self.

"He did get trapped at the end. It worked well for him in the beginning; as far as I know, he raised no objection. [Michael] Browning used to feed stories to the *Truth*, which was the rag newspaper published in Melbourne, the scandal rag. Browning used to feed them silly stories about Bon because he didn't have this bad-boy image before AC/DC. People who knew him well knew that he did some really stupid things but his general image was not the bad boy. So that was sort of manufactured: you know, the old bad dude and the young guys, his young apprentices or whatever in *badness*.

"But I think towards the end that cost him, personally. He was trapped in that. It certainly caused problems for me because in a way he was forced into that role all the time. He had to be *that* person. He was always a bit cheeky but that [bad-boy] side was really developed *for* AC/DC. It was draining him. Because that's the person people want you to be. There's nothing more draining. I spent the first decade and a half of my life being *told* who I was; not being *who* I was, just being *told* what I was. And it's really hard, really hard."

It is a profound insight from both women. While the Youngs were serial denouncers of other musicians to the point of rudeness and obnoxiousness, Bon could be just as bad. Led Zeppelin, the Stones, Jeff Beck, Eric Clapton, Rod Stewart, The Sweet . . . very few top-line musicians of the 1970s escaped AC/DC's ire when it came to doing press: they did interview after interview dumping on other musos.

For a band that abhorred the "punk" tag, their record company was happy to promote them as such and they did a fine line in playing up to it. A good example of this is a 1978 interview in

Punk magazine with John Holmstrom. Bon didn't cover himself in glory.

HOLMSTROM: What kind of girls do you like?

ANGUS: Dirty ones.

HOLMSTROM: Girls who don't wash?

ANGUS: No, just dirty cows.

BON: A nice clean dirty one. Clean cunt. Dirty mind.

HOLMSTROM: You're not married, are you?

BON: Nah, divorced. And you can understand why!

HOLMSTROM: Why?

BON: I'm divorced.

HOLMSTROM: Oh. What's the most depraved thing you ever did?

BON: Fucked an Abo in the nose. Fucked an Aborigine's nose. Big flat nose.

Later in the interview Bon is asked, "What did you do last night?"

BON: Ah, went out. I had this fantastic dream. I got really drunk — you saw me yesterday afternoon — I went home and went to bed. And I dreamed I had these two big fat New York groupies sucking my cock and me ass and me balls and all. One was Linda Lovelace. She got the — you know.

ANGUS: And you woke up and it was true.

BON: First time I ever fucked a lung from the mouth — and I couldn't say it was trite. Well, when I woke up there was no one there, so maybe it was true.

It was puerile stuff and Bon was fulfilling his brief. The big-city critics might have been unimpressed by his stage performances and AC/DC's American record company unconvinced of his commercial appeal, yet how could *anyone*, let alone the notoriously ruthless Young brothers, conceivably sack him? Bon elevated AC/DC to another level: lyrically, in performance and, most crucially of all, in spirit. For all his crassness, there was a roguish charm to him that is impossible to deny. The Youngs could not have got as far as they already had without Bon; they instinctively would have known this and have admitted as much in press interviews since he died.

Without Bon, there simply wouldn't have been a band by 1979 — AC/DC would have been dropped by Atlantic had *Highway To Hell* not broken through for them and we'd be reading about them today in a retrospective in *Classic Rock* magazine, a historic curiosity like Michigan band Brownsville Station. Bon was the best thing to ever happen to AC/DC — and still is to this day. He gave the band the edge it required, on the stage and off.

But as the band's roadie Barry Taylor thoughtfully ventured, Bon was lucky he'd found the Youngs: "The meaning of the music isn't in the lyrics alone." In AC/DC, he said, "There's actually a war going on between the lead guitar player and the singer. There's a conditioned environment of tension . . . the language of rock is emotive not discursive. You *feel* the meaning of rock music. And that's why the meaning is hard to isolate. You can't determine the meaning of a song from the lyrics alone."

None of that mattered, though, with a singer hellbent on self-annihilation.

"Angus and Malcolm didn't think anybody else was worth the shit on their shoes," says Grahame Harrison. "They thought they were supreme in every way. Malcolm ran the band but you had to be on Angus's good side to get in the band, and in order to maintain your position in the band you had to make Angus happy as well as Malcolm happy. Angus was like a precocious child."

The two brothers had an important decision to make.

CHAPTER 7

HELL AIN'T
A BAD PLACE
TO BE

In a 1969 press release for The Valentines, Bon said his loves were his parents and his pet Crater Critter, a plastic toy that appeared in Kellogg's cereal boxes in Australia in 1968. He liked red painted rooms, showers, swimming, long-haired blondes and sex. He hated "being disturbed while thinking," washing and ironing. As sweet and naughty as you like.

Very little in Bon's background gave clues to the life that would follow. His family was exceedingly normal. The second son of Isabella Cunningham Mitchell (born 18 February 1919) and Charles "Chick" Belford Scott (born 24 August 1917) of "Ravenscraig," Roods, Kirriemuir, Scotland,[13] Bon was born in Forfar, seven miles southeast of Kirriemuir, on 9 July 1946. He left with his family for Australia on the *Asturias* from Southampton, departing 5 March 1952, and 25 days later arrived in Fremantle, Western Australia, according to the *Inward Passenger Manifests*. The Scotts had £1500 to their name after their passage and were on their way east. Bon's Scottish heritage meant something to him later in life. He had a coat of arms tattoo on his inside right forearm and, according to Roy Allen, "was proud that he could play the bagpipes; maybe the only thing he ever bragged about to me." Yet as Irene Thornton pointed out, there "wasn't a trace of a Scottish accent on Bon . . . he was a true-blue Aussie."[14]

Charles was 34 and Isa 33. Their occupations were given as "baker" and "housewife" on the shipping records — Charles had been a baker for 19 years in Kirriemuir — and the family was marked as "V. Good Type Family (2 Boys)" on immigration papers. Charles, it noted, had "several jobs offered" in Australia.

"Master Ronald Belford," as Bon was referred to in the documentation, was six years old and younger brother Derek was two. (Their elder brother, Alexander, had died before his first birthday.) In their medical examinations Bon was marked "good" for Standard at School and Intelligence; Derek was "average." Bon's youngest brother, Graeme, would be born in Australia a year later. The Scotts' temporary address in their new country was 89 Couch Street, Sunshine: the home of Eleanor Laing, Isa's youngest sister. It was the same Melbourne suburb where the film clip for the AC/DC single "Jailbreak" would be filmed in 1976.

The family stayed in Sunshine for four years, Bon attending the local primary school. After Graeme was diagnosed with asthma, the Scott family moved permanently to Western Australia in 1956, finding a home at 54 Harvest Road, North Fremantle. In the 1963 electoral roll, Chick gave his job as a "fitter." While Bon was tearing it up in America in 1977, the Scotts were living at 306a Rockingham Road, Spearwood, about as working-class Aussie suburban as you can get. His two brothers might have been off seeing the world, but Derek, a glazier by profession, was happy to move into a modest home nearby at 17 Dion Place, Coolbellup, with his wife, Valarie.

According to electoral records, at the time of Bon's death Chick was working as a storeman and Isa as a cleaner. She was a dutiful and proud mother. Bon would tell Pattee Bishop that Isa kept the first T-shirt he was ever given with the AC/DC logo on it. But she hadn't been able to protect her son from the violence of the playground, as Bon remembered.

"My new schoolmates threatened to kick the shit out of me when they heard my Scottish accent. I had one week to learn to speak like them if I wanted to remain intact. 'Course, I didn't take any notice. No one railroads me, and it made me all the more determined to speak my own way. That's how I got my name, you know. The Bonny Scot, you see?"

He left high school early, quit drumming in the local pipe band he'd joined with his father and in 1963, aged 16, as Vince Lovegrove would recall, got in his first serious stoush with officialdom, being "committed to the Child Welfare Department for 12 months. After being arrested for brawling, he gave a false name, escaped from custody, stole 12 gallons of petrol, and added a charge of unlawful carnal knowledge to his CV before being arrested again and committed to Riverbank, a jail for uncontrollable boys."

Bon explained it differently: "I was singing a couple of songs with a band at a dance in Fremantle and a couple of guys started giving me a hard time. I got off the stage and got stuck into them. The cops tried to break it up and I finished up on a charge of assaulting the police. I did 11 months."

Depending on what you read, Bon's "11 months" is everything from nine to 12 to 18 months. His records have not been released. Either way, he went inside — of his own free will.

"That incident itself, that thing that I find hard to explain about him, just misbehaving or doing something that was really destructive either for himself or for somebody else, it all started way back then because he had a choice of coming home," said Silver Smith. "He was given the choice in the court of going home, but he didn't want to see his parents.

"I think he was really embarrassed. His grandparents had arrived from Scotland. And back in the day, it was really expensive to travel. These were not well-off people; they were working-class people on low salaries. His mum was a tea lady in a university, his dad worked in a biscuit factory. So the grandparents, this was the one chance they'd get to see their grandchildren and Bon wasn't there because he chose to stay in and do the time in reformatory because he was embarrassed. But he regretted it. Really, *really* regretted it. He never saw his grandparents; they'd passed on before he got to England. So he was doing that self-destruct stupid thing *waaay* back. Maybe it was just some fatal flaw in his psyche."

Silver, frequently portrayed as a cold-hearted bitch, was actually close to Bon's parents: "Chick and Isa met me at the Fremantle docks the first time I came back to Australia, and I stayed with them for three days. I enjoyed it very much.

"I could see why Bon was the second best housemate I ever had: because of Isa and Chick. Staying with them was very familiar. The house was spotless, and major household purchases were obviously carefully planned, chosen and budgeted for and maintained. The boys' shoes would have been repaired in a timely fashion. Every dollar used to its best advantage, no waste. I was impressed by Isa's acceptance of Bon the way he was. All three boys seemed to have been really different to each other."

Clinton Walker makes a case in his biography, largely on the testimony of Silver, that Bon's arrest in '63 and subsequent incarceration at Riverbank filled him with enduring shame. His desire to succeed in the music business was matched by his desire to make amends to his family for the embarrassment he'd caused them. Now that is very possibly true, albeit a long bow. But what it almost certainly did was affect the feelings a young Bon had about himself, which were then compounded by an aborted musical career with The Valentines and Fraternity, then his failure as a husband to Irene. It's tempting to psychoanalyse the person Bon was in 1977, yet ultimately guesswork.

However, it's a safe bet that his compulsive drinking masked some sort of inner struggle. Close friends speak of a profound darkness that befell him, especially in late 1979, when he went off the rails so badly.

Far from being just another dumb rock star throwing his life away through booze and drugs, Bon was hungry for new experiences. He was restless, uncommonly sensitive and, in many respects, exceedingly contradictory. He was vain and loved order but had no issue waking up at the bottom of a flight of stairs. He cared about his vocal cords but abused his body mightily with alcohol and drugs. He was an adept writer and prodigious correspondent, but wrote his lyrics in clumsy capital letters and was a chronically bad speller.[15] He had an impenetrable inner life but was always willing to do anything for friends and very mindful of his fans' needs. He wanted to be famous but craved a life outside music. He could be deceitful yet was selfless and generous in a way few people are. He could be the life of the party but he could also be lonely. He was a romantic — it was clear that he was driven by love and the idea of love and being *in* love but ill equipped to let go of the other romantic streak in his life: his own freedom, his sexual liberty and the image he'd created of himself in his own mind and projected to the world. He told women what they wanted to hear, changing his stories for whose company he was in; not something unknown among womanisers. He cavorted with prostitutes. As one man who'd played with Bon in AC/DC and wished to remain anonymous for this book told me: "Bon was very sleazy. I wouldn't have trusted him with my grandmother."

So it came to be that a man who could shag multiple women in a day or gleefully participate in group sex (one woman I spoke to who knew Bon in Florida remembered an occasion at his hotel room when "literally 10 chicks would be lined up on the beds and he'd do them all") was also capable of producing something as tender as "Love Song," the much maligned track off AC/DC's first album, the Australian release of *High Voltage*. It was written, Bon said, "to make housewives sort of cry into their tea towels as they're doing the dishes, you know. That was the whole idea of writing lyrics to the song."

Malcolm joked that the band "tied him up and made him write some nice clean lyrics for us for a change."

Bon himself had two intersecting stories about how he joined AC/DC. The first was that he was recovering at home in July 1974, two months after a near-fatal motorcycle accident in Adelaide had put him in a coma, and heard "Can I Sit Next To You Girl" on the radio.

"I heard the song and I sort of went, 'Oh, yeah.' You know, cleaning the house 'cause my wife was the nine-to-fiver and I was the housekeeper. And I'm cleaning the house, and I'm sorta, you know, polishing the kitchen table, [singing] *Can-I-Sit-Next-To* . . . and the song finished, and the guy said, 'The newest thing from Sydney, AC/DC.' I thought, 'Yeah, right. Sydney pack o' poofs, for sure.' And two weeks later I'm singing, *Can-I-Sit-Next-To* . . ."

The second had him on the wharves. Bon clearly liked to spin a yarn.

"I was painting ships in Adelaide Harbour with the Painters and Dockers Union, getting very old and grey, and this bloke called Dennis Laughlin, an old friend of mine who was the manager of the band, says, 'You want a job with a rock 'n' roll band?' And I thought [*adopts geriatric voice*], 'I don't know if I could do that, mate. They're all pretty young looking fellas,' 'cause I'm a bit of a granddaddy . . . and so there I was with this band, and I was really worried 'cause I thought, 'These blokes are 19 and 20 and I'm gonna have to keep up with them.' So I bought a stack of Methedrine and anyway . . . we got together and I kept up. I dragged them here and there, like down [*laughs*]."

Laughlin invited him to AC/DC's gig at the Pooraka Hotel in Adelaide.

"The band walks out in crimplene, you know, shirts and things. And [there's] this silly little bastard with a school suit on [*laughs*] and I stood there for the whole half hour they were onstage and laughed."

He was "knocked out" by what he was seeing but "didn't like the music, I didn't like the way it was played." Bon admitted he was "really sneaky" and "organised a blow" at Fraternity bandmate Bruce Howe's place on Prospect Road "because they had gear set up in the cellar." Bon played drums, Howe bass, "and we had the most incredible jam, you know, it was really good."

Bon, who was working as a driver for an agency owned by Vince Lovegrove, said he "got [AC/DC] on the road to check out what they were really like," and it was then that he decided he wanted to give them a go. The Youngs asked him to join before he said yes, but he still knocked them back anyway and went to get a job at Port Adelaide Fertilisers. The medical check showed a clean bill of health. Bon was supposed to start the following day but he had "gone home and thought, 'No, I can't do it.' So I picked up the phone and rang Dennis, and I said, 'Hey, Dennis. Is that job still going with the band?' [*laughs*] He said, 'Yeah.' I said, 'Well, send me 60 bucks for a plane. Be there tomorrow.'"

Having Bon replace the band's first singer, Dave Evans, Grahame Harrison argues, was the best thing the Youngs could have done.

"Dave Evans was never right for the band. He was the wrong kind of arrogance out the front. Bon was a cheeky-arrogant party boy. Brian Johnson is just a car lover who just has to stand there and sing, and bounce around the stage a little bit, and that's about all. Whereas Dave Evans was just a rooster, a real *rooster*, out the front. Dave, invariably after a gig, would do what Dave does possibly still best of all: make a gigantic goose out of himself after he's had a few drinks at the bar and strut around like a fucking rooster and everybody would go, 'You *wanker*.' He's just one of those guys who didn't offend you but he irritated you just by being there. 'Badass' Dave he calls himself now. That's the kind of dick-head he is. From the word go when I first saw them I didn't think [Dave] was going to last. Because it was pretty obvious even then that the band was under the control of two guitar players."

Harrison's dim view of Evans was shared by Bon: "He wasn't cutting it and, besides, he was a bit of an ass."

⚡

Three years later and Bon was resting up in a hotel room in New York City. The menial career he could have had at Port Adelaide Fertilisers must have seemed a world away — because it was. He'd made the right choice even though stardom in America and the financial security that would come with it remained elusive.

AC/DC's British and European tours had been successful, the album entering the *Music Week* charts in the United Kingdom on 12 November 1977 at #42. By 10 December it had got as high as #37, the band's debut in the top 40, but then it fell away again before Christmas. While Earth, Wind & Fire was filling 35,000 seats at the Capital Centre in Landover, Maryland, AC/DC was back for the winter leg of the *Let There Be Rock* tour, booked into small theatres and auditoriums in the Northeast, Southeast and Midwest as a support act. They then returned to New York for the recording of *Live From The Atlantic Studios*, a special promo-only release that was issued just prior to 1978's *Powerage* in the hope that radio stations would play it "in its entirety."

Silver Smith spent some time with Bon on the road in the United States before their eventual break-up in 1978 while sharing a motel room in Sydney's Coogee. It was her decision, and Bon wasn't happy about it.

"I wanted a *life*. I didn't want to be someone's caretaker. You'd never feel the least bit secure [with Bon]. You could not plan for [what he'd do]; some shit was going to come down that you couldn't have possibly allowed for. He just did stupid things every now and then that [even] he couldn't explain why he'd done it; he could see the damage that it had done.

"I'd already been affected by the things that Bon had done without thinking that had really quite serious consequences. It wasn't like he was like [this] all the time. The danger was you just never knew when he was going to go and do something really, *really* stupid that he couldn't explain. He could give no reason for doing it and it was pretty obvious it was a disastrous thing to have done. But [what he did] could really affect your life.

"I couldn't see how it was meant to work. Not what he wanted, anyway. It was just not doable. I wanted to get back to just having my own life for a bit and to work out whether that was what I wanted or not; whether I was prepared to take that on. I mean, it must have been the same for Irene: really difficult. You're sort of trying to do all the hard work, normal things, and Bon slips in and out being Bon [*laughs*]. He would give me 12 months' space and

I would give him [space], but, of course, he never gave me the 12 months. I didn't get three months [*laughs*]. When I arrived back in London, he had already been there for a month, and had spent it driving everyone I knew crazy, looking for me. I felt hounded and embarrassed and just wanted to hide."

She estimated that over his lifetime Bon wrote her "300 or 400 letters, 50 or 60 telegrams," all of which she lost. They are gone forever.

⚡

Living off a meagre allowance, Bon couldn't afford to cover Silver's travel expenses on the road in America, and the Youngs certainly weren't going to contribute, being wary of if not hostile to her presence, so she paid her own way. From New York she went to Milwaukee, where she met Pattee Bishop's friend and Cliff Williams's girlfriend, the late Candy Pedroza, a "half-Mexican, half-Italian little firecracker . . . a hot potato."

A one-time girlfriend of Kinks tour manager Ken Jones and Humble Pie's Steve Marriott, Candy was known to use heroin. She had reunited with Cliff in Chicago after their first meeting in Florida. Candy and Silver went on to spend a few days together in Chicago before Silver reluctantly returned to Manhattan, which was "such a shithole back then." She and Bon booked into the Holiday Inn on West 57th Street for their last night together in New York and decided to sample the nightlife.

"Bon and I tried to find [live-music club] CBGBs in the freezing cold and found six sad drunks propping up the bar."

At the Mid-South Coliseum in Memphis, Tennessee, AC/DC opened for the biggest touring attraction in North America — Kiss — in front of 12,000 people. They did it again the next night in Indianapolis, Indiana (which Silver attended before heading out to California en route to Australia), then a third time in Louisville, Kentucky. For their shows in Indianapolis and Louisville, the band was paid just $1000 per night. Local radio station WLRS promoted the Louisville concert as "The Show of Shows!" and in front of their biggest crowd yet, over 18,000 people, AC/DC was determined to upstage the headliners.

"This audience was with both groups all the way," wrote the *Courier-Journal*. "It went berserk over a little electronic device that sustains a guitar note long after the string is plucked and the hand is removed from the guitar. That passes for virtuosity among Louisville rock crowds."

AC/DC's winter run ended with two shows later that month, supporting Kiss in Largo, Maryland, in front of 19,000 people, where they stood in for Bob Seger and the Silver Bullet Band, and Pittsburgh on a bill with Blue Öyster Cult. When it was all over, reminisced roadie Barry Taylor, it was "five trucks and 50 crew and we're off and we're running."

⚡

In Greensboro, North Carolina, AC/DC played its first ever show with Illinois band Cheap Trick. Embarrassingly, the Australian band's name was misprinted on the ticket as "AC/BC."

"Both bands were in similar spots in their respective careers," says Cheap Trick drummer Bun E. Carlos, who was inducted into the Rock & Roll Hall of Fame in 2016. "We both had a goofball lead guitarist, cool singer and rocking bass and drums. Both bands were out there in the trenches. Cheap Trick was a bit heavier in concert than on record. Bon always came off as a regular, hard-rockin' guy who was always up for some fun. The only health problem we ever noticed was his excessive boozing in his last year. No one was surprised, sadly."

Was AC/DC's management in that last year doing enough to get on top of Bon's drinking problem? Was the rest of the band conscious of how bad it was?

"Nobody seemed to be doing anything about Bon's boozing, but that wasn't unusual back then. No one had ever heard of rehab, or 'babysitters,' stuff like that. Management was some guy in a suit who showed up in L.A. or New York City."

Silver Smith said Bon never mentioned rehab: "No, I've never known him to do that." But she confessed, "I was pretty ignorant; I didn't know rehab existed until the mid '80s."

"[Rehab] wasn't even on the horizon," says Mick Jones. "AA? Alcoholics Anonymous? What the fuck is that? That wasn't even on the table. It was just, 'You need to dry out or something or go away.' I used to do that, actually; I used to go away for three or four weeks sometimes to a restful environment somewhere, sometimes a health farm, which I guess is somewhere in that family of trying to get better; putting a Band-Aid on it."

Until Jones got sober, he was wary of AA.

"Whenever I met AA people I was like, '*Whooah*. Get away from me.' It's like the devil."

Did you have an intervention?

"No. Apparently many had been planned [*laughs*]. But eventually I did it of my own free will. A friend had sort of set something up for me and I went down to the Caribbean, and it was the best thing I've ever done. It really saved my life. Because I guess I was trying to live this dream of debauchery, stardom, all those things all shoved into one horrible mess. I realised that I was jeopardising my relationship with my family, jeopardising my career, jeopardising everything. Everything I could have lost, I would have lost. I'd have lost my life, for starters. That's basically the long, tall and the short of it. I'd seen that happen to many people, to Bon. Bon was one of the earlier ones of our generation — the '70s, into the '80s. It's tragic.

"Musicians are very sensitive-type people. Driven not by hunger, not necessarily by power and money; it's more about the *glory*. It's more about getting that feeling onstage that you're connecting with all these people out there and you're moving a whole shitload of people. And it's trying to sort of somehow keep this dream going on when you're really not capable of it any more. There were so many times when I knew that I had to do something about it, but [after abstaining] a few days later I was back: 'Oh, I haven't had anything for five days, now I deserve to go and *really* have a party this weekend.' It was a continual cycle of that: you know, *denial*. There's no such thing as one drink for an alcoholic, or one drug or one whatever. I knew if I didn't get my shit together I'd better just forget about music."

Some of that denial could be found inside AC/DC itself.

"By the way he carried himself, you really thought that Bon Scott was immortal," said Angus Young. "He would drink like a fish, and when you saw him the next morning, he'd be no worse for wear. And you'd think to yourself, 'How does this guy do this?'"

How did he indeed.

PART TWO
1978

CHAPTER 8

WHAT'S NEXT TO THE MOON

I book a return ticket from New York to Miami, Amtrak's Atlantic Coast Service, a journey of over 1550 miles — one way. Within minutes of leaving Manhattan's Penn Station the *Silver Star* is riding parallel to the highway, a rolling panorama of water towers, shipping containers, trucks, buses, concrete overpasses, electricity grids, swamps, uncut grass, junkyards, scrap metal, coal piles and billboards. New residential developments are springing up in Harrison, New Jersey. By Trenton, the state capital, the landscape starts becoming more suburban: American flags hanging on poles outside tidy clapboard vinyl houses in neat little streets, plastic outdoor table-and-chair sets on manicured front lawns, above-ground pools. In Virginia I start seeing tractors. By nightfall, after half a day travelling, I've only got as far as North Carolina with its forests, wooded groves and open fields dotted with sheds and farm machinery. It was into this vast industrial-pastoral America that Atlantic Records sent AC/DC in 1978. The big cities had yet to be won over.[16]

That time, that era, will never come around again. It's lost. So is that exceptional music. And so, soon, will be the people who knew this remarkable man called Bon Scott. It's an almost impossible task to recreate Bon's time in North America. Why are so many people, including me, motivated to produce books, films, stage shows, documentaries, Instagram posts and Facebook pages about him? Why do countless AC/DC cover bands around the world, from bars in Yokohama to fan fairs in Germany, choose just to cover *his* songs, not the ones that were written after he died? The devotion to the man is clear in the band names themselves: Let There Be Bon, Bon But Not Forgotten, Whole Lotta Bon, Bon Scott Experience, Bon Scotch. There are hundreds of them. It's not just about the music; it has to be more than that. I'm not sure, but I think that at some point, maybe, like a lot of these same people, I realised my life, as much as I tried, was never going to be like Bon's. He packed more into a decade in the 1970s than most people do in their lifetimes. By being fans, perhaps we hope a little bit of whatever he possessed that made him the man he was might touch our otherwise mundane existences.

I didn't want to hear another recycled, wildly embellished story about Bon. In writing this book, I wanted to meet the people who knew another side of the man, who weren't afraid to upset the members of AC/DC or Bon's family and didn't have something to hide or anyone to protect. They are rare and elusive. To do that, I had to travel to a city on the edge of the Caribbean, far away from Sydney, Melbourne, Perth, Los Angeles, New York and London. A place where, very possibly, Bon saw a glimpse of the future he'd always wanted: a good-looking woman he could be happy with, a country that was offering him new chances. There are only so many people who knew him and who haven't spoken before. Finding them is one challenge. Finding those who are prepared to talk is another.

I realise now that what we draw from Bon's story and the broader story of the band is ultimately personal: the music, the legend, the myth or all of it. It doesn't really matter. If anything, the majority of fans would probably prefer to go on thinking of Bon as a sort of Peter Pan figure rather than confront the deeply flawed human being he really was.[17] As Tony Platt, engineer of *Highway To Hell* and *Back In Black*, told me: "AC/DC fans should make their own minds up; that is the nature of celebrity. Your fans take the bits that suit them best."

But I'm equally certain that Bon, the real Bon, struggled with the same sort of questions every one of us faces. *What do I want out of life? Who do I want to end my days with? End it early? Grow old? When do I know I've done enough to be truly happy?* The bald truth is Bon died pitifully, not heroically. For a man who inspired so many people, he let himself down to end his life the way he did.

It's worth taking the train just to see the stars over South Carolina and the sunrise in Georgia. By the time the *Silver Star* stops in Jacksonville, Florida, the landscape changes again: trailer homes, palm trees. With each mile travelled it's like I'm going back in time. The skies get bluer and wider. Orlando. Fort Lauderdale. West Palm Beach. Hollywood. *Miami.* In her 1987 book about the city, Joan Didion calls Miami "not a city at all but a tale, a romance of the tropics, a kind of waking dream in which any possibility could and would be accommodated."

Waiting for me, patiently, at Miami Amtrak station in a black, green and white dress, even when I'm running two hours late, is American Thighs.

⚡

When I spoke to Holly X over the phone from New York and proposed coming to meet her in Miami, she had one important condition if we were to go ahead and publish her story: anonymity. There were two main reasons. The first was a prestigious professional position she wanted to protect. The second was her membership of Alcoholics Anonymous.

"The world is just too overly connected now," she explains. She's in her mid 50s, taller in person than I expect her to be, curvaceous, with high cheekbones, long white-blonde hair and heavily mascaraed eyelashes. "I don't want a bunch of old photos appearing anytime someone Googles my name. I don't want AC/DC fans contacting me. Anonymity is the foundation on which AA was built and why it works. People who are famous and who have their booze and 'drugalog' documented in the media and then who get clean will talk and write songs about their recovery. They never had anonymity to begin with. There are many more famous and not-so-famous people who are in AA and no one knows who they are. Humility is at the heart of AA. People don't need to know *me*, just my story. Through AA, I feel I help many people and none of them know my last name. This is just what I feel is right for me as a member of AA."

We're driving around Miami in Holly's Toyota Prius with its "Native Miamian" plates and decide to order some Indian takeout on her iPhone. It's a hot Friday night in May. The traffic's bad heading towards the beach and the Indian restaurant can't manage to take our order because they're understaffed so we drive there and pay in person. The place is full. While we're waiting for our food to arrive, we have time to talk.

The conventional record has it that Silver Smith was the great love of Bon's life. AC/DC biographer Mick Wall said as much, floridly, to *Classic Rock* magazine in 2015: "The closest Bon Scott ever really got to love, after Irene [Thornton], was with Margaret 'Silver' Smith, hippie trail enchantress, heroin user and queen of the long nights." According to Clinton Walker in his biography of Bon, "He had never gotten over her."

I ask Holly: Did Bon ever talk about Silver?

"No," she replies, almost curtly. It's clear to me she's never heard her name. "He didn't talk about any women."

*

Holly X was born in Miami in 1959 and graduated from high school in 1976, starting work for the *Miami News* as a photographer and going on to sell one particularly famous image of a now dead rock star to *Rolling Stone*. Revealing it would identify her.

"I went through my 'rocker lifetime' from about 1976 to 1980 or so. I had a relationship with my first musician at age 17. He, like Bon, was not really famous when we first got together. He and I shared a long history and we only stopped speaking to one another a couple years ago, although I had stopped our physical relationship in the 1990s. I even brought my daughter to meet him at a concert in 2009."

She tells me his name and I'm taken aback: he's one of the legendary figures of 1970s rock, someone rarely out of the news. They met in Lakeland, Florida, in 1976. He and Bon met each other and were, to all intents and purposes, friends. They even played on the same bill a few times but neither man knew of the other's involvement with Holly.

When she moved to New York in 1977, Holly enrolled at the New School's Parsons School of Design and for extra money worked as a model and promo girl, which was how she met Bon. She did promo work not just with AC/DC but with J. Geils Band and Foreigner.

"Bon and I had a great friendship first and foremost. I dated other rockers during that time as well, although Bon and the person I mentioned were the men I cared most about back then. It was a wonderful, intoxicatingly exciting and crazy time. I have no regrets. All the alcohol and drugs I did back then and the struggle with addiction that I shared with Bon has made me the woman I am today. My entire career is really dedicated to helping those afflicted with this terrible, often fatal illness. I got clean and sober at 26 and, other than a couple of short relapses, I have enjoyed many years of sobriety and recovery."

We share a plate of curry puffs. The food is taking longer than it should.

"At first I wasn't going to talk, because it brings up a lot of sadness. I haven't read a lot that's been written about Bon but everything I have read it's all about his addiction and him getting high and stories about him being wasted and all this, and that was part of it but he was a really, really *neat* guy. I cared a lot about him. He was a lot of fun. He was a gentle person, gentle soul, in spirit, and very, very sensitive."

She says they were together from "1978 till Bon died," starting around the time AC/DC decamped to Miami for a two-week holiday before the 60-plus dates for the summer tour promoting *Powerage*.

"We really cared a lot about each other, but there was no, like, 'Okay, I'm just going to be with *you*,' we never had that talk, [but] it was getting to that point."

Holly, a doctor and academic, has written a book under her former married name. She's devoted the latter part of her life to teaching students about addiction. She's the real deal; no jobless, publicity-seeking trashbag like so many former lovers of rock stars seeking to relive — and cash in on — events that happened decades ago. She also believes in her "version" of God.

"I am a Christian and a professional and have nothing to gain by embellishing anything I have told you. I'm a recovering addict and I teach about addiction now. I have a quiet, happy life and *definitely* do not seek, nor wish to be in, the spotlight. I thought long and hard before [agreeing to be interviewed] and only did so in order to let people know how wonderful Bon was. I feel I owe this to him for all of the joy he brought to me during that short time in my life. He really was an amazing person. I just want to put out what a lovely man he truly was.

"We were more friends than anything else although we were lovers as well. I wasn't initially attracted to him. Bon was kind of like a little elf, this bizarre little elf guy; he was so tiny. I was this tall blonde, but he was a total sweetie pie. He was one of the sweetest men I've ever known and very loving. So I don't remember anything bad about him."

How did he change when he was drinking?

"Bon was very accessible when he was sober. Very loving, very emotive. He told me how much he cared about me. And when he drank he just kind of shut down. He became very dark. He didn't become violent or anything. He became sad. He became a different person and a very unhappy person. We also did Quaaludes together and things like that.

"When he was drinking he'd do anything, pretty much anything that was in front of him, and then he changed into that different person, as all of us with the disease of addiction did. But that wasn't him, you see, and that's mainly what's been written about him: that he was this 'partyer.' Yeah, he was, but he was *not* his addiction. Underneath his addiction he was a really good man. Way too sensitive, probably."

⚡

The portrait Holly paints of Bon's relationship with AC/DC, especially Malcolm Young, is very different from what people might expect.

"Bon's relationship with Malcolm was not, I mean they weren't, like they didn't hang out, they weren't . . ." She trails off for a moment to process what she needs to say. "To the best of my knowledge there was *something* going on there. I don't think Malcolm really *liked* Bon and I think it was because of his addiction. I just got that impression from Bon; and I don't know if it was just through Bon's eyes because he was drinking or whatever but Malcolm, every time I was around him with Bon, he just didn't really smile, he wasn't really nice, he wasn't really friendly. That's what I remember. But then again Bon and I were partying a lot.

"Bon was this big puppy, really sweet, and Malcolm was this kind of hardass. I didn't really like him, to tell you the truth. There seemed to be a lot of tension between them; I didn't think too much about it. I figured it was because of Bon's drinking and drugging. Bon was this very gentle soul and he was a lost boy. Bon was very unprofessional because of his addiction and he couldn't really be relied on."

But Holly says Malcolm was doing what he thought was right for the band.

"Dealing with someone with the disease of addiction is the hardest thing in the world; I know that. Bon felt that very deeply, he saw that very deeply, he knew that very deeply. I met Malcolm towards the end of Bon's addictions and he basically was done [with trying to deal with it] by that point. I don't know why nothing was done for Bon. I don't why rehab [didn't happen]. It was just because of the time.

"It must have been extremely hard for Malcolm to watch his very gifted and talented lead singer self-destruct on a regular basis. And, of course, Bon's frequent forays into oblivion impacted the overall health and well-being of the band. Anyone would have become frustrated. In 1980 [when he died], I was only 20. It was another lifetime and I have had many other 'lifetimes' since then, as we all have since our adolescent years. Even though Bon didn't say, 'I want to stop drinking and drugging,' he did talk to me about how his partying affected the relationship that he had with Malcolm and the rest of the band, especially Malcolm, and how Malcolm really didn't approve of it.

"He would get very angry at Malcolm when he was drinking, but when he was sober — it's not like we would talk about it a lot or anything — it was more a sadness. I really felt like he wanted to stop but the demons had him by then. He couldn't stop. He would go for times without partying a lot at all, when we hung out together, but it was only for very short periods of time that he could do that because he was already so far into his addiction by that time in his life. So, while there was much tension between Malcolm and Bon due to his substance abuse and his concern about disappointing the band but being unable to stop using and drinking at that point, it is completely understandable that Malcolm *was* frustrated with Bon."

Our Indian arrives and we get back in the Prius.

⚡

After I unpack in her guest room and shower, Holly calls me to dinner and pulls out her old photographer's bag. It's covered in backstage passes. Led Zeppelin's 1977 North American Tour. An old CEDRIC KUSHNER PRESENTS, NEW YORK sticker. The Knack's first world tour. A Criteria Studios sticker. An All Areas pass for the 1979 "The Return of Kiss" tour with "Aucoin," for Kiss's late manager Bill Aucoin, scribbled on it. Swan Song Inc.

Eric Clapton. Gulf Artists Productions' Black Sabbath with Van Halen at the Hollywood Sportatorium. ZZ Top's World Wide Texas Tour with Nils Lofgren at the Beacon Theatre. QUEEN U.S. WINTER TOUR 1977 — GUEST PASS, NO ON-STAGE ACCESS. Jeff Beck and Tommy Bolin 3 December 1976 in Miami, Bolin's last ever concert. SUNSHINE JAM '76: A BENEFIT FOR JIMMY CARTER IN JACKSONVILLE AT THE GATOR BOWL FEATURING CHARLIE DANIELS BAND, LYNYRD SKYNYRD, MARSHALL TUCKER BAND, OUTLAWS, .38 SPECIAL, RICHARD BETTS, CHUCK LEAVELL, JERRY JEFF WALKER & FIREWORKS! Kiss with Uriah Heep at Lakeland, 1976. Leon and Mary Russell. Santana. Outlaws. Rod Stewart. Aerosmith. The Who. Journey. Starz. Foghat. A roll call of 1970s classic-rock legends. And there, in crinkled blue cloth, RON DELSENER PRESENTS AT THE PALLADIUM, DICTATORS, M'S BAND, AC-DC.

The same circle of cloth is visible on Holly's jeans in the photo taken of her with Bon by photographer Chuck Pulin. She shows me a card Bon sent her from the road that she kept. It's of marijuana leaves. It's simply signed "Bon" with an X and a trailing squiggle. To this day she doesn't know what he was getting at. She didn't smoke pot but Bon liked a puff.

Roy Allen tells me he got a similar card with nothing else on it — just "Bon."

"I remember Bon sent me a card one time, still not sure why but he was just that way, little surprises — like saying 'Hey' to me on the radio." The station was KLBJ Austin. "It was a Snoopy and Woodstock card, they were saying something to each other and it was written in French, signed 'Bon.' No 'hope you're well' or anything like that. I never did find out what it said. I remember my dad saying I should get it off the floor of my pickup before I kicked it out and lost it. I didn't and I'm sure it fell out in some beer-joint parking lot. After it disappeared I remember telling him that it was no big deal; that I was sure I'd be seeing him before long."

Said Angus Young: "He made a lot of friends everywhere and was always in contact with them too. Weeks before Christmas he would have piles of cards and things and he always wrote to everyone that he knew, keeping them informed. Even his enemies, I think [*laughs*]. He certainly was a character."

That night, after dinner, Holly and I walk three of her five dogs around the streets of her leafy nook of tropical Miami. It's a quiet neighbourhood. Her rock 'n' roll days are well and truly in the past.

Holly is not the first person who believes Bon wrote a number of songs on *Back In Black* — "several," as she puts it — but her opinion is probably one of the most significant given her history with Bon. She was especially incensed that "Have A Drink On Me" was included on the album as a "tribute" to him. So furious was Holly that she personally confronted Malcolm about it at an AC/DC gig on the *Back In Black* tour but "I was pretty wasted and upset. I was going really downhill with my addiction and I went to one of their concerts . . . I just remember thinking, 'Why am I here? This is insane.'

"I have absolutely no doubt the immense grief I was experiencing at that time — he had only recently died — contributed the most to why I felt compelled to confront Malcolm. The main reason I went was that I felt they were mocking him in a way, especially by including 'Have A Drink On Me' on that album. I felt it necessary to say something on Bon's behalf. I had contacted someone I had met with Bon and had gone backstage to specifically ask Malcolm why he had not given Bon credit on 'You Shook Me All Night Long,' as well as other songs, and to share my anger about the inclusion of 'Have A Drink On Me' since Bon had died as a direct consequence of drinking too much. It was egregious and in very poor taste, not to mention horribly disrespectful to Bon's memory — he had just *died*. I had always been very protective of Bon because I knew how badly he really felt about his drinking and he just could not stop at that point, at least not for long. I guess [at the time] I had made Malcolm the 'bad guy' although now, I completely understand his frustration. I left right after speaking to him and felt angry, sad and quite embarrassed."

I ask Holly what Malcolm said in reply but she can't recall his exact words, which she puts down to her being drunk and the conversation taking place nearly 40 years earlier.

"Whatever happened, it did not go very well."

Either way, it's a fairly damning insight from Holly, especially when Angus Young was once asked in an interview, "Did Bon Scott's death come as a surprise to you or were you well aware of his heavy drinking?"

"That's always been a bit of a myth especially with someone like Bon," he replied. "I can only tell ya what I know of him and we, as a band, saw a lot of him and how he was. I remember him as a real professional and conscientious guy when we worked in the studio. He looked at it as his art. If we had a couple of days off, then he might go out and get a bit crazy. He had a great constitution. He was always the first one out of bed and always looked fit and healthy. He was a guy who really enjoyed life."

In another interview, Angus went deeper into denial: "Bon was not a heavy drinker." Even though Bon's own mother, Isa, confessed: "We were aware that he had a drinking problem and it worried me stiff."

A bit of a myth. Bon was not a heavy drinker. They are remarkably ignorant, almost unbelievable, comments about someone who was slowly dying from alcoholism.

"Bon *was* a heavy drinker — once he got started," says Holly. "Bon could stop drinking for short, discrete periods of time but he just could not *stay* stopped. Especially as the years went by, his disease became more progressive and severe."

He was surrounded by fans, groupies, sycophants and yes-men, but Holly assures me the spectre of the homuncular but fearsome Malcolm intimidated him.

"I think Malcolm made Bon really look at himself, which isn't a bad thing, but he felt a lot of shame because of that. He couldn't stop."

All of which is ironic given Malcolm took leave of the band

in 1988 to battle his alcoholism. But the difference was it was *his* band. He could do it. Bon could not.

"I read stuff that the band considered disbanding [after Bon's death] and I can't imagine that they would have disbanded. I can't recall kindness between Bon and Malcolm. No matter what, [AC/DC] would go on. They wouldn't disband just because Bon died because I don't think he meant that much to them. That's what I thought. I've questioned a couple of the songs that were on *Back In Black*. I really think Bon wrote those, like 'You Shook Me All Night Long.' But he didn't get any credit."

⚡

When we return to her house from our walk, I tell Holly I have my own strong suspicions about "You Shook Me All Night Long." Doug Thaler, AC/DC's American booking agent who with Doc McGhee would go on to manage Bon Jovi and Mötley Crüe, had told me for my first book on the band: "I don't care who tells me anything different: you can bet your life that Bon Scott wrote the lyrics to 'You Shook Me All Night Long.' It's Bon Scott's lyrics all over the place."

She doesn't hesitate: "I never would have brought this issue up with Malcolm in person after Bon's death had I not been abso-lutely certain that Bon had written those lyrics. As always, quite possibly [he wrote them] in tandem with the Youngs but they are *his* ideas. I have one last thing to say about that song: the lyric is 'chartreuse eyes' not 'sightless eyes.'"

She had the sightless eyes. On reflection, it's a line that makes no sense. Could it have been changed because no one in the band knew the meaning of chartreuse? Under the kitchen lights, Holly asks me to tell her if her eyes are chartreuse. They are. Most people don't know what chartreuse means. Had Bon penned lyrics to "You Shook Me All Night Long," it doesn't seem com-pletely implausible that the Youngs and Brian Johnson might have changed Bon's original wording, not just to that song but to others on the album, wherein anything too clever or likely to go over the heads of fans was removed or modified. But they have always maintained their exclusive authorship of it and all the remaining tracks on *Back In Black*. According to them, Bon had no part to play at all apart from jamming on drums in rehearsals on barely formed song ideas that would later become "Have A Drink On Me" and "Let Me Put My Love Into You."

"A memory I have which is so clear is that Bon and I were sitting out in the sun behind the Newport Hotel [in Miami] and he turned to me — the sun was on my face — and he suddenly exclaimed, 'Your eyes are *chartreuse*!' I remember this vividly because I had no idea what colour 'chartreuse' was and immediately took it to be something bad, like bright pink or some ghastly colour. He referred to my eye colour by that word many times.

"I was wearing a lime-green shirt and he told me my eyes matched my shirt. It's funny that I would remember that so clearly. My mother told me my eyes were olive-green growing up, so who knows? To me, they're just green."

But not to a poet like Bon.

Silver Smith was not only certain Bon wrote the song, but, somewhat astonishingly, said it predated his arrival in North America.

"I know for sure that one was written at [my flat in] Gloucester Road [in Kensington, London] back in '76. 'She told me to come but I was already there' — he wrote that in a letter to somebody, one of his grotty mates, just after we got together, actually. He always kept notebooks and added and subtracted to them and so on. He put in 'American thighs' even way back then, because that was the market they were going to try and crack. So that was written a long time ago."

CHAPTER 9

KICKED IN THE TEETH

Bon fighting with Malcolm? Rick Springfield told me, "Bon was a sweetheart of a guy." Ken Schaffer said pretty much the same thing: "Bon I remember as very sweet." But Malcolm was the polar opposite. One of AC/DC's former managers, talking off the record, doesn't remember him fondly: "I always found Malcolm to be the antithesis of anybody I wanted to spend more than five minutes with."

When I ask Barry Bergman, AC/DC's former American publisher and self-described "surrogate manager," to define Malcolm's relationship with Bon, he seems unusually hesitant, even cagey.

"Probably contentious," he answers. There's a *long* pause. "I'm sure it was the alcohol and the other stuff . . . I think it was chemistry. They were all headstrong. I think the tamest one in the band was Cliff. He was cool and calm."

How then did Bon's *drinking* affect his relationship with the band? Bergman seems lost for words.

"That I honestly don't know. I don't believe it was good. I was in shock [when Bon died]. I was angry because I know that

I sat him down on a few occasions and told him he would die. And he didn't seem to care."

Any concern Bergman had about Bon's well-being was "between me and him." It never went to Malcolm.

"I didn't think it my job to tell them . . . it wasn't my band. Yeah, [music publisher Edward B. Marks Music Corporation] had the band, we represented the band, but it's not my band and it's not my job to change people. I can only tell people what I think and then they're going to do what they want. And I wasn't about to start a war with the band because that was not me: to go start a war, to rile everybody up against Bon. There weren't going to be any interventions here; that was not going to happen."

For his part, Phil Carson, who was probably closer to the band than anyone inside Atlantic, downplays the significance of the Bon–Malcolm rift. But, tellingly, he also has no knowledge of Bon ever wanting to go to rehab, considering leaving the band, doing drugs or wanting to do a solo album.

"Inevitably, tensions can arise in any bands that comprise of members who drink a lot and some who don't drink at all," he says. "But these were just normal tensions and there is nothing peculiar in that."

Pete Way of UFO agrees: "Bon and Malcolm got on like a house on fire. They didn't mind [Bon's drinking] at all. It wasn't a question of: 'Hey, we've got a show to do, better sober up.' It'd be like: 'Got a show to do, better drink *twice* as much.' With Bon, anyway. He was always totally alert and a livewire onstage. Malcolm liked to drink, too [*pauses*]. I think they made sure that by the time they were walking on to the stage, if there'd been any drinking in the afternoon, they were ready to take that crowd by the neck."

To Malcolm, at least publicly, Bon's drinking was just part of who Bon was and never a serious problem; nothing to be concerned about.

"[Bon] was what he was. And it's so rare to have something that's real be real for real . . . he knew what life was. Bon never was on a deathwish, you know." But he'd also concede: "I think Bon taught us in a way not to end up like him."

It was a bittersweet comment coming from someone who put himself through AA in 1988. Bon, of course, wouldn't get the same chance.[18]

$$\lightning$$

"By 1979 I saw Bon a lot," says Holly. "He came to my house; he met my parents. Bon was very polite and proper with my parents. He really wanted them to like him. But, again, he really wanted everyone to like him — at least when he was sober and 'himself.' He was very sweet and eager to please. It was very important for him to feel accepted. If I'd kept up my partying, I'd have died long before 33. I'm glad I wasn't a rock star. I don't think Bon really had a chance. He was older so it had gotten worse with him. There were a lot of nights where he had passed out and things like that, but there were also a lot of times he wasn't drinking and he wasn't high and we had fun. That was when I was able to see the real Bon and he was able to see me.

"I have great memories of taking a trip with him to the Miami Seaquarium where he got splashed by Hugo the Killer Whale, and we laughed and laughed because [Bon] looked like a little wet cat. He came out to watch me ride my horse, a chestnut thoroughbred jumper with four white stockings named Doubletime. He was very sweet and gentle with Doubletime. Bon was quite fond of him and met him on at least two occasions when we went to the barn. He did not attempt to ride him but I know he enjoyed watching *me* ride him. We were like kids — in fact, I *was* a kid — and had a great time playing, goofing around and laughing together. Bon loved my horse."

Doubletime? Brian Johnson was working double time on his seduction line in "You Shook Me All Night Long."

"Bon was an incredible man, not just as a 'rock star.' Back then and even now, I just cannot see him as a rock star. He just did not carry himself that way at all. When sober, Bon was a truly humble person who did not seek attention — he was even a bit shy and definitely more than a bit vulnerable. No ego. When drinking, or when he felt he had to 'perform' onstage or in interviews, he'd start strutting and say all kinds of stuff to sound like a tough, arrogant, worldly rock star. But that was a performance he gave because he thought that was what he was expected to do."

This precisely mirrors what Irene Thornton and Silver Smith said about Bon: in public he was playing a role that didn't reflect who he really was in private. Holly clearly knew the very same Bon intimately.

"He was able to blow off some of his anxiety by laughing and being cavalier about the really crazy stuff he did do while under the influence by making it seem like it was all just part of being a rocker. But those things ate away at him — the shame and regrets about how his behaviours hurt those he loved, including Malcolm and the band — and no doubt fuelled further drinking and drugging. He was the polar opposite when sober and away from the spotlight."

Some fans, appallingly, have poured alcohol on Bon's grave as a way of paying homage to him or left behind beer cans or whisky bottles.

Airplay. In 1978, rock groups in the United States and Canada lived and died by it, and station jocks were kings. AC/DC's road map of the USA that year was a spider's web of radio stations with call signs starting in W or K, broken up into blocks of distinct music programming. The band's mission was to get "added" to stations pumping out album-oriented rock (AOR), progressive rock, and the Holy Grail, top 40.

AC/DC would ultimately get most of their play as album cuts on stations programming AOR, which took hold as a format in the mid 1970s and would evolve into what today might be called "classic rock," but they still had to earn that coveted exposure the hard way: touring. What they didn't have was a hit single — and it was causing Atlantic Records some deal of anguish, which was why the band's booking agent, Doug Thaler, on vacation in Sydney over the New Year of 1978, broached the subject of a change of producer directly with Harry Vanda and Angus's and Malcolm's older brother George Young, who together had produced all of AC/DC's

CHAPTER 10

ROCK 'N' ROLL DAMNATION

albums to that point. It was also why, after Atlantic's first listen of the band's new album, *Powerage*, recorded between January and February 1978, AC/DC was sent back into the studio to record "Rock 'N' Roll Damnation." The first track listing of the album simply wasn't radio-friendly enough.

$$\lightning$$

In May that year *Powerage* was released in the United States with a retail price of $7.98. Atlantic's instruction to AC/DC to come up with something more commercial was a wise move, at least in the United Kingdom, "Rock 'N' Roll Damnation" becoming AC/DC's first top-40 single, debuting at #51 and reaching #24. The album went to #26. Angus Young described *Powerage* as "the classiest we've done" in Sydney's *Sun-Herald*, while America's powerful music-trade magazine *Billboard* gave it a rave review: "AC/DC has transcended its punk image with nine searing cuts of high-energy rock."

Radio told one story. AC/DC was getting added to stations in Madison, Eugene, Nashville, Reno, Rochester, San Diego, Albuquerque, Allentown, Rockford and San Jose. But the charts told another. For the week ending 24 June, the first date of the 1978 summer tour, *Powerage* entered the charts at #186, beginning a slow creep to a high of #133. The greatest album AC/DC ever made couldn't get anywhere near the top 100. Meanwhile, *Saturday Night Fever* was the #1 album and "Shadow Dancing" by Andy Gibb was the #1 single. Disco wasn't going away any time soon, especially on AC/DC's own label, Atlantic, which was making more money from Chic than any of its other acts.

AC/DC was going to have to do it the hard way all over again: on the road, without a hit album, without a single that was being played nationwide on radio, with an alcoholic, drug-abusing lead singer who was well and truly on Atlantic Records' and the Young brothers' shitlist.

The pressure to change Bon had been there since even before AC/DC got to the United States, as the band's former bass player

Mark Evans and manager Michael Browning have revealed in interviews over the years since their sackings. When confronted about it by *Countdown* host Molly Meldrum on Australian television, Angus Young played dumb. He seemed affronted at the very notion.

"Browning was always open to people's earholes, you know," he said. "But I mean, for us, that's the first time really I've heard something like that."

The Youngs hadn't sacked Bon for his heroin overdose in 1975 but they'd come close. The second alleged OD the following year had likely escaped their attention. But what was the point of doing all the hard work in the studio and then live if there wasn't going to be a financial pay-off? In nearly five years playing together, Angus and Malcolm (and from the wings, the all-seeing eyes of older brother George) had shown a remarkable willingness to sack musicians in every position in the band but their own. The body count was high. Atlantic's president Jerry Greenberg wasn't going to write cheques for tour support in perpetuity if the band couldn't make inroads on radio and on the charts. The band was heavily in debt to the record company. Bon was supposed to be suddenly immune? The fact is he wasn't, never had been and never would be.

Even Bon himself had gotten into the act, personally sacking bass player Paul Matters in 1975, not long after the pair had spent a day on the beach together. Far from being everyone's friend, Bon could be as cold, heartless and ruthless as the Youngs. Matters, an uncommonly handsome sight in AC/DC, a kind of hard-rock Chris Hemsworth who could play (Malcolm Young inelegantly described him as "a pretty rock bass player" just after he joined), has not given an interview for over 40 years but agreed to speak to me for this book. He lives in a small town on the Central Coast of New South Wales, Australia.

"I was only with them a short time. I did the *High Voltage* tour around Australia, starting in Melbourne and then Adelaide and Sydney."

How were you told you'd been fired?

"*Bon*. Bon Scott. He got out the back of a truck, he was getting changed, I think, and he told me I wasn't going back to Melbourne with them. We were up in Sydney doing a concert for schoolkids. So I didn't play that day. I just turned around and didn't say a word to him. I turned around and walked out."

What had you done to lose your job so abruptly like that?

"George Young was doing the studio stuff when I was there. Playing live was great; I loved it. The only time I didn't get it together was going into the studio. I was just a bit lazy, I think. I didn't have any food in my stomach. They didn't give us any money to buy food or anything. I was a bit cranky about that, so I just laid down on the lounge and said, 'Stuff this. I'll go to England with you, but not now.' No money for the tour. No money to buy food. No proper bed. I couldn't stand it. I thought they were expecting too much. We weren't getting paid at *all*. The tour manager came in with a bundle of 20s and he gave $20 out to each of us. Malcolm got a bit more; I think he got about $40. [The tour manager] was going to forget about me. He was just going to walk out. And I said, 'Listen, mate, if you're not going to give me any money, I'll go *now*.' So he gave me $20. That's pissweak, isn't it? It was a bit of a shame but it could have been worse, couldn't it? I could have gone to England and carked it like Bon did."

Matters says rumours his sacking had to do with drugs are incorrect.

"I smoked pot. That was all. I didn't get into any heavy drugs."

It was the last time Matters saw any member of the band. He sold his Fender bass and was so heartbroken he quit music altogether soon afterwards. Today he lives on a disability pension.

How did that make you feel?

"Terrible. I was gutted. Every day I kick myself, mate. It can be a ruthless business, can't it, mate. *Money*. It can break a person. It's a shame what money can do to people, hey."

His replacement, Mark Evans, was similarly dispatched with a striking lack of mercy and compassion, this time in London by a most reluctant Michael Browning, who'd been asked by the Youngs to do their dirty work right before AC/DC's first American tour.

"Mark was always quite clear thinking . . . quite smart," said Silver Smith. "He was a decent kettle of fish. Phil was a nice guy but he wasn't all that smart. And the Youngs were just, *uh*, the Youngs. They were an exclusive society of two."

Angus, Malcolm, Bon and Phil gathered in stony silence in the Youngs' apartment while Browning delivered Evans his marching orders. Bon, rather ignobly, didn't raise a word in protest, even though he thought it was he and not Mark who was going to get axed.

Said Silver: "Bon thought that he was going to get fired that night. It was around about the time that the band was under pressure from the American [record] company to get rid of him and get somebody that was more photogenic or something."

Evans's departure from the band has been recorded in a number of accounts as of his own volition, even that he was "tired of touring." Malcolm, disgracefully, said the bass player had "quit" in an interview with *Metal CD* magazine in 1992. Australian press explanations that it had come down to musical differences and "as always, everyone involved maintains there are no bad feelings and that the split was amicable" were also false. The truth is, like Matters, he was sacked and, again like Matters, he was devastated about it. To put it bluntly: Evans was knifed in the back.

"We were on tour with Black Sabbath," he told me. "We were going straight to Helsinki and [then] to America. Yeah, I was disappointed . . . at that point I hadn't been to the States. I was the last piece of what people want to call the original lineup, what people think [of] as that Bon-led lineup . . . but it's nowhere near the original lineup, you know; there were plenty of bass players before me."

Not that you'll ever hear the Youngs talking about them.

⚡

Where has this myth sprung up that Bon was untouchable? It was largely created by the Youngs through the solemn interviews they've given since his death about how he pulled them all together and the guileful memorialisation of the *Back In Black* album. VH1's *Behind the Music* special on the band spelled it out plainly. *Back In Black* was "AC/DC's musical memorial to Bon Scott."

Yet according to many people who personally knew the band at the time, it's an album that contains Bon's songs. If it's true, as many suspect or allege, what does that say? All along, the only people pulling the band together were the three Young brothers: Angus, Malcolm and producer brother George. It was their band and theirs alone. If AC/DC couldn't break through in North America, something had to give eventually — and it wasn't going to be Angus or Malcolm. Who would stop them firing Bon?

Angus was feeling the pressure. He told Argentinean magazine *Pelo* it took four albums for AC/DC to make it in the United States: "It was particularly hard for foreign bands because in 1977 Kiss was on top and there was no audience, no press promotion for anyone other than them."

Says Barry Bergman: "Angus had said at one point, 'Radio doesn't want to play our records, I don't know what's gonna be.' I said, 'Angus, you just keep doing what you do. The pendulum will swing and you will have your day. And then in 1979 I remember getting a call from him. I was in Syracuse [in upstate New York] and he called the office. And I called him back and he said to me, 'Barry, the pendulum is swinging.' That's when *Highway To Hell* started to go. The pendulum is swinging."

⚡

For their first four American shows of 1978 — in Virginia, Kentucky, Alabama and Tennessee — Bon would be the support act to an American singer whose drinking problem had eclipsed his own.

"I was worn to a nub," Alice Cooper wrote after the *Lace and Whiskey* tour of 1977. "I was flat-out exhausted from the constant recording and touring, no time off, and nonstop drinking." Cooper's vice was beer, a case a day, a bottle of Seagram's VO, and he was "the most functional alcoholic you could ever meet" who'd be "throwing up blood first thing every morning."

"If you took my alcohol away, I couldn't walk from my bed to the door. I became the classic alcoholic, if there is such a species, because I was using alcohol to self-medicate and sustain my productivity. If there were five interviews to do and you gave me a beer and whiskey, I could do them all. If I had a show to do that night, I would keep drinking. But take away the alcohol and it's no show, no interview, no production . . . no life. That's when you know you're truly an alcoholic."

I ask Holly if she thinks Bon shared some of those characteristics.

"I know Bon felt ashamed about not being able to stop using and the effect his behaviour had on the band. Alice Cooper seems further along the progression of addiction than Bon was when I knew him. However, I have no doubt Bon either got to the same place, or was headed there fast, when he died."

Roy Allen agrees: "Alcohol affects the body, mind and spirit. Alice's story is a common one in regard to later stages of alcoholism. You have to have the booze — it's your best friend and worst enemy. The reason you throw up every morning is that you have to drink to get well which makes you sick and you have to throw up, but you keep drinking and throwing up, hoping and trying to keep a little down to ease the nerves that are sticking out through your skin. Usually, the blood is caused when you bust a vessel in your throat from dry heaving which can look like a lot of blood, but you get used to it somehow. Once you get some alcohol back in your blood, things smooth out and you are good to go for a while."

What's remarkable, though, is that far from looking like a dry-heaving alco, Bon appeared to be in the best shape of his life at the start of the *Powerage* U.S. tour of 1978: muscular, toned, and sporting a shorter hairdo. What his body didn't show was the torment that came with his addiction.

"Bon used because he was an addict," says Holly. "He was not physically dependent, at least not when I first knew him, although his use increased over the years. Like most, *all* addicts, Bon had a tremendous amount of self-doubt — even though he was so obviously gifted — so he usually drank more right before shows than he had done during the day. When there was no pressure, such as when we visited Doubletime or just hung out doing non-band-related stuff in the daytime, I do not recall either of us being high or using anything.

"Everyone with addiction has a different 'key' or 'keys,' a particular substance that 'turns on' the specific reward centre in our brains. Mine were mainly alcohol and sedatives, as were Bon's at the time I knew him. We did other drugs, such as cocaine on occasion, but only to bring us back up when we got too down on the depressant substances. I do not recall him ever using cocaine alone. Neither did I. We were both high-energy people and stimulants alone would have caused us to become way too anxious and jittery."

Says Roy: "I think it says so much about Bon, him being able to do what he did in spite of being so sick."

⚡

AC/DC's shows with Alice Cooper at Norfolk and Lexington flew under the radar with critics. In fact, the review in the *Lexington Herald* didn't even mention the opening act: "Fans were on their feet and worked into a lather by the time his final tune, 'School's Out,' chugged to a halt . . . the 'new' Alice brought along a top-flight band, dancing chickens, teeth and spiders, an eight-foot Cyclops, his snake and a guillotine." But buzz was forming for the support band, especially their lead guitarist.

"I heard about this crazy guitar player and I went out to see Angus being carried on a roadie's shoulders into the crowd while he soloed like a madman," says Alice Cooper keyboardist Fred Mandel. "They sounded great. I knew they were going to be big."

By the time they got to Knoxville, Tennessee, for the last of their shows with Cooper, AC/DC had pulled the rug right out from under the feet of one of North America's biggest touring acts.

"Cooper might be wise to finally give up the theatrics and give a concert," wrote the *Kingsport Times-News*. "The music was, for the most part, lacking. Those who came to rock and roll, however, were not totally disappointed . . . AC/DC, the punkers from Australia, blasted their way through a lengthy opening set which pleased the young audience . . . the outrageous antics of 19-year-old [sic] guitarist Angus Young proved popular, and didn't appear to be as affected as those of Cooper."

AC/DC's next road stop, Texas, was about to get its second dose of high voltage rock 'n' roll. Bon was also about to get a reunion with his favourite drinking buddy, but the Youngs wanted to put a stop to that.

CHAPTER 11

GIMME A BULLET

The Leber-Krebs office on West 55th Street in Midtown, Manhattan, had a pinball machine, exercise bike, fish tank and big stereo system. The principals, Steve Leber and David Krebs, were known to get around in denim jeans, Pucci ties and velvet jackets. It was the heyday of the 1970s music industry and times were good.

The rock 'n' roll management firm had earned a full-page profile in *Rolling Stone* and, in 1978, its acts were selling close to eight million records combined. Leber and Krebs were doing so well they had begun diversifying. Krebs ran the management division (the rock side), profits from which went to Leber's "other areas" such as musicals. And they had had a hand in just about anything that might turn a dollar: a nightclub called Privates on the Upper East Side; planned musicals on Elton John, Marvel superheroes, disco, and a rock 'n' roll history of the world; a play and movie of Eagles' *Desperado*. They even wanted rising tennis star John McEnroe to star in a movie version of *Archie*. Their biggest

Broadway success, Beatlemania, ran from 1977–79, notching up a thousand performances.

Indisputably, Aerosmith was Leber-Krebs's most important client. Signed by Columbia's Clive Davis in 1972 after seeing them at Max's Kansas City in New York, by 1976 they had sold four million albums. The same year "Dream On" was a top-10 hit and *Rocks* went platinum. In 1977 "Walk This Way" also went top 10 and *Draw The Line* became the band's fastest platinum seller. The 82-date tour mounted to promote it brought Aerosmith in July 1978 to Leber-Krebs's Texxas World Music Festival (aka the Texxas Jam) at the Texas State Fairgrounds' Cotton Bowl in Dallas. In front of 80,000 people on 1 July, Aerosmith headlined Ted Nugent, Atlanta Rhythm Section, Head East, Heart, Van Halen, Frank Marino & Mahogany Rush, Eddie Money, Walter Egan, Journey and Texas "Battle of the Bands" winner Blackstone. Cheech & Chong hammed it up between sets. Temperatures were so hot — around 40°C — the crowd close to the stage was fire-hosed by a stagehand.

"A scorching hot Texas sun beat down relentlessly on the Cotton Bowl," wrote *Circus*, "giving the appearance of a giant, unoiled frying pan on the verge of spontaneously igniting."

But the lowly AC/DC wasn't big enough for the main event. Instead they were relegated to nearby Fair Park Arena on 3 July with Blackstone and Virginia band Artful Dodger. Willie Nelson's Annual Picnic, featuring Nelson, Waylon Jennings, Kris Kristofferson and more, took place the same day.

"It would have been just before Willie's barbecue kicked off," says Paul Harwood, bass player of Mahogany Rush. "It was a free show as there was no time to promote it and was very poorly attended."

But Artful Dodger drummer Steve Brigida was thunderstruck: "I will never forget AC/DC. One of the best bands ever. Bon seemed under the weather that night, though. We had the ungodly task of following them."

When Bon got to Lubbock on 4 July 1978, Roy Allen went looking for him.

"I had to call around to the hotels to find Bon. After that, he would always call when they were in Austin and let me know where they were staying. I was living in Lubbock with my late uncle Gary White, a pharmacist. I had been going to South Plains College and again was out for summer. It was my third school to attend. I was drinking a lot and using drugs that my uncle would bring home from work. Somehow I found out the band was playing in town."

AC/DC was playing the Municipal Coliseum with Aerosmith and Mahogany Rush. Paul Harwood was impressed by Angus Young but struck by how little spontaneity there was in AC/DC's stage show.

"It seemed that the act was very much following some game plan. AC/DC kept to themselves and out of sight until they rushed up onto the stage and did their very tightly scripted act."

He's right. There was nothing very spontaneous about the band and never has been with AC/DC, as an editorial in Australian music newspaper *RAM* once observed: "AC/DC have a calculated approach to whipping audiences into heat. Everything 'spontaneous' is in fact carefully pre-planned, right down to the sole thickness of Angus Young's feet when he makes his 'daring' leap from the top of a stack of loudspeakers."

After they'd finished their set, Roy approached security backstage.

"I passed a note to the doorman to take back to the band. Malcolm came and got me and we walked to the room they were in. Malcolm and I always got along fine but Angus, he could be a real asshole and act like a spoiled child. All I remember of that concert is that Bon was with this girl."

Bon and his unknown companion, another blonde, went with Roy to his Uncle Gary's house in Lubbock. It didn't go so well for Roy.

"Bon and this girl and Gary and his girlfriend were there. They stayed for a while visiting; we always smoked weed. Bon and the girl were not drinking much and he was not drunk but I must have been extra fucked up because I fell and hit a metal bookcase with my lower left jaw and cut myself pretty bad: lots of blood but not bad enough to see the doctor. I still have that scar."

By then Bon had broken whatever remaining ties he still had with Silver Smith in Sydney and attempts to go sober — including hypnosis — had failed. What Bon saw go down that night in Lubbock might well have affected him. Seeing a friend, another alcoholic, at his worst while he himself was trying to stay off the booze would likely have jolted him into some sort of resolution, or, at the very least, given him some clarity about his own problematic relationship with alcohol.

In Irene Thornton's memoir of Bon, *My Bon Scott*, she reproduces a letter from 1975, very early on in his time with AC/DC, in which he writes that he doesn't want to settle with anyone because of the demands of life on the road, yet "on the other hand there's 20-30 chicks a day I can have the choice of fucking but I can't stand that either. Mixed up." There was a nasty tone in some of those letters, something Irene remarked on in her book. The deeper he got into the band and the persona of Bon Scott, the AC/DC rocker, the cruder he became; and Bon was not a pleasant drunk.

"His drinking was completely out of control," she wrote. "If he wasn't pissed he was sleeping it off, preparing to get pissed the minute he woke up."

Bon's only ex-wife deserves high praise for her candour and willingness to expose his faults to the world. When I wrote to her in 2016 to express thanks for her courage in bucking the Bon myth, she replied: "There isn't enough honesty and the myth building is really annoying (to say the least). He could be a real pain in the neck; the same as anyone else."

Seeing Roy cut up his jaw and ruin the evening for everybody might have been the awakening he needed.

"The next day was the first time Bon asked me if I had ever thought about not drinking," says Roy. "It was a question that has always stuck in my mind. He said I had been way too drunk and it looked pretty bad. I don't remember what my reply was.

I was riding to Austin with them the next day and recall Gary coming down on me for being so drunk too."

⚡

Bon and his Amazonian guard picked up Roy the following morning for the long drive to Austin. Roy believes the girl may have been hired by the band to make sure Bon didn't drink.

"I don't remember her name but it didn't take long to realise that this girl was not a very nice person — she was such a bitch. She was a Texas girl from Houston and she drove a brand new Firebird; nice car but with a little back seat. She was very particular about that car. I remember thinking, 'Where in the *hell* did Bon find this girl?' She would not let us drink or smoke and all she did was bitch about little things and was constantly saying no to everything. I remember wondering if [AC/DC] put this girl on Bon to make sure he made it to where he needed to be and in decent shape.

"That's how it looked to me, because there was no way Bon would hang out long with someone like that. Her looks were her only good quality. I remember it being one of the longest seven hours of my life; she made the ride back miserable. As soon as we hit town I told her, 'Let me off right here, I can manage to find my way,' so I got out in front of a Mexican restaurant on the west side of town, and told Bon I would see him later. He understood. They had that whole day off. I know I hooked up with them again later that day, but it is very foggy."

While all this was going on, Aerosmith tour accountant Peter Mensch, on the payroll at Leber-Krebs, was being wooed by Malcolm Young — or the other way around. Michael Browning has made no secret in various interviews and his autobiography that he believed Mensch was sweet-talking AC/DC behind his back as early as 1978. But according to Mensch it was Malcolm initiating it: "They called me."

AC/DC was upstaging Aerosmith but Bon wasn't leaving much of an impression on him. Mensch remembered Angus getting on "a small guy's shoulder, the singer, who's just yelling into the microphone, unintelligible words, as far as I'm concerned." After the two bands parted ways in Lubbock, "AC/DC called me almost every day in my office just to give me news of them."

$$\textit{\textbf{f}}$$

The next day Roy travelled for six hours on the band's tour bus to Austin for AC/DC's first show with San Francisco band Yesterday & Today. Bill Martin, Roy's friend from Rockdale who'd been in the audience for AC/DC's concert at the Armadillo World Headquarters the year before, was there to meet him with a group of friends.

"We, of course, didn't believe that my friend's brother Roy was actually *friends* with Bon, so when they played the Opry House he told us to meet him and Bon would get us in the show. Again, we didn't believe Roy so we showed up early and bought our own tickets."

They needn't have bothered. Roy appeared with Bon, "who went to the ticket office, grabbed up a stack of tickets and started writing 'comp' on the back of them."

Martin still has the ticket Bon signed for him.

"We got to go backstage and watched the concert from the side of the stage. Pretty cool, to say the least. AC/DC was an important part of our music growing up, especially after seeing their very first concert. Because of Roy we got to meet them and spend some time with Bon."

"The show was great, maybe the best show I saw them do," says Roy. "They had really found a groove."

But away from the stage, something was clearly up with Bon. AC/DC's lead singer drove to Corpus Christi with his girl minder.

"I remember feeling sorry for Bon. I didn't ever see the girl again. I had the impression she had a job to do and was being a real bitch about it. Or maybe he liked her for her looks or something; she was damn good-looking. Haven't we all kept bitch girl-friends around just for their looks? I have never been able to figure out exactly what that was all about."

Supporting Roy's suspicions about the girl, Yesterday & Today singer and lead guitarist Dave Meniketti says Bon was unhappy about not being allowed to drink or have groupies on the AC/DC tour bus. He didn't want to travel with AC/DC. In Yesterday & Today's modified Dodge van, no such restrictions applied.

"Bon was not happy with the fact that he felt he couldn't party in the way he wanted on the AC/DC bus," Meniketti tells me. "He would try a few days travelling with a bunch of kids — us — in a Dodge van, drinking booze in the back and carting groupies around from gig to gig. I think that setting was more to his liking, where he could do as he wished. I remember stopping for fuel and the guys jumping out of the van and buying what I believe was a bottle or two of Jack Daniel's from the gas station liquor store."

Joey Alves, Yesterday & Today's late rhythm guitarist, remembered Bon hitching an altogether better ride on their voyage around Texas.

"One warm day travelling to the next town on the open highway, a car with some wild-looking ladies raced by our van then slowed down to get our attention. It was Bon sitting in a car with five ladies from the previous night's show. He was in the back seat waving to us, telling us to pull over at the next road stop. We did. While we were stocking up on cold drinks he filled us in on his wild night with his newfound friends. Bon had a great way of telling stories and always kept you entertained when doing so. One would think that living life in the fast lane would take its toll on one's live performance but that was not the case with Bon. He was spot on every show, as was the band."

Even so, in San Antonio on 8 July 1978, legend has it that Bon "was so incapacitated that he polished off an entire bottle of aftershave in a single gulp, mistaking it for whisky." It's a story that superficially seems ridiculous — surely he wasn't that hard up for something to drink — but UFO's Paul Chapman had also seen Bon drink aftershave. It may have been just a lark, another one of Bon's party tricks, but his behaviour disguised an addiction that was beginning to cause him inordinate pain.

CHAPTER 12

UP TO MY
NECK IN YOU

More shows with Aerosmith followed in Utah, California and Oregon, most notably a poorly received 15 July 1978 gig at Selland Arena in Fresno, where Angus Young interrupted his solo in "Bad Boy Boogie" to return some fire to hecklers who'd taken to throwing things at him from the audience. "Hell. *Oi!* Out there! Hey! *Prick.* Fucking come here. If youse wanna fuckin' throw things at us, we can fuckin' heave 'em back, alright?" He then launched back into his solo like nothing had happened. They didn't finish their set and were booed from the stage.

"We were all at the hotel after that incident at Selland Arena in Fresno, when AC/DC were ushered off stage and basically kicked out of town," says Atlantic Records' West Coast regional promotion director Barry Freeman. "I remember it being a warm night. We were all sitting outside, and I guess they were expecting some cars to come because the police were waiting for them to get out of town."

AC/DC were not faultless; they invited trouble.

"I don't know if I should tell it, but I will tell you this story," says an Atlantic staffer who has requested anonymity. "It's a true story, I promise you that [*laughs*]. AC/DC had an interview at a radio station at San Rafael, which is about 10 miles north of San Francisco proper. You have to go over the Golden Gate Bridge and you head up north and there was what they used to call a free-form rock radio station, KTIM."

It was the second American radio station after WPDQ/WAIV in Jacksonville to play AC/DC.

"I got a limo and we all got in the limo, me and the band and the driver. And off we go to San Rafael and we've come over the Golden Gate Bridge and we're now kind of heading towards San Rafael, about 10 or 15 miles. And there's a bus, a church bus, and it was filled with kids — nine, 10, 11, 12, not older kids, but *younger* kids. And the band, for a little respite while they were waiting to get to KTIM, had a copy of *Hustler* magazine.

"In those days there was a thing they called Scratch 'N' Sniff and the naked girl on the centrefold you scratch their private parts and it supposedly smells like a real person. And they took that magazine and they spread it on the back boot of the Cadillac limousine, between the back seat and the back window. They spread it out and they pointed. I don't know if these girls knew who was in the car. They weren't yelling out or holding up album covers or any of that stuff. So [AC/DC] started scratching as we were going by, and I remember saying to them, "Oh, guys, you *can't* do this; we're going to be arrested. *Don't* do this." They all started laughing and they kept doing it. And they were pointing to the girls to look at this magazine as we're driving by in the limo. So the limo driver probably figures discretion is the better part of valour and he moved over to the left and slowed down and the bus went on ahead. It was funny then but not funny in retrospect. It's so typical of that day and age."[19]

⚡

Dawn broke in Oakland, California, and AC/DC was up early for the most important show of their lives: the 10:40 a.m. opening act at Bill Graham's Day On The Green concert with Aerosmith, Foreigner, Van Halen and Pat Travers. It was the third of five Days On The Green that year and the first of three major festivals for AC/DC in the Bay Area in 1978–79.

"Great shows, Days On The Green," says Mick Jones. "That was a huge kind of stage to pass through. It was almost like you'd been baptised or something into the higher echelons. I remember Bill, who I'd known many years, way back, took me aside and said, 'Mick, I wanna see you up here at like 11 o'clock on the stage. I wanna show you something.' So I met up with him onstage. And he said, 'Okay, 11 o'clock.' *Bang*. All the entrances to the stadium opened at once and people were coming out like rats. *Sheeeeuuuuwwww*. Just running to try to get up front. It was an unbelievable sight to see that. I think he wanted to just punctuate, make me appreciate, what was going on a bit."

Eddie Van Halen was on the main stage at noon and he had become a fan of AC/DC.

"Eddie went in their trailer," says Van Halen bass player Michael Anthony. "AC/DC was right next to us. In '78, half our tour we opened up for Black Sabbath throughout Europe. The thing that really kept us all going on our tour bus — it was our first tour, we'd been out for a long time, everyone was kinda burned out — was *Powerage* on cassette tape. We were just blazed. *Everything*. 'Sin City.' All those songs. That kinda kept us all in good spirits. That was like one of the only cassettes we played every day. That is one of my favourite albums. After playing with them at Day On The Green, we got ahold of the cassette, and man, I tell you, at that point then that's all everybody was listening to when we were going through Europe."

Anthony says the two bands had more in common than just virtuoso guitarists.

"Alex Van Halen was a big drinker. Alex and Eddie, both. We all drink obviously because you're thrown into this lifestyle that you only read about. Opening up for some of these bands it's like, all of a sudden that door opens up to you and, 'Let the games, let the partying begin.' Alex really had affection for Schlitz Malt

Liquor and he would drink quite a bit of it. And it got to the point we played a show in Chicago [in the late 1980s], he fell off his drum kit. We actually sent him to rehab. His drinking had kept escalating to a point where he had to go somewhere. It was either going to kill him or he had to stop."

Jones also went to rehab.

"I was using through the '80s, I was using into the '90s. It was at the end of the '90s [that I went to rehab] so I had a good long run in that battle. Coke and vodka: great recipe. Being the leader of the band I guess nobody had the balls to tell me [to stop]. And I didn't realise how gradually more and more it was affecting my relationship with the band. It certainly took a toll on [Foreigner lead singer] Lou Gramm's and my relationship. Both he and I were going along the same path a bit and he chose to do something about it in the early '90s and it took another seven or eight years for me to start battling back. Bottom line was that I think I lost probably a good 10 years of creativity and life while I was an addict and an alcoholic."

Do you think you've made up for it by having that clarity now and re-embracing your life in a different way?

"Oh, yeah. The main thing, or perhaps the biggest thing for me, was trying to get my family back, my kids. To be somebody they could rely on, somebody they could trust, and not this guy that came staggering in at six o'clock in the morning, waking everybody up and ready to party. It just caught up with me and I realised that I was in danger of losing everything. Liquor and drugs were unfortunately the most important things in my life. When you're in that trap, it's very hard to get out of it."

Something Bon was just starting to discover.

CHAPTER 13

RIFF RAFF

That North American summer of 1978 Aerosmith's Steven Tyler and lead guitarist Joe Perry were at the height of their addictions to heroin. As July turned into August, AC/DC did seven shows with Aerosmith: Vancouver, Spokane, Billings, Winnipeg, Rapid City, East Troy, and Chicago's Summer Jam festival at a sweltering Comiskey Park. Spokane's *Spokesman-Review* sensed the changing of the guard.

"Aerosmith's lead singer, Steve Tyler, thinks he's hot stuff. But judging from the reaction of last night's capacity Coliseum crowd, his popularity here has cooled considerably . . . what Spokane fans needed last night was something new. That they got when the warm-up band, AC/DC, appeared and lead guitarist Angus Young began his hour-long rock blast."

But while they were tearing up the Northwest, Canada and the Midwest, AC/DC still had onerous obligations to their record company. In Nashville, Tennessee, they played a set at the fifth annual Record Bar Convention, along with Memphis band Creed, coming onstage after the attendees' dinner to perfunctory applause.

"QUIET AREN'T YA!" screamed Bon to an accompanying power chord. "We'll change that!"

With little happening for AC/DC on FM radio, the band was going to pull out all stops in their live performances. In Salem, Virginia, and Fayetteville, North Carolina, a town servicing nearby U.S. Army base Fort Bragg, AC/DC did back-to-back shows with Cheap Trick and Nantucket.

"I was standing there at the monitor desk while they roared into their first few tunes," says Nantucket drummer Kenny Soule. "[Lead guitarist] Tommy Redd and I looked at each other and went, 'Holy *shit*.' AC/DC would hammer a groove, like the beginning of 'High Voltage,' until the audience went bonkers. It was like Chuck Berry on 12; the way I had always dreamed of experiencing that kind of rock 'n' roll. They rocked that place so hard and so passionately it was kind of scary. I was almost horrified that a band could kick that much ass. Other than seeing James Brown a few times in the late '60s, I had never seen such a thing. As soon as I got a load of Angus Young, it was like James Brown. Tommy and I were kind of dumbfounded."

While AC/DC could unleash hell onstage, they were sweet as pie off it.

"On our way out of town, we stopped at a Waffle House for a takeaway coffee. There they were, all crammed into a small booth having a bite."

⚡

After the band's gig with Cheap Trick at Atlanta's Symphony Hall, Bon took a limo back to Peachtree Plaza, which had only recently been surpassed as the world's tallest hotel. He was exhausted.

"I guess I have always had the idea of being rich and having a lifestyle to which I was suited," Bon told Australian photographer Rennie Ellis. He was also in an unusually expansive mood with Vince Lovegrove, who was in Atlanta to film AC/DC for *Australian Music to the World*, a spinoff TV special of his 5KA radio series in Adelaide.[20] Silver Smith told me she believed Lovegrove as a friend was more intimate with Bon than anyone else, only Fraternity bass player Bruce Howe coming close.

"The more we work, the more we tour, we're getting more ideas," Bon said to Lovegrove. "It's gonna get better and better. I can't see an end to it. It's like infinity rock 'n' roll."

Bon, Lovegrove would recall years later, was "dressed to the nines" but "ragged around the edges." Off camera, he admitted his dream was still to make it as a rock 'n' roll star though self doubt had started to creep in and he was wondering whether the sacrifices he'd made were all worth it when he had so little to show for himself.

"He thought I got the best deal because I was settled down and I wasn't on the road any more. And [Bon] said, 'I really envy that. I wish I was [settled down] . . . to be honest, I'm really getting sick of this. We're on the road nonstop and I need a break. I want a break . . . I can afford to take a break. I've got a lot of cash coming my way.'"

Bon wanted to "live an ordinary life like anyone else and just play guitar." Lovegrove believed "there was a deep core of unhappiness" and "an undertone of sadness" in his friend from Western Australia. There were doubts about whether AC/DC was going to make it: "He had been touring nonstop on an upwardly mobile track of making it in a rock 'n' roll band since [1966], people forget that . . . the others [in AC/DC] hadn't been."

These were haunting words when juxtaposed with Bon's own in a 1977 interview with Molly Meldrum in London. The band was about to head off on its second leg of American touring.

"You've just got to have a break, you know," he said. "You've just got to have a break occasionally."

But Bon would go on feeding the press white lies when it suited him: "I've been on the road 15 years and I have no intent to stop. We meet a lot of people, we drink lots of stuff and we have lots of fun."

Bon, 32 in late 1978, had started to noticeably age. Yet despite being worn down from constant touring, drinking and drugging, he had retained his winsome manner. Lovegrove attempted to describe this side of Bon, saying there "was something about Bon that was a touch effeminate, that was subtle, very subtle, and certainly not overtly exploited by him, but [it] definitely was [there]." When you "took away all the showbiz," Bon "brought an ordinariness and a slight edge of amateurishness about rock 'n' roll to the fore, something that wasn't slick."

In *Live Wire*, Mary Renshaw writes that she is "angry" at Lovegrove for revealing the Atlanta conversation with Bon "because this was possibly the only time Bon had ever been vulnerable with Vince, and he then used that against Bon . . . years later, Vince was working with an American film producer, trying to make a movie about Bon's life. She emailed me, saying, 'Bon was in a really dark place; he was going to leave the band.' Vince had told her that, and it was total crap."

Or was it?[21]

Lovegrove was in doubt: "He told me that he'd had enough; that he couldn't stand the touring lifestyle any more but that he had to keep going because the big money hit was just around the corner. In many ways, Bon was not suited to be a pop star, in many ways he was. But he longed to get out, settle down, have kids and just write and sing music, that's for sure. No matter what anybody else says, he wanted out, but the addiction of it all was too much. He was hooked like we're all hooked on music. It's just a matter of how hooked, what we do about it, and under what circumstances we try and let it and its side effects take over."

Lovegrove, who would go on to reinvent himself as a journalist and biographer, would write a number of stories about that same Atlanta meeting. In Adelaide's *Advertiser*, he claimed Bon told him, "[AC/DC] were nearly there, that he could smell the success, but if they didn't make it in the next year or two, he would leave the band. He said there still wasn't much money, that he was still broke. He told me he would come back to Australia if it didn't happen soon for AC/DC. He told others he would stay in America. I am sure he told different people a different story. But he was certainly lonely."

In *Australian Worker* magazine, he asserted that Bon "was all but broke" when he died.

"[Bon] enjoyed being in the band but wanted to see some money for his efforts. He wanted a break. He wanted somewhere to lay his hat . . . the question is: How does a working-class Scottish immigrant with a police record, who, in the 1960s, lived in the rough, tough, blue-collar suburb of North Fremantle, end up as a multi-millionaire — after he's dead? At the time of his death AC/DC had sold around three million albums, respectable sales it's true, but touring expenses, record company touring advances, management and agency percentages, and promotion and recording costs had all but swallowed the lot."

It's a very good question from Lovegrove, one that up to now has never been adequately answered.

CHAPTER 14

DOWN PAYMENT BLUES

AC/DC might have been building steam as a touring act in North America but record sales were still poor. And this was at a time when the record industry was booming, especially at Atlantic Records, part of the giant WEA conglomerate.

Understandably, the executives that mattered at Atlantic — co-founder Ahmet Ertegun, president Jerry Greenberg and chief financial officer Sheldon Vogel prime among them — had reservations about coughing up any more "tour support" for AC/DC. By Atlantic's lofty standards, *Powerage* had been another commercial turkey. Greenberg and his lieutenants promptly began angling for producer Mutt Lange to replace Vanda & Young.

"When [Leber-Krebs] first got involved with AC/DC," says David Krebs, "Steve Leber and I together went to see Ahmet Ertegun, *not* Jerry Greenberg, to say, 'Look, Ahmet, because the group has such a weak record deal that they had made through Phil Carson with Ted Albert, we want Atlantic to pay us, the managers, a couple of extra [royalty percentage] points.' Don't laugh. We had balls. [*Laughs*] He, of course, said no . . . but we did try that."

The true terms of AC/DC's contract with Atlantic were punishing, according to Krebs.

"AC/DC signed with Phil Carson for five years, three albums a year, so they had a *15-album* commitment. Do you know how onerous that is? Nobody ever was signed for more than two albums a year. Nobody could do three albums a year, certainly not of quality material, even though we're talking about two sides of vinyl. When we had huge success with, I think, *Highway To Hell* but it could have been *Back In Black*, [Peter Mensch's management partner] Cliff Burnstein and I took a meeting with Sheldon Vogel, who was the right-hand man of Ahmet. And *Back In Black*, being an amazing album, was the eighth album out of 15 [it was AC/DC's eighth release but their sixth original LP with Atlantic].

"So I said to myself, 'Shit. Only so many records. We're gonna get *shit*.' So I was prepared to give Atlantic more records for a much higher royalty, immediately, because I thought it didn't matter. If I owe you seven at this point, what's the difference if I owe you *nine*? I'm not sure I was right looking back. But the group said no to that deal, so we let that go. The fact that they were [stuck] in a 15-album deal is quite incredible.

"It's a question I've never quite understood. Why did Ted Albert agree to sign with Atlantic for three albums a year for five years? It was a stupid deal. Nobody can do three albums [a year]. Which meant that a five-year deal probably became a 12-year deal, or whatever, you know what I mean?. If you didn't deliver the third album it just got extended. *Nobody* fucking did three albums a year, not that I ever heard of."

It was a view shared by Mensch: "[AC/DC] signed the worst record deal I have ever seen in my entire life with Atlantic Records."

⚡

Ted Albert was the second of three sons born to the late J. Albert & Son chairman Sir Alexis Albert and Lady Elsie Lundgren Albert, who owned a two-storey, multimillion-dollar mansion with 38 metres of water frontage in Vaucluse, Sydney. It was a charmed life. Albert liked to sail on Sydney Harbour and competed in Dragon Class sailing competitions when he wasn't countersigning foreign record contracts.

"An absolute straight arrow," says Phil Carson. "Dead straight; a complete gentleman."

But Carson maintains he did his super-profitable deal with Albert in good faith and everyone was happy about it; nobody was duped.

"At that time, nobody really cared about bands from Australia. Both Alberts and AC/DC desperately wanted a release. They also wanted to be convinced that whoever signed them was the right person to get the band started. Yes, they paid a price, but the result was incredible. I stuck by that band when everyone else at Atlantic had turned their back, to the point that they actually dropped the band when they first heard *Dirty Deeds*."

That is true, according to Barry Bergman: "Jerry Greenberg did not believe in the band. [Atlantic in New York] didn't believe in the band; they didn't sign the band. It was signed through Phil Carson. I remember when one of the albums came [in], Jerry wanted to drop the band before *Highway To Hell*.[22] And Michael [Browning] called me up and told me all about the situation and we discussed it and he was really upset, as I don't blame him, and he said to me, 'You know, Barry, I don't know what I'm going to do. [Jerry's] thinking about dropping the band, he wants to reduce the advances.' I said, 'Take whatever you can get. Don't worry about it. You'll make it up after the band makes it. We're better off with a record coming out than no record at all any more.' And he took, I think, a major advance cut."

Carson says he reversed New York's decision.

"I worked extremely hard to break the band, and the rest is history. All my people at Atlantic in London were believers in AC/DC and the ideas that we came up with were novel and effective. I broke AC/DC because of their hard work, quality playing and writing, stellar performances, and the right marketing and promotional expertise. From their side of it, while the terms of the deal may not have been financially what they wanted, all the rest of it fell into place. Once I got the ball rolling in the UK and later in Europe, I was able to convince Jerry and the team at Atlantic in New York that this was a band they could break. Atlantic Records was the right company for AC/DC."

Said his Atlantic UK colleague, label manager the late Dave Dee: "We ended up signing [AC/DC] to a ridiculously long deal for a ridiculously cheap fee, because they were just happy to get a deal of any sort in those days, and we were able to sign them without telling anybody at Atlantic where the money had come from. It was a brilliant scam."

$$\frac{1}{7}$$

Though it was standard industry practice for bands to renegotiate royalties in record contracts when they became successful, the problem for AC/DC was they had no bargaining power.

Explains Krebs: "With AC/DC still owing seven albums, I think, you had very little leverage to get the label to make that move, especially with a guy like Sheldon Vogel, who was really a penny-pinching kind of guy; not the easiest guy to get along with, but doing his job, of course."

Mensch has boasted that he "solved that problem" when he became AC/DC's manager, but Carson plays it down: "Peter came in and asked for more. And he got more. But he didn't get much more, I can tell you that. [That's his] ego telling you it was sorted out, but he certainly didn't get any relief from having to deliver 15 albums under the contract. Peter talks away a big game and he's very good at what he does but he was up against Sheldon, who was very protective of Atlantic's bottom line. I'm quite sure AC/DC got a better royalty rate but they certainly didn't get any albums back [on the contract]. So big deal, Peter. You know, *great*. You improved the royalty, excellent news. But not by much.

"Peter is correct in that the deal was renegotiated and AC/DC received a more appropriate royalty and bigger advances as time went by. However, Atlantic still had a 15-album deal. They sold the last album under the terms of this contract to Sony for $10 million. Whoever signed AC/DC is undoubtedly a legend and genius. Oh, wait a minute: that's me. I signed AC/DC for $25,000 for the first album in a contract that called for Alberts to pay for them to come to England for promotion, and gave Atlantic a further 14 albums at $25,000 each. This is undoubtedly the most profitable deal in the entire history of the recording business."

$$\lightning$$

What did all this mean when it came to the money that went into Bon's pocket?

A source who has asked for anonymity confirms that Alberts got a 12 per cent royalty for AC/DC from Atlantic Records. It was an "all-in agreement," meaning two of that 12 went to the producer, in AC/DC's case, Vanda & Young (this percentage later rose to three or four when Mutt Lange produced the band).

"Harry once said to me that they only really got rich when AC/DC took off overseas," says Vanda & Young biographer John Tait. "He said something like, 'Two points on every AC/DC album they produced.'"

Then Alberts took its cut. Whatever else was left went to the band and their manager. To give an idea of how little money was actually flowing to the band itself outside of songwriting royalties, Bon received a royalty cheque from Ted Albert in the second half of 1976 for $3957.29 out of the band's cut of $24,733.06. Of that $24,733.06, Michael Browning took $4946.61, his 20 per cent manager's cut, leaving a total of $19,786.45. The band members were left to divide the remainder equally, giving them $3957.29 apiece. So, on that occasion at least, Browning was actually receiving a bigger cut than each of AC/DC's five band members, which might go some way to explaining Angus Young's antipathy to him.

"A large part of the Australian rock 'business' has always been disgusting, not only Alberts," says Grahame Harrison. "I spent most of my time with Harry Vanda. He was great. Harry had a very amenable nature. Lovely man, lovely individual, who knew exactly how to get results out of the musicians he was working with. George Young was a cunt. *Full stop*. To his due, he was totally focused on what was going on, the business, but he was a very tightly wound individual with a short temper, a short fuse."

It's well known that Vanda & Young had a stake in Alberts through Albert Productions, the recording arm. Ted Albert had agreed to extend the producers a partnership agreement as part of a deal to lure them back from England in 1973 and begin writing and producing in Sydney. This agreement has been variously described as "a share in Albert Productions in lieu of cash," a "partnership" and a "three-way partnership including regular generous advances in return for royalty earnings." Vanda likened the agreement to "falling into a bloody goldmine." So how, then, did Vanda & Young, who never made any money from their own band, The Easybeats, get so fabulously rich?

⚡

Under U.S. copyright law a songwriter and the songwriter's publisher get an automatic payment each time a copyrighted song licensed to the record company (a "published" song) is pressed or sold by that record company, usually in the form of a compact disc or a digital phonorecord delivery (downloads, ringtones). That payment, called a mechanical royalty, is typically divided into half to the songwriter and half to the publisher. In 1978 recorded music was predominantly sold in the form of LPs and cassettes, and the statutory mechanical royalty was 2.75¢ a song. With various increases over the years, the full rate for CDs and permanent downloads is at the time of writing 9.1¢ (or 1.75¢ per minute of playing time for songs five minutes or over), but record companies typically insist on clauses in contracts limiting the rate to 75 per cent of the full statutory rate and putting a cap on the number of "controlled compositions" on an album. These are songs that are owned or written by an artist and derive mechanical royalties.

AC/DC hasn't covered another artist's song in the studio since Chuck Berry's "School Days" in 1975. "Fling Thing," an instrumental B-side from 1976, is based on a Scottish traditional song. A share of publishing rights (in effect, the copyright on the song's lyrics and melody) is highly valuable, not least because any other artist who covers AC/DC's songs also has to pay them royalties for the privilege. AC/DC had an industry-standard 50:50 "life of copyright" deal with Ted Albert.

"A publishing deal is not a life sentence," says the anonymous insider who worked closely on AC/DC's contracts. "It has a term attached to it. So in other words, you can assign the song to the publisher in perpetuity. But you can't be *signed* to a publisher as a writer in perpetuity. The share of artist revenue that comes from publishing is now much greater than the share for performing the actual music, as an artist royalty. Publishing is not diluted by anything. Record royalties are. A record royalty is diluted by a manager taking a commission and the record company charging any 'tour support' to it. There are no deductions in publishing."

Tour support refers to recoupable or deductible expenses charged against royalties.

"It was rather unusual that Albert would own 100 per cent of the publishing [mechanical royalties] of AC/DC," says Krebs. "That's why I asked for half of it back in my one meeting with Ted, because I thought it was onerous. I thought it was unfair. That's a 50:50 deal obviously on every dollar [of mechanical royalties: half to the publisher, Albert, half to AC/DC's three songwriters]."

How much, then, of Albert's own share might have been shared with Vanda & Young, Albert's partners in Albert Productions and the producers of AC/DC's albums? Michael Browning confirmed to me that even he, as the band's manager, wasn't privy to the precise division of publishing royalties but to "the best of my recollection" Atlantic's deal with Albert was through Albert Productions. While J. Albert & Son was the publishing arm, it seems inconceivable that Vanda & Young, a producing team which included Angus's and Malcolm's own brother, didn't receive a share of publishing royalties from AC/DC.

Says Tait: "The older they got the more canny they got regarding their entitlements, so I would guess 'yes,' but it's only a guess."

I put it to my anonymous informant that George Young was possibly earning more money than Bon did from Bon's own songs.

"I'm sure he was. I'm sure he was, yeah."

Krebs agrees. George, he says, "was probably making a lot of money" from AC/DC. Which is extraordinary given Bon lived out his remaining days in relative penury.

"It is, really," says the informant. "George also got a producer's share as well, so he was making a lot more money. I have no knowledge if George also acquired part of the publishing although it does seem likely given his financial position. AC/DC is a family business, and George was also a part of Alberts. My guess is that the brothers had something going on between them that was not shared with the rest of the band. Publishing is more important to AC/DC than record royalties, particularly in the United States. Royalties are based on the retail price; mechanicals are paid at the statutory rate. The retail price has gone down while mechanicals have about doubled since 1975. There are more participants in the royalty pool than in the publishing stream.

"It has always been my belief that a renegotiation occurred at some point where the Youngs acquired part of Alberts' side of the AC/DC income stream. It would seem odd that a band such as AC/DC would not have renegotiated the initial deals at some point as the band became more successful. There is nothing illegal or questionable in the initial publishing deal. AC/DC started from square one and signed a boilerplate agreement. That agreement would have called for the income stream arising from markets outside of Australia to be diluted by whichever entity collected the income in any given market. Initially, there would have been sub-publishers appointed by Alberts collecting funds in each market and then passing the income through to Alberts after taking a share, which could have been as much as 50 per cent.

"For example, if a song earned $100 in Germany, the German publishing company may have passed on as little as $50 to Alberts. Alberts in turn then would have taken half of that. The net result under those circumstances is that the writer ends up with $25 or 25 per cent of a song's income in any foreign market. At a certain point, Alberts established their own publishing companies in most of these markets and it would not have been illegal for that separate publishing entity to keep the same share as the original sub-publisher. However, the question remains as to how this was dealt with as the band became more and more successful. The standard practice for a major artist is to look for a 10 per cent at-source collection agreement. That would mean that if $100 was earned in Germany, $90 would be passed on to the writers, as against the $25 that they would have received under the original agreement."

Who was collecting for AC/DC's publisher in Germany?

"I believe they had yet another Young brother running the publishing company in Germany at one point."

The brother being referred to is the late Alex Young, who died in Hamburg in 1997.

⚡

AC/DC is an extraordinarily lucrative family business for the Youngs, these days largely through assets from touring: ticket sales and merchandising revenue. Vanda & Young have done very well out of their handshake deal with Ted Albert.

As the informant argues, it stands to reason that as AC/DC became more successful, especially after the sales of *Back In Black*, the original royalties split between songwriter and publisher was renegotiated to give a greater return to Angus and Malcolm, who have solely shared writing credits on AC/DC albums for decades. After the release of 1988's *Blow Up Your Video*, Brian Johnson was shut out of the songwriting process completely before he sensationally parted ways with the band in 2016.

Another crucial revenue stream for AC/DC is performance and synchronisation royalties, the money that is owed when a song is broadcast or performed live in a commercial venue, used in advertising, TV shows or movie soundtracks, played on radio or streamed. It's nice to think these royalties are equally split five ways between each band member, but they only go to those who have writing credits.

Just to be sure they got all their entitlements, though, Cliff Williams and Brian Johnson took the precaution of hiring longtime Led Zeppelin attorney George Fearon, a step that caused immense friction within the band, so much so that some longlasting friendships were lost. At AC/DC's 2003 induction into the Rock & Roll Hall of Fame, tensions were running high. Fearon represents both men to this day.

AC/DC has long been a no-nonsense business for all its members, as much as it remains a rock band. It was always thus. But Bon, whose flair for words and showmanship started it all for AC/DC, didn't live long enough to see any of this river of gold beyond a piddling share of concert receipts and the occasional royalty cheque. By contrast, the Albert family (including Ted Albert's widow, Antoinette "Popsy" Albert) cashed in big. Its collective personal wealth was estimated to be $45 million as far back as 1992, two years after Albert's death from cancer. The company was sold for an undisclosed amount to the German music giant BMG in July 2016. Crucially, it retained its stake in AC/DC's publishing.

"Bon never did have much money," says Roy Allen. "I didn't know why that was. It's a damn shame because he worked so hard. I wished he could have got to enjoy some of the fruits of his labour."

Silver Smith, according to Doug Thaler, had taken off with Bon's money back in Australia: "They had a little savings account and she just up and took off and cleaned out their bank account. He wasn't quite right after that."

Silver categorically rejected this: "I have never in 65 years held a joint bank account with anyone." In fact, she said, Bon was a slippery figure with other people's possessions: "He had an 'easy come, easy go' thing with not just his own money and possessions, but other people's, that they'd worked really hard for . . . he spent everything he got on trivial things, didn't have a bank account even, with the attitude that the people around him would do the boring stuff, like get references, find flats, pay electricity and phone bills, et cetera, and work hard in mundane jobs in order to do that."

Yet Pattee Bishop remembers Bon telling her something about the joint bank account: "His sister-in-law [Derek's wife, Valarie] kept a lot of his money after that. He had cash given to him from management like an advance. He had to invest his money. I heard that from Bon. He had money in '78, '79. Before then Bon had Silver keep his money; he got his money sent through Western Union and his cheques went to her when he travelled. He told me he would never get married again and would end up living where it's warm year round.

"He was very generous when he finally had money. He gave me $1200 when I left Florida for California in '79. I left home and needed money to get a place in Beverly Hills, so he came to my house and gave me a bank leather pocket thing with $1200 in it, for a gift. It was all tens and fives. I wonder where Bon got the money to give me. I never asked. Bon called me from the Sunset Marquis, and I went and stayed that weekend with him."

So what did he say he wanted to do? What was his plan?

"He told me he would never marry again, but his parents, he loved. He never wanted to buy a house."

Bon never wanted to buy a house?

"A car or nothing."

Silver said Bon talked a bigger game than he actually delivered.

"He knew he owed [his ex-wife] Irene [Thornton] a big favour, and he talked about helping her with a deposit for a house all the time because she had taken him in after the bike accident [in 1974], but he didn't do it, did he? I thought he should have *done* it, not went around to visit her with expensive booze and just talked about it."

I ask Pete Way if Bon ever complained about his financial situation while AC/DC was on the road with UFO.

"Um, I think they possibly used to moan about, I forget his name, but Angus used to say, '*Mehhh*, fucking Browning.' That'd be that. But then again to us we were probably thinking the same because between us we were getting, like, $18,000 a night and a lot of it was going on production and that, and suddenly you'd think, '*Mmm*, where does the money *go*?'"

The truth is stark and can be revealed for the first time. Bon died with just $31,162.52 in assets, of which $30,846.09 had been banked into a savings account. A total of $316.43 was in shares. That was the sum of Bon's entire estate at the time of his death. He did not own any property in London or California.[23] Before he died, though, with *Highway To Hell* on its way to platinum in the United States, he had good reason to believe he'd finally be rich.

Back in black.

CHAPTER 15

SIN CITY

From Atlanta, AC/DC returned to Florida for two shows with Cheap Trick: the Coliseum in Jacksonville and the University of Miami's Maurice Gusman Concert Hall. It was the start of a much-needed five-day break for the band. The same week they had a top-10 album in Holland, but not with *Powerage*; instead, *Let There Be Rock*. The good news continued: "Rock 'N' Roll Damnation" was chosen as a "Recommended" pop single in the influential *Billboard*. Finally, the pendulum had started to swing, as Barry Bergman had predicted. It had been a successful tour.

AC/DC fan Robby Gregory was front row against the stage at Gusman Hall.

"I heard Bon Scott say that he loved South Florida and considered it his home in America when they first came here. When you're 16 years old and you hear your hero say anything about where you were born and raised, you never forget it. Bon was just bigger than life when onstage — even with his smaller stature, he was a *giant*. He was very polite and then when the music would start he would take control of the crowd and whip everyone into a frenzy. I have seen all the big bands in their prime. Bon Scott was the best frontman ever."

Even so, a WQAM-AM "South Florida Pop Music Poll" of 1000 listeners later adjudged AC/DC's show at Gusman Hall "worst live performance" of the year. As Bon knew more than most, there was no pleasing everybody.

$$\lightning$$

Pattee Bishop has a warning for me: "Please find the one thing us girls had in common that Bon liked and please don't get caught up with the girls that had a crush on the lead singer but not the *man*. Us real girls of Bon Scott were not groupies: we were girls he rang up and came and stayed with, who he went for walks with, who he laid in the grass with."

The Real Girls of Bon Scott would have been a good name for a reality-TV show about Bon's sex life. He had many bed partners in the United States, but Pattee says she was closer to him than the others, even when she told him she wasn't interested in anything serious. Her hands were full enough. She rolls off a list of celebrity conquests that are probably best left private. Bon, she says, was open to her about his other relationships. Silver Smith said she didn't know about any of Bon's American girlfriends but Pattee knew about Silver.

"Bon told me about her, with nothing but kind stories . . . we both, her more than me, didn't want to be married, or be a girl-friend, but we were the ones he cared about, and we know the secrets [*laughs*]. Silver like me was full of herself; she and Bon weren't a couple any more but still depended on each other and were friends. Silver like me was wild, and Bon didn't care. You could be and do as you please, and Bon never was jealous."

What did Bon say about Silver?

"Just she'd been there for him. He never spoke badly of people. He told me she was a junkie. I'm happy for Bon [this book is being written]. I'm glad I'm here to see and hear the truth during that time. Just makes me smile to hear about all his other girlfriends [*laughs*]."

Did Bon ever tell you he loved you?

"He would say, 'You know you got me right?' Or: 'Pattee, you're all I can handle.' Or call me his 'One.' But we never told each other we loved each other. I didn't want him to love me like that. I was about to leave for a whole new life in Los Angeles with four of my best friends. But he saw me every time he was here [in Miami]. If I saw Bon, we got together. We had sex. I never called him my boyfriend; he was my friend who liked to have sex a lot and hang out and drink and he was up for anything.

"I took good care of him; he ate right. I groomed him: cut his hair, pubic hair, nose hair. So he appreciated how much I cared about how he looked. I never knew him to be depressed, or sad; just always ready to do something. I never saw Bon do any drugs. Bon's lower back was hurting him. I knew he was half-deaf in one ear. He always told me I was his 'best-looking one,' and he got lucky because of me. I wish I had been in love with him, because he would still be with us. He asked me if I would marry him so he could get his Green Card. But I was too wild and he was very set in his ways. I swear he would say in '77, 'Let's do some shakin'.'"

Sometime after the Gusman Hall concert, Bon stayed for two nights with Pattee and her housemate, a shy, aspiring amateur singer called Marian Pizzimenti, at 7211 Miami Lakes Drive West, Miami Lakes.

"I remember Bon giving me some singing advice," says Pizzimenti. "I took a piece of notebook paper and he wrote some things down. I was taking voice lessons at the time."

Says Pattee: "It was a three punch-hole tear-out, the one he tore out for Marian; an old-school hardback. Notebook thin. Bon drove a golf cart once just to see Jackie Gleason's house." She pauses for a moment. "What did he always have in the back pocket of his jeans?"

I have no idea.

"A toothpick. Never without one. He would change it at hotels. If you knew him you knew about that pick."

Pattee took Bon to meet Tight Squeeze, a local punk-rock band with a club of the same name, at Big Daddy's on Johnson Street in Hollywood, because she wanted to make keyboardist and heart-throb Michael Dirse jealous.

"I was in love, puppy love with Michael, and I wanted to show off by bringing Bon into the club [*laughs*]. Bon and I had just left an AC/DC concert. You should have seen their faces. Bon got up and sang 'Sin City' to me. He said, 'This goes out to my lady, Pattee.' He sang one more song and then we left. [Bass player] Teddy Rooney and Michael were pissing in their pants. The whole club died that night."

"We were all somewhat in a drug- or alcohol-induced stupor in one way or the other," says Dirse. "Bon was like a comet out of control. He was in this, like, frenetic but simmering rage that came out when he performed. No one could touch it."

Pattee, Bon's #1 go-to fuck buddy, still misses him.

"Why was he so good to me? I was a handful back then, but he and I were fun together. He wasn't my boyfriend. That was because of me. But I was his safe place. He liked to be with just me and hang out. He'd want me to pick him up and take him any-where when he was in town. He loved Florida."

⚡

But Bon wasn't just seeing Pattee and Holly. He was also sleeping with a third woman in Miami, a brunette called Beth Quartiano, who is now deceased. In unusual circumstances, she ended up having a sexual relationship with Angus after being let go by Bon. Malcolm Young, meanwhile, had hooked up with Beth's friend Robin Jackson-Fragola, while Cliff Williams had a brief fling with another of Beth's friends, Maria DeLuise. Beth and Robin had been underage girls when they first met AC/DC at the 4 O'Clock

Club show in Fort Lauderdale. A year later, now legal, they were having the time of their lives hanging out with AC/DC.

"Malcolm and I were a special kind of friends," says Robin. "We had some great times. It was very funny to go to upscale department stores, into the boys' department to buy clothing, seeing as [the Youngs] couldn't buy jeans and such in the men's department due to their size. It was also a hoot when we went to restaurants to have dinner, and the staff thought that we were their paid companions, due to the fact that we were much taller than the boys, especially with five-inch heels. Mal and I had lovely moments, many times. Not lovers, friends. We were like oil and water due to our personalities. We understood the limits of that lifestyle. Life is good when you don't expect more than what is. We enjoyed each other's company."

Did your "special" friendship with Malcolm ever cause issues with Linda? (O'Linda Irish, also known as Linda Irish, had been seeing Malcolm for some time before Malcolm met Robin. Linda married Malcolm on 14 April 1979 at the Westminster Registry Office in London, the day recording finished on *Highway To Hell*.)

"I would never put he or myself through that."

What about Beth and Bon?

"She was seeing Bon and we were at a show at Gusman Hall. Beth spent time with [Keith Richards's drug dealer] Fred Sessler and the Stones back in the day, so that is how she met up with others. She got a bit wasted so I left and went home. The next morning she called me from the hotel crying because she woke up in Ang's room. I drove down there and read everyone the riot act for this and that is how Mal and I became sidekicks of sorts . . . the Beth–Bon–Ang thing kind of drew us together."

When you say Beth ended up in Angus's room, do you mean she slept with Angus?

"Yes. She actually got involved in a tiff with [Angus's future wife] Ellen in West Palm Beach at a show."

23 August 1980, West Palm Beach, *Back In Black* tour?

"I suppose. I know it was West Palm Beach."

Why was she upset? What was the nature of the altercation that followed?

"She got wasted at the [Gusman Hall] show; Bon was pissed. I left her there and went home. When she called me crying from Ang's room, I ran down to the hotel and gave everyone a piece of my mind . . . Bon shrugged it off as any ladies' man would. Beth and Ang carried on."

So she woke up in Angus's room naked and had no idea how she'd got there?

"That just about sums it up."

Beth and Angus "carried on"? What do you mean? Fighting? Or having sex?

"My anger surpassed hers. That is when Mal took a liking to me . . . Beth carried on sexually with Ang."

What was the tenor of the conversation between you and the group when you arrived at the hotel room?

"I was a bit enraged and said, 'What does she look like, a piece of meat to pass about?' With some of the responses, I bopped them."

Who had been with her? Just Angus?

"I guess."

So when Beth first slept with Angus, this was a one-off? Or did she continue seeing Angus through 1979?

"Continued. Yes. That's how she ended up in a tiff with Ellen."

So Beth was still seeing Angus in 1980 while he was with Ellen?

"Evidentially."

⚡

Pattee seems like a natural person to ask. Did you know of Angus or Malcolm having girlfriends in Miami?

"[Laughs] Bon would laugh when I asked that. I know my friend tried with Angus, but he couldn't do anything [laughs]. I only know Malcolm was in love with some girl from home; I want to say London. [Tour manager] Ian Jeffery was the groupie guy. He would pick up girls and bring them to the boys. He always handed out the passes. Ian was always treated like shit by them. So was Bon. There were these types that always were with the roadies, after the band got done with them. They would smoke cigs, and weren't the pick of the litter, as we say [*laughs*]. Ian could tell you every girl's name, because he had them first, or the other guys did. He was so funny."

Do you remember a woman called Robin Jackson-Fragola who was seeing Malcolm?

"Malcolm was with this small brown-haired girl. She smoked."

I show her a picture of Robin from the 1970s. Was this her?

"Yes. *Wow*, I remember this one."

So he had an affair with her while he was with Linda?

"Yes, I saw her more than once. Florida girl. She was with him. She had a girlfriend; brown hair, too, I remember. I was a stylist, so I remember faces. It was part of my job."

I show her a picture of Beth.

"That's her friend, yep. Those two were *around*."

CHAPTER 16

COLD
HEARTED
MAN

Opening for Ritchie Blackmore's Rainbow at Calderone Concert Hall in Hempstead, Long Island, things weren't going so well for AC/DC. It was deteriorating into another Fresno.

"A guy in the fifth row started heckling them," wrote Australian music magazine *Juke*. "Angus Young strode to the edge of the stage and yelled back at the heckler. The heckler spat at Angus, so Angus spat back. A spit battle started. Mind you, this was happening over four rows of people. A woman sitting next to the heckler started yelling at him, asking him to stop acting up. The heckler retaliated by punching her in the face. Angus saw this and dived from the stage over the four rows to king-hit the cretin."

Wee Angus dived over *four* rows and *king-hit* him? Impressive. It wasn't unlike a yarn Malcolm told about Bon after he was hit with a full beer can during a gig in New Zealand. Atop a stack of amps, Bon "jumped straight off the amps then off the stage into the crowd and he was piling into these four Maoris when the bouncers got there." Bon was handy in a fight but four adult

Maori men would have torn him apart. The actual truth of the matter in Hempstead was quite different. Steve Stokking was one of the hecklers.

"The crowd wasn't too receptive at first. Bon started making gestures at the crowd, mostly me and my friend. We were a bit jacked up and started to head to the stage, but some guys held us back. Angus may have scruffed with someone. That's it. By the end of the show we thought they were pretty cool [*laughs*]."

But the truth didn't matter so much as hype. The band's performances and Angus's attendant antics were getting noticed in the right places, including America's biggest selling rock magazine.

"Malcolm Young doesn't believe that AC/DC's tremendous onstage energy results solely from the band's youthfulness," wrote Ira Kaplan in *Rolling Stone*. "Nor does he worry about AC/DC getting too old to rock and roll. Appropriately, he cites Ted Nugent's years of touring in search of superstardom as an example to emulate. 'Now that he's famous,' says Malcolm, 'he's not going to get old.' Malcolm sees no reason why his group can't do the same.

"If nothing else the members of AC/DC are enthusiastic, able to see the bright side of being an opening act (you get to go home early) and to laugh away the bad shows, like a performance at CBGBs . . . in front of the punk patrons, the band played what its members say was one of their best sets ever, yet they were met with silence. The experience was not in vain, for it taught them one of the truisms of rock concerts. As Malcolm puts it: 'You play shitass, the kids go wild. Play great, and everybody sits there.'"

Fresh towns and cities were falling to AC/DC: Wilkes-Barre, Boston, Morristown, Albany. A year to the day from their first show in New York City and the night Bon met Holly, AC/DC was back at The Palladium. Ritchie Blackmore was clearly rattled by AC/DC's well-drilled stage routine, according to *Billboard*.

"Rainbow cut short its set at the Palladium in New York recently when lead guitarist Richie [sic] Blackmore stormed off-stage 15 minutes into the set, claiming there was a hum in the sound system. A makeup date was promised. Rainbow's semi show followed a blistering performance by AC/DC which took the cordless guitar to new heights, literally performing from the Palladium's balcony."

♪

However at the very next concert, a 25 August appearance for Providence radio station WPRO at Rocky Point Park in Warwick, Rhode Island, Bon's drinking took a turn for the worse. For the first time since joining the band it caused the abandonment of a show.

"I was no more than 20 feet from the stage," remembers AC/DC fan Ed Fagnant, who was 17 at the time. "Bon was wasted and barely understandable. The show ended after about five songs or so when Angus tried to ride Bon's shoulders, causing him to lose balance, and they toppled the speaker stacks at the right side of the stage. The place turned into a near riot. The announcer on the PA system at the park was constantly asking people to return the band's equipment. I left the park with my friends and saw a guy loading the mike stand. The Warwick Police were patrolling the parking lot and saw him, and arrested him. We were also patted down, but had already smoked our contraband hours earlier [*laughs*]."

So Bon was *really* wasted?

"Yes."

It came as no surprise to Barry Bergman: "I loved the band from the beginning and I really loved who they were as people. But there were issues. Bon had his drinking issue, which was not a secret. My boss [Edward B. Marks Music Corporation president Joseph Auslander] used to give the band for the holidays a quart of alcohol. Bon had drunk it before he even left the office. It was a mistake to ever give him alcohol."

After shows in Willimantic, Connecticut and Owings Mills, Maryland, AC/DC flew to Seattle for two nights supporting Ted Nugent and Cheap Trick, followed by a Portland date with Cheap Trick, and another Day On The Green in Oakland. They weren't just selling seats but getting all-important radio adds in California, South Carolina, Connecticut, New Mexico, West Virginia, Ohio,

Missouri and Florida. That they were making such headway with Bon in the grip of full-blown alcohol addiction was remarkable.

"I definitely got the feeling that they were trying to outdo us," says Blue Öyster Cult drummer Albert Bouchard. "They were very reserved. We didn't really socialise. I think Bon liked being an iconoclast. I was shocked when he died. Honestly, I wish I'd made more of an effort to get to know him."

In Denver, BÖC made it clear who was headlining, preventing AC/DC from using their full lighting rig.

"The stage around us was really dark," recalled Cliff Williams. "At that gig I was really worried about Angus careering off the end of the stage."

Bouchard regrets what happened: "I sometimes wonder if we treated them badly as an opening act and at some point someone in the [AC/DC] organisation decided to get back at us. As a musician you sometimes have no idea what's going on with the crew and management . . . I never got the sense that they didn't like us."

But Kenny Soule of Nantucket is in no doubt how they felt: "AC/DC *despised* Blue Öyster Cult as much as we did. [*He impersonates Malcolm Young*] 'They gave us six *fucking* lights. Fuck Blue Öyster Cult.' I can't imagine them having to follow AC/DC."

Or anyone else. AC/DC had become unstoppable.

⚡

Bon was back in L.A., this time for a live taping in Burbank of "Sin City" for Burt Sugarman's *Midnight Special*, a one-and-a-half-hour music program on NBC that ran from 1973 to 1981. He'd had his hair cut by Pattee — "it looked so good that night" — and in the slow breakdown during the "ladders and snakes" part of the song, he did his best Alex Harvey impersonation.[24]

"Bon really delivered with his talkin' stuff," said Malcolm. "The audience, they were all like, 'Shit, is this the devil?' . . . you could see they were stunned . . . he's a little bit of an actor, Bon; he could really pull it off."

Bon fancied his dramatic abilities: "Now that I'm in AC/DC

I realise I'm not very musical — I'm more of a showman . . . an actor. I'll do anything to get a reaction from an audience." He described the feeling of being onstage as almost being at one with the crowd: "It's all so close to you, it's all right on top of you, and like you don't have to look out through the crowd to be *in* the crowd. You're just there anyway on the stage. It is really exciting."

The thrill of their first — and only — major U.S. network TV appearance was just what Bon and the band needed, segueing into a full run of commitments with Cheap Trick, Thin Lizzy, UFO and The Dictators that took them from the Southeast to the Midwest to the Northeast: Wheeling, Johnson City, Columbus, Milwaukee, Royal Oak, Schaumburg, Cleveland, Allentown, Huntington, Chicago, Kansas City and Omaha. The pace of touring never bothered the band.

Said Angus: "We just like being in the womb of the road. That's the greatest thing for us — just going from gig to gig."

By the end of September *Powerage* had spent 15 weeks in the *Billboard* 200, all in the lower reaches. Chart position couldn't rescue the album for Atlantic but the harder won success AC/DC was having as they went from city to city, state to state, showed Bon had what it took to overcome the barbs of critics and even silence the sniping inside his own band over his future. He was a hard worker, even when he was sick.

"It was a great and memorable experience playing with AC/DC, especially so early on, and getting to watch their inevitable rise to stardom," says Dictators rhythm guitarist Scott Kempner. "It was well deserved. They did everything right, wrote great songs, worked their asses off, never dogged it, and I never saw their audience go home anything but happy, sweaty, and simultaneously tired and energised."

Dates in Buffalo, South Bend, Toledo and Fort Wayne saw AC/DC and Aerosmith share the same stage for the last time, Bon hoisting Angus on his shoulders each night because that had become the band gimmick all the fans were talking about. Somehow, against all odds, AC/DC and its alcoholic lead singer were actually coming good.

"Bon was there doing it when nobody else was doing it," says Barry Bergman. "One of the reasons the band really stuck out when it started to connect was because, you know, there's a saying: 'The trend is your friend.' Rock 'n' roll was not the trend. It was disco that was the trend. They didn't fit in so there was lots of attention when things started to work. We went from the era of disco in the mid '70s to New Wave in the early '80s and this thing came out of nowhere, this *party* band. Somebody wants to call it heavy metal, hard rock or whatever . . . it was a party band; the people's party band. That's the way I always saw it. It stuck out and it became very relevant because there was nobody else doing anything.

"Everybody was signing the New Wave acts or they were doing Donna Summer, the Ritchie Family and the disco acts. The difference is very simple. I think AC/DC have held on to a lot of that early audience, even today, because lots of people grew up with them that were starved for rock 'n' roll. They had no real rock 'n' roll at that time. This was basic rock 'n' roll with a phenomenal live show . . . there's been nothing else that comes close to it. It's unique; it stood out because it was of its own genre."

⚡

But Bergman isn't quite correct. California's Van Halen was a "party band" and was on a similar highway to AC/DC at the time. Like AC/DC, they were invited as a support band on Aerosmith's *Live Bootleg* tour. Like AC/DC, they made a habit of embarrassing Steven Tyler and Joe Perry. Like AC/DC, they were panned by critics. And most like AC/DC, their fans just didn't give two shits what anyone else was thinking.

"We didn't even really start headlining until our third tour," says Michael Anthony. "So like '78, '79, we were pretty much playing everywhere opening up for as many people as we could. We opened up for everybody that was big at the time, like Nugent, Foreigner, Boston, Aerosmith, all those bands. None of them would even give us the time of day [*laughs*]."

Van Halen is one of the few bands, like AC/DC, that arguably went on to be bigger though not necessarily better when they replaced their best singer. INXS fell into a heap and never recovered. Why do you think Van Halen and AC/DC got it right?

"Man, you know what, I don't know. Especially AC/DC. Obviously they even became more successful when Brian Johnson joined the band but they were on their way there with *Highway To Hell*. That next album with Bon Scott would probably have been the one that did the same thing *Back In Black* did. It's just a lucky draw, I think . . . maybe it just has to do with the chemistry and the timing and obviously the music.

"The only way I really remember Bon is through the music and the videos, basically, besides the one show that we did together. I love the way the guy sang. He had a very unique voice. Between him and the stuff that Brian did, the funniest thing for me is to see people try to play that AC/DC stuff; the singer trying to sing it. I'm sure there are singers out there that can sing it but not that I've heard. That's actually kinda cool, that your singer is the kind of guy that nobody can really imitate. Bon's was a very unique voice that, to me, *was* AC/DC. The guy was just on the brink of his band getting to that next level and all of a sudden it was gone."

⚡

Powerage spent 17 weeks in the charts and, at the time, sold more copies than *High Voltage* and *Let There Be Rock* combined. Atlantic Records had been smart enough to realise AC/DC had something very special in concert, and by the middle of October 1978 the first copies of the *If You Want Blood You've Got It* live album (though it wasn't quite all live — there were plenty of studio overdubs) were rolling out in trucks from Atlantic's pressing plant in Olyphant, Pennsylvania.

Meanwhile, Atlantic's Nesuhi Ertegun and Michael Klenfner flew to Italy for a WEA Roadshow at Castello di Sammezzano in Florence, where they promoted AC/DC. Klenfner, derided by Angus as a record-company "earpiece," flew on to Sydney to deliver last rites to Vanda & Young, telling George Young, "You haven't got a commercial ear."

The band's European and British tour of nearly three-dozen shows kicked off in West Germany and ran through to the third week of November. *If You Want Blood* got as high as #13 in the UK charts and was released in the United States at the end of the band's commitments in Europe. By December, AC/DC was on its biggest roll yet in North America, *Billboard* giving *If You Want Blood* a plug in its "Recommended LPs" slot — "the spirit is the thing here, and a bit of that can go a long way sometimes" — and Atlantic taking out a very expensive full-page ad. But most crucially of all, things were finally starting to happen for the band on radio, especially in the all-important Northeast and West.

"Even though I was not a big fan of live albums, I was impressed with the raw energy of *If You Want Blood* and decided to add 'Whole Lotta Rosie' right away," says Robert Shulman, then music director of KRST Albuquerque. He'd previously resisted AC/DC.

"It sounded good on the air so I moved it to a higher rotation. At that time, I had a 1953 Chrysler New Yorker that I was foolishly trying to keep running with the idea of restoring it. It was in the shop quite often. The mechanic, a young kid, who was probably about 20, had a radio playing on his workbench that was tuned to KRST. The kid did not know that I worked at the radio station. He was in the middle of telling me the bad news that the car's fluid torque transmission was completely shot, when 'Whole Lotta Rosie' came on the radio. He stopped in mid-sentence, walked back to the little transistor radio and turned it up to the point of distortion. The song's pounding drums, wailing guitars and Bon Scott's powerful vocals echoed through the shop. For a moment, I forgot about my car problems as I looked at the young man's face. He was transfixed. He was so happy. That's when I knew AC/DC was going to be the next big thing."

Bon would spend the end of 1978 in Australia, doing demos for the band's new studio album at Alberts in Sydney with Atlantic's anointed replacement for Vanda & Young, South African producer Eddie Kramer, and *Powerage* engineer Mark Opitz. But he was fast becoming a liability. Already on thin ice with some important executives at Atlantic Records, his alcoholism was now starting to impact the band in the studio, and his criminal record (a bust for pot possession in September 1969 the most likely sticking point) had prevented a planned tour of Japan in March 1979 from going ahead.

If the band hadn't been on a career upswing at that particular moment, about to cash in on all the hard work they'd put in on the road by creating the album that was going to finally get them on to top-40 radio, their merchandising profits starting to outstrip revenue from ticket sales, Bon would probably have been just another casualty of the Young brothers' diarchy (a triarchy if you count big brother George). Yet even they couldn't ignore the numbers that were starting to roll in. AC/DC was in the charts, albeit not quite where Atlantic wanted them to be. They were on the airwaves. The days of playing in dingy clubs and small theatres were coming to an end.

By the start of 1979, Bon and the band were back in Miami, a place he publicly liked to mock: "Horrible place, Miami. Like a Jewish graveyard. Full of rich old crocks who flock there for the winter."

But in his heart it was where he wanted to be.

PART THREE
1979

CHAPTER 17

WALK ALL
OVER YOU

One early morning in January 1979, at the tiny Tight Squeeze club at A1A and Johnson, Hollywood, Florida, right by the beach, Henry Laplume, the good-looking, six-foot-five bass player for North Miami punk-rock band Critical Mass, was weighing up whether to stay drinking at the bar or go home.

"That particular night my bandmates left me there. They all went home and I stayed and partied a little bit later than I should have, probably, but as it turns out this little guy walks in the door and I go, *damn*, that's Bon Scott! Right away I knew it had to be him, tattoos on the arms and all. He went straight to the bathroom and I followed him in there and the first thing I said was, 'By the way, *listen*, I'm not stalking you, I'm a big fan, my band plays a lot of your songs,' and introduced myself: 'My name's Henry.' Bon turned around after he got done doing his business, washed his hands, and said, 'Hey, *Harry*, how you doin'?' So from then on he called me Harry. I guess he didn't hear that well but I thought that was kind of neat."

Tight Squeeze Fine Food & Spirits, "Florida's New Home of

Rock and Roll," where the cover charge was $2, was nondescript from the outside: diagonal timber cladding and bricks, some high windows, hanging plants, and even a patch of soil with plants out front. Two lanterns on either side of the door. Inside, large letters spelling the word SQUEEZE hung over a beam over the cramped main stage, a jumble of wires and amps.

"The Tight Squeeze has been open now for a little more than four months and already it has developed a national reputation," wrote the *Miami Herald* in 1979. "It has been mentioned in *Rolling Stone*'s Random Notes, in *Hit Parader* and other music magazines. And no wonder. The club has not only booked national acts such as Horslips, Iron Butterfly, Pure Prairie League, The Winters Brothers, and Desmond Child and Rouge, but also managed to attract rock entertainers who are just passing through the area. Among the notable who popped in to jam with local bands are Ted Nugent, Pat Travers, members of Bad Company and Bob Seger."

They forgot to mention AC/DC. Henry and Bon went to the bar to have a few drinks, "slamming cocktails, Jack Daniel's." The barman called for last drinks. Bon was with Holly, and Henry needed to get home.

"I'm stuck for a ride. My bandmates left me here."

"No worries," said Bon. "We'll give you a ride back to our hotel. You can call your bandmates from there and they can pick you up."

"No problem."

Henry, Bon and Holly left the club and drove to the Newport Hotel on Collins Avenue, now the Newport Beachside Hotel & Resort. The Newport, where Tommy Bolin had died of a heroin overdose in 1976, had a reputation for being a rock 'n' roll hotel, Miami's own version of L.A.'s Riot Inn. Henry used the room telephone to call up Critical Mass's drummer, Mike Barone.

"Listen, you guys bailed out on me and I need a ride home now."

"Ah, fuck you," said Barone. "No, you get your own ride home."

"Well, I'm hanging out over at the Newport with Bon Scott."

"No you're *not*."

"Well if you come and pick me up you'll meet him and the rest of the band."

Barone was there in 10 minutes. The next day Henry called Michael "Fazz" Fazzolare, Critical Mass's lead singer and rhythm guitarist, to tell him what he'd missed out on. Fazz had been in the audience for AC/DC's set at the Day for the Kids in Hollywood, 1977. AC/DC was his favourite band.

"You shoulda been at the club last night, Fazz. Bon Scott was there."

"*The* Bon Scott?"

"How many fucking Bon Scotts do you know of?"

Says David Owen, Critical Mass's lead guitarist: "Mick was the person who bought import albums; he had *everything*. He bought everything that came out that was hard rock. We were even doing some of their stuff in our cover material; half a dozen or more AC/DC songs at that point, even though this was before *Highway To Hell* and before they became popular."

By Fazz's admission, "I practically *lived* at Tight Squeeze. I was ramming my head into the wall, kicking myself, pissed off beyond all comprehension that I missed meeting the lead singer of my favourite band in the known universe."

He went to Tight Squeeze the next night hoping there was a slim chance Bon would be there again. He was. He'd also brought along Phil Rudd, Cliff Williams and Malcolm Young.

"Immediately Bon walks over to Henry and me," says Fazz. "That was the beginning of an adventure I'll never forget."

⚡

The year 1979 couldn't have started much better for AC/DC.

If You Want Blood was sitting at a respectable #127 in the *Billboard* 200 and made the top five "National Breakouts" in "Album Radio Action" behind Rod Stewart's *Blondes Have More Fun*, The Blues Brothers' *Briefcase Full Of Blues* and Jean-Michel Jarre's *Equinoxe*. It was a "Top Add-On" in the Southwest and Southeast, as well as a "Breakout" in the Northeast and Western regions, getting heavy play at WIYY Baltimore, KSJO and KOME in San Jose, KTIM San Rafael and WLVQ Columbus. Shifting to Miami from Sydney, at the urging of their frustrated producer, Eddie Kramer, had been a blessing in disguise.

"We did the album in a totally different way this time," said Bon. "Usually we'll write the songs while we're working on them in the studio. But instead we took two weeks in Miami to write them so we didn't have to waste valuable studio time."[25]

When they weren't hanging out at Tight Squeeze, picking up local girls or eating pizza and drinking cold milk back at the Newport, AC/DC was writing and rehearsing songs for what would become *Highway To Hell* in a 750-square-foot sound-proofed room with a wooden stage, mood lights, and a lounge area at Musicians Studio Rentals (MSR), aka "Mary's Place," at 1926 NE 151st Street, North Miami. They were so skint, Angus Young recalled, "We'd $10 between us."

"AC/DC were in Studio B," says Fazz. "At the time, MSR had two studios, A and B. Studio A was completely carpeted, padded, and had the ambience of a recording studio. *Dead*. Studio B had a carpeted stage and some sound-sucking materials on the wall, but the floor was bare concrete. It was very much a live room. The reverb off the floor was way more conducive to their sound than what a studio could have afforded them."

Owen remembers MSR being "a sort of a warehouse complex where this big warehouse had been chopped up into studios for bands to play. They had stages, they were all carpeted, they included a PA system in each stage area."

When AC/DC plugged in, there was no mistaking them for anyone else.

"Critical Mass had the place rented out for a couple of weeks and we were just rehearsing one night, just like normal, and you could hear other bands playing around because there were probably five or six rooms in this complex. All of a sudden this band started playing right next door to us in the biggest studio and it was like the walls were *shaking*. We just heard the thunder next door."

Frank Prinzel, electronics maintenance engineer at the nearby Criteria Recording Studios, where AC/DC was doing demos, says there was "tea and Foster's on the tables. The boys were working with Eddie and there was some tension. There was a story going around that they slagged off one day and did some work with [late engineer] Steve Gursky at Criteria. Steve was frequenting the Tight Squeeze club at the same time AC/DC were visiting."

The Bee Gees, Elvin Bishop, Eagles, Bob Seger, Thin Lizzy and Little River Band had all rehearsed at MSR. Criteria, owned by the late Mack Emerman, had four 24-track studios, all equipped with the latest technology, and had seen the likes of Eric Clapton, James Brown, Aretha Franklin, Eagles and Fleetwood Mac all record landmark music on its premises. The Gibbs, Australia's other great musical family, had worked on their last three studio albums and the *Saturday Night Fever* soundtrack at Criteria, turning Miami into a city crawling with studio musicians and engineers. Barry Gibb lived just minutes away. Atlantic had sent AC/DC to Miami to make a hit.

"Malcolm asked the band if they were all aboard in going with this more refined, slightly more dynamic commercial style," says Fazz. "They were writing 'Girls Got Rhythm,' and Bon was singing some racy lyrics: *The girl's got rhythm, she's got the free-style rhythm.* [*Laughs*] Malcolm stops playing and says, 'Mate, those words are a bit too *strong*. We need to tone it down a little.' Of course, the lyric became *the back seat rhythm*. To be honest, I didn't see the difference. Then again I was 23 so my imagination was very active. They let our drummer, Mike Barone, jam with them on 'Beating Around The Bush.'"[26]

Says Barone: "I'd come and go and once in a while someone would come in and jam with them. The day I was there, a member of Tight Squeeze, Teddy Rooney, was actually jamming with them."

"Shazbot Nanu Nanu," Bon's bizarre sign-off on "Night Prowler" and the last words Bon ever uttered on an AC/DC album, had nothing to do with *Mork & Mindy* being one of Bon's favourite TV shows.[27]

"It was something we were all saying when we hung out, which was started by Teddy," says Fazz. "He was the one who went around using the phrase. We would all chime in on occasion. I would guess it winding up on the album was either a nod from Bon to Teddy himself or a nod to the entire Miami gang."

The true reason for Mork's catchphrase being Bon's last words on *Highway To Hell* could have gone to the grave with Rooney when he passed away, aged 66, in July 2016. He never did a press interview about it.

"*Mork & Mindy* was on TV at the time," says Owen. "It was a very popular TV show. It's just one of those kind of things from TV that just passes on, like [the Wendy's slogan] 'Where's the beef?' It works its way into general language. Bon had a great sense of humour. He was always trying to get a laugh out of someone. He didn't mind playing the clown."

Bon himself was also playing drums at MSR.

"When he was up there," says Barone, "I kind of made the gesture, 'Do you mind if I sit in?' Bon said, 'No problem,' so I went and jammed with them for a song or two. Bon was the one I hung out with the most. AC/DC would come to the Tight Squeeze. Bon was usually pretty annihilated so I just kind of watched over him at the time."

Were you worried about his drinking?

"I was probably 20, 21. I didn't think much of it, you know what I mean? [*Pauses*] I'd say maybe a little. You never thought [his death] was going to happen. It was quite a shock."

In the same rehearsal studios, the title track off *Highway To Hell* was created.

"Mal was banging on the drums," said Angus Young. "I went to the toilet for a minute, and I started singing the words 'highway to hell' for the chorus. And then Bon put his pen down and came up with the verses."

Critical Mass went to a few more AC/DC rehearsals. Fazz, a huge fan of the band, was in heaven.

"I was blown away by the sheer power of 'Walk All Over You.' I was so impressed by the fact that their sound didn't need any studio gimmickry. This was *the* band. A *real* band. In your face, rock 'n' roll. No pretence, no bullshit, just balls to the walls *rock*. I learned from AC/DC to not dwell on too much detail, just let the music fly: 'We're a rock band, not Beethoven.'"

Back at a packed Tight Squeeze with Critical Mass onstage, Bon got up and tore through a set of half a dozen songs including "Whole Lotta Rosie," "Let There Be Rock," "Gimme A Bullet," "Sin City" and "Up To My Neck In You."

"It was stellar. Never forget it," says Fazz. "We were running around like three Angus Youngs on speed. Bon's drink was two shots of Jack Daniel's and Coca-Cola or, as he put it, 'double Jack 'n' Coke.' *All night long.* I was amazed how he could stand up, never mind that he remained somewhat lucid."

"Bon was pretty lit by then," says Laplume. "He completely fucked up the lyrics. Mick, of course, was up there trying to help him out and stuff."

Fazz: "After the first tune, Bon goes, 'These fuckers have gone *crazy*!' [*Laughs*] So we finish our set and we're all sitting together. I asked Malcolm if he had any tips for our band. He said, 'You could do with a bit more *dynamics*.' Best advice anyone ever gave me. Improved my tunesmithing exponentially. A short time after that, Bon had gotten so hammered by that point, he picked up what he thought was his drink, and *gulp*, right into his mouth. Only it wasn't a drink; it was an ashtray overflowing with cigarette butts. He didn't give a shit. He starts laughing his ass off, which, of course, caused the rest of us to howl in laughter as well."

Laughs Owen: "He drank an ashtray full of ashes just because somebody had spilled a beer in there. He was completely smashed but it was awesome. We probably did 30 minutes with Bon up there. What was remarkable about it in my recollection was that he was extremely intoxicated *before* he got up onstage. He was staggering and kind of stumbling and mumbling, just generally partying and drinking. When we started playing, he grabbed a hold of the mike stand and it was like Dr. Jekyll Mr. Hyde. He got his balance. He was rocking out from side to side. He was completely into it. He loved it. From my perspective as a musician to be up there doing AC/DC songs with Bon Scott singing the vocal part and I look out into the audience and I see the faces of Malcolm, Cliff and Phil sitting there looking at us — and they were having a great time — it was surreal."

How do you think Bon was able to perform so well when he was so intoxicated?

"There's a certain amount of nervousness that you have any time that you get up to perform. And up until he got up onstage with us, he had no inkling that night [that he was going to sing]. He didn't show up to perform that night; he showed up just to party. So he was there to have a good time and relax and everything and then I think when those musician instincts kick in, those kinda nerves tighten up inside you. It was just like the *adrenalin*."

But the very same night, after the show, Critical Mass literally lost Bon. Tight Squeeze closed at 6 a.m., when the sun came up. Bon was gone in more ways than one. The band was partying at a table at around 4 a.m. when they realised he'd disappeared.

"We're still there hanging out at the club and all of a sudden we notice that Bon was missing," says Owen. "We were like, 'Where'd Bon go?' And nobody had an answer to that. He didn't tell anybody that he was leaving. We didn't think anything of it for a while and after about half an hour, 40 minutes, he still hadn't showed up, so we started getting a little worried. We started looking for him, looking under tables and behind curtains and stuff like that. There was no sign of him. We were thinking, 'He was pretty drunk so maybe he's passed out in the street or the sidewalk or something.' So we walk out and start searching, me and the other guys in my band and a couple of guys from AC/DC; I don't remember who was what at that point — I think Phil was still there. We're looking for Bon, we're looking in the parking lot and we're like looking between cars and stuff like that and somebody finds him inside a car and he was passed out in the back seat of a car. And we woke him up."

"Whose car is this, Bon?" Owen asked him.

"*Yaaaarrrridunnooo.*"

"You mean you just came out here?"

"Yeah, it was open and I was tired. I had to lay down."

As Owen explains it, "Bon had walked out into the parking lot, and pulled on a couple of doorknobs, and found a car that was unlocked and just went in and passed out on the back seat of a car."

Did Bon come to fairly quickly or did it take a while?

"It took him a little while. He was groggy. He was extremely inebriated."

How did you react when you heard he'd died?

"His death really hit me hard. It was like hearing that a brother or an uncle or somebody in my family had died. I think Bon went all over the world and he was the kind of person that was gregarious and he loved people, he loved partying, he liked having a good time. I think he made friends and had a network of people all over the world that had the same kind of relationship and feelings that I had about him. So when he passed away it's like he had a family of 100,000 people that were in shock."

Did you think that he was indestructible or that his lifestyle could handle it?

"He sure gave the impression that he was indestructible because he was very take-no-prisoners. He was very sure of himself. He didn't hesitate when he wanted to go out and do something. When he had an idea he was not the kind of person to mull it over. He was very impulsive."

Did you ever perceive any conflict between him and Malcolm or any of the other guys in the band?

"I think they thought Angus was a little bit weird. I remember telling him a couple of times, 'What's up with Angus?' And he was like, 'Ah, he just doesn't like to have fun.' I think Angus probably had a certain sense of responsibility. I think Angus was maybe a lot more serious about what he was doing. I think he looked at music and looked at the band as a business and as a job. He was very sober about his approach to it, whereas the other guys saw the opportunities to have fun. Of course there were many of those.

"The ones who came out, it was always Bon, Malcolm, Cliff and Phil. You would never see Angus. He never went out and partied with the band. I don't recall seeing him outside of the studio once. You know, it's all in your attitude. I kinda gotta hand it to Angus. What we saw as odd or weird, I think he was wise beyond his years simply because at 25 he saw the moneymaking potential that AC/DC had and he didn't want to blow it. If I knew at 20 what I know now I would have had a very different attitude about a lot of the dealings, especially the business dealings, that my band had."[28]

Fazz doesn't remember seeing much of Angus either: "I saw Bon and the gang mostly at the bar late nights till the wee hours."

When you say "the gang" — who?

"Everyone except Ang."

So Mal?

"Often as well."

How did Mal get on with the others?

"Great from what I saw. Friends in a band."

You ever sense tension?

"Not once. But we were usually in an altered state of consciousness."

Robin Mendelson is a pediatric ICU nurse in a hospital in Miami and is friends with both Holly X and Pattee Bishop. In 1979, she was called Robin Kuster and was Holly's "best friend" when Bon and AC/DC were hanging out in Miami. The Tight Squeeze club is where Holly and Robin first met and it's where Robin, a 17-year-old bartender/cocktail waitress after leaving home at 16, says she hooked up with Cliff Williams.

"We were all a little starstruck of Bon Scott and AC/DC. Holly came into the club with Bon and Cliff and I accosted her in the bathroom and said, 'Is that *Bon Scott*?' And she was like, '*Yeppp*.' And I was like, '*Oh my God*, I want to meet the guy he's with,' and that's how I ended up meeting Holly and I ended up going out with Cliff. He'd come over to Holly's parents' house at Key

Biscayne. I spent a lot of time there. Holly had the whole bottom floor of this three-storey house, and [Bon and Cliff] used to come over a lot."

How long did you go out with Cliff?

"Not very long. It was a short stint. It was maybe a month or two . . . but when you're 17 years old that's like forever."

Were there issues between Malcolm and Bon?

"I've been a drug addict and an alcoholic and I've been in recovery for 33 years. I think that there comes a time when you're always out there having fun, partying, and there are people who are serious and want to live life and [when] they see you destroy yourself they become a little bit distant. Looking back at it now, there was *distance* from Malcolm — to protect himself, and to some degree to protect the band. That's how I would perceive it today. Back then I don't know if I would have perceived it that way."

What about Cliff? Was he concerned about Bon's drinking?

"Yes, absolutely, 100 per cent. Everybody was concerned about Bon's drinking. *Everybody*. At the time we were doing a lot of drugs, too. Fortunately at the time I was personally very hooked up in the cocaine cartels here in South Florida. I had an ultimately abundant amount of cocaine at my disposal all the time so I used to bring it to have a party. When you're young and you're pretty — back in those days, *oh my God*, forget it — I am grateful to be alive, to tell you the truth. I surely shouldn't be here either."

Robin, Cliff, Bon and Holly would go out together. She visited Criteria with Holly.

"I can honestly tell you as an outsider looking in that Bon was so smitten with Holly. He looked at her as if she were a goddess. She was this big, voluptuous, big boobed . . . he used to go between her boobs and shake his head and he'd go, 'I'm finally *home*!' We used to wear stiletto high-heeled shoes, like six-inch [heels], and he would look up at her — because [when she wore them] she was six feet tall and he's this little, *pfft*, five-foot whatever he was, a little guy — and just . . . the *look* on his face. I remember one time thinking to myself, 'This guy absolutely loves this girl.'"

It's not hard to imagine that Bon might have written songs about Holly or Pattee or both. "Girls Got Rhythm" and "Touch Too Much" are two songs off *Highway To Hell* that could conceivably be about either one of them, especially the lyric *The body of Venus with arms* from "Touch Too Much." Indeed, Fazz is convinced of this: "I still say 'Touch Too Much' is about Holly." Fazz describes her in 1979 as being "a knockout." The song was in the British top 40 when Bon died.

But the track that stands out the most as a possible ode to Holly is one Bon was never credited for, off an album he never sang on. Instead the song credit has "Young/Young/Johnson" after it. When I put it to Robin that Bon might have written some of the lines that found their way onto "You Shook Me All Night Long" about Holly, she is in no doubt.

"I 100 per cent believe that is true. 'You Shook Me All Night Long.' He used to say that about her all the time. He said, 'The girl shook my world.' He used to say, 'THIS GIRL SHOOK MY WORLD! SHE SHOOK MY WORLD!' *Yep*. There's not a doubt in my mind, not a *doubt* in my mind that he had written songs about her. Holly doesn't listen to [AC/DC] because it's very painful. She was very in love with Bon and vice-versa. I really believe that he was very in love with her, as much as two people who are crazy and young can be and be that messed up, you know? You can tell when somebody looks at somebody how they feel about them. You can look at two people who love each other and you can see that look. They *look* at each other."

But Cliff, interviewed in 2007, denied Bon had had anything to do with the writing on *Back In Black*: "No, no, no . . . that was all, you know, lyrically, from Brian Johnson's influence from when he came into the band."

⚡

Fazz and Bon went for a drive around Miami.

"There were six of us riding in one of our piece-of-shit cars. Bon was in the back seat, between two girls. I said, 'Hey, Bon, here in the States we call that 'riding whore' [*laughs*]. He goes, 'Well, that fucking fits, don't it?' I *peed*. We put on the Sex Pistols and Bon's singing along, screaming, didn't know the words, but he's just screaming along with Johnny Rotten and after about 45 seconds he goes, 'TURN THAT FUCKING SHIT *OFF!*' So we end up at a restaurant called Sambo's. There's six of us and Bon is in rare form. He says to the waitress, pointing at the pictures illustrating the menu items, 'What I order better look like *this*!' She answers, 'I can't guarantee that, sir.' He didn't order anything. I ordered the chilli. He asked if he could taste it. He ate the entire *bowl*. I ordered another. I started to inhale it, and in that classic voice of his, just like his singing voice, Bon yells loud enough for the restaurant to hear, 'LOOK AT 'IM *GOOOO!*' Meanwhile, he starts dipping his spoon in the bowl. Poor guy. I don't think he'd eaten in days."

By 5 a.m., Fazz, Bon and Frank Prinzel, the electronics maintenance guy from Criteria, were back in Bon's room at the Newport Hotel.

"Bon whips out a bottle of Blue Nun wine and asked us to hang," says Fazz. In the 1970s, Blue Nun was a German Liebfraumilch, a semi-sweet white table wine from the Rhine. "I had to go, since I delivered appliances for my dad's appliance store. Bad enough I had to be there at 9 a.m., but with a hangover to boot. We felt sorry leaving Bon. It was on that drive home when it dawned on me that I'd really started to feel a bond with the guy, and I first felt a twinge of worry about him."

Prinzel remembers the morning with Bon at the Newport like it was yesterday.

"This was a high point in my life. In the room there was some small talk and friendly banter. I remember Angus being there and being very quiet. Cliff may have been there too. I remember seeing their boots lined up against the wall and thinking how very, very *small* they were. There were practice cassettes lying around. It was very late and we opted to go and I remember Bon being very disappointed and standing before the doorway asking us to stay with a bottle of Blue Nun in his hand, smiling."

Says Fazz: "I don't think during the entire time we spent together I saw Bon get angry. Back then, I weighed around 250 pounds. I asked Bon if Rosie from 'Whole Lotta Rosie' was as big as me. He grimaced and said, 'Mate, yer a pickle in an elephant's ass compared to Rosie!' People call it *Power-age*. Bon told me it's *Power-ij*.[29] Maybe Bon was being funny. We were so damn coked up, God knows what the hell we were talking about."

How did you feel when you heard he'd died?

"It didn't sink in right away. When it did, it consumed me. Yet I wasn't that surprised. I saw firsthand how his drinking habit was. Someone had nicknamed him Bombed Scott. Horrible feeling. I wondered what was to become of the band."

Did you ever sense why his drinking had got so out of control?

"I just thought he liked it. No dependency issues or emotional reasons. He was always happy."

But you said it was on that drive home from the Newport when it dawned on you that you'd really started to feel a bond with the guy and had a first twinge of concern. So what was it that made you worry?

"What made me worry on that drive home, I guess, was [that he was] tethered to that bottle of Blue Nun at four or five o'clock in the morning in the hotel room and while everybody else kinda knew when to stop, Bon didn't. He just kept *going*. And I think the alcohol thing was an obsession inasmuch as it was something he enjoyed very much but I don't think at that point he was able to control it, and therein lies the problem.

"There was one incident where I was shocked because I had brought a joint into his hotel room and I'm going, 'All right, Bon. Wanna fire this baby up?' And he's going 'No, *no, no*. Not going to do it today. No, no, *nope*. Going to go clean today.' I was kinda proud of him. And, I swear to you, within *two fucking minutes*, he goes, 'Well, are you going to fire it up or what?' Within what seemed like a nanosecond, from one point not wanting to smoke it, to *let's go*.

"That was perhaps another indication that there may have been a problem. *May have been*. There *was* a problem. But I don't want you to think that everything was Bon being fucked up, because it wasn't like that at all. I mean, there were times when he was very lucid, when we got together during the days and hung out and stuff. Once again, he was the sweetest guy you'd ever want to meet and just an incredible talent — a unique talent. I loved him. In the short time that I got to spend with him I got to *know* Bon Scott. He didn't stay that rock hero that I idolised, the whole band actually. I became his pal. Bon in particular was just so unique, an incredible person. I hate to sound corny, cheesy and sappy but it's really how I felt about him."

Prinzel agrees: "Bon made a deep impression on me. Yes, he was a rock idol of sorts but he impressed me as a deeply sincere, guileless and genuinely jovial person. He was the antithesis of the rock idol. I could possibly be wrong but the message I got was that Bon was one of the good souls."

"I just thought he was a partying guy," says Henry Laplume, himself a recovering alcoholic. "I thought his drinking was the norm. But then again it took me 40 years to figure out what I was. It was a rude awakening."

As far as AC/DC was concerned, it was back to business as usual.

"Bon always knew what he was doing, you know," said Malcolm Young. "I never saw Bon drunk onstage. *Ever* in my life . . . he had his own rules, Bon, you know, but he was always in control. Afterwards . . . if he had a great night, a couple of nice chicks hanging off him, hey, that man was the happiest man in the world. I'm sure he didn't want to get drunk and collapse with two beautiful chicks hanging off him, you know. He'd make it last."

But his time was fast running out.

CHAPTER 18

NIGHT PROWLER

In 1979 Miami was the centre of drug trafficking in the United States. According to the book *The Pursuit of Oblivion: A Global History of Narcotics*, the illegal drug trade was worth $7 billion a year in Florida.

"The Medellin cartel's U.S. power base was South Florida: Miami became a city of murders . . . cocaine sniffing became regarded as a pleasurable accoutrement of worldly success. Its paraphernalia was commercialised. The number of people with cocaine-related problems seeking admission to federally funded clinics climbed by 600 per cent from 1976 to 1981."

Says David Owen: "There was quite a bit [of cocaine going around]. This was a time before AIDS. A lot of the stuff out now that can kill you wasn't around back then; things weren't as permanently deadly back in those days. It was a very loose, swaggery kind of time. It was a great time to be a musician and to be young, that's for sure."

Michael Fazzolare, who was born to play a character role in a Mafia TV series with his FM radio voice and faint resemblance to the Stallone brothers, was right in the scene as well.

"Ever see *Scarface*? You see the shit he had? That wasn't *dick*."

Pattee Bishop is shocked when I tell her about the extent of Bon's drug habit.

"I find it all hard to believe, really. How did a guy I knew pretty well, who told me a lot, because I talk a lot, hide that from me? He liked hard alcohol and his back hurt. He took aspirin. Robin Mendelson is telling me all this drug crap with Bon. 'Oh *Pattee*, Bon did a lot of drugs.' I told her, 'Not with me, with *you*.'"

Did you see Bon taking Quaaludes?

"We all did, and speed . . . I never saw Bon do heroin, but Robin says he did heroin. We liked Nembutal, speed . . . if he did [heroin], he didn't do it with me. Dark liquor and a line. He knew I would leave if I saw it."

I ask Robin straight up if Bon was doing hard drugs in Miami. She tells me a different story than whatever she was allegedly telling Pattee.

"The 'game' was doing heroin. I think I was just doing downers. I never *saw* Bon doing heroin. We did a lot of pills though. A *lot*. A real lot more than any normal person. It's part of the addiction. I believe like 30 Quaaludes a day; maybe a quarter ounce of coke daily. It was a crazy time . . . *crazy*. It's actually like another lifetime ago. I'm not that same person, that's for sure. We used to do a line of coke and at the end of the line of coke would be a Quaalude."

Thirty Quaaludes a day back in 1979?

"Yep. We all got *wasted*."

It's an extraordinary thing to contemplate that in all the innumerable articles, TV specials, books, tribute shows and possibly soon-to-be-made films about Bon, no one has ever mentioned his Quaalude intake.

Says Roy Allen: "Bon and I took Quaaludes. I remember one time we were at a friend's house and Bon showed up. [The friend] held out a Quaalude in his hand and Bon picked it up and the guy turned around for a second and Bon popped it in his mouth and the guy says, 'Hey, where's that Quaalude?' Bon goes, 'It's in me *gut*.' He just put it in his mouth right there. We weren't above doing drugs. We never did heroin or speed or anything like that. If we did get something, I think it was pretty much the Quaaludes. He didn't even ask. He just put it in his mouth and swallowed it, which was pretty cool — at the time, anyway."

⚡

Quaaludes (also known as methaqualone or Mandrax) are among the most dangerous drugs to combine with alcohol, a sedative hypnotic on its own. When Quaaludes were available over the counter in West Germany as an insomnia and anxiety medication in the early 1960s, up to 22 per cent of all drug overdoses were related to Quaaludes. In Japan, the figure was 40 per cent. By the middle of the decade, they were being manufactured in the United States, prescribed "as a non-addictive alternative to barbiturates." By the 1970s, cocaine, Quaaludes and alcohol were a common mix in backstage dressing rooms, parties and nightclubs. The year Bon died, Quaaludes could be legally obtained at so-called stress clinics.

As Justin T. Gass explained in his book *Drugs, the Straight Facts: Quaaludes*, "Beginning around 1980, these clinics provided an easy way to legally acquire a prescription for Quaaludes."

You could either front up as "extremely stressed" and get a prescription from a doctor after a physical examination and accompanying "stress-based survey" or pretend to be.

"Non-stressed people could imitate the signs and symptoms of a clinically stressed person and obtain a legal prescription for Quaaludes. Some patients would keep the pills for themselves; others, however, would sell the Quaaludes to make a quick profit."

An American teenager called Karen Ann Quinlan combined alcohol with Quaaludes in 1975, fell into a coma and died a decade later from pneumonia, following her parents' successful court battle to have her disconnected from a respirator. Roman Polanski gave 13-year-old Samantha Geimer a Quaalude and champagne when he sexually assaulted her in 1977. Candy Givens, the lead singer of Tommy Bolin's band Zephyr, drowned in a jacuzzi in 1984 after passing out from Quaaludes and alcohol.

To give an idea of how much they were a problem in Miami around the time Bon was with Holly X, in 1980 there were 66 deaths alone related to the drug in Dade County (now Miami-Dade County, the most populous in Florida): one more than the previous four years combined.

If that weren't concerning enough, in South Florida there was an endemic problem of counterfeit Quaaludes. Fake ones were sold at rock concerts. Made in Colombia for 13c and sold for $2.50 a tab in Miami and $5 elsewhere, in 1981 three million counterfeit Quaaludes were seized in Miami by Drug Enforcement Administration officials, each containing dangerous quantities of Valium.[30] The fake ludes could be lethal.

Just one was enough to kill a "schoolchild" if mixed with alcohol. Quaalude overdoses could also cause vomiting, respiratory depression, seizure, and cardiac or respiratory arrest. Bon already had trouble breathing because of asthma.

Quaaludes were made a Schedule II drug on the Controlled Substances Act in 1973, meaning they had "a high potential for abuse" but "a currently accepted medical use" and could only be obtained by prescription. Quaaludes are now Schedule I, meaning high potential for abuse with no currently accepted medical use. Florida was the first state in the U.S. to reschedule Quaaludes in the early 1980s. By 1984 they were banned nationwide.

Users are known to become tolerant to the highly addictive drug and have to increase doses to get the same effect every time they use. Bon was addicted to alcohol, but what about Quaaludes? Had he developed a so-called cross tolerance, where his metabolic tolerance to booze was matched by a tolerance to depressants? Depression is a common side effect for people who have used Quaaludes then stopped. By numerous accounts Bon experienced depression. He loved to drink and "lude out," slang for combining booze and Quaaludes, and he was getting most of his Quaaludes from Robin and Holly.

"My husband David Shaffer [now deceased] was a huge drug dealer back then, he gave them to us," says Robin. "All his connections were Colombian."

So on average how many pills did you take in a session? Can you remember?

"Me or Bon?"

Bon.

"Oh, I don't remember. We just drank and did drugs. We didn't count [*laughs*]."

So one was not enough?

"And a thousand never too many. We drank and did drugs till we all passed out."[31]

Give me a number, then, for how many you could do on a typical "get wasted" drinking session with Bon.

"I don't know. Maybe *10*."

They were Quaaludes supplied by David?

"David supplied me with cocaine and Quaaludes before we got married in 1982. He was my boyfriend-dealer. I got pregnant with his child and ended up marrying him. David did eight years in prison and his partner is still doing time."

Did Bon source his Quaaludes from David as well?

"No, he got them from us. There's actually a little bit of responsibility that goes along with saying that, because I don't think [Bon] did pills until he met Holly and so it's kind of the healing process to admit that he started doing drugs because of us; not that he wouldn't have done them anyway, but just the thought of having turned him on to harder drugs is kind of sad."

It's quite an admission from Robin. Bon was taking hard drugs a long time before Robin and Holly entered the picture; he'd broken whatever promise he'd made to the Youngs. I tell her I don't think she or Holly should feel responsible. The man was old enough to make his own choices.

"That makes me feel better. He made it seem like it was a new thing for him. I know it was probably a new thing for Cliff. I think Cliff just tagged along to try to keep him out of trouble. But unfortunately he just got sucked in."

Was Cliff doing coke with you?

"Yes, [*laughs*] oh yes."

Did you ever see anything harder than cocaine?

"Cocaine was just the drug back then; that and alcohol. And a lot of pills, a lot of downers. Cliff's a very quiet guy. Just like everybody else I'm sure now that he's married and has kids, he's probably a decent man; like us all, we change. I'm sure he got very hooked up. You can be swayed easily. There's a fine line between which road you should travel, especially when you're young. I can't imagine being young and in a band like AC/DC. Do you go off with the party people or do you stay and hang out and party just a little bit and do what's right for the band? I just feel bad that Bon didn't make it out alive. Nobody I knew from back then who didn't get into recovery is alive. I can honestly say we were hardcore. And Bon definitely could keep up with us."

Holly X's 20th birthday was due to fall in the second week of March 1979 so she threw a big party — fully catered, lobsters, the whole shebang — at her parents' house at Mashta Island in Key Biscayne while Bon was still in town. Holly's father, according to her childhood friend Liz Klein, was "very laid back" and his house was "over-the-top beautiful." Critical Mass turned up.

"I met Bon at a private party one time while they were down there and he had a local girlfriend at the time whose birthday it was," says David Owen. "Bon needed some 'party materials and inspiration' and he wanted me to meet him over there and bring some, so I did that. Bon called me a couple of times when he needed help procuring some 'fun stuff.' And I would usually meet him and kinda hang out with him outside of that. I ended up spending a number of hours there and basically the whole time Bon and I sat on the couch next to each other and partook of party substances and just kinda watched the world go round us and talked about music and life in general and it was *awesome*."

CHAPTER 19

TOUCH TOO MUCH

Owen says they had "some substances on the table in front of us . . . it seemed like people were just swirling around the house and coming and going, and we were sitting there, talking about music like the rest of the world didn't exist. Being that [AC/DC] were from out of town and [Critical Mass] were the guys that were in town they kind of relied on us to help them sort of navigate around and acquire certain things that they desired, so I'm not trying to be vague but you know what I'm talking about."

Was Bon's intake of the "fun stuff" more prodigious than others?

"It was prodigious on shall we say a 'civilian' level but I've seen musicians do a lot more than he did. But it was more than just a casual average person at the time."

This party was out at Key Biscayne?

"Yeah."

Was the girl called Holly?

"*Holly!* That's it. Yep. It was Holly's birthday party. I didn't know her personally. I remember seeing her a few times back in the day, and seeing her with Bon a couple of times; she was an attractive blonde, kind of a surfer chick from what I remember. Good-looking girl."

Mike Barone, Henry Laplume and Michael Fazzolare all independently confirm that Holly was Bon's girlfriend in Miami. Bizarrely, Pattee Bishop also turned up to Holly's. It was the first time Bon's two girlfriends found themselves under the same roof. Bon, claims Pattee, had invited her to come.

"I was at the party. Bon was there, but I had a boyfriend. It was at Holly's parents' house; it sucked. I saw no love there [with Holly]. I never heard him call any one of us his girlfriend. I'd never heard of Holly before that party, but I was with Bon that day. Holly is the only mystery to me because I was there in '79, and I'm still at a loss with that. I never heard Bon say he liked someone, that he had a girlfriend. Silver was his girl back home, the one he stayed with, and she kept his money. He told me that. I never heard Holly was his girlfriend or Robin was Cliff's.

"When I hear Bon was Holly's *boyfriend* it makes me laugh; I didn't care who was whose boyfriend. If I was having fun, I just did my thing. But Bon, if he had had a girlfriend, he would have told me — because he was like that. He never was [into] bullshit or told lies. I always had someone I was seeing or who was paying my bills [*laughs*] and Bon knew that I did my own thing; but we liked each other. He called me from London and Australia. I think he liked to keep me in the know. In Florida, he always hooked up with me at least once when he was in town. Bon told me AC/DC were in Miami because of the weather, to record, and the band could keep an eye on him. He got into too much stuff at home [in Australia], drinking too much. He got Malcolm upset. He had to apologise."

Did Bon hook up with you in Miami?

"Yes. I had been with Bon *that* day. That's how I knew where the party was. Bon I had seen the night before Holly's party; he and I went to a bar, then back to my place. I took him back to his hotel early that next morning; he called me later and asked me to come to this party. Trust me, it's because of me any of them got to meet Bon. Why would Bon invite me to his girlfriend's party? It was no big deal. Robin Mendelson remembers me being there. I didn't even say goodbye to Bon. We just ran out of there [*laughs*]."

Holly doesn't remember Pattee coming to Mashta Island but is aware of her now through their mutual friend, Robin. She prefers to keep her memories of Bon positive, even if he was effectively two- or three-timing her.

"Bon looks like a little devil, right? He had this child-like quality, this innocent kind of child-like quality. It was real. It wasn't put on. He had this sense of wonder about him, and joy, and exuberance, enthusiasm. He was a *lot* of fun to be with. You'd be laughing very easily with him."

Did you ever see him do harder drugs when he was with you?

"Yeah, I mean, he did, *yeah*. We did Quaaludes together, we did cocaine together. It was the late '70s, the beginning of the '80s in Miami, 'cocaine cowboys.' Bon could do whatever was in front of him. People gave him stuff all the time. It used to get me really upset. We would go out clubbing in Miami. There were some big clubs down here, so we were always out seeing local bands and did all that in the clubs.

"People, once they found out who he was, obviously everybody wanted to be around Bon and gave him all kinds of stuff. I remember confronting him. We were both trying not to use anything other than alcohol, I think, and he had done some cocaine and he was really high and I asked about it. And he denied it. People were constantly shoving things at him and it got me really angry. I felt really protective of him there for a while."

So you say he did cocaine but you didn't see him do heroin?

"No. He didn't do that around me. But it's all heavy: cocaine, Quaaludes. He liked downers; he liked pills. When you mix those with alcohol . . . barbiturates were around back then. We did barbiturates together. You know, *Valley of the Dolls* kind of stuff. Like Marilyn Monroe died on, and all that, when you mix alcohol and barbiturates."

Monroe died from a toxic overdose of chloral hydrate and Nembutal, a downer. Jimi Hendrix died from a combination of alcohol and barbiturates. Barbiturates are also lethal combined with heroin.

"A big no-no in my head was mixing barbiturates with heroin. Any kind of barbiturate," says Paul Chapman of UFO. "Tuinal, Nembutal, Seconal, any of those, even Valium, stuff like that. Don't mix those with smack. I mean, you take acid with it and take coke with it and stuff like that but don't do any barbiturates with it. It puts you further down than you know."

⚡

Three weeks of sessions at Criteria came to nothing, the band hating Eddie Kramer's methods and doubting his ability, the producer rightly appalled at Bon's drinking and unable to get the Youngs onside. Kramer has given a few interviews over the years that have all told the same story: "Bon Scott was having problems with the lyrics and problems with drinking and problems with everything else." He's spoken of his "obvious difficulty with the singer" who was "drinking like crazy and didn't have any lyrics." The band arranged to leave Miami for London, where they'd been booked to record *Highway To Hell* with Mutt Lange at Roundhouse Studios.

"We were under a lot of time pressure on that one," said Cliff Williams. "That album had to be out so quickly that I wouldn't be surprised if one or two of them were first takes."

Critical Mass went with AC/DC to the airport bar to say their goodbyes.

"Angus and me were in the coffee shop as neither of us were fond of alcohol," says Fazz. "The lady working the coffee shop was a grump. She was yelling at us to not make a mess while we made our coffees. Angus stood up, smiled and gave her a military salute. Hysterical. I asked him if they had a name for the album, and he told me he was thinking about calling it *Slipdisc*. Of course that never happened. One of the last things Bon ever said to me was, 'If this one doesn't fly, they'll be holding a funeral for our record contract and me along with it.' He gave me a hug and said, 'Loved meeting you, Fazz.' They then boarded the plane. He was the nicest guy ever."

CHAPTER 20

LOVE HUNGRY
MAN

In North Miami Beach I have lunch at New York's Big Apple Deli on Biscayne Boulevard with Michael Fazzolare, his friend Jackie Smith, Holly X and Neal Mirsky, a former program director of WSHE Miami, the biggest rock station in Florida in the 1970s, and later coordinating producer of MTV and Howard Stern. The placemats have a map of Florida on them with drawings of palm trees, gators, dolphins and Cape Canaveral. Don Henley's "The Boys Of Summer" is playing. On the map, Jacksonville, where it all started for AC/DC on radio, is just inside the state border, one dot down from Fernandina Beach.

"To me Jacksonville is like South Georgia rather than North Florida," says Mirsky, who moved to Florida in the 1970s from New York. The group agree, telling me it's still a place where some folk get around in pickup trucks adorned with Confederate Battle Flags and "truck nuts," or plastic testicles, hanging off rear bumpers. I ask them where the divide is in Florida. Where's the DMZ line on the placemat between the rednecks and civilisation? The response is unanimous.

"Anywhere north of Miami."

Mirsky joined WSHE just before Bon died, but interviewed him in May 1979 for WDIZ Orlando. He says American radio since then has changed beyond all recognition.

"I worked my way up from Sarasota to Orlando to Tampa and then Miami. For decades now listeners have been telling us what they didn't like about our product: too many commercials, too much repetition, not enough variety. This is the feedback we would get from listeners. But our attitude, not mine personally, was 'So? Where the fuck are they gonna go?' And now of course they have so many places to go, whether it's YouTube, Pandora, SiriusXM. And as the laws change where one company can own hundreds of stations, what used to make us great for listeners was the *competition*. It was that competition that made us all better, trying to outdo each other, and the listeners benefited. But now your competition is down the hall: you've got a ClearChannel cluster with eight, nine radio stations, so it's really just a matter of divvying up the pie; nobody's competing. It's really not about the listeners or the advertisers, it's about the corporate owners' stock price. Now it's just kind of a joke."

Today rock 'n' roll is just holding on in formats such as Classic Rock and Album Rock/Active Rock (a heavier kind of classic rock with new artists thrown in). Classic Rock has the larger market share.

"There's your CHR [contemporary hit radio], your top-40 kind of radio, the Katy Perry stations, but really it's muzak; it's *their* muzak. But it's not about music discovery like it was for us [in the 1970s]. Radio represented music discovery. I grew up just outside of New York City in the '60s where top-40 radio was at its best. WABC in New York is where I first heard the Stones and The Kinks, The Zombies. And then in the '70s and '80s WNEW in New York or WSHE in Miami is where you discovered Elvis Costello or Pink Floyd or whatever."

WSHE was also the first major station in South Florida to play the Bon Scott–led AC/DC.

"It sucks because I'm sorry, I don't care, that was the best version of the band," interjects Fazz. "The songs were better, it rocked, it was in your face, it was full speed ahead. Don't you think? Not that it needs to be a contest but it just friggin' figures, man. The problem is that Bon should have been on friggin' at least *Back In Black*, as far as I'm concerned. The discerning listener can tell the difference between who wrote the lyrics. The poor fucker never got to experience it. Bon's were extremely clever, tongue in cheek, play on words, very clever. Brian Johnson's just like some guy pandering to however many metaphors for his dick he can come up with. Let's take a cliché and write a song about it: 'I Put The Finger On You.' You know what I mean? 'Sink The Pink.' Let's find a cliché and we'll build a song *around* a cliché. It got almost, like, embarrassing to me after a while. Whereas Bon was just like a . . . I don't know; he was crazy and a genius. And I could never quite figure it out. Because he was like this sweet, personable guy."[32]

I turn to Holly. Why don't you have photos of you with Bon?

"I don't have 'personal' photos of Bon even though I was taking lots of band photos, although much less by the time I got to New York. I didn't want him to think I was a 'groupie' or in any way *impressed* by him."

She didn't take photos of her previous lover, the huge rock star, for the same reason. I tell her people might question the veracity of claims she makes for that very reason, and she seems slightly affronted. But Fazz didn't take pictures either.

"I regret that we didn't have camera phones then," he says. "Can you imagine?"

"Oh my gosh," says Holly.

"You had to have somebody with a Kodak Instamatic with a flash cube."

"*Yeppp.*"

⚡

After lunch we take a tour of Miami in Jackie's Mercedes, stopping where the Tight Squeeze club used to be on Hollywood Beach, right by the Halifax River ("The Intercoastal") and the Atlantic Ocean. The neighbourhood is part of "Floribec," nicknamed thus for its high concentration of Québécois tourists. On first impression it seems to be made up exclusively of low, brightly painted short- and long-term apartments and thick clusters of Tow-Away Zone parking signs. There are signs outside the motels that betray the clientele: COMPLETELY FURNISHED, FRENCH TV.

"You could do whatever you want here," says Fazz. "Long term, seasonal. The Montreal crowd; French Canadians. Guys my size with ponytails walking around in thongs."

If ever a man was missing out on his calling in life both as a famous rock musician and character actor in Hollywood, it's Fazz. In the laidback Miami of 1979, he explains, the Tight Squeeze club was surrounded by shops selling nothing but "suntan lotion, sunglasses and thongs." Nearby there was also a bar called Nick's, which still operates.

"Is *this* it?" he says, pointing to a partly boarded-up building site with a couple of migrant labourers milling about with hammers. "This is it! That's *it*. Right *there*. That was the Tight Squeeze."

There's nothing to see — the place has been stripped bare to nothing but a shell — but we walk inside anyway. Fazz is pointing in all directions.

"From here, from that wall, *this* was Tight Squeeze. Where those boards are going horizontally that's where the stage was. You walked in and the main entrance was right in the front there. The oval bar was here. Spent many moments with Cliff Williams there. And all the tables and everything were in here. The bathroom was back there. That's where it all originally happened [*laughs*] with Henry taking a piss in the bathroom and he looks over and he goes, 'I know you. You're Bon Scott!'"

When we get back to the "Broadwalk," as the boardwalk along the beach is called, the heat and humidity is unbearable. It's a sauna.

"I could just sit out here all fucking day," says Fazz, furiously perspiring in a black short-sleeved shirt. "Over the years it's all changed. But if you turn your back on this and you look that way," he says, gesturing towards the beach and ocean, "you're in 1966."

I point out that Jimmy Buffett's Margaritaville Beach Resort is being built nearby.

"Well, he's the patron saint of alcoholic Key West residents."

We go to the Newport Hotel, where Fazz hung out with Bon. For a lark, he knocks on door #617, Cliff Williams's old room, and tries the handle but no one answers. Instead, to get a feel for the place as it might have been in 1979, we walk into an open room being cleaned down the hall.

"This is different," he says. "This wasn't here before. Totally renovated."

Holly, who's been quiet, pipes up: "This is a very bittersweet experience."

Have these halls changed at all, Fazz?

"Probably a coat of paint."

So, how many times did you come out here to the Newport when AC/DC was in Miami?

"Fuck. *Shit*. Every night [*laughs*]. A bunch. I'd say at least a dozen times."

We take the elevator to the lobby and walk out to the beachside pool to see the spot where Bon told Holly she had chartreuse eyes. The Newport building as it was in 1979 is still largely intact, but just like the rest of the Sunny Isles strip it's in the shadow of a residential tower. All the old motel-style places bar The Sahara are being demolished and replaced with glass monstrosities. Donald Trump has seven branded developments between Sunny Isles and Hollywood, 10 minutes' drive north.

"I love this part of town but I don't recognise it," says Fazz, getting into the car. "None of this was here. If you want to rec-reate that Miami/Sunny Isles [of the '70s], go to Daytona Beach Shores. Those same hotels are still there."

It's not all glitz and glamour. At traffic-light stops at major inter-sections, homeless people and drug addicts shuffle between vehicles, holding up cardboard signs asking for food, money or employment.

Holly sees a lot of "undocumented" people in her line of work as a doctor: Mexicans, South Americans, Central Americans, Jamaicans, Haitians, Cubans, Dominicans, Bahamians, even Russians. There's a massive illegal immigration problem in South Florida as well as a synthetic drugs crisis that authorities claim has been contained. We're certainly seeing some real-time "Faces of Meth" as they walk past the car's windows. The era of the cocaine cowboys in Miami seems almost innocent in comparison to the devastation being wrought by prescription opioids and cheap but deadly street drugs on America's towns and cities.

"These poor fuckers," says Fazz. "There's a lot of them on these corners here."

"Oh yeah. There but for the grace of God go I," replies Holly.

When we pull into Criteria, the studio where AC/DC did demos for *Highway To Hell*, there's not much to see. It's now called The Hit Factory Criteria Miami and a very high wire fence has been erected around it, keeping out intruders. The nearby Musicians Studio Rentals, the rehearsal space where Bon heard Teddy Rooney say "Shazbot Nanu Nanu," has become a mechanic's workshop. The sign out front reads: VANTAGE MOTOR WORKS, FINE VINTAGE & CONTEMPORARY MOTOR CAR SERVICE.

Half an hour's drive south in Key Biscayne, Holly's parents' house has also disappeared. When it was built in 1960, there were no other houses around it. The floor plans are still held at the University of Florida but the original house has been knocked down, replaced by a modern two-storey mansion. Bougainvillea enshrouds the garage and there's a huge black wrought-iron gate out front.

"Key Biscayne is all cocaine money now," she says. "You can't even see the water any more from the street. Billionaires' row."

We knock on the door and it gets answered by a Russian called Evgeny. He's very pale and wearing a Hawaiian shirt. I introduce myself and tell him I'm writing a book about AC/DC. Evgeny tells me he's in real estate back in St. Petersburg and this place is a holiday house. Not a bad holiday house. I ask if we can go around the back.

"Yeah, okay, sure, no problem," he smiles and gestures for us to walk around the side to the pool by the water's edge. His wife comes out of the house with a book about Key Biscayne. The view that greets us is incredible, like something out of *Miami Vice*. There's a speedboat in the distance. Stone pavers around the pool have replaced what used to be a natural beach. A small wooden jetty juts out into a turquoise-blue bay. There's an iguana on one of the steps of the pool. This is where Holly grew up and where Bon would spend some of the most important moments of the last year of his life. He ate at the local yacht club with Holly. He'd go boating with Angus, Malcolm and Holly, wearing Holly's cutoff shorts. It's also a long way from where he died, in a junkie's car on a grey day in East Dulwich, London. How things might have turned out differently had he never gone to England.

⚡

That night in her kitchen, Holly confides in me.

"It was the end of '79. Bon wanted me to go to Perth, something that was very meaningful to me. I'd never been to Australia before. He wanted me to meet his family. And then he left Miami. In early 1980 I got a call from a friend of mine who had heard it on the radio that he'd died. I was devastated. I was just really sad. You don't expect people to die when you're young."

But why didn't you go to Australia with him?

"We spent time together when we could. Our relationship was a series of comings and goings. We both had lives apart from one another but we did speak on the phone from wherever he was, although the constant connection we have now with cell phones was unheard of back then. I think me going to Perth was even more meaningful to him. He wanted me to meet his family. He'd suddenly gotten quite serious about 'us.'"

Christmas 1979 was the first time Bon had seen his parents in three years. Why didn't those plans come to fruition if he was suddenly so serious about you?

"It may have been due to me drifting away a bit. I have no doubt that Bon recognised that I was becoming dangerously distracted by someone else."

Holly had a brief affair with an internationally celebrated guitarist who lived in Miami, knew Bon and actually shared some of his last concert bills with him. She surmises Bon possibly knew about it, as well as her meeting the man she'd marry and have a child with, a singer in a well-known local band. She's convinced that's why Bon suddenly got serious. He felt he was losing her. *Taking more than her share/Had me fighting for air.*

"I was supposed to go meet Bon sometime in 1980. The plan was to meet me back in Australia after the [*Back In Black*] shows at some point. I don't recall why we didn't choose Christmas [1979] for the rendezvous."

Was Bon's plan to bring out Holly to Australia a prelude to settling down? The 20-year-old Holly was definitely a catch for 33-year-old Bon; she was wanted by other rock stars, some of whom were Bon's own friends. Why wouldn't Bon ask her to come meet his family? Holly's chartreuse eyes. Doubletime the chestnut mare. Clean motors. American thighs. Was "You Shook Me All Night Long," the title, perhaps a rough first verse and chorus, worked up in Bon's lost notebook?

⚡

Robin Mendelson backs up Holly's claim about being asked by Bon to come to Australia.

"Holly said, 'I want you to come with me.' She was young and scared to go by herself. I was still seeing Cliff. So she was like, 'Why don't you come?' We had these plans that we were going to meet his parents and go touring with them over in Australia. This was right before [Bon] died. I was only 17."

How did it end with you and Cliff?

"Well, after Bon died, it pretty much was over. The only connection we had was Holly and Bon. I don't really believe that we were boyfriend and girlfriend. It was just a moment in time and we were having a good time. I don't even look at it that way. From my perspective, he was just some guy who I used to, pardon the French, *fuck*. I was just having the time of my life and that's what it was all about . . . and that went along with it. It was sex, drugs and rock 'n' roll. I don't know how else you say it."

Do you think Bon and Holly could have had a happy ending had he not died?

"Had Bon gotten clean, yes, I do believe there might have been a happy ending to their story. The reality is that nobody I know from that time that didn't get clean, I don't know one person that's alive. Not *one*. They're all dead."

Liz Klein also supports Holly's story. She saw Holly and Bon make out on the floor of the house in Key Biscayne after falling out of a closet.

"All of a sudden a closet door fell into the room and made a slamming noise and there they were making out. They had fallen from the back of the closet and they continued to make out on the ground with the closet door there. Bon was madly in love with Holly. She was always gorgeous, still is; just a beautiful woman, really beautiful inside and out. She had just like a perfect body. I would definitely think that 'You Shook Me All Night Long' is about her if it was written in that timeframe."

Liz even tells me there was talk of engagement.

"I remember Holly saying, 'We're getting engaged and we're going to be married.'"

Engaged?

"Yes, yes. I remember that conversation."

They were planning on getting engaged or they actually got engaged?

"She said they were engaged. I'm positive she told me that."

But Holly reacts awkwardly when I tell her: "I feel kind of weird Liz brought that up."

So were you engaged to Bon?

"I think it would have happened in Australia."

⚡

Leaving Miami on the *Silver Star*, I get time to reflect on what I've seen and what I've heard. It all seems so perfectly neat. Like all the things I've ever suspected about Bon, all the hunches I had about the lyrics for songs on *Back In Black*, are being confirmed. The whole thing seems too perfect. I begin to entertain the idea it could be a conspiracy to fool me, an elaborate practical joke hatched by someone with a grudge against me. But, as with Roy in Texas and Pattee in California, there are too many people involved, people I've come to trust, and far too many independent corroborations. It all checks out. When I get back to New York, Holly sends me an email.

Dear Jesse

I feel a wee bit apprehensive. I'm afraid you'll uncover something that I don't want to hear, like he had other loves all around the world and wrote songs for each of them too . . . we weren't exclusive, as you well know, although we were definitely heading that way before he was taken away. There's absolutely no doubt about that and I recognise this truth with all of my heart.

Bon's story ended far too abruptly. We will never know how it would have played out. Would he have gotten sober? Would he and I have married and had kids? Was he meant to have been one of the great loves of my life? I'll never know and that's just a terrible pity. But, when all is said and done, we need to move forward from great pain and loss and keep living and loving those who are still here.

You have given me the golden opportunity of being able to go back into the past to heal old wounds and to remember someone who was incredibly precious to me. It was such a different time back then; the halcyon days of the '70s which dovetailed on the awakening of sexual expression of the '60s. No one worried about HIV; in fact, it was quite incestuous in those music circles back then and that was just the norm. Since I have such a completely different perspective on sex (and drugs) now, I cannot help but still cringe a bit but thank God I have people like Robin [Mendelson] who give me the much-needed reality check I sometimes need. And a reminder that anytime I use substances, really bad things will happen that I will feel horrible about later. I am actually grateful for that because without that knowledge — and pain — I would not be sober today.

Bon continues to bring good things into my life. I would not have met Robin, then my ex-husband and then the most important person in my life — my daughter — had it not been for Bon. Quite amazing when I think that my relationship with that one incredibly special and wonderful man led to so many important moments in my life. I certainly cannot say that about anyone else; it is kind of mind-blowing. If he could hear me, I'd thank him with all of my heart. And come to think of it, the most important moment in my life — choosing recovery over addiction six years after his death — was also due, in a large part, to watching the person I cared so much about die from this horrific disease.

It is an incredibly sad fact, well known in Alcoholics Anonymous/Narcotics Anonymous, that "others must die so we can live." Without painful consequences, such as the incomprehensible loss of those we care about, we would continue using. So Bon's death moved me closer to life, although I wish so very much he were still with us. Another gift from him to me, albeit one I never in a million years would have chosen if I had been given an option.

I got clean and sober in 1986 and, other than two relatively short relapses, I am extremely grateful to report I have had many long years of abstinence from all substances. The second relapse, in 2012, served to skyrocket my passion for teaching about preventing burnout and addiction.

The reason for these relapses was because I had stopped going to meetings and had stopped working the "Steps." They say this is a disease of "forgetting" and when we forget the pain and despair of active addiction, it won't be long until we are destined to relive it. I've learned the hard way that unless I make my recovery the number-one priority in my life, my chronic disease — active addiction — will recur and be even worse than before.

Those experiences have enabled me to help others who are struggling even more than I ever could before. I know I have a deadly disease, the same disease as the one which killed Bon, and have learned the hard way that if I become too complacent, or hold resentment or bitterness inside for too long, I am at very high risk for relapse. One day at a time, I'll never have to go back there again. God's grace is so amazing and I am so grateful for each day I have in recovery.

Holly

⚡

From New York I fly to São Paulo to launch a Portuguese translation of my first book on AC/DC. Brazil is the only country outside Argentina that can really be said to have the most passionate AC/DC fans in the world. At the bookshop Livraria Da Vila in Higienópolis, I buy *Let There Be Rock*, *Powerage*, *If You Want Blood* and *Highway To Hell* — the four essential Bon Scott–era AC/DC albums — for about $4 each, brand new and sealed. In nearby Pinheiros, there are "You Shook Me All Night Long" pillows for sale at Museu da Imagem e do Som de São Paulo, the São Paulo Museum of Image and Sound.

AC/DC T-shirts, pins, books, records and posters can be bought virtually everywhere in São Paulo, Rio de Janeiro and Porto Alegre. In Brazil, as elsewhere in South America, Bon is a god — which is extraordinary when he never set foot on the continent. *Back In Black*, the biggest rock album of all time, didn't achieve what it did for AC/DC in isolation. There was a reason for it; there was groundwork and foundation to the triumph. Most of it had to do with Bon, his words, his melodies, his phrasing, his range and most of all the spirit he, not the rest of the band, continues to represent even in death. AC/DC no longer connotes electricity, bisexuality or (in some crackpot evangelical households) satanism. It means rebellion. It's the very same reason those football stadiums in South America get filled. Without Bon, none of it would have happened.

At the book launch, as I'm speaking in English to a roomful of Portuguese-speaking AC/DC fans patiently waiting for my answers to be translated by the moderator, Renata Simões, a guy in the audience, Ricardo Artigas, puts up his hand to ask me about Alistair Kinnear, the last man who saw Bon alive. Where is he? Did he have anything to do with Bon's death? When it comes to signing books, a charming young man who introduces himself as Fernando Lima gifts me a postcard of Bon to welcome me to his country. There isn't a part of the world that Bon hasn't touched.

That weekend my wife, Flavia, and I drive down to stay in a friend's house in Praia de Pernambuco, a beautiful tropical beach, 60 miles away. The caretaker and cook, a shy, plump, middle-aged woman called Rita who only has a Labrador for company when the owners are away, keeps largely to herself but suddenly pipes up when I play "Ride On" on my laptop. Bon once described the song as "about a guy who gets pissed around by chicks, and he heads for the horizon . . . he can't find what he wants, so he keeps on looking."

"Eu amo esta música," Rita says wistfully in Portuguese.

I love this music.

We all do. So why, Bon, did you have to head for that horizon so early?

AC/DC skipped the Califfornia (one F wasn't enough) World Music Festival at the Los Angeles Memorial Coliseum on April 7–8 1979 because they were recording *Highway To Hell* in London. The troubled handover from Vanda & Young to Eddie Kramer to Mutt Lange had been a masterstroke.

"[Lange] really injected new life into us and we brought out things we didn't know we were capable of," said Bon. "For instance, we put harmonies in the backing vocals, which is something totally new to us. We're really trying to be acceptable for American radio without becoming drippy like those stupid American bands. And it works, too. The raw AC/DC sound is still there but it sounds a lot better."

The Young brothers, however, were still troubled by what to do with Bon.

"Angus and Malcolm were getting tired of him being sick," says Pattee Bishop. "Bon was tired of carrying Angus on his back; his shoulders would be rubbed so red. It would piss Bon off, how long Angus would stay on. He didn't like that he felt he

CHAPTER 21

IF YOU WANT BLOOD (YOU'VE GOT IT)

owed them anything; after a while we would laugh at how long Angus would steal the show. Bon would go to the side of the stage, and grab his drink, and wait. He said to me, 'All I do is show up and do the tracks,' his parts."

Do you think any of Bon's lyrics ended up on *Back In Black* after he died?

"They never wanted his lyrics, he told me that. He really didn't care."

Bon didn't care about the band or the lyrics?

"He knew the band was the [Young] brothers. He said to me, 'It was a dream come true to sing with them,' but they never hung out. Sometimes he was sober, then other times not, but he drank that hard shit. The brothers were selfish, he would tell me. Bon would tell me how they put him down sometimes. The band would have meetings with him [about his drinking], and I know Mutt spoke to him one time he was on the wagon."

In 1979, according to Mick Jones, the notoriously reclusive Lange had won his own battle with alcohol and would have been in a position to give Bon some desperately needed guidance. Foreigner's main songwriter and lead guitarist had met Lange to consider him as producer for 1979's *Head Games*. Jones was a fan of City Boy, the English band that initially had got Lange attention from Atlantic and AC/DC. At the time, says Jones, "We were really rolling, we were big, it was starting to get to my head a little bit; even if it wasn't blatant, it was probably working on me." He ended up choosing Queen, Cars and Journey producer Roy Thomas Baker over Lange.

"I was really impressed by [Lange's work with City Boy], so he came over to New York to meet up and talk, and he'd been going through a bit of a rough passage; he'd had some problems at that time too. We decided to go with Roy and then Mutt kind of became insistent; we did have a good rapport when we met, somehow. He wasn't in the best of shape, apparently, but was probably in a lot better shape than I was."

Drinking?

"Drinking. I don't want to besmirch his name in any way. I never saw him do anything, drink, drugs, anything. He was a complete vegetarian when I met him, living a very clean life."

⚡

On 8 May 1979, the *If You Want Blood* tour began in Madison, Wisconsin. With UFO, the band travelled through Iowa, Ohio, Indiana, Kentucky, Illinois, Tennessee and Georgia. In Nashville, Malcolm coldly dispensed with the services of band manager Michael Browning, who'd only just come from meetings in New York with Atlantic Records over the cover of *Highway To Hell*. Aerosmith tour accountant Peter Mensch, whom Malcolm had been secretly wooing since their first meeting in Texas, replaced Browning. Leber-Krebs had long ago been shrewd enough to sense the commercial opportunity presented by AC/DC and signed the band to a two-year management deal.

Tales that have sprung up around *Highway To Hell* — that the record company was up in arms about the title, the devil horns and tail on Angus, the pentagram hanging from one of Bon's chain-link necklaces — are contradicted by Atlantic's art director, Bob Defrin.

"Atlantic didn't give a shit about the covers. As long as the band, their manager and Atlantic's legal department approved, it was fine with them. This was a gigantic plus for me. Regardless of who the act was I would work directly with them. In many cases the first time Atlantic would see a cover was when final artwork was done and of course approved by the band. All the label really cared about was that the band liked it and that it came in on time and on budget."

Five days later Bon and AC/DC were back in Florida for a stadium event at the Tangerine Bowl in Orlando alongside Boston, The Doobie Brothers and Poco. The four members of Critical Mass drove up for the day to see them.

"We saw AC/DC only at the show, in their trailer," says Michael Fazzolare. "I spent it mostly talking to Malcolm about The Who.

They were waiting to perform so it wasn't the same as when we partied in Miami."

But Neal Mirsky got a chance to interview Bon: "WDIZ was broadcasting live from the press box. I would run backstage and conduct interviews with a portable cassette recorder, then run the tape up to the press box where we would feed the audio over the air as if it were live."

MIRSKY: Welcome to Florida.

BON: Thank you, Neal. It's a pleasure to be here and I love the place [*laughs*].

MIRSKY: Have you ever been to Florida before, playing?

BON: Gee, we used to spend five weeks down here, a couple of months back, to write the new album, which is, like, the *Highway To Hell* album.

MIRSKY: Is that the name of it, *Highway To Hell*?

BON: Ah, tentatively, yeah, yeah. We were down here on Miami Beach for five weeks.

MIRSKY: That must have been real hard to take.

BON: It was actually, you know. God's waiting room.

MIRSKY: Did you record the album in Miami?

BON: No, it was recorded in the Roundhouse Studios in London. [Hopefully it will] . . . go number one around the world . . . make us a million dollars.

MIRSKY: And then you'll retire?

BON: Ah, no, I've still got a lot of debts to pay [*laughs*].

MIRSKY: How long has AC/DC been together?

BON: About five years.

MIRSKY: With the personnel that's in the band?

BON: As of now, two years, two-and-a-half years. We've just changed people as we've gone along, like, you know, a chain's broke, you put a new piece in the chain.

MIRSKY: The band is known to be rooted from Australia but you actually don't live there now, do you?

BON: No, we're not actually rooted to anywhere right now for reasons most bands live in the Virgin Islands or whatever. But we're mainly Australian, three of us. The three Australians were born in Scotland, one Englishman and one Polish guy. We're what you might call "international."[33]

MIRSKY: Something for everybody. An international rock 'n' roll band. AC/DC's reputation as a live band is very well known. How did you feel about the live album that you just had out?

BON: Yeah, well, I thought that was really good. It was a pleasure doing it as well. I've seen the video. They videoed at the same time as they did the recording, I think . . . it was mainly from one gig . . . in Glasgow, Scotland, which to me is the home of rock 'n' roll in the world. People say Detroit is the home of rock 'n' roll. To them I say, "Shit," you know [*laughs*].

MIRSKY: What's the new album going to be like? Is it going to be pretty consistent with the sound that AC/DC has come up with in the past: straight-ahead rock?

BON: The sound hasn't changed, although we've got a new producer so I guess the sound has changed a little bit. The basics of the sound are still how we want it to be like, how we play it. The songs? It's really hard to put your finger on what the commercial side of it is. There's a definite difference there. It's much better. Every album is better than the last. When you get to the stage where it isn't better, then you sort of got to start thinking about doing something else. Like playing country and western [*laughs*].

MIRSKY: Where we see it from the radio station point of view, people seem to want to rock 'n' roll now more than ever before. I don't know — maybe it's just the price of gasoline going up, the cost of everything getting outrageous, people are just into partying and rock 'n' rolling.

BON: Yeah, they can stay home and play a record and have a good time. You don't need no gasoline for that.

MIRSKY: How do you like playing these big outdoor shows?

BON: I love them. I don't care. Here or 200 people, it doesn't matter. As long as it's kicking on . . . there's lots more to choose from out there. Like you see some pretty faces in that audience out there.

MIRSKY: Oh, for sure. Well, thank you very much, Bon.

BON: Thank you, Neal.

MIRSKY: Have a nice set today.

BON: Thank you, mate.

MIRSKY: And good luck to AC/DC.

BON: Much obliged.

CHAPTER 22

GIRLS GOT RHYTHM

The band toured the Northeast and Midwest at the end of May and June 1979, joining UFO for a string of shows that took them to Buffalo, Rochester, Davenport, Peoria, Erie, Allentown, Largo, New York City, Albany, Toronto, Pittsburgh, Poughkeepsie and Philadelphia. In Davenport, Iowa, on 3 June, AC/DC played the Mississippi River Jam II festival on a bill with Heart, Nazareth, UFO and Seattle band TKO. Bon's sexual adventuring was catching up with him. Says Paul Chapman: "I can remember Pete Way, Bon and Dan McCafferty [from Nazareth] in the bathroom and everybody had scabs on their lips like in *Spinal Tap*."

UFO was nominally headlining AC/DC, but already in the eyes of the media and the fans the Australian band was the main attraction. In Allentown, local journalist Jack McGavin wrote that AC/DC's very short set was "a blessing to some and frustrating to others as some people had come mainly to see AC/DC and had hoped that the band would be headlining the show. Either way all got their money's worth." In New York,

Billboard confidently declared: "Atlantic's AC/DC all but stole the show from UFO." But Alan Niester, a staunch AC/DC hater, wasn't impressed with either band in his review for Toronto's *Globe and Mail*, calling it "one of the most furious extended evenings of sonic overkill the bedraggled old edifice has ever seen." All the same, he knew he was seeing history being made: "If audience reaction is any indicator, it certainly won't be too long before Australia's AC/DC are headlining the largest venues in town . . . AC/DC do absolutely nothing novel musically, [but] you can't help but cheer for a band that puts out 110 per cent."

⚡

On 17 June 1979, during a short break before touring recommenced in Texas, Bon headed out to a rain-marred Outlaws show at Meadowlands Stadium in East Rutherford, New Jersey. It was co-headlined by Boston, with Todd Rundgren and Poco the support acts in front of 60,000 people.

"Bon chugged almost an entire fifth [a fifth of a gallon or 750 millilitres] of Crown Royal in our dressing room before our show, showing no visible effects to his demeanour," says Outlaws guitarist Freddie Salem. "But Bon's drinking did not strike me as unusual for the reason that we were also heavy drinkers. The 1970s and '80s were the time of all the substance abuse that you could handle [*laughs*]. Bon connected with us on the spot. He was one of us from the time he walked in the dressing room. Bon watched our entire show from the side of the stage. He loved it and was complimentary beyond belief."

Backstage, Bon met Outlaws manager Charlie Brusco and found out they had more in common than a love of Southern rock.

"Bon and I both had the same girlfriend in New York, and I don't think either of us knew about the other guy," he laughs. "We both found out at the Meadowlands. I don't think she knew he was coming and she was there."

The "she" in question was Valeria Parker, an employee of the late Cedric Kushner, a walrus-like South African concert promoter who had briefly co-managed AC/DC with Michael Browning.[34] After AC/DC he switched to boxing promotion.

It occurred to you that they were seeing each other?

"Oh yeah [*laughs*]."

How did you work it out with Bon?

"There was a discussion, let's say [*laughs*] . . . I think Bon was expecting to ride back with us to [New York] and he had to make other arrangements. Bon was a character. He fashioned himself as a tough guy and everybody from the South fashioned themselves the same way. He ran pretty hard. I ran around with a lot of rock musicians back from those days and there were two that I spent a few different nights with and both of them were kind of the same: Phil Lynott and Bon.

"To me, as far as drinking and drugging and doing everything that there was to do, Lynott and Bon were kind of cut out of the same thing. Lynott just didn't play that tough guy thing. Bon always had, I felt, a little bit of a chip on his shoulder. Just like a lot of the guys were back then; he was a little bit of a mean drunk when he got drunk."

It's not the first time I've heard Bon being described as a mean drunk.

"Yeah, he was. Ronnie Van Zant was the same way and that might have been why Bon and Ronnie I think got along and Bon and Gary Rossington got along because they were all the same."[35]

So how did it work out with Valeria in the end?

"I thought it was good. I think Bon did too. We both kept coming back for more."

Brusco has lost contact with Valeria but says "she was very good-looking."

I ask Freddie Salem if he remembers her.

"Is a pig's ass ham? Of course I remember Valeria. A very young, pretty, slender girl."

Bon was clearly getting around but no closer to being truly happy.

⚡

From New York, AC/DC flew to Fort Worth for the start of seven consecutive shows with Journey, five of them in Texas. On 21 June 1979 at the Municipal Auditorium in Austin, Bon reunited with Roy Allen.

"Bon and I drank a whole fifth of whisky before we left for the show, right out of the bottle," he says. "Looking back, we had probably both crossed the line to real alcoholism by this time. We rode to the show from the hotel with AC/DC in their bus and hung out in the band room at the auditorium.

"When the show was over Bon was standing by me before he went out for the first encore; it had been all good; a great performance. He ran back onstage and picked up the microphone and they did their first encore; no big deal, except when Bon came back over to me after the song. I could tell something was wrong from just looking at him. He had his hands in his hair, he was pacing and was saying something, talking, but not necessarily to me. He was obviously very upset. I remember getting him to look at me. I had never seen him this way. It was like he'd messed up. He was so scared; it was like he was frightened."

The conversation that followed would last less than 30 seconds.

"What's wrong, Bon? What happened? Are you okay? What's wrong?"

"I fucked up. I started singing the wrong song. This is bad, this is *bad*."

"It wasn't *that* bad. I didn't notice anything at all. Calm down, everything is okay."

"That's not it, Roy. You don't understand. They are going to hurt me."

"Nobody's going to hurt you. I'm here."

Bon then went back onstage for the next encore. Someone was going to physically *hurt* Bon? Or he was going to pay dearly for his mistake? Bon had messed up his lyrics before. Why was he so anxious about this occasion? Did he think this time it was going to cost him his job? It's an extraordinary story from Roy, almost unbelievable, but he swears it happened.

"I don't remember talking to Bon any more that night. We never got the chance to talk privately. I only saw Bon one more time, in San Antonio [in September 1979]. It never made sense to me that someone would want to hurt Bon for making a mistake, but that's how I took it. Surely, I must have misunderstood. I had been drinking and I know you have to give that some weight — the crowd must have been loud too. And there was the problem of Bon's Australian accent. But, at the very least, his error had a huge impact on him and his reaction was extreme.

"I wanted to talk to him about it and find out what the deal was. It has always bothered me not knowing. It was something I would have had to ask while we were by ourselves, but I never got the opportunity. I ask myself now: What were the consequences for Bon for making that error? If someone was going to hurt him, in what way? How could a simple little mistake be so bad?"

How did you perceive Bon's relationship with Malcolm?

"Bon and Malcolm were close but there was a tension in the air the last time I saw them that I had not noticed before. Something had changed, people looked at me differently and there was something with Bon and the band that was different. I always assumed it had to do with me but maybe there was more to it."

*

On 4 July 1979 AC/DC performed "Outdoors Under the Sun and Stars" at Winnebago County Fairgrounds in Pecatonica, Illinois, in front of 35,000 people with Cheap Trick, Molly Hatchet, The Babys and Climax Blues Band. Though they were about to start a run of dates with Cheap Trick through Wichita, Sioux Falls, Des Moines and Omaha, Bon wasn't so enthused about Rick Nielsen's band, dismissing them as "just . . . just . . . pure *pop!*" AC/DC's time as a second-tier concert attraction had come to an end and Bon was confident enough to say it publicly.

"We're beginning to make an impact [in North America] at last. I reckon we'll still have to push a bit harder to get to the top. We tour there constantly. Our last tour supporting Cheap Trick was great, but [it was] to support them . . . our next tour has us headlining. You know, we've been going full blast all year . . . I've lived out of a suitcase for three years."

When AC/DC got to Southern California for an "Intimate Amphitheatre Style" gig with Mahogany Rush and St. Paradise, they weren't in the mood for fraternising: it was just business. Mahogany Rush's Frank Marino told me that after three shows with AC/DC he failed to meet a single member of the band. St. Paradise's Derek St. Holmes, also a member of Ted Nugent's band, had a similar experience. But after "three or four days of touring together," what he calls "a real brief encounter," he came upon Bon walking down their hotel corridor with two girls, one in each arm.

"They were young and they were cute. They looked about the same size, they looked like twins, but I don't want to bolster the story too much [*laughs*]. I'm standing outside my hotel room in the hallway and here Bon comes down the hallway with a fifth of Jack Daniel's, bare feet, no shirt on and a girl on each side of him. He comes up to me [*laughs*] and I said, 'What are you guys doing?' Bon goes, 'We're just partying, man. Aren't you that bloke from Nugent?' I said, 'Yeah.' He goes, 'Man, you're a *great* singer.' I said, 'Oh, man, *you're* a great singer.' We started chitchatting back and forth a little bit. I said, 'You wanna come down to the room I'm in? Roll down to the room, we're partying.' And Bon looks at the two chicks [*laughs*] and the bottle of Jack and he goes, 'I'm probably not going to make it this time.' I laughed my ass off and he laughed and he turned round and walked down the hall. It looked like he was going to be awful busy [*laughs*]."

The next day Bon did a fan meet-and-greet, the "Travelling Rock & Roll Circus," organised by radio station KSJO in San Jose, ahead of AC/DC's 21 July appearance at Oakland's Day On The Green. Local fan Bill Kaye took photographs of Bon signing autographs and his blonde female companion. They're some of the best images ever taken of Bon, showing a side of him people like to remember: the smiling, friendly, kind-hearted, take-the-shirt-off-my-back-for-anyone Bon, not the man he became tortured by drink.

"It's 11 a.m. and Bon shows up with a beer," recalls Kaye. "I was young and naive. Couldn't even bring myself to shake his hand."

The girl?

"She just sat in the back of the van; very quiet. No words spoken. She was a beauty. Taking it all in, I suppose. Rock stars. Only to realise six months later he would be no more. Well, in the material world anyway."

In Oakland, the lineup was Ted Nugent, Aerosmith, Mahogany Rush, AC/DC and St. Paradise.

"That's a *newww* one," Bon said after they'd wrapped up "Highway To Hell," not without some poignancy.

Interviewed by KSJO's Sheila Rene after the show, Bon was asked if he wanted to or would go back to playing smaller clubs. The answer was an unequivocal no. Bon was so close to achieving his lifelong dream.

"We're just getting to the stage where we're making money, we're doing a lot of big shows and it's really exciting getting out, like, through the crowds . . . why go back to the clubs, if you can turn 20,000 people on, like today: 80,000 people? Clubs have got 1000; it takes 80 times that amount of shows to turn that amount of people on. So give us some big shows."

"He likes the big venues, but he's getting old," interrupted Angus Young. "He's got his coffin ordered."

Bon continued his answer: "I'd like to do a whole string of concerts, headlining, as big as this one is today. Why settle for anything less? The more people they can give us out front, the harder we play . . . I'm more in love with rock 'n' roll. That grows. I'm more in love with a couple of things. I was in love with one but, uh, she left me. I just hope rock 'n' roll never leaves me."

AC/DC backed up for another big festival, this time the World Series of Rock at Cleveland's Lakefront Stadium with Aerosmith, Ted Nugent, Journey, Thin Lizzy and German band Scorpions, who had just been signed by Leber-Krebs. It was the fourth highest grossing concert event of the year (the biggest was Supertramp) but most notable for Steven Tyler firing Joe Perry backstage after their headline set.

St. Holmes says getting signed by Leber-Krebs was "hugely" important to AC/DC.

"They had all the power back then so they could get all these tours to put AC/DC on. I know for a fact that Leber-Krebs helped break AC/DC. They were lucky. They had so much momentum that all David had to do was pick 'em up and put 'em on the right tours and that's what he did."

Krebs cheerily deflects some of the credit: "I personally was directing the careers of Aerosmith and Ted Nugent myself [so] I was happy to have Peter Mensch on behalf of the company do AC/DC and I thought it was a great idea to set up an office [in London]. My contribution to AC/DC was putting them on the best tours that were possible for their career. Cliff Burnstein and I were over at Atlantic Records. Cliff worked Atlantic. He was a very experienced guy in the business.

"When the moment came when Bon died and there was a funeral in Australia, I decided that I should not show up and I should let Peter take the entire spotlight because he had been the day-to-day manager. I was not the front guy for AC/DC. I thought we delivered 200 per cent based on what happened during our period . . . I think the results of what took place during that three-year period speak for themselves. There were shows where it was Aerosmith, Nugent and AC/DC. Now that had to be an amazing show if you were a kid."

Cleveland was Scorpions' first gig in the United States and they had shows lined up with Aerosmith, Ted Nugent and AC/DC, with whom they'd go on to play Fort Wayne, Indianapolis and Pittsburgh. The band's drummer, Herman Rarebell, befriended Bon, the pair going out to drink together a number of times.

"Somehow we liked each other. I had the best contact with Bon [of anyone in the band]. We went to the local clubs and sometimes we would just go up there and jam with whoever was there. We never played Scorpions or AC/DC songs, just other stuff. We tried to pull chicks, got drunk. We were young guys. We just had a good time."

How successful were you pulling chicks?

"We were *always* successful. Come on [*laughs*]. We were young and good-looking. In America, it's not too difficult when you are a rock star to be successful."

Pete Way confirms Bon was never short of female attention wherever he went: "Bon and I had a girl in every port, as they say . . . don't forget there's a lot of cities in America; he would always have an evening's company after the show."

⚡

AC/DC's tour wrapped up with two shows supporting Ted Nugent: Madison Square Garden in New York and the Philadelphia Spectrum. *Highway To Hell* was in record stores nationwide, virtually two years to the day that they'd played their first gig in North America.

Billboard also offered qualified praise for the band's new album: "Just as a tiger can't change its spots, this veteran Australian band can't change the style it has been playing since its inception. High energy, lowbrow heavy metal is what this quintet plays and it is played well . . . however, the pulverising instrumentation and sameness of subject matter (girls) gets to be wearing."

By 11 August "Highway To Hell" was the #1 most added song nationally, heading the Southwest, Midwest and Western regions and second in the Southeast and Northeast. From nearly being dumped by Atlantic, AC/DC was now arguably the hottest band at the label. The disco era was coming to an end. North America had turned on to the band. All it had taken to turn its fortunes around was a change of producer and a change of scene in Miami, which Bon was only too happy to concede.

"The change did us a power of good," he said.

So why, when everything he had always wanted was laid out before him — money, American celebrity, and Holly X, a beautiful young woman who could have given him a child — did Bon proceed to blow it?[36]

⚡

After a quick flurry of European dates, including the Bilzen Rock 79 festival in Belgium and a Wembley concert supporting The Who, AC/DC turned up in Munich to record songs from *Highway To Hell* for the *Rock-Pop* TV show on German public broadcaster ZDF. Bon was badly off-key and drunk when the tape rolled. He seemed stiff, almost lockjawed. Uncharacteristically for a man with such a tremendous vocal range, he struggled in the choruses. His voice was hoarse and discordant, more of a shout than usual. Realising he was flat, he stripped off his jacket to energise the audience, an old stage trick he'd done thousands of times before, but the muscular body of 1978 had noticeably softened, become more square.

"The last time I saw him, he looked bigger in the belly," says Pattee Bishop. "He was the biggest and fullest I had ever seen him. To me he looked great, but he had filled out. Looking at him naked from the back it looked like he had no waist. He couldn't clear his voice from crap in it, like a smoker almost, after a night with him."

Bun E. Carlos of Cheap Trick saw the train wreck unfold.

"Bon was pretty drunk and pissing off the director and camera crew. In Nürnberg, where we both opened for The Who, Bon was pretty hammered all three days we were in town. The morning after the concert Bon was in the hotel coffee shop. Our singer [Robin Zander] sat down with him for breakfast and Bon said something like, 'Let me clear the table for you,' and proceeded to sweep his arm across the table, sending everything on it crashing to the floor."

Along with all that he had worked so hard for.

The week ending 1 September 1979, AC/DC had cracked the American top 50 (at #50) for the first time. The following week they were #42, the next #36. After two years of relentless slog, they were a top-40 band at last. But this wasn't *Rocky* with an Oscar waiting at the end. Bon was on an alcoholic deathwish at the worst possible time: the start of another North American tour with a breakout album to promote.

Bon wrote to Irene Thornton that the LP was selling "like hot crumpet" and "I think we've done it with this one." He fed her his usual whim of the day — "I wanna buy a house in California" — and played up his virility: "I'm still a very single man and having a ball right now. America's certainly the place for a good time." But for once there was a rare, jarring note of real candour: "I've become a bit of an alco."

The Young brothers, resigned to the fact Bon was going to drink no matter what they did or said, were hardly helping fight his addiction with a tour rider that allowed for a full bar to be kept backstage.

CHAPTER 23

HIGHWAY TO HELL

"The bar was part of the band's rider with bartender," says Moses Mo, guitarist of Mother's Finest. "It was there at every show, every night when it was time for Angus to ride on the shoulders of his crew into the audience. Bon would seat himself at the bar for the duration, as if he had gone to the pub, and return to the stage when Angus would come backstage to dismount. They never missed a beat. I just found that amazing."

He was also buying coke from roadies. Geoff Chang worked on the California leg of the tour. At the time he was 22 and Yesterday & Today's drum tech. Later that year he began working as the manager of Elvin Bishop.

"AC/DC's bus had broken down. Yesterday & Today had kindly loaned some equipment to help out. Some of the amps were from the days when Yesterday & Today and Journey shared management. So I went along to keep an eye on the equipment loaned and just hung around with mostly Bon, Angus and Malcolm. I sold Bon a gram of cocaine. Never saw Angus even drink a beer. Malcolm would have his two beers after the show, and he and his brother would discuss the whole thing.

"I was working for Yesterday & Today making $60 a month. I would deal coke. I cut it with French baby laxative. I think I went back up from Santa Cruz to my home near Richmond to get Bon a gram. I remember Angus apologising for the plain looks of the sweet black girl he slept with the next morning and me thinking, 'This is Angus Young apologising to me for the not-quite-knockout looks of the girl he was with last night.' Bon I didn't quite connect with like I did Angus and Malcolm, who were really nice, gentlemen-like guys. Bon would have three plain girls kind of chatting with him after the gig, and when I said, 'Come on, we're going to the hotel,' he acted like he was being mobbed à la Beatlemania. It was humorous, but maybe a tad pathetic. It was all fun."

By the fifth show, at Long Beach, Bon was a mess. Just as in Munich, he was hoarse, having to scream to hit the right notes. Pattee Bishop slept with him the night of the concert.

"I would get my backstage passes from Ian Jeffery, all my drinks, and he would seat me during a concert. Ian would get blowjobs from all the groupies. I was never one of the blowjob girls, or knew any of them. The ugly girls backstage got there because of being with the roadies; it was kind of a joke. I did a lot of living in those four years, from Florida to L.A., but I always had time for a night with Bon — or a day, depending on what was going on. It wasn't always sex with us. Sometimes we had no time to be together, so we would see each other and kiss and hug, and he would do the [AC/DC] show, and I would leave."

But he had become very sick.

"Bon had x-rays of his liver done. I knew he threw up blood sometimes. He had back pains. He would take a lot of turns."[37]

"No one could drink that much Scotch and not damage their liver," said Silver Smith. "He had an iridologist/chiropractor called Ross Partington in Paddington, Sydney, with whom he had gone to school, but I don't know of any doctor."

Barry Bergman was worried for his friend. He says he warned Bon on multiple occasions that he was in imminent danger: "I had said to him many times, 'You gotta stop drinking.' All through the years. And his philosophy was 'I live for the day . . . I'll be alright.'"

Rehab never came up with him?

"No."

The band themselves, were they concerned?

"I think they were very concerned about it. Yes. I think they loved him."

⚡

AC/DC went from California to Texas for 10 shows in 11 days with Molly Hatchet: Amarillo, Lubbock, Midland, El Paso, McAllen, Corpus Christi, Houston, Dallas, San Antonio and Beaumont. The day of the San Antonio concert, *Highway To Hell* had moved to #32. Roy Allen tried in vain to get a moment to talk to Bon about the 21 June show in Austin, when he'd come off stage shaken, convinced someone was going to hurt him for starting to sing the wrong song.

"I never got the chance to talk to Bon in private that night. I don't remember he or I drinking too much before the show. Backstage after the show, someone pulled out a giant joint that a fan had thrown on the stage during the performance. It had to be over a foot long and at least an inch or so in diameter, and had 'AC/DC' in big letters written on it in ink. Angus or maybe Malcolm said to break it up and roll some joints where we could smoke it. My friend Bob took care of the rolling. He was a little concerned because police were around but they did not hassle us about it.

"We all went to the hotel bar and were drinking there; lots of girls were around and it was shaping up to be a perfect night. But Bob got so drunk he insisted on leaving, in that insistent way only a very drunk person can do. He was way too drunk to be driving so I had to leave with him; I drove us home. I'll always remember seeing Bon and all the guys waving bye as I left."

With support acts alternating between Sammy Hagar, Mother's Finest, Molly Hatchet, Point Blank, Blackfoot and Pat Travers, the tour cut northeast to Tennessee for shows in Memphis, Nashville and Johnson City, then southeast to Charlotte and Greenville. By the end of September, *Highway To Hell* was #28. Shows with Blackfoot and Mother's Finest in Knoxville, Greensboro, Birmingham and Dothan the first week of October proved lucrative, Knoxville topping the "Top Box Office" charts in *Billboard*. And it kept trundling on: Jacksonville, Atlanta, Columbia, Norfolk, Wheeling, Charleston, Towson, Buffalo and Cleveland.

By the Norfolk show of 13 October, AC/DC had made its debut entry in the *Billboard* Hot 100 singles chart at #82. Two days later, "Highway To Hell" was tied as the 20th most added single in the country according to "Universals" analysis by *Fred Magazine*, a radio-industry tipsheet.[38] But at Chicago's Aragon Ballroom, Doug Thaler, who'd set up all of AC/DC's North American tours, saw Bon as he really was: tormented by an addiction he could not control.

The following month at the Holiday Inn in Liverpool, England, Bon described his drinking to Kent North Radio interviewer Angela Morgan as being part of his daily routine.

MORGAN: The press is keen to comment that you demolish the whisky bottle.

BON: [*Laughs*] Demolish the whisky bottle? Yeah, I do about a fifth of a Jack Daniel's a night . . . being on the road; that's easy. I don't think it's any good for my voice . . . [but it] keeps the head together.

The truth though, says Thaler, is that the combination of his drinking and the emotional barrenness of life on the road was slowly destroying him.

"In the late summer of 1979, I put together the *Highway To Hell* tour with AC/DC and Pat Travers, both personal clients of mine," he tells me over lunch at Virgil's Real BBQ near Times Square in Manhattan. "I normally went out and covered a couple of shows a month but I didn't do that on this last tour. The only show I went to was Chicago. I arrived mid-afternoon. I was staying in the hotel where both bands were booked. I was waiting for the elevator when I saw Bon with a couple of girls. He was really super out-of-it [drunk] and didn't even notice me. I don't remember much about the show; I do remember spending more time with Pat than with AC/DC. I believe it was Ian Jeffery that told me that Bon was doing some very hard drinking on a very regular basis by then. He characterised Bon's behaviour as getting drunk, passing out, waking up to do the show and repeating the process daily. I had never known him to behave like that."[39]

Thaler got a phone call from Bon just before he died.

"He wasn't drunk or fucked up in any way. It was a surprise call because he had never called me unless he was in New York. It seemed like he just wanted to chat for a little while. *Highway To Hell* was just about platinum by then and I congratulated him on that — I said something like, 'You'll finally have some real money for your pocket now.' He said that with all the newfound success, nothing had trickled down to him yet so his life was still the same as it had been. It was only a couple of weeks later that I got the call from David Krebs that he'd been found dead in a car in London."

In Toledo, Ohio, on 20 October 1979, the same day "Highway To Hell" jumped 12 places to #70 on the singles chart and the album went to #22, Bon gave an interview to Dennis Frawley of WABX Detroit in the parking lot of the Sports Arena. Bon was asked if there was a follow-up to *Highway To Hell* "in the oven."

"Yeah, it's in the oven, but it's in the needing stages, I think; we *need* songs," he replied. "We haven't got the full thing happening yet, you know. We've been too busy . . . it's worn me out completely. I feel like a 10-year-old pair of shoes that hasn't had a retread. And after tomorrow night we've got two days off . . . tomorrow night we're playing Columbus, Ohio, and that's the last date we're doing in the States this year . . . we've got to go back and record a new album . . . yeah, I wanna say that we'll be coming to Detroit this year; I just hope that everybody who likes the band comes along to see the band. We'll be by ourselves and doing our own thing in our time; we'll kick ass."[40]

Bon's last ever show in North America took place at St. John Arena in the grounds of Ohio State University. The tickets were just $8. In three years of touring the United States, AC/DC had gone from a cult bar band in Texas, Ohio and Florida to both a national headliner in its own right and a very profitable recording artist for Atlantic Records. Phil Carson's gamble on them had paid off in a big way. The week ending 27 October, the band had a top-20 album (at #20) and a *Billboard* Hot 100 single (at #69). Two weeks later, the album had reached a high of #17. On 8 December the single peaked at #47.

"The truth of the matter is they needed the magic song," says Bergman. "The live show was the greatest show in rock 'n' roll. The song, the magic song, wasn't there very early on. They needed that magic hit. And that's what came with 'Highway To Hell' in '79."

It was time to collect. On 6 December 1979, *Highway To Hell* was officially certified gold by the Recording Industry Association of America (RIAA). Before AC/DC headed to the United Kingdom and Europe, Atlantic Records welcomed the band at its New York headquarters with a placard that read: "Atlantic Records Congratulates AC/DC in Highway to Hell GOLD!" The band cheerily smiled for photographs with executives who'd wanted to wash their hands of them only a year or two before.

Bon, however, was thinking of leaving it all behind.

⚡

Early that December, Roy Allen got a call from Bon, who was in a hotel room in France. It was morning in Rockdale, Texas, but Roy was already "stoned on weed" and had been drinking beer.

"It was a day I'll never forget and I have carried much regret since then. I was at home. The phone rang. I answered. It was Bon. I have replayed this conversation over in my mind a million times through the years; so many questions. I have told this story to very few people."

Bon got straight to the point.

"Roy, I want to come to Texas. I'm coming into a good bit of money soon. I've had it: the living on the road, the shows, the drinking. I'm ready to leave the band. I've got to get out. It's all killin' me and I know it. I want to know if I came to Texas I could stay with you. We could try quit drinking together."

Roy still kicks himself that he wasn't quite alert to what he was being told. He was more hung up on the news Bon wanted to come visit rather than the fact the lead singer of AC/DC was telling him he was thinking about stepping down from a band that had just scored the biggest hit of its career. It tallies with what Vince Lovegrove was told before Bon died. He wanted out.

But why did he want to come to Texas and not follow through with his plans to take Holly to Australia? It could be explained by Holly's suspicion that Bon sensed she was "drifting away" into the arms of someone else, either the famous guitarist or the local singer she'd go on to marry. He would have instinctively known that his hopes were dashed: the engagement, the house, the kids, all of it. Pattee didn't want him. Silver didn't want him. It would appear that this was a phone call from a depressed, lonely individual on the road who didn't know what he wanted to do and had few people he could genuinely call friends, perhaps least of all the members of his own band. There is a crushing pathos imagining the loneliness and isolation Bon would have been feeling in that hotel room when he made that call.

"Bon always talked about coming to Texas to spend time when he got the chance; we talked about it often. So, it was not a total surprise when he called and asked about coming," says Roy. "I just got too excited and was not listening closely to what he was saying. I wish I had that day to do over again. I didn't get the feeling Bon had a lot of close friends back then. Somebody like a good friend you'd call and shoot the bull with, all that; somebody he could really fall back on and trust.

"We had always talked about him coming and maybe living in Texas. He loved Texas. He loved our culture. We were so much the same, the way we lived, how we partied, the food we ate, barbecues; that was appealing to him. I had told Bon many times that he was welcome to stay with me if he ever decided to come. My dad had recently built a nice home on the golf course at the country club in Rockdale; he had to live in town because he was a judge and had to reside in his precinct, so I lived there off and on.

"When it was my turn to talk, I said, 'Of course, you're welcome to stay,' and then went off on a rant about partying, women and fun. Bon told me that that was what he was trying to get away from. I told him I was willing to do whatever, just come and we'd figure it out. He sounded discouraged, said he had to go. The conversation didn't last long. He didn't sound like he'd had much, if anything, to drink. He was not drunk. He sounded more like he was desperate, anxious, talking fast.

"As I stood there by the red rotary wall phone, hearing that dial tone in my hand, what he had really said to me and asked me finally sunk in. I had a really bad feeling; uneasy. There was something in his voice. He was my friend before anything else. I was really worried and wanted to talk to him again; convince him to come and, yes, I would give no booze a try. Maybe we could do it."

Roy didn't have Bon's number so he rang around whoever he could think of that was connected to the band until he got hold of someone from Atlantic.

"I explained a little of the situation and that I needed to talk to Bon again. 'Do you know where they're staying or how I can find them?' I remember [the Atlantic staffer] saying he knew Bon had some stuff going on but he couldn't help me because he didn't know where they were staying or how to find them. He kind of laughed, if I remember right. I just couldn't think of anyone else or any other place to call, so I had to give up. So that was it."

He hung up the phone. I ask Roy again: Are you absolutely sure what you heard, that Bon was going to quit AC/DC?

"*Definitely*. He said he's going to have to leave the band to [get] cleaned up, is what he said; he had to get away from it, the way he put it, in his words, 'cause it was killin' him. He said it was just too much; he couldn't handle it any more. There was something in his voice that it took me a little bit to pick up on and I wish I could have got to talk to him again that day. I would have done anything if I could have got back hold of him."

It was the last time they'd speak.

PART FOUR
1980

CHAPTER 24

SHOOT TO THRILL

The name Alistair Kinnear looms over the Bon Scott story like Moriarty in *The Adventures of Sherlock Holmes*: a figure of pure evil made more evil by the fact no one knows exactly who he is. The man who many people think killed Bon, if not by intention then through neglect. He should never have left him in a parked car on Overhill Road, East Dulwich, that frigid early London morning of 19 February 1980. What was he thinking? What wretched low-life scum could do such a thing to any man, let alone the lead singer of the hottest rock 'n' roll band in the world?

Over the years Alistair has been described, erroneously, as "another junkie acquaintance of Silver's . . . an aspiring bass player," "allegedly a would-be musician; apparently a bass player," and "a would-be musician, although he may have been nothing more than a ligger and a drug slut." Worse, at one time he didn't even exist. He was a ghost.

The nonsense began with AC/DC biographer Mark Putterford in 1992: "There is strong evidence to suggest that Alisdair [sic] Kinnear was, in fact, a false name given to the police and press to conceal the true identity of the man who accompanied Bon on the last night of his life." *Classic Rock*'s Geoff Barton had even more cloak-and-dagger notions: "Alistair Kinnear — who some claim was a rock journalist, not a musician — may have changed his identity . . . Putterford, who raised the issue of heroin being involved in Scott's death, was reputedly aware of Kinnear's new guise."

Meanwhile, Bon Scott biographer Clinton Walker was convinced Alistair was simply a name made up by someone he'd already interviewed.

"No one spoke to him before or after the event. He just doesn't seem to exist," he told the *Guardian*'s Richard Jinman for an article on the 25th anniversary of Bon's death. If there were any doubt what Walker really thought and was saying, Jinman dispelled them in his story: "Walker believes Kinnear was a name adopted by one of Scott's associates who did not want to be identified." Jinman said pretty much the same thing in AC/DC biographer Paul Stenning's *Two Sides to Every Glory*: "People like Clinton Walker have been convinced that Alistair Kinnear was a made up name."[41]

It's not hard to deduce who Walker thought was masquerading as Kinnear: the Australian musician, roadie and alleged drug dealer Joe Fury, who operated under various *noms de guerre* and was sleeping with Silver at the time of Bon's death. There was no one else it could be. In his book, Walker spells his surname as "Furey." Walker told *Classic Rock* in 2005: "Alistair, I believe, was another guise used by one of the characters already in my book — and I did try to very gently imply that. I have met this fellow, but I've left it at that. What I'm saying is, I met the guy who might have been 'Kinnear' but that feeling is based on no real evidence, just a hunch."

It was a shitty hunch. Alistair was a very real person, as any basic bit of investigation would have proved. Joe and Alistair were friends, according to Silver Smith.

"In early '77 Bon and I got a flat in Abingdon Villas, Kensington, which was a few doors away from my friend Carol [ex of Rolling

Stones horn player Jim Price] and her little boys. We met Alistair at Carol's. Joe met Alistair and Carol a year later."

Silver said she even gave Walker information on Alistair's family to follow up. Alistair's doctor father Angus, whom she described as "wonderful," had treated her at home for pleurisy within five days of Bon's death.

"I gave [Walker] enough information to have easily found Alistair and his kind and gentle parents and check everything, but he stuck with his theory, causing them to endure further unnecessary suffering."

Alistair, she said, was so devastated by his portrayal in Walker's book that he became a virtual recluse. Silver and Joe were also deeply impacted by their association with the book's telling of Bon's death.

"Alistair was really traumatised, and I don't think it's a coincidence that he 'disappeared' after the release of Walker's book. I was upset by some of it and asked my oldest sister of whom I'm very fond not to read it. It also caused me to become extremely wary of press and media, and to be very reclusive and careful.

"Joe chooses to keep his privacy. You have no idea what it was like for Joe and Alistair and me. Alistair was always looking after other people, often to his own detriment. Joe and I never did an unkind thing to anyone, so how do you deal with the whole world being told you are some kind of evil creatures by people who don't even know you, or worse, people who do? We have families, too. The only consolation is the support and outrage of people who *do* know you, and love you.

"So Alistair disappeared for decades before he told his story, which only differs from mine in unimportant detail which one of us has misremembered; Joe changed his name, and I never told anyone who didn't already know that I even knew Bon. If his name came up in conversation, which it often did, I would quietly leave the room. I didn't work in the music business here in Australia, although I had good references, so I didn't need to change my name . . . when the negative stories started to gain momentum, fortunately it never crossed my workmates' minds that they were about me."

Alistair was flushed out of hiding in Spain in 2005 by an American woman called Margaret "Maggie" Montalbano, who wrote crosswords for rock magazines. She died in 2009. He was living at Calle del Plátano, No. 167, in Estepona, near Marbella, and released a full statement through Montalbano giving his side of the story about the evening and morning he spent with Bon on 18–19 February 1980. But no one foresaw what was to come next: the following year Alistair disappeared while sailing from France to Spain. His family raised the alarm on 19 July 2006 with the Maritime Rescue Co-ordination Centre (MRCC) in Falmouth, Cornwall. It wasn't until 2010 that Alistair's banker son, Daniel Kinnear, made a public statement about his father's fate for a story in Sydney's *Daily Telegraph*.

At this point you might have expected Bon's biographer Walker to fess up to his mistake — every writer makes one or two — but he'd begun the process of furiously trying to spin his way out of it.

In 2006 he wrote in Australian *Rolling Stone* that "the strongest conspiracy theory" of Bon's tale was that Alistair was an alias used by "another person close to the action." In the piece, no surprise, he directly named Joe Fury as that person. But Walker claimed whatever he'd said to Jinman for the *Guardian* had been misconstrued: "I told Jinman it was my belief that everything on the night of Scott's death was as it seemed — but as long as Kinnear remained a phantom, I could never be 100 per cent certain. I knew that Furey [sic] wasn't Kinnear, but after 10 years of searching, I still didn't know who Kinnear was."

Walker even went on to claim that Alistair's emergence as a real person and the 2005 statement to Montalbano "put to rest . . . all the outrageous conspiracy theories" and capped off his theory about Bon's demise all along.

"The final piece of the jigsaw fitted perfectly into the puzzle," he wrote in the 2015 edition of *Highway to Hell*.

Pardon? The most outrageous conspiracy theory was Walker's *own* that Alistair was an invention. The biographer was undeterred: "When Alistair Kinnear . . . issued a very belated statement on that fateful night, it confirmed how right I'd got my original reconstruction of it in the first place, despite the pressures exerted by various erstwhile conspiracy theories."

The problem is that Walker's reconstruction isn't "right" at all. It is riddled with holes. This is not schadenfreude on my part involving another writer. I subscribed to Walker's account myself until I began researching Bon's story. This is history; a man's life. It's important to get it right for Bon's sake, his family's sake, AC/DC fans' sake and history's sake. The publicity for the latest Australian edition of Walker's book even claims that "thanks to new information, [the author] finally dispels the myths surrounding Bon's death." This is simply not true. Somewhat comically, he boasts his book has "hardly had to stand corrected on matters of fact."

Walker explains away what he said to Jinman in puzzling fashion.

"[I] was quoted exasperatedly [in 2005] asking the one final question that neither [Jinman] nor anyone else was ever able to answer: What happened to Kinnear? His disappearance was so complete, his identity so shadowy, it was as if he never even existed in the first place . . . and indeed it was this idea — that Kinnear never existed — that formed the basis of the major conspiracy theory: that 'Alistair Kinnear' was merely another alias among many of Joe Furey's [sic] and, co-dependently, drugs were involved in Bon's death."

Yet, once again, this is Walker being disingenuous. It was Walker himself who in 2005 publicly proposed the same "major conspiracy theory" that the man didn't exist to both *Classic Rock* and the *Guardian*. We now know that is wildly wrong. Alistair was no phantom; he was flesh and bone.

So who exactly was he?

CHAPTER 25

HELLS BELLS

Alistair Kinnear was born on 20 April 1950 in Ootacamund, India, the son of Angus Kinnear, an author, composer, missionary and doctor, and Jean Austin-Sparks, the daughter of evangelist Theodore Austin-Sparks. In 1959, along with his brother Neil and sister Fiona, Alistair came to London with his parents. They had a house at 4 Hengrave Road, Forest Hill, right next to East Dulwich.

"Jean worked for social services in Lambeth," says Daniel Kinnear. "Angus practised as a GP in South London. Al was born in India while his parents were working there. They were committed Christians. Angus wrote a biography of [Christian Chinese church leader] Watchman Nee."

Against the Tide was published the same year Daniel was born: 1973. He was six years old when Bon died and hardly knew his own father. Alistair went to sea at Port Saint Louis du Rhone in Marseille, on 6 July 2006, completely haunted by what had happened to Bon. He was never allowed to forget it. Grieving fans had taken to affixing pictures of Bon to Alistair's front door in East

Dulwich, which must have been deeply unsettling when he came home at night.

"That event fundamentally affected Al," says Daniel. "It is probably the key factor that pushed him into his drug addiction and saw his music career take a dive. Al was a sensitive person and having to deal with such a tragedy was hard for him. It was a story that I was unaware of until adulthood. It was never discussed."

Do you think there was more involved in Bon's death than alcohol poisoning?

"No. I think this was a tragic accident that resulted from over-indulgence in alcohol. I do not suspect any foul play."[42]

What do you think happened to your father?

"Unfortunately, no bodies were ever recovered. He — along with two others — had renovated a boat, which they then proceeded to sail from Marseille to Estepona. This voyage was never completed and [the family's] working assumption is that the boat sank mid journey, resulting in the death of all three onboard."

Danara was a 13.5-metre, single-masted, wooden-hulled sloop sailing under a Spanish flag. The three people on board were the Dutch owner, Adrian Root, formerly a resident of Estepona, along with Alistair and fellow Briton Gino Yuile. The boat had spent three years in Marseille being refitted. It was last sighted by a French customs patrol boat near the Frioul Islands, off Marseille.

"Given the fact that we have never heard anything more from Al and that one of the pensioners onboard ceased drawing down on their pension, we're confident that this assumption [that they perished] is correct. Due to Al's particular lifestyle we would have expected him to make contact with the family to draw down funds. He was not fully financially independent and often relied on support from his mother."

Alistair's siblings, especially his sister, don't want to talk about him publicly.

"I think my aunt's resistance stems from the fact that she had a polar opposite lifestyle to my dad. She is very religious. Like her parents she too worked in India teaching at a missionary school. I don't believe she was comfortable with Al's lifestyle and simply wishes to sweep it under the carpet. Al's family was *hardcore* religious. I imagine this was one of the reasons that drove Al's rebellious nature."

⚡

There was nothing "aspiring" or "would-be" for Alistair when it came to music. He really could play, according to his son: "Al was an incredible musician. He taught himself to play the guitar one summer as a kid. Could play anything with a string, from fiddles to sitars. Drugs can really mess you up."

By the end of the 1960s, Alistair was well involved in Swinging London.

"I knew Alistair from about 1966 from a folk and poetry club in St. Peter's [Church] Crypt we used to go to in Streatham," recalls Jon Newey, editor of *Jazzwise*. "He was a couple of years older and already had quite long hair for the time and was musically quite aware: the blues, Dylan, Stones. He was also a quite capable guitarist and had a jug band.

"He was quiet, very friendly and charming and by 1967 was getting into the emergent psychedelic scene and countercultural underground. I went with him to The 14 Hour Technicolor Dream, one of the first big happenings in April 1967, and saw him about at underground clubs such as Middle Earth and Implosion at the Roundhouse over the next few years. He did a bit of road managing for hippie bands and the next I heard he was playing with an underground group called Screw, formed from musicians from the Streatham blues scene."

Recorded at Lansdowne Studios in May 1969 and produced by Pink Floyd's Nick Mason, the tracks were "Banks Of The River" and "Devil's Hour," but they were only issued on 10-inch vinyl in 2006. The release was dedicated to "Alister [sic] Kinnear." The highly obscure Screw was most notable for opening for The Rolling Stones at Hyde Park in London in July 1969, a performance that wasn't well received. But Alistair had left the band a few weeks earlier.

Sam Cutler, Screw's manager, described them as "a punk band, more than a decade before Malcolm McLaren got involved with the Sex Pistols and well before anybody had a clue what 'punk' actually was . . . one of the only bands I have ever seen force an audience into dumb and befuddled silent surrender. After hearing Screw play, people simply didn't have a clue what to think, let alone say. Screw rendered them appalled and speechless. This was, we thought at the time, a considerable achievement."

By the winter of 1972, Alistair was playing guitar and violin with England's Glory, fronted by Peter Perrett and with Jon Newey on drums.

"Alistair was somewhat spaced out by this time, almost like a Syd Barrett–type figure," says Newey of the band's rehearsals at Underhill Studios in Greenwich. "Still charming and quiet but not really *there*. People told me it was too many LSD trips. We couldn't really use him with England's Glory for the reasons mentioned and he was too untogether, sadly. Later he got into harder drugs and the next I heard was that his parents had paid for him to live in Spain to get away from drugs.

"The last time I spoke to him was in 1995 when I was told he was at his parents' house for a few weeks and I wanted to ask him a few questions about Screw for a book I was working on at the time. Alistair had such potential, but sadly other things got in the way. He owned a flat in Estepona before he went missing at sea. During [Maggie Montalbano's] investigations into Alistair's disappearance in late 2006 she got a phone call from the British Consulate in Malaga, Spain, saying Alistair was still alive but did not want to be contacted."

The Salvamento Marítimo Español had led the search for the missing vessel but it was officially called off on 25 August 2006 after the MRCC La Garde near Marseille sent the following fax to all MRCCs: "Missing person Alistair Keith Kinnear from the yacht *Danarah* [sic] has been located safe in Ibiza. Please cancel all enquiries." The French website *Sail The World* reported: "*Danarah* is safe. *Danarah* is safe in some Mediterranean harbour. The 58-year-old [sic] crew member the family was looking for doesn't want [them to] know where he is. We respect his wish."

Daniel, however, says the report was false: "When Al disappeared an initial alert was sent out to all coast guards. It was via this channel that we received a message back from the Ibiza coast guard that Al had left [this] message. However, upon further investigation it was discovered that the message was from one of Al's associates. While I don't recall the detail, we viewed this as unsubstantiated and misleading."

Who was this associate of Alistair? And if the report were erroneous, as you say, why would he claim that your father was alive?

"We have no idea why the person said what they said. Maybe it was miscommunication; that is, they meant they had seen him but at an earlier date and time. I think the guy was Armin Gerd Habermann. Ultimately we will never know what happened. The belief is that the boat simply sunk en route to Estepona. However, anything could have happened. Yet another mystery in the life of Al."

When Bon died in February 1980, Alistair was 29. He was 56 when the words "lost at sea" went up against his name on the Kinnear family tree. His death certificate was only issued by the Spanish civil registry in Madrid on 30 December 2015.

⚡

So, far from being someone who didn't exist, Alistair was someone's father, someone's brother, someone's son, someone's friend, someone's bandmate, someone's shipmate. Bon's death — and the inadvertent part Alistair played in Bon's demise — had a profound impact on young Daniel's life. When he was seven, his late mother, Mo Jasmin (not her birth name), had a mental breakdown and for a period was institutionalised. Daniel went to live with his grandparents. Alistair went to jail at one point and Daniel remembers feeling "very embarrassed about it" when he visited him inside. Mo died of cancer just two months before Alistair's disappearance and prior to her death relayed to her son her belief that Bon "may have experimented" with heroin but "wasn't a habitual user."

Walker's major revision to his 1994 biography of Bon appears to be solely concentrated on the passages related to Alistair, a talented musician from a very good if religious and conservative family whose life was wrecked by heroin.

Silver conceded Alistair used the drug, "but only in the same way I was [using it]; no big deal."

Addict or not, he obviously meant something to Daniel and his family. But Walker didn't find out what happened to Alistair. He didn't talk to Daniel. He panned the sensational testimonies of UFO's Paul Chapman and Pete Way, who were interviewed by Geoff Barton for a 2005 *Classic Rock* story about Bon's last hours and would again be interviewed by me for this book, as "the garbled and conflicting accounts of these recovering addicts," which, "along with other conspiracy theories, never added up. No, the way Bon died was pretty much as the 'official' version always had it, as [I] too concluded."

Walker admitted to Barton in written correspondence that he "never spoke to Chapman, but in the interviews with him I've read he sheds no light, and I even doubt his claims of closeness. Therefore I was content to speak to the people who saw Bon on that very last day: his then girlfriend [a Japanese girl he'd recently dumped, referred to in Walker's book as "Anna Baba"], his old girlfriend [Silver Smith] and 'Alistair Kinnear.'"

Lest there be any doubt Walker didn't believe Alistair was a real person, Barton writes, pointedly: "The quotes around 'Alistair Kinnear' are Walker's own."

How wrong Walker was — and in more ways than one.

CHAPTER 26

SHAKE A LEG

Paul Chapman and Pete Way did heroin in the late 1970s and '80s, by their own admission. It has affected their memory. Some details simply cannot be extracted. As Chapman explains, "It was a fucking *long* time ago. The early '80s was like a blur. Whatever I say, it's only what I remember." But on matters of import to Bon's fate both have exceptionally good recall and tell substantially the same story, despite recounting events that happened nearly 40 years ago.

And one name sticks out: Joe Fury.

Chapman is adamant that he saw Bon the night before he died and spent the late evening of 18 February and early morning of 19 February 1980 with Joe waiting for Bon to return to his flat in Fulham with a supply of heroin. Bon never turned up and Joe left Chapman's place just after dawn on the 19th.

Soon afterwards, Chapman says he was phoned by a distressed Joe to tell him that Bon was dead. The call was made some time between 6:30 and 8:30 a.m. and Way, independently of Chapman, vouches for it being true because soon afterwards he got a phone call from Chapman, asking for a phone number for either Angus or Malcolm Young.

"I can remember as plain as day what happened. I can remember as plain as day even the condition [Joe and I] were in," says Chapman. "Prior to that, Joe worked for me for almost a year. He was my guitar tech for quite a long time and I used to go around Joe's to score [heroin]."

$$\lightning$$

Joe Fury operated — or at least was known by or has been referred to — under various aliases: Joe King (as he was known at the time to Chapman), Joe Silver, Joe Furey, Joe Blow, Joe Bloe, Jo Fury and more. Take your pick. In written correspondence with me, Silver Smith frequently referred to him as "Jou."

Just like Alistair Kinnear, the reclusive, even apocryphal, Joe has become a sort of bogeyman in the Bon Scott story. Before this book, he'd only ever given one interview — to Clinton Walker — while AC/DC biographer Mark Putterford managed to get his phone number but died before getting around to making a call.

What I could gather about him from friends and acquaintances was that on his return to Australia from living and working abroad in the early 1980s, Joe played bass in various bands with the likes of Dave Tice, ex-Buffalo, and Pete Wells, ex–Rose Tattoo. Later he gigged regularly with a band in Sydney called Rough Justice. He got married, had a bunch of kids with an actor and painter called Dolly, moved to the Central Coast north of Sydney and fell off the radar. No one I spoke to who knew Joe or "Joey" could remember his real last name — or wanted to tell me.

"A bunch of crap went down with them and nobody wants to know either of them," said one informant, a person well plugged into the Sydney hard-rock scene of the 1970s and '80s. "Nobody has seen or heard of them for over 20 years since they moved to the Central Coast."

Just getting this information about Joe was difficult enough. My source was reluctant to dig any more, warning me that prying any further would be fruitless: "A lot of people keep their mouths shut about the old days and some of them do not like writers."

Darryl "Spyda" Smith, who played drums in Rough Justice, worked as a roadie for Rose Tattoo and was a mate of Bon's, told me he hadn't seen Joe for years.

"Joe and I played with Pete Wells in a band called The Rent Is Due, Punch, a couple of other bands. I introduced Joe to Dolly. I know Joe very well. Joey's a nice enough bloke, mate. Good guitar player. Crazy enough fucking individual. Pretty straight down the line. Collected. *Crazy*. But then again he could be totally secure. Just one of those types. He'd been in and out of situations and became, how should one say, a 'person for the season.' He was available, shall we say, at a moment's [notice] to party on. He just did what he had to do, mate."

I asked Spyda whether he was aware of Joe working as Bon's "assistant." (Mark Evans had once described Joe in an interview as "Bon Scott's personal assistant in London until Bon had this girlfriend Silver Smith and Silver left Bon for Joey. That was in 1979 and it fucked Bon up.")

"I'm not quite sure about that," he replied. "I wouldn't like to say anything on that, mate."

But you're aware of the rumours of Bon using heroin?

"Yeah, I'm aware of everything you like, mate, but I still wouldn't say anything about that; I'd leave that to the people who were there."

⚡

Then, in September 2016, after a year of trying to establish any trace of the man, I made contact with Joe. I found him to be friendly and nothing at all like the piranha-toothed, drug-addicted rock zombie I'd been expecting. We spoke for over five hours.

Today he runs a business called Godspeed Garage at Erina on the Central Coast. But in the late 1970s and early '80s he was a backstage fixture in the international live-music scene, working as a roadie for UFO, Wild Horses and even Little River Band.

Of Italian heritage, his real name is Joe Furi. He told me his "original family background was not terribly enjoyable," which was partly why he changed his name to Fury. His sister, Jan, is the widow of late Australian music journalist and magazine editor Ed Nimmervoll. That was how Clinton Walker came to be introduced to Joe and also how that writer originally found Silver.

As Silver explained, "I got a message from [Joe] saying his brother-in-law told him Walker was okay if I wanted to talk to him."

Joe said he never read Walker's book. He regrets he facilitated the introduction to Silver: "I was a bit reluctant. I feel a bit responsible still to Bon for really probably not protecting [Silver] as much as I was supposed to do."

He hadn't read Barton's *Classic Rock* article containing the allegations made about him by Paul Chapman. I had to email it to him. He got back to me soon afterwards and wasn't impressed: "It's the greatest amount of drivel and crap I've ever read . . . I don't know where [Barton] is now, but if he'd said that [to me] at the time he would have got a smack in the fucking head."

He wasn't even aware suggestions had been made that he was Alistair Kinnear. He knew nothing of Alistair's 2005 statement to the press. Astonishingly, he was totally oblivious to the fact that Alistair was dead.

As Joe put it drily, he'd been occupied with "other things than following late '70s rock 'n' roll."

⚡

Bon and Joe had become friends back in Sydney in early 1978, Joe meeting AC/DC's lead singer and his girlfriend Silver through Rose Tattoo guitarist Mick Cocks, who was lodging at the three-storey, 21-room rehearsal studio-cum-boarding house Joe ran in Kings Cross. Joe even visited Albert Studios for the recording of the band's seminal album, *Powerage*. He was immediately struck by how little Bon factored in AC/DC's overall musical strategy.

"There was no [chance] of Bon having any input in the studio, *ever* . . . he wouldn't get past Malcolm and Angus, let alone the big boys [George Young and Harry Vanda] who Malcolm and Angus followed the direction of. They were pissed that Bon had even come into the studio [during the *Powerage* sessions] with anybody else."

When soon afterwards Bon and Silver broke up/took a 12-month break from each other, she and Joe travelled "overland" through Asia. Bon, says Joe, "didn't really want her heading off on her own," so Joe accompanied Silver with his friend's blessing. Bon even paid for Joe's ticket.

It was during this trip that Joe and Silver would become intimately involved. On arriving in London, they worked together at the Tudor Rose, a pub in Richmond, and shared a single-room flat nearby, where Bon visited them. Yet Silver denied that she was in a relationship with Joe when Bon died.

"People quite reasonably kind of assume that [Joe and I] were [in a relationship], but as soon as you got to know us you realised it was something quite different. We were just incredibly alike. Like twins . . . we just really hit it off; we had a lot of interests in common as well, quite esoteric stuff."

Joe, she said, was also "the ideal travelling companion," a far better proposition than Bon. "I knew that I'd never [travel overland through Asia] with Bon because one, when would he get the time off, but the other thing is I would never have gone anywhere like that with Bon. It's quite possible he'd get you killed [*laughs*]. You wouldn't choose Bon as a companion to travel somewhere like that."

But Joe tells a different story. He says he and Silver had formed "an unusual relationship" where they'd "merged into a bit of an entity." Bon well knew what was going on between them yet didn't feel threatened by it because, as Joe puts it, the affair was nothing more "than me sort of treading water with her until Bon finished up with AC/DC." He presented "no challenge to Bon and Silver being *the* couple."

"Friends of mine said, 'What the fuck are you doing, you're going to get killed. You're screwing AC/DC's lead singer's fucking *girlfriend*. How long do you expect to live [*laughs*]?' Looking back on it a couple of years later [after his death], I thought, 'Jeez, I'm surprised he didn't fucking hit me over the head with a baseball bat' [*laughs*]."

Silver, says Joe, was Bon's true soulmate, the woman with whom he might have returned to Australia to settle down.

"If you saw the two [of them] together, they were like an old couple even back then when they weren't very old. Bon almost had the slippers and the pipe out and she'd be making him a cup of tea. It was that sort of relationship. It had none of that rock hysteria, fucking fame, showbiz [element to it], anything at all. They were like two Aussies from South Australia. Bon could have been out mowing the lawn and fixing things in the shed and she would have been saying, 'The scones are ready.'

"I don't think Bon was ever going to be emotionally invested with too many women other than Silver. Whatever they had going, the bond, the history, and whatever, was more important to him than having a *chick*. It was having some sort of grounding to his real self as opposed to the façade of the wild rocker.

"I have no doubt that as soon as he had achieved his goal and his fame and his fortune, whatever, he and her probably would have packed themselves off to somewhere in Australia and that would have been it. I didn't want to horn in on [the relationship] and I never really felt that there was anything that I could do that would ever break it up."

But Joe suspects Bon had also moved on.

"There was an American girlfriend. When [AC/DC] were doing the *Highway To Hell* tour, he dropped over. Silver and I were sharing a small flat in Richmond. I remember Bon coming by and dropping in and giving me some T-shirts from the *Highway To Hell* tour.

"The flat was obviously pretty small. It was only one bedroom, so I think at that stage Bon was aware that Silver and I were sort of together. There was no animosity . . . it was one of those things where it's like, 'This is obvious, that's obvious, you know, I know,' and I had that feeling that maybe that's when I knew he had another girlfriend in America."

Bon, however, had already immortalised his lost love Silver in the song "Gone Shootin'" off *Powerage*, which he explained to an audience in Columbus, Ohio, in September 1978 was about "a lady who took it upon herself to do whatever she wanted to do."[43]

As for a longstanding rumour that Malcolm Young had Joe beaten up after Bon's death, for reasons unknown, it never happened. In fact, neither Joe nor Silver would ever cross paths with AC/DC again.

"It wasn't Joe that was the problem between me and Bon," deadpanned Silver.

So Bon's problem essentially was Bon?

"Yeah," she replied with a raspy laugh.

CHAPTER 27

LET ME PUT MY LOVE INTO YOU

Like Mark Evans before him, Paul Chapman says that when Bon arrived in London in January 1980, Joe Fury was "assigned Bon's, well, minder if you like, his lookerafterer-type person." There have been whispers that Bon and Joe even shared a flat. But the truth is Joe was never employed by Bon and never lived with him. Bon lived alone in Victoria, a district of the City of Westminster.

Joe shuttled between Silver's new apartment in Emperor's Gate and a flat he sometimes shared with Mick Cocks on Kensington Church Street. Bon, he says, was already doing more than enough for him financially to even contemplate going to work for him or moving in with him.

"Bon had that sort of air about him of someone who wasn't desperate to claw over anybody's dead body to do anything. He was an incredibly genuine sort of guy. Whenever he took you anywhere, of course, he'd have to pay for everything. When he came to [London] he was incredibly generous. Straight away it'd be like, 'I'll take you out to dinner.'

"So Silver, myself and a couple of others would go out to dinner [with him]. He'd take us to restaurants that were the ones to be at for an emerging rock star of the time that was doing well. I remember [one time] I caught a glimpse of the fucking bill at the end of it and it was like £900 or £1000 [*laughs*]. It was almost like you were embarrassed to go out with him when he'd ring and say, 'What are you doin'?'"

But Chapman says Joe didn't need any help from Bon moving up in the London social scene.

"I'd meet all these kinds of people around [at Joe's] that I hadn't met before. I met [late Rainbow, Wild Horses and Dio bass player] Jimmy Bain in Joe's bathroom and Jimmy and I became really close friends after that. It was weird who you would meet around at Joe's house."

At the time Bain was co-writing some songs with Phil Lynott, Silver's friend, on Lynott's *Solo In Soho*. He played synthesiser and piano on the same track, "Girls," on which Silver's backing vocal would appear.

"Joe was going out with Silver," continues Chapman. "This was after Joe [had] worked for me. I hadn't seen him for a while. I can't remember Joe working with [UFO] in the U.S. I can remember him in Europe and I can remember him in Britain and Ireland; it must have been less than a year that he worked for me."

Chapman says eight to 10 months, possibly a year, later, Bon turned up with Joe for either the second or third of UFO's Hammersmith Odeon shows on their *No Place To Run* tour in February 1980. There were four consecutive concerts, from the 4th to the 7th. Bon had completed seven shows in France and two in Newcastle and Southampton the previous month, his final appearances with AC/DC. Band preparations for the recording of *Back In Black* were afoot. He was free of touring commitments.

"We were all big into the 'brown stuff.' Joe immediately came up to me and said, 'Hey, great to see you,' and I shook hands with Bon. I hadn't seen him for a while. I think it was Pete [Way] who said, 'Bon's just gotten back here,' and it was hugs and 'Hey, how you doing, we haven't seen you since the last time,' which was probably months ago."

Joe, however, disputes he was there: "I never went with Bon to the Hammersmith Odeon to see a UFO gig."

Chapman stresses he'd "never seen Bon do anything like" heroin but says he wouldn't be surprised if Bon was using the narcotic. He was around it constantly. One of Bon's friends in London was Joe's part-time flatmate, Mick Cocks. He and Joe would spend time around at Bon's apartment in Victoria, his sanctuary from the Youngs, listening to the records he wanted to listen to. Behind his own front door, Bon didn't have to be Bon Scott, the lead singer of AC/DC. He could just be Bon Scott, himself.

Recalls Joe: "Mick and I would go down and hang there a bit and Bon would play records, like The Pretenders. Mick and I would look at each other and go, 'The *Pretenders?*' [*laughs*]. Bon really liked The Pretenders. Who would he talk to about that? Who could he sit down with and not be Bon Scott? [*Adopts Bon's voice*] 'Yeah, mate, fuck, yeah, *rahrahrah*.' He got trapped in that role."

Cocks, seemingly just like everyone else in the London rock scene of the time, was a heroin user. In fact an anonymous source close to Rose Tattoo alleged to me that a non-playing figure involved with the band around that era "was a criminal who was a smack dealer." Adding fuel to suspicions Cocks was seen as a negative influence on Bon, he himself admitted to Clinton Walker before he died that Malcolm Young had tried to punch him following Bon's death.

"Unfortunately, Michael [Mick Cocks] was a difficult person to manage on the road," says the band's longtime roadie, Grahame Harrison. "Completely unreliable due to serious drug and alcohol issues. There were times when Bear [roadie Greg Horrocks] and I had to break into his flat in Kings Cross [in Sydney], drag him out of bed and throw him in the sleeper in the truck and proceed to the gig.

"We had to take that action just to guarantee that he'd make the gig. And Michael never improved as a musician. He got to one level, enough to keep him in the Tatts, and was too lazy and out of it to improve himself. Yes it's sad, but it's also an indication of the man himself. He was sacked by the Tatts several times and replaced by Rob Riley. Rose Tattoo these days is just a very sad approximation of the original band and I call the lineup these days, 'the band currently trading as Rose Tattoo.'"[44]

"*Everybody* was doing [heroin]," says Chapman. "Almost everybody there [at UFO's shows at the Hammersmith Odeon] did; all the people who were backstage. I could drop a lot of names here but it's really not fair. Every single person that I knew that would be backstage pretty much had a little stash of that."

So when you say you didn't see Bon do heroin, you still wouldn't be surprised if he was using heroin?

"No, I'm not. Not at all."

⚡

Pete Way was photographed with Bon, one of the last images of Bon alive. It was thought to be from one of the Hammersmith shows — Chapman and Way both believe it was taken at the Hammersmith — but photographer Ross Halfin insists it was from 18 February 1980, adding weight to rumours that Bon was in the company of UFO the night before he died. Whatever the case, it will do little to quieten scuttlebutt that members of the band know more about his death than they are letting on.

"I only took two frames," he says. "Bon, for all his good-guy image, was always a dick to photographers. I got Pete to pose with him. Can't remember who the band was. Bon left and was dead the next day."

Are you absolutely sure Bon died the day after the photograph was taken?

"Yes, because Peter Mensch accused UFO of giving him drugs. It was *not* at a UFO show. I'd gone out with Pete and Wilf [Wright], UFO's manager . . . it was the night [before] he died. I remember being quite shocked after I had the photo the next day."

The Clash played at the Lewisham Odeon on the 18th. Is that a possibility?[45]

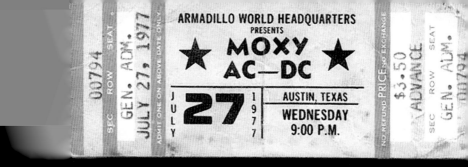

ARMADILLO WORLD HEADQUARTERS
PRESENTS

★ **MOXY** ★
AC—DC

00794 SEC ROW SEAT

GEN. ADM.

JULY 27, 1977

ADMIT ONE ON ABOVE DATE ONLY

JULY **27** 1977

AUSTIN, TEXAS
WEDNESDAY
9:00 P.M.

NO REFUND PRICE NO EXCHANGE

$3.50 ADVANCE

SEC ROW SEAT

GEN. ADM.
00794

Eighteen-year-old Wade Smith had come to Armadillo World Headquarters in Austin, Texas, in July 1977, to see Canadian band Moxy, but was blown away by the support act from Australia playing its first-ever show in North America. AC/DC was paid just $350 for the gig. "[Bon] exuded confidence and had control of the audience. His jeans were so tight, along with the navy-blue muscle shirt he was wearing; it looked as if he were poured into them . . . I just remember thinking, 'How do they make the guitars sound so good?'" Wade has saved this untorn ticket stub for 40 years. COURTESY OF WADE SMITH

Long-haired Texan rebel Roy Allen in 1976, a year before he met Bon. He offered a ride to the AC/DC singer after the Armadillo gig. "Bon insisted on driving. I was cool with that as I already had two DWIs and we were not that drunk but neither of us would have done well on a sobriety test." COURTESY OF ROY ALLEN

A tanned Bon flanked by Angus Young (LEFT) and a shirtless Malcolm Young (RIGHT) performs with AC/DC in Hollywood, Florida, August 1977. Pattee Bishop met Bon following the show and not long after began a casual relationship with him. COURTESY OF PATTEE BISHOP

Bon loved blondes with money. Pattee Bishop says she first became involved with AC/DC bass player Cliff Williams in August 1977 but soon became Bon's lover and remained in a casual sexual relationship with him until the end of 1979. COURTESY OF PATTEE BISHOP

The Palladium, New York, August 1977. Bon with his future girlfriend Holly X (FAR LEFT), Angus Young and Holly's friend Gigi Fredy backstage. Holly didn't keep many mementos of her time with Bon, but one was a photography bag (ABOVE RIGHT) with a cloth sticker from the show. An identical sticker can be seen on Gigi's jeans. WARING ABBOTT/GETTY IMAGES & JESSIE FINK

Holly modelling in Miami, Florida, in the early 1980s. Holly says Bon was getting ready to make a proper commitment to her in late 1979. Yet Pattee Bishop painted a very different picture about Bon's ideas of domestic bliss: "He told me he'd never get married again." COURTESY OF HOLLY X

A young Holly and her horse, Doubletime. Holly says Bon "loved my horse." If Bon did indeed write lyrics for *Back In Black*'s "You Shook Me All Night Long," as many of his former friends and lovers believe, the words "double time" in the first line of the second verse could well be a nod to the chestnut thoroughbred jumper. If not, it's a remarkable coincidence. The *Back In Black* album is officially credited to Young/Young/Johnson. COURTESY OF HOLLY X

In Cleveland in August 1977, AC/DC booked into the Bond Court Hotel. Janet Macoska was called in to take some photographs of Angus and Bon. "They were doing a press interview thing in their hotel suite. [Afterwards] I asked if I could take a couple of candid portrait-type shots before I shot them live.

"There was a deli food tray put out for them and the press, and Angus jumped up on the table, put his foot in the middle of the deli tray, and Bon put a pickle up his nose." These are two photos from the session.
JANET MACOSKA

All smiles before AC/DC's breakthrough performance at Bill Graham's Day On The Green in Oakland, California, in July 1978. But the bigger AC/DC became in North America, the more Bon's drinking increased, bringing him into direct conflict with Malcolm. Former AC/DC manager Michael Browning, sacked the following year, is behind them. **RICHARD MCCAFFREY**

"I wasn't initially attracted to him," says Holly X. "Bon was kind of like a little elf, this bizarre little elf guy; he was so tiny." Bon backstage at Day On The Green. **RICHARD MCCAFFREY**

"The Youngs might have had a heap of reverse snobbery about me," Silver Smith told me before she died in December 2016, "but the reality was that they didn't have to pay for a minder to keep Bon out of trouble if he was with me during his free time." In this photo, Silver appears to be wearing the same pentagram chain Bon wore on the cover of *Highway To Hell*. COURTESY OF JOE FURY

Angus in costume during the *Powerage* tour, Rochester, New York, September 1978. Bon can be partially seen behind him. COURTESY OF ROBERT VALENTINE

Vinyl hunt in New York City. The cover of *Highway To Hell* is one of the most iconic in rock, designed by Atlantic Records art director Bob Defrin, who came up with the international covers for *Let There Be Rock*, *Powerage*, *If You Want Blood You've Got It*, *Highway To Hell* and *Back In Black*. *Highway To Hell* photographer Jim Houghton is now out of the business, according to Defrin: "Jim, one of the best photographers I've ever worked with, has disappeared into the haze. I asked his representative and he told me when last seen he was selling ice cream in Philadelphia."
JESSE FINK

Circa 1979, a line forms outside the hottest club in Hollywood, Florida: Tight Squeeze. This is where Critical Mass bass player Henry Laplume met Bon while in the men's restroom.
PHOTOGRAPHER UNKNOWN

Critical Mass

Career Direction:
Sid Bernstein Associates/
Irwin Meyer & Stephen R. Friedman
180 W. End Avenue
New York, NY 10023
(212) 595-5515

Exclusively On:
MCA RECORDS

Critical Mass, AC/DC's buddies in Miami, were signed by MCA and released their one and only album in 1980. FROM LEFT TO RIGHT: Mike Barone, David Owen (FRONT), Michael Fazzolare (REAR), Henry Laplume. The talented band, unfortunately, never made it. COURTESY OF JACKIE SMITH

The poolside area at the Newport Hotel where Bon told Holly she had "chartreuse eyes." Holly believes this description was changed to "sightless eyes" for "You Shook Me All Night Long." Adding considerable weight to mounting anecdotal evidence that Bon wrote lyrics for *Back In Black*, Silver Smith maintained that she saw lines from the song in one of Bon's letters in 1976. JESSE FINK

Biscayne Bay from the rear of Holly's former family home in Miami. Bon spent much time here in the final year of his life. "Key Biscayne was really high dollar back then," says Henry Laplume. "It was a real nice place. Massive amounts of alcohol and then anything and everything that was available. Cocaine was a big thing in Miami back then. We were all partying like rock stars." **JESSE FINK**

Bon got no favours from critics in North America — even when he was dead. Reviewing Bon's magnum opus "Ride On" off the American release of *Dirty Deeds Done Dirt Cheap* in 1981, the *Milwaukee Sentinel* wrote that "it demonstrates Scott really couldn't sing, even if he was a top notch macho shouter." The *New York Times*, reviewing *Let There Be Rock*, the film, in 1982, said Scott was "oafish." **ROBERT ALFORD**

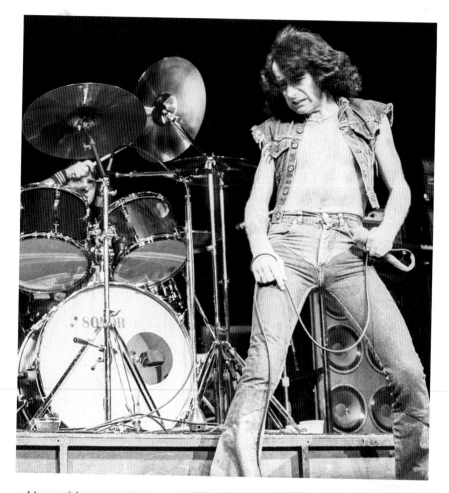

It's one of those curiously unremarked things that Bon was almost as compelling a performer on stage when he *wasn't* singing. He knew how to command attention from an audience, stretching the microphone cord tightly and wrapping it around one of his fists like he was about to garrote some unfortunate soul in a real dirty deed. Bon admitted in a radio interview in November 1979 that he didn't listen to his lead guitarist on stage: "Angus will probably kill me for saying this, but I don't listen to any guitar playing. I just listen to the rhythm. It's all I work on — and the *feeling*." LISA TANNER

Before another Day On The Green, Bon was pictured at KSJO's Travelling Rock & Roll Circus in San Jose, June 1979, along with (RIGHT) an unidentified blonde companion. Mick Jones of Foreigner grew to be a fan of the Aussie band: "I never realised, because Foreigner were so engrossed with what we were doing, how powerful and what a great live act AC/DC was." It's something people from all walks of life came to realise every day about AC/DC. Especially when it had Bon, a performer whose cheeky personality and scallywag character would have made him a bona fide video star had he lived to see the MTV era. COURTESY OF BILL KAYE

Bon and Pattee on their last night together. COURTESY OF PATTEE BISHOP

Alistair Kinnear has been accused by many AC/DC fans of being responsible for Bon's death. This is the only photo of Alistair that his son Daniel still owns. "[Alistair] was a bit of a space cadet," said Silver Smith, "but he was *our* space cadet and we all loved him." Kinnear used hard drugs, while Bon was the drinking champion of the world and the proverbial life of the party. However, Bon also didn't mind the odd "toot," Silver's word for snorting drugs. So it begs the question: What were Alistair and Bon *really* doing together that late evening and early morning of 18–19 February 1980? COURTESY OF DANIEL KINNEAR

Página 1/1

Tomo: 51509   **P.** *057*

Registro Civil Central

Sección 1ª   Certificación Literal

Anotación Soporte
ANOTACIÓN.- D./DÑA. ALISTAIR KEITH KINNEAR , hijo/a de ANGUS IAN e hijo/a de JEAN ALISON , sexo VARON , nacido/a en SELBORNE NURSING HOME - OOTACAMUND , REINO UNIDO , el veinte de abril de mil novecientos cincuenta . Este asiento constituye una simple anotación, tiene mero valor informativo y carece del valor probatorio propio de la inscripción, practicándose al exclusivo fin de que sirva de soporte para la sucesiva inscripción de DECLARACION DE FALLECIMIENTO .
Hora :   diez horas veintiocho minutos
Fecha :   veinticuatro de agosto de dos mil quince

(SIGUEN FIRMAS)

CERTIFICO que la presente certificación literal expedida con la autorización prevista en el art. 26 del Reglamento del Registro Civil, contiene la reproducción íntegra del asiento correspondiente obrante en Tomo 51509 página 057 de la Sección 1 de este Registro Civil.

Madrid , treinta de diciembre de dos mil quince

D./Dña ROSARIO MARÍA ACOSTA GARCÍA. Funcionario Delegado

Kinnear's disappearance while sailing from France to Spain in 2006 remains a mystery, and his body has never been found. Still, a Spanish court issued a death certificate in 2015. COURTESY OF DANIEL KINNEAR

FULL particulars and value of the estate and effects at the date of the death of the deceased chargeable with duty under the Stamp Duties Act, 1920.

ASSETS	*	VALUE	
		$	c
REAL ESTATE			
Real estate possessed by the deceased at death, and Real Estate liable to duty under section 102 of the Stamp Duties Act, 1920 .. .. as per Schedule No.	Nil		
PERSONAL ESTATE			
Landed property held under lease .. .. as per Schedule No.	Nil		
Rents accrued but unpaid .. .. as per Schedule No.	Nil		
Furniture .. .. as per Schedule No.	Nil		
Watches, jewellery, etc. .. .. as per Schedule No.	Nil		
Money in hand or house or at business	Nil		
Money on current accounts .. .. as per Schedule No.	Nil		
Money in banks or financial institutions on deposit including Interest accrued on same .. .. as per Schedule No.	1	30,846	09
Life Policies (including Settlement Policies and Policies for payment of Death Duty) including Bonuses .. .. as per Schedule No.	Nil		
Payments under any scheme of superannuation .. as per Schedule No.	Nil		
Monetary value of long service or other leave, etc. .. .. as per Schedule No.	Nil		
Payments under any Medical Benefits or Hospitals Contribution Fund .. .. as per Schedule No.	Nil		
Funeral donations or other payments from any Lodge or Society .. .. as per Schedule No.	Nil		
Taxation credits (Provisional tax, Group Certificates, etc.) .. as per Schedule No.	Nil		
Shares in companies listed on an Australian Stock Exchange as per Schedule No.	Nil		
Shares in companies, not so listed .. .. .. as per Schedule No.	2	316	43
Dividends declared but unpaid, including dividends on shares valued "ex-dividend".. .. .. as per Schedule No.	Nil		
Government Stock .. .. as per Schedule No.	Nil		
Debentures (including interest accrued) .. .. .. as per Schedule No.	Nil		
Mortgages (including interest accrued) .. .. .. as per Schedule No.	Nil		
Debts due to Estate .. .. as per Schedule No.	Nil		
Interest in a partnership .. .. as per Schedule No.	Nil		
Interest in a deceased person's estate .. .. .. as per Schedule No.	Nil		
Motor cars, Vehicles, etc... .. .. as per Schedule No.	Nil		
Plant, Farming implements, Tools, etc. .. .. .. as per Schedule No.	Nil		
Stock (as per stock sheets) in shop or business .. as per Schedule No.	Nil		
.. per Schedule No.	Nil		
.. per Schedule No.	Nil		
.. per Schedule No.	Nil		
.. per Schedule No.	Nil		
.. per Schedule No.	Nil		
.. per Schedule No.	Nil		

**In the Supreme Court
Of New South Wales
Probate Division**

No 900159 of 1980

The Estate of

RONALD BELFORD SCOTT

Late of

SPEARWOOD in the state of Western Australia

Deceased

Died on 19 FEBRUARY 1980

BE IT KNOWN that upon a search being made in the Registry of the Court, Probate was made on 11 JULY 1980 in the above estate and was granted to:

JOHN MCEWEN as Attorney of CHARLES BELFORD SCOTT and ISABELLA CUNNINGHAM SCOTT claims that Administration of the Estate be granted to him until the said CHARLES BELFORD SCOTT or ISABELLA CUNNINGHAM SCOTT shall come in and obtain a Grant and that the Administration bond be dispensed with.

A copy of Letters of Administration & the Inventory of Property is hereunto annexed.

GIVEN at Sydney in the State of New South Wales on 15 January 2016.

A/Deputy Registrar

Supreme Court of New South Wales documents showing the Letters of Administration and the Inventory of Property relating to the Estate of Ronald Belford Scott. That Bon ended his life with just over $30,000 in assets when the Young brothers went on to amass a fortune of several hundred million dollars is the bitter reality of this story. He died with no heirs and the money that was to enrich his estate went to members of his family who he saw very little of in his final years. SUPREME COURT OF NEW SOUTH WALES

Contrary to appearances and prevailing band history, Bon wasn't very close to the rest of AC/DC — that's the opinion shared by three of his most significant lovers: Pattee Bishop, Holly X and the late Silver Smith. Away from gigs, he largely kept to himself and was interested in reading, going to art galleries and listening to The Pretenders and Steely Dan. Pictured with (FROM LEFT) Cliff Williams, Angus Young, Phil Rudd and Malcolm Young in Munich, August 1979, Bon had taken a dramatic turn for the worse with his drinking. It was so bad he contemplated quitting the band altogether. ROBERT ALFORD

Roy Allen at a New Year's Eve party, December 1979, the same month he got his last phone call from Bon, asking if he could come and stay with him in Texas to dry out. Says Roy: "I told him I was willing to do whatever, just come and we'd figure it out." **COURTESY OF ROY ALLEN**

Bon with Pete Way, bass player of UFO, London, February 1980. This is widely considered to be one of the last photos of Bon. Way himself believes it was taken at a UFO gig at the Hammersmith Odeon early that month: "I think it was the last photo [of Bon] by a professional photographer. That was probably walking down to [UFO's] dressing room after the show." But Way's friend and the image's photographer, Ross Halfin, says otherwise, insisting it was taken on 18 February, possibly at The Clash's gig at the Lewisham Odeon. **ROSS HALFIN**

THE HIGHWAY TO HELL IS PAVED WITH PLATINUM.

ATLANTIC RECORDS AND WEA INTERNATIONAL CONGRATULATE AC/DC ON THE SUCCESS OF "HIGHWAY TO HELL" SD 19244

PLATINUM
UNITED STATES

GOLD
CANADA, FRANCE, GERMANY

SILVER
ENGLAND

An Atlantic Records/WEA press ad from the back cover of *Billboard*, 26 April 1980. The success of *Highway To Hell* would come too late for Bon. One prominent American rock musician, who shall remain anonymous, told me, "I've heard rumours for years that there are recordings of Bon singing the same lyrics that Brian sang. I'm sure, if true, that George Young has them tucked safely away." COURTESY OF AMERICAN RADIO HISTORY

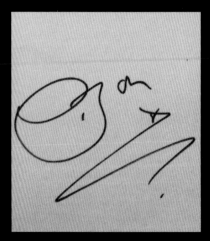

Bon's distinctive signature on a card kept by Holly X. Said a letter writer to *Sounds* magazine on 8 March 1980: "AC/DC has still got Angus Young, but Bon Scott was the vocalist, the communicator with the audience. Without him the magic is gone." Bon was a great writer as much as he was a rock star, if not superior as a writer, but one who never committed a word to a book. That his lyrics are renowned around the world despite being written in a less-than-encouraging band environment in which anything too clever was "censored" by Angus and Malcolm Young, is a testament to just how good a writer he really was. JESSE FINK

"Yes, that makes sense as Bon was found dead in Catford, which is next to Lewisham. East Dulwich/Catford, same area."

What was the tenor of Mensch's accusation? Were you privy to it?

"No, but he was trying to put together what happened and, as at that time everybody was doing drugs and UFO liked to indulge, he presumed Bon got drugs from Pete, which is *completely* untrue."

Maybe so, but it gives an insight into the possible thinking of the AC/DC camp after Bon died. Acute alcohol poisoning appears to have been the furthest thing from their minds.

Way says he didn't know Silver Smith but remembers Joe being with Bon on the night they turned up at the Hammersmith for one of UFO's shows in early February 1980. In his autobiography, *A Fast Ride Out of Here: Confessions of Rock's Most Dangerous Man*, published in May 2017, he says it was the seventh.

"After a few drinks or whatever, I just went home . . . that night Bon went off with his Australian friends."[46]

Paul Chapman and Joe, he maintains, "spent an awful lot of time together when we were off the road."[47]

"I saw Bon and I saw the guy you mentioned, Joe, who actually did bring down certain drugs for us, and that was it really. It's always so busy when you play in London when you're from London. Obviously my time would have been spent talking to Bon because he was, *erm*, a great pleasure to talk to. I knew that Joe was there because there was magically drugs available in the dressing room."

An angry Joe again rejects any suggestion he was at the Hammersmith: "Pete Way wasn't the brightest fucking tulip in the fucking patch, I can tell you. He was as thick as a fucking brick. I don't recall doing that. There may have been a time when [a person within the UFO organisation] asked me to fucking carry the drugs or take drugs or something [else] to [Way]."

Way is undeterred.

"I think [Bon and Joe] were so close at that point, him being Australian too. I think they were making the [*Back In Black*] album, and Bon had time off so he probably hung around with him. But as I say, Joe, I think it's 'Joe Silver' he was called — I'm not sure if that was his real name — I certainly wouldn't want to slander him by saying, 'Yeah, he was providing drugs and then Bon took drugs and [was] drinking.' There you get a difficulty with alcohol, because if you're taking something *and* you're drinking, you can run into trouble. It was *very* available."

Was Joe guitar tech for Paul Chapman, as Chapman claims?

"No, he wasn't actually, unless he got a job without us knowing, *no*. He was just basically somebody that we saw [around the band], possibly with Paul Chapman, on a regular basis because he would bring cocaine and heroin to our shows."[48]

It's an odd statement, as Way referred to Joe as "a friend of mine" in his autobiography, though in the book, he doesn't actually reveal his identity beyond calling him "an Australian guy." I ask Way: Did you take Quaaludes with Bon?

"If I took a Quaalude I'd take them in the privacy of my own dressing room. No, I wouldn't take a Quaalude until after the show. Any drugs we kept pretty private, actually."

So you never saw Bon doing Quaaludes?

"No, but I'm sure he probably would sometimes [take them] to get him to sleep. It's quite possible he may have taken cocaine. And then, of course, Quaaludes being a sleeping tablet would put you to sleep, because from what I heard, Bon was left to sleep in the back of the car [outside Alistair Kinnear's apartment]. They probably thought, 'Oh, he's fine; just let him sleep and he'll get out of the car' and come into, *um*, I think it was a flat. I never went there. But Quaaludes actually can also heavily affect [sic] the opportunity to find yourself choking.

"I was somewhat thinking there was a possibility [of that happening] and I've never seen Bon take heroin but that can also make you, *er*, throw up. *Erm*, and it can also make you go to sleep. So [*pauses*] there's *something* that could have happened. I can imagine if I'd been [in Alistair's apartment] at the time, it'd be, 'Yeah, Bon's alright. He knows where the front doorbell is, he'll come out.' So I could see why they left him in the back of the car, because they probably didn't want to disturb him."

Do you suspect that there was more involved in Bon's death beyond alcohol poisoning?

"Whether or not he took any drugs, *well*, that has always been at the back of my mind because Paul Chapman called me at six in the morning the day he died and said to me, 'Pete, Bon's dead.' Which, of course, was a terrible shock to me."

What do you remember about that call?

"[Paul] said, 'Have you got any numbers for the band? Because we need to let the band know what's happened.' And, as it happened, I had Angus's and Malcolm's numbers. So I gave Paul Chapman Malcolm's number.[49] I preferred not to tell . . . *well*, I really didn't want to be the one *telling* them, but they just needed a number. And this came via Paul Chapman. So I don't know if Joe called Paul Chapman.[50] I don't even know if Paul Chapman was there [with Bon and Alistair] or not."

Did you know Alistair?

"Probably. I mean, the name rings a bell. At the time I knew a lot of people and in a way they were familiar faces. But really and truly, unless they were members of AC/DC's road crew, then they were just friends of Bon's. Obviously he would have no problem accessing [backstage] passes for his friends. Quite possibly I knew him."

So how did you get your drugs?

"I didn't particularly go out to clubs, but we might rehearse and somebody would pop down with some sort of substance. Yeah, I did heroin at the time but I also did cocaine. I used to mix it. Speedballs. Which is what made me wonder if possibly Bon who really, *um*, [was] very sort of, *um*, oh I can't really put it into words; [I'd] say *open-minded*, that's the wrong word, but, you know, I can see him doing a line of what he thought was cocaine. He wasn't to my knowledge a heroin user by any strokes. *Um*, I think he *possibly* could have done that, which might have brought on [his death]. It's quite possible because I know he did coke. But, I mean, once again he did it privately. He didn't advertise it."

I get the impression Way is driving at something but not quite prepared to say it. John Belushi and River Phoenix died from the same thing: a speedball.

Bon never spoke to you about using heroin?

"No, *no*, not at all."

But you mention the possibility of Bon doing a speedball. You once said, "If you're not skilled at the art of heroin, then you do [a] dance with the devil." Do you think early that morning Bon might have just met with a drug accident? That he was so cavalier with his own safety that he would do something like that?

"I think if there was [a speedball] it would have been by accident. I wouldn't say [Bon was] careful, because he didn't really look to see how much was left in the bottle; so for me it could have been an accident. He was very level headed. I never really saw him drunk. You never saw him being carried out anywhere. He was very fit as well, you know."

There is some merit to Way's thinking: Why would Bon use heroin knowing full well he'd already had problems overdosing on it and just weeks from recording the most important album of his career? He either met with an accident, was unbelievably selfish and stupid, wanted to get out of it, or, most likely, all of the above.

CHAPTER 28

GIVEN THE DOG A BONE

UFO's Hammersmith Odeon gigs took place around two weeks before Bon died. Paul Chapman has previously stated in an interview with American radio host Eddie Trunk that he went from the Hammersmith with Joe Fury and Chapman's then wife, Dutchwoman Linda Melgers, back to his flat in Fulham and "Bon was supposed to meet us back there and he didn't." The following morning he was informed of Bon's death. But as UFO didn't have a gig at the Hammersmith on the 18th, this could not be possible.

When I pointed this out to Chapman, he was as confused as I was, though he had prefaced his comments to Trunk with the warning, "There might be a discrepancy here." There certainly was. It may be one of those things that can happen to a former addict's memory. Snippets of images and recollections meld into each other, timelines blur, details become vague. Disputes over the location and date of Ross Halfin's photo of Bon do not help matters.

In Chapman's defence, he also once stated that his alleged encounter with Bon and Joe was "some days after our Hammersmith gigs," and he would concede to me, "I thought it happened after a Hammersmith show. Obviously it couldn't have." These irregularities do need to be acknowledged and considered, but what they don't do is necessarily disqualify his story. For when it comes to the thrust of what happened on the evening of 18 February 1980, Chapman is absolutely convinced: he, Joe and Bon met up somewhere in inner London (where exactly is a detail lost in the wormholes of Chapman's memory). He says Bon "went off" to get some heroin.

"Joe said, 'I got some great blow,' some smack. And I said, 'So do I. But I haven't got very much and I was going to stop on the way home and pick up some more.' And he said, 'Well, I've got a bit and if you've got a bit that'll tide us over until Bon gets back.' And I was like, 'Gets back from where?' And Joe said, 'Oh, he's gonna go and pick up some more.' This is all I can remember. This is on my daughter's *life*. And I said, 'Well, why don't you go with him and make sure he does what he does and then come back to my house?' And he said, 'I have a better idea. Why don't *I* come back with you and he goes and does what he does and then he'll meet us at your place when he's done, which will probably be about 2 a.m., something like that.'"

They went together to Chapman's place in Fulham to wait for Bon.

"I had no idea Bon was going out to [The Music Machine]. Otherwise I would have stopped on the way home and got some more [heroin] myself and then not have to wait and sit up with Joe till 5:30 in the morning. I haven't seen Joe since then. Even the days after, the weeks after, I *never* saw Joe. And I don't think I've seen him to this day. Wherever [Bon] was going [that night] he was going to score.[51]

"Why [Bon] went down [to Alistair Kinnear's flat in East Dulwich] I have no idea . . . I haven't got a clue. [Heroin] was everywhere then. Obviously because of the condition we were all in, everything is a blur. None of this, anything to do with this, is mentioned in any of the *Behind the Music* things or any of the [AC/DC] interviews or any of the other books or anything like that.

It's all kind of glossed over. I thought a lot about it. I've seen a lot of documentaries, stuff on VH1; it's a pile of shit. All the *Behind the Music* shows with people I know are usually incredibly wrong.

"To sum it up, I think there was an incredible mistake on whoever's part it was that left him in the car and all these fingers are pointing at Alistair Kinnear. Joe and I stayed up, well, till it was light and there was no sign of anybody. My wife [Linda] had gone to bed. I can remember it was about 5:30 [in the morning] and [Joe] going, 'I better get going. It looks like he's not coming.' And 'I gotta get back' to wherever he was staying."

Chapman offered to call Joe a minicab.

"He went, 'No, no, *no*. You don't have to do that. I'll just walk to the end of the street 'cause Wandsworth Bridge Road is pretty busy and you've got a really good chance at getting a cab really quick.'"

Chapman walked Joe down to the front of the building, through a locked door and down a hallway.

"As I walked him out, the sun was just coming up and I can remember looking at his face and it was green — as green as a palm tree, as green as a plant. As if he was just about to throw up. And I went, 'Are you okay?' And he went, '*Ehhh*, I'll be fine.' And he took off and walked down the road."

Chapman went back inside his apartment.

"I didn't have any furniture. All I had was like cushions everywhere . . . and I laid down right next to the phone and I drifted off into this slumber, nodded out, and within about an hour the phone went and it was Joe."[52]

Chapman was puzzled why Joe was calling so soon after he'd left.

"Did you get home okay? What's the matter? You stuck or something? Are you still down the end of the street? Why are you calling me?"

"Are you sitting down?"

"I'm lying right where you left me."

"Bon's dead."

"What?"

"Yeah." Joe began crying, according to Chapman. "I need a number [for the band]. Can you give me Pete's number?"

"No, not really." Chapman didn't want to give out Way's telephone number to Joe. "Give me your number, I'll call you back."

Chapman immediately rang Way and got Malcolm Young's number for Joe. Chapman says Way was "pissed off that I woke him up. Pete gave me Malcolm's number and then I called Joe back and gave him Malcolm's number and that's all I can remember."[53]

What about Alistair?

"I don't know anything about this Alistair guy. I have no idea who he was. I think this Alistair Kinnear bloke is full of shit by the sound of it."

I ask Chapman if he ever bought heroin from Silver Smith. She'd been to his place in Fulham.

"Yeah, all the time. Her and Joe. Sometimes he had [the heroin], sometimes she did. She had a really annoying laugh, if I remember, like *Hehhh hehhh hehhh hehhh*." But he says Silver was "very nice . . . almost to the point of gushing."

Which raises the obvious question of why Bon would need to go off to get heroin on his own when a simple phone call to Silver — Bon's ex-lover, Joe's "twin" and a dealer herself — might well have solved the issue for everybody. She knew other people in the drug trade too, as did Joe. The possible answer, as much as it might surprise some people, is that she did not condone Bon doing harder drugs, knowing how destructive he could be when not in control of his faculties. Bon would have avoided asking Silver for heroin.

But how, at least in Chapman's version of events, could Joe have got the news so early? He was close to Silver and she was a friend of Alistair's. Is it possible that Silver was informed of Bon's death the *morning* of the 19th? Or could Chapman have got his dates wrong, confusing the morning of the 19th with the 20th for when he got the phone call from Joe?

To be fair, there is a distinct possibility that Chapman's heroin tale involving Bon actually did happen after one of UFO's

Hammersmith shows and he has simply conjoined that event with what Silver and Joe insist happened on the morning of the 20th.

Both of them think a blurring of dates is the source of the confusion, as the two stories are diametrically at odds in their timelines.

According to Chapman, Joe was with him the entire evening of the 18th and the early morning of the 19th while waiting for Bon. According to Silver, Joe was "probably" with her during the same timeframe, as well as at King's College Hospital on the evening of the 19th, when she was informed of Bon's death and asked to come in. As Joe tells it, he was with Silver from the evening of the 18th through to the evening of the 19th and into the early morning of the 20th, though he too is not 100 per cent certain where he was exactly for the duration.

"I don't know if [Joe] stayed [over at my apartment] for sure, but probably," said Silver. "The 18th seems to have run late in the evening for everyone, so if it was after the Tube stopped running — in those days that was reasonably early — then probably . . . Joe rang Chapman from my attic when we got back from the hospital [on the 19th], in the wee small hours [of the 20th]."

This is completely feasible, and Joe backs her up on it. He says he was at Silver's apartment when Bon first rang her on the evening of the 18th and was there when Alistair called twice early on the morning of the 19th. But where Silver said, "[Joe] had his own place . . . a flat in the city; I think a caretaker's flat in a business building," Joe remembers the circumstances very differently.

"We were at home. I was sharing a flat with her by that stage . . . on the particular night [Bon] died he'd rung earlier and sort of said, you know, 'Let's go out' sort of thing. I can't remember [why I] made the decision not to, but part of it would have been, one, keeping up with him was hard work, because when he went out he *went out* . . . you knew what it was going to be; you were going to be in the trenches [*laughs*]. And second it was hard because it wouldn't have entered into his head, Bon, that you should be paying your own way when you go anywhere or buying the drinks. He loved to *give*. He loved to share whatever success he'd had.

"The night of Bon's death [18–19 February] I may have gone somewhere afterwards or whatever but [Silver and I] didn't go out with Bon that night . . . he certainly wasn't asking to get drugs or anything like that. He was just going out and hitting the clubs."[54]

Joe says Chapman's alt-story has him lost for words, bewildered. So much so he says it's "out of *The Twilight Zone*." He suspects it may be motivated by Chapman wanting to "get back in the press" or simply a desire to take revenge for some perceived, unknown personal slight from the past, such as "[I] screwed his fucking wife or whatever."

In particular, Chapman's story about Joe's skin turning green in the morning sun is worthy of "romantic novels . . . it gets a bit flowery and flamboyant."

"This is *fact*," says Joe. "I never saw Bon [doing heroin] or even imagined Bon had *much* to do with heroin. He might . . . you know . . . I mean, like, let's face it: in those days those drugs were fucking *everywhere*. But there was never any moment [when Bon] would have been getting heroin from me or Paul Chapman that I know about. I certainly was never waiting anywhere for Bon to come with heroin. That's fucking ludicrous . . . there was never Bon, Paul Chapman and I in the one place at the one time.

"Bon was never a heroin type. Bon was a *drinker*. He'd dabble in everything else he thought that was sociably what everybody else was doing. He was never one to sort of stand [there] and moralise or anything. His forte was drinking; drinking Scotch. He'd just drink. I never saw him have any association [with heroin] or ever have any inclination to find out where there were drugs or anything like that, either. He was happy as long as he had a bottle of Scotch.

"That last period [before he died] he was not really drinking that much as he did in the [mid to late] '70s . . . he had his downsides, Bon, too. He'd pass out on a couch, wake up in the night and think he was in the toilet and piss in the middle of your lounge-room floor and go back to the couch [*laughs*]. He was high maintenance . . . so I imagine that was probably part of the drawback [of Bon] for the Young brothers, managing that side of things."

However, the detail of Chapman's account (especially his recounting of dialogue with Joe) of 18–19 February 1980 does contrast dramatically with the vagueness of Joe's and Silver's recollections of what happened during those hours and especially where Joe was precisely: he may have gone out, he stayed in at Silver's, et cetera.

It also doesn't explain something absolutely fundamental: If both Chapman and Way are correct in saying that they got their phone calls about Bon's death, asking for AC/DC's number, sometime after dawn on the 19th, why did AC/DC only find out about it sometime after midnight on the 20th?

Joe told me at one stage that "I imagine I probably wouldn't have thought of ringing Chapman or anybody until the next day [after Bon's death]; it wouldn't have been that night, I don't think . . . it would have been the day after Bon died . . . it might have been two days after Bon's death that I called him after other [people were contacted] or whatever, I'm not sure . . . he wouldn't have been the only person I rang."[55]

Pinning down and confirming details with Silver and Joe was difficult. Before her death, Silver had grown deeply irritated by my repeated questions regarding the timeframe. The more I pressed her, the angrier she became.

"No one knew Bon was dead in the morning [of the 19th]. And I don't know how long it was after Alistair found him in the evening that the hospital rang me, how long it took to get there, or how long it took me to get home with Joe to try and make the phone calls. It was a *long* way; I know that. [The] closest I can get with the timeline was that it was bloody late at night, probably in the wee hours [of the 20th], but definitely still dark. I was sick, in shock, and on top of that the next day trying to help [Bon's ex-girlfriend] Anna Baba and Alistair, who were both in an even worse state. I was not looking at clocks."

But if, as Silver said, she and Joe called Chapman in the "wee hours" of the 20th after they returned from the hospital — she was absolutely insistent on this point to me: "It was the *middle* of the night by phone, not the previous morning" — why does Way confirm Chapman's story that he got a call sometime after 6 a.m. on the 19th? The sun rose in London that day at around 7:10 a.m.

If Joe left Chapman's flat after daybreak and returned an hour or so later, then the phone call Chapman alleges he got from Joe most likely would have come sometime between 8 a.m. and 10 a.m.

And it couldn't have been dark.

CHAPTER 29

HAVE A DRINK ON ME

AC/DC's account of events is that they were informed of Bon's death sometime after midnight on the 20th. They could not have found out *before* Pete Way because it was he who provided Paul Chapman with AC/DC's number to give to Silver Smith and Joe Fury, who then called AC/DC.

Which means that for the Silver account to match UFO's, Chapman would have to have made his phone call to Way in the very early hours of the 20th, likely sometime between 12 a.m. and 2 a.m. Both Chapman and Way specifically mentioned the call being made *after* dawn when the sun was out.

But though Way told me the call was made at around "six in the morning the day [Bon] died" and he informed Geoff Barton it came "early in the morning," in his autobiography the timing had changed to "late one night." Chapman insists there was daylight: "As [Joe] left my house, my front door faced directly where the sun came up. Which is why I could see he looked so green. Which is why I remembered it. My front door was underneath my living-room windows . . . the sun would come up and it would be *right* in your face . . . it had been up for a couple of hours at that point."[56]

Silver was unrepentant. She denounced the Chapman version, calling it "an insane wild, wild tale . . . it's all a bit sad. And then the angels came down from heaven and lifted him towards the sky, which was filled with tiny pigs with wings. There were no sinister plots, just something awful for all of us, especially Alistair, who had done everything he could to prevent it.

"Bon wasn't the sort of person that even scored for himself with smoko or anything. People just gave him stuff. So the idea of him catching a train from Westminster to Fulham to go somewhere in South London to score smack, of all things, for Paul Chapman and then the Tube back to Fulham, it's just nonsense. It's just *insanity*.

"Either the guy [Barton] completely made it up or whatever. When I heard that, it just made me worry about Paul Chapman. The writer guy [Barton] probably made half of it up and Paul was probably just really confused because he certainly wouldn't lie on purpose. He just wasn't that sort of a guy. I can't imagine Paul doing it in any sort of malicious way, so he was either confused in what he told the writer and then the writer just made the rest up, because it's just absolute nonsense."

The subject of Barton's article especially raised Silver's hackles when I queried her over Chapman's insistence that Joe was not with her but with him on the evening and early morning of 18–19 February 1980 and his allegation that Bon left Chapman's apartment to score heroin.

"Joe and I both knew a handful of people within walking distance who could have supplied heroin," she said. "So did Bon. Bon going to [East] Dulwich to score heroin is absurd. Bon scoring heroin for anyone in my humble opinion is absurd."

Silver did, however, tell a similar tale to Chapman in one crucial respect: the phone call to Way.

"Joe's part in the death story only began when he came with me to the hospital, and if he hadn't worked occasionally for Paul Chapman I would have had no way of finding a phone number for the Youngs to give them the bad news. On the way back [from the hospital] we were just like, 'What the hell, how are we gonna let them know?' Then Joe remembered Paul Chapman saying one of the other [UFO] band members had gotten friendly with Malcolm. I didn't like the idea of anyone else being told before the family and the band, but what else could we do? I should have rung [Bon's mother] Isa myself, but I had sort of shut down, shock probably."

This UFO "band member" would be Pete Way?

"Yes, it was Pete Way. So [Joe and I] rang Paul Chapman and he rang [Way], who had Malcolm and Angus's number."

It was the first time Silver mentioned both Chapman and Way and corroborated what UFO's guitarist has said all along: that he got a call from Joe asking for help in getting the Youngs' numbers. The enduring dispute is *when* Chapman got the phone call from Joe. On the morning of the 19th, as Chapman says, or around 16 to 18 hours later, after Alistair supposedly discovered Bon's body in the car and when Silver and Joe went to the hospital? It's a crucial discrepancy.[57]

"If Joe hadn't have worked for Paul, I don't know what we would have done," continued Silver. "It's a huge burden when you're the only person who bloody knows [that] this has happened. So that was just luck that we were able to contact Malcolm and Angus the same night."

⚡

Joe, unusually for someone who was supposed to have been in tears when he called Chapman, can't recall much of what happened: "There would have been an effort made to contact AC/DC . . . I might have rung Paul Chapman knowing that he might know somebody . . . those two bands played and toured together a bit and whatever."

Did you know Alistair at all?

"No, not really. A Pommy guy. Silver knew him. I'd met him recently I think at the time."

Clinton Walker's suspicion that Joe in fact was Alistair is totally new to the man himself.

"I wasn't Alistair Kinnear."

Silver couldn't even recall which of the Youngs she telephoned: "I don't even remember if it was Malcolm or Angus that I spoke to, to this day."

But she was sure of one thing.

"[The Way/Chapman story] doesn't make any sense. None of it does. Joe did not sit around all night at Chapman's from early evening the day before. Why the fuck was he *green*? Joe was not sitting around all night in the seventh circle of hell with Chapman, waiting for Bon. It's ludicrous."

Joe agrees with his late girlfriend that the truth has been lost in Chapman's telling of the story. He told me there was simply no reason for him to have been in Fulham.

"[Chapman had] done a lot of *hard yards* in the music business when I was working for him. I wasn't working for him or anything then. So it must have been quite a time after I had much contact with him. I wasn't really socialising with him that much.

"I don't know if he's cross-referencing with something that happened earlier. Bon was never one to go and try to get drugs. Sure he took 'em if they were there on occasion but he'd just want to go and have the Scotch. He wouldn't have been out looking for *that*. He wasn't a sort of person that would go back to your place and just get wasted *there*. He was always [one to] *go out* and get wasted. He'd go where people were.

"UFO were having their own internal dramas. I know Paul Chapman liked the 'slower type' drugs. Maybe he thought while I was housesitting and minding [his wife Linda] for him [that] we became a bit more 'friendly' than we should have [*laughs*].⁵⁸ He might have thought that but we didn't. Yeah, so I always had a soft spot for Paul. I thought he was a nice guy, really. He wasn't one of the baddies that are out there."

One of those baddies, Joe revealed to me, was a prominent band manager of the time who was supplying his own band members with hard drugs that they'd pay for with the per diem he was giving them. He'd pocket the profits while keeping them hooked on smack.

Somewhere between Chapman's version, Way's version and Silver's and Joe's, there might just be some long-awaited truth in the story of Bon Scott's final hours. The problem is the deeper you get into it, the more confusing it becomes.

$$\text{\Large \textbf{\textit{ϟ}}}$$

Clive Edwards was a good friend of the late Jimmy Bain and the drummer in Bain's band, Wild Horses. What he has to say may offer an important break in the Bon Scott case. He claims he was with Silver at Bain's house on the evening of 19 February when she got a phone call to come to King's College Hospital. He says he didn't know Joe, even though Joe worked as a roadie for Wild Horses and was a personal friend of Bain's. Edwards doesn't remember any "Joe" being there.

"Silver was hanging out with Jimmy a lot; in fact she [was] round at [Jimmy's] flat in Richmond the night Bon died."

So you knew Silver from the drug scene?

"Yes, they were all at it, and they all loved smack. I was there too; it was a shock. I would spend a lot of time at Jimmy's. I didn't do very much of the bad stuff, just smoked a lot of dope."

So you were with Silver and Jimmy at Jimmy's place while they did heroin?

"Yes, and there would be Sophie, Jimmy's wife. There was a small circle of people coming in and out most of the time."[59]

What do you remember about the phone call?

"All I heard was that there had been a call and Bon was dead and I think they wanted Silver to identify him; that's what was said."

What was Silver like?

"I didn't know her that well as I wasn't one of the junkies; just simple banter talk-wise before they all nodded out after having a line."

So they were snorting heroin. To your knowledge was Bon caught up in the London heroin scene along with everyone else?

"Not much social interaction with smack. Just scratching your face before passing out. I didn't have much contact with Bon so couldn't say."

You didn't have much social interaction with it?

"No, just in general. Everyone would go round to someone's house, do a line or two and then not speak for hours and hours. Not like Charlie [cocaine], where you chat like fuck for hours. Never saw needles with Jimmy and the boys. I didn't see Phil Lynott with a needle either but he was doing it by the end."

Did you ever wonder about Bon and the circumstances of his death?

"Well, I was not happy that he was left in the back of the car. What I heard was some others had let themselves in [Alistair's] flat and left him outside. They should not have left him in the car and that pissed me off."[60]

How many people were in Alistair's flat? Do you know them?

"No, I don't know them. I just heard from Silver that he had been left outside pissed with a bottle of whisky."

But there was more than one of them?

"That's what I heard. Bandmates would never have left someone on their own like that, so it would have been hangers-on."

Silver had previously said she received two phone calls from Alistair early on the morning of the 19th. She told him to put a blanket on Bon and leave him in the car to sleep it off. Does that surprise you?

"Yes, that does. But she would have been smacked out when she got the call. You don't need to call someone; you just get them in the flat, full stop."

That's what perplexes me. Why wasn't he carried inside?

"You don't leave a buddy," Edwards replies.

You most certainly don't. Especially in the middle of winter. So why was Bon left in the car?

Bon's death is arguably to rock music what the JFK assassination is to American political history: the great unsolved mystery of our time. The players involved contradict each other, pieces of crucial information are missing, and very little of what has been presented as fact stands up to rigorous scrutiny; all of which fuels the various conspiracy theories.

Much of the generally accepted version of events has been built around the testimonies of Alistair Kinnear, Joe Fury and Silver Smith, three people all allegedly associated in some way with heroin; the tight-lipped members of AC/DC; and a Japanese girl, Anna Baba, a school friend of Ian Jeffery's wife, Suzucho. Anna had only recently been dumped by Bon after a casual relationship that lasted less than four weeks and wasn't actually with him on the night of his death.[61]

Now what I believe is the true story can be told. And it's easy to tell it simply by deconstructing Alistair's 2005 statement to Maggie Montalbano. It began:

CHAPTER 30

BACK IN BLACK

In late 1978 I met Silver Smith, with whom I moved
to a flat in Kensington. She was a sometime girlfriend of Bon Scott. Bon came to stay with us for two
weeks, and he and I became friends. Silver returned
to Australia for a year, and I moved to Overhill Road
in East Dulwich. On the night of 18 February 1980,
Xena [sic] Kakoulli, manager of The Only Ones,
and wife of bandleader Peter Perrett, invited me to
the inaugural gig of her sister's band at The Music
Machine in Camden Town (renamed Camden Palace
in 1982).

Peter Perrett and his wife of 10 years, Xenoulla "Zena" (alter-
nately spelled as "Xena") Kakoulli, were good friends of Alistair,
according to Silver: "They'd known each other forever. I only met
Peter and his wife once, but I know they were very close."

They were also well known for their fondness of heroin.
Guitarist Richard Lloyd of the band Television had a heroin overdose at the Perretts' after (according to Perrett himself) snorting
heroin, drinking and taking downers, and was rushed to University
Hospital Lewisham. Recalled Perrett, Lloyd's "mouth had turned
blue. He was totally fucking completely gone."

In 2009, Perrett described to *MOJO* magazine the London
drug scene of the time: "In America I could spend $500 a day and
not even get straight because the heroin was so weak. The street
stuff there, it was between two- and six-per-cent heroin because
it had been controlled by the Mafia and organised crime for so
long and that was how they cut it. That's why so many American
junkies ODed when they came to England . . . we were awash in
this Iranian brown heroin, on account of the rich Iranians fleeing
their country, taking their money out in drugs. It was easier than
smuggling gold.

"You see, in the '60s junkies got most of their stuff from doctors, pharmaceutical stuff, which isn't the same. There was the
occasional white heroin, which was from the Golden Triangle.
That was normally quite weak, but there weren't that many

junkies around and there just wasn't a black market in it. Plus, you had to inject that stuff, and it seemed a big step to go from smoking a joint or snorting a bit of coke to sticking a needle in your arm. But, with the brown heroin, you could snort it, or just smoke it, and smoking it just seemed less threatening."

Which itself is a furphy. While injecting is by far and away the most lethal method of heroin administration, snorting and smoking also claim lives. Jim Morrison is widely acknowledged to have died from snorting heroin in Paris in 1971, although the medical examiner officially put down the cause of death as heart failure.

A 2003 paper by researchers at the Karolinska Institutet in Stockholm, *Fatal Intoxication as a Consequence of Intranasal Administration (Snorting) or Pulmonary Inhalation (Smoking) of Heroin*, found that of 239 heroin-related deaths in Stockholm from 1997 to 2000, 188 were from injecting, 33 were undetermined, 11 were from snorting and seven from smoking.

Of those 18 deaths from snorting or smoking, 83 per cent were male with a median age of 32. Five of the 18 were casual or "party users." In eight cases there were eyewitnesses to the deaths. Three dropped dead immediately after smoking or snorting, "the other five fell asleep and were found dead later on." The research team also found that factors such as alcohol and the presence of other drugs were "important" contributors to causing death from heroin overdose.

Brown heroin burns at a lower temperature than white heroin, hence it being used for smoking. White heroin needs the addition of an acid to make it soluble and turn it into a salt for injecting. In London in early 1980, the in-thing was to smoke or snort brown heroin. Then there was the method known as "chasing the dragon," described by Richard Davenport-Hines in his book *The Pursuit of Oblivion: A Global History of Narcotics* as "placing the heroin on aluminium foil, heating it and inhaling the vapour."

Says Paul Chapman: "In America, heroin was taboo at the time. So you get back to London, the first thing you do would be to dial up somebody you knew that had a bit of it. I was thinking,

'[Bon's] only just got here . . . if he hadn't connected [with heroin] already, if everybody around him is doing this, I'm surprised that he's not, you know, partaking like everybody else.'"

Silver told me that the heroin trade in London in 1980 was "a hippie thing on a small scale. It was very small scale. The importation was a couple of ounces at a time; it wasn't sort of organised bloody container loads."

Users in London mostly sought brown heroin to snort it, and she snorted herself, as did most of her friends and acquaintances. A few others smoked it, but she "never saw a needle, never a saw a gun, nothing like that, there was nothing sordid."

"A few travellers would bring in what was called 'Thai white' or 'China white.' [Heroin dealing] wasn't a disreputable occupation at the time. You had to have a few things going for you. You know, *discretion*. That was another thing. Bon was horribly indiscreet. He just didn't think about things."

⚡

Alistair's story went on:

> I phoned Silver, who was once again living in London, to see if she wanted to come along, but she'd made other arrangements for the evening. However, she suggested that Bon might be interested, as he had phoned her earlier looking for something to do. I gave him a call, and he was agreeable, and I picked him up at his flat on Ashley Court in Westminster.

This is where things get problematic because Alistair's version of events clashes with Silver's. The differences between these accounts are not "unimportant," as she claimed, but significant. Silver lived not in a flat in Gloucester Road, Kensington, as widely believed, but in what she described as a "tiny attic" in Emperor's Gate, South Kensington, about a 20-minute drive from Bon's flat at Ashley Court, Victoria.

"Bon's flat was just . . . *ugh*," she said. "It was pretty hideous. It was very luxurious, it had no natural light . . . his flat was cold. It was all sort of smoked glass and marble and crap. I mean, it wasn't cheap but it was *horrible*. It was really dark. I'm pretty sure Bon wouldn't have chosen something like that.

"I just got such a horrible vibe off the flat. I couldn't have lived there. I would have been unhappy staying a night there. The reason why I didn't ask him whether he chose it or someone else chose it was that he was so proud, possibly [for] the first time ever, certainly [for] the first time in a very long time, that he had a place that was actually *his*. He was always living with someone else. That first year I supported him at Gloucester Road. He was getting £50 a week and it wasn't even covering his Scotch bill. Irene and I supported him for years."

Silver had lived in various parts of London: Kensington, Richmond and South Kensington. From where Alistair lived in Overhill Road, East Dulwich, it's roughly a 40-minute drive to Emperor's Gate in South Kensington.

She told Australia's ABC Adelaide in 2010 that on the evening of 18 February 1980 Alistair was planning to visit. When Bon called at around 7:30 p.m. asking her to go out, she declined, having already made plans, and suggested that he hook up with Alistair. Bon wanted to go to the club Dingwalls in Camden Lock.[62]

Silver said she told Bon, "'Alistair's coming over later, do you want me to get him to ring you? He might go with you.' And that's what happened. They set off together."

Yet in the original 1994 edition of Walker's *Highway to Hell*, she described another scenario altogether: Alistair was already in her flat when Bon called. She said, "Oh, Alistair's here, I'll see if he wants to go."

How did those details come to change so dramatically in 16 years? Why was there no mention whatsoever of Joe sharing her flat, as he claimed when I interviewed him for this book?

Alistair and Bon were quite the odd couple, but they knew each other well and were friends. Silver told me the pair had first met years before at the flat she was then occupying in Abingdon Villas,

Kensington. Alistair even moved in with them for a period. On this detail, Alistair's statement to Montalbano is substantiated.

"He actually stayed with us, Bon and I, for a couple of months because he had work up in the city."

After that, they lost contact, but "the night that Bon died, we hadn't actually seen him in quite a while."

Adding some weight to Alistair's claim that he knew Bon, Walker's book established that Anna Baba called Alistair after Bon's death. She had his number. It appears with his name on the inside back cover of a pocket book allegedly owned by Bon but in Anna's possession.

"When I saw him at the flat, [Bon] was already so drunk," Anna quotes Alistair as telling her. In a short interview with London's *Evening Standard* in 1980 Alistair said the same thing: "[Bon] was pretty drunk when I picked him up."

So it's odd that Alistair makes no mention at all in his statement to Montalbano of Bon being drunk when he arrived sometime between 11 p.m. and midnight at Bon's flat.

Joe Fury thinks it was out of character for Bon to be drunk at home so early in the evening: "I found it a bit funny . . . [it was] unusual for [Bon]. He must have been pretty damn drunk when Alistair picked him up [for Alistair] to say that Bon was drunk; 'cause he could drink a bit and you wouldn't really know it."

What's even more odd is that on Bon's death certificate, Bon's address is given as "Morford Crescent," yet Morford Crescent doesn't exist — at least in London. It does, curiously, in Sheidow Park, a suburb of Bon's old home of Adelaide. The certificate should read "Morpeth Terrace." It's a detail so startling it beggars belief it hasn't been raised before. Why would an address that doesn't exist be on Bon's death certificate? A transcription error? Unlikely.

Was it a false address given to police and, if so, why and by whom? To give unknown persons adequate time to go through Bon's flat before police arrived? It's one possible explanation. But why wasn't it ever picked up? Already there is enough information to cast some doubt on the veracity of Bon's death certificate.[63]

In an interview with a Canadian podcast, Colin Burgess, AC/DC's first drummer, said he and his musician brother Denny may have been at The Music Machine that night, though he conceded, "I'm not sure . . . we went there with Bon . . . I can't remember; it was a long time ago." He's on the record elsewhere as saying Bon didn't appear intoxicated: "Bon was sober . . . I cannot remember Bon being drunk enough to kill himself in a car. I mean, come on." Yet, if we are to accept Alistair's earlier comments, Bon was already drunk and got drunker as the night went on, reputedly drinking seven double whiskies.

> It was a great party, and Bon and I both drank far too much, both at the free bar backstage and at the upstairs bar as well; however I did not see him take any drugs that evening.

Not *seeing* him take drugs is different from him not *taking* drugs. Lonesome No More was the band playing that night. Lead singer Koulla Kakoulli, sister of Zena, had done backing vocal work for both solo artist Johnny Thunders and Peter Perrett's new band, The Only Ones, in 1978. Contrary to reports in some AC/DC biographies, future guitarist for The Cult, Billy Duffy, wasn't playing guitar that night with Lonesome No More — but he was there at the club.

"It's very simple," says Duffy. "I had been invited down to watch Lonesome No More play that night with a view to I think replacing the guitarist, which eventually happened, but I don't think at that point I played with them.

"I was at the sidestage bar at the venue and I remember seeing Bon and another guy walk by, probably grab a drink at the bar and then disappear backstage. That's it, really. I had seen AC/DC play in Manchester a couple of years previously and was a huge fan so there was no mistaking Bon."

⚡

At the end of the party I offered to drive him home. As we approached his flat, I realised that Bon had drifted into unconsciousness. I left him in my car and rang his doorbell, but his current live-in girlfriend didn't answer. I took Bon's keys and let myself into the flat, but no-one was at home. I was unable to wake Bon, so I rang Silver for advice. She said that he passed out quite frequently, and that it was best just to leave him to sleep it off.

Again, Alistair's account is at odds with Silver's. Silver said that "the keys got jammed inside the door" while Alistair was attempting to enter Bon's flat. Alistair makes no mention of this.

"According to Silver, when they got to Ashley Court, Kinnear couldn't move Bon," wrote Walker. "He roused him, but Bon couldn't, or wouldn't, move. Thinking he could usher him inside if he cleared a path, Kinnear took Bon's keys and opened the flat, leaving the door ajar. The building's front door, however, presented Kinnear with something of a problem, and although he managed to open it, he subsequently locked himself out."

The keys jammed or he locked himself out? It's another inconsistency made more puzzling by the fact that the important factor of Bon's house keys isn't referenced in Alistair's statement to Montalbano. As for the phone call, why would Alistair be ringing Silver asking for "advice" when he was already inside Bon's fourth-floor flat, #15, and a natural course of action would be to carry him upstairs or at the very least attempt to do so?

He'd already driven drunk, by his own admission, from The Music Machine. How hard could it be to throw an arm around Bon's waist and try to get him inside? Silver said she got the call from "a very distressed Alistair" around 1 a.m., saying, "He's passed out. He's half passed out. What do I do?"

It wasn't uncommon for Bon to drift off into a stupor from alcohol so, again, why would Alistair call Silver in such a panic from inside Bon's flat if he thought it was just alcoholic intoxication?

"I suggested he take him home [to Alistair's flat in East Dulwich]," said Silver, "where he might be able to get some help to get him up the stairs."

Or in other words, she was suggesting to an intoxicated Alistair, who had the passed-out lead singer of AC/DC in his car, that he travel twice as far as he needed to, rather than drive the shorter distance to her flat in Emperor's Gate, where she (and Joe, who she failed to mention was there) could conceivably be of at least some assistance.

"I was up five flights, he was up three, so that seemed sensible, 'cause I was six and a half stone and used to wear four-inch heels . . . I'd been in that situation with Bon many times and it was difficult, believe me."

Whose help exactly was Alistair going to get at that time of the morning? Why couldn't Silver get help from Joe or offer Alistair a hand herself? Why hadn't Alistair called his own father, Angus, a doctor who lived in Forest Hill, next to East Dulwich, if he was worried about Bon's health and didn't want to go to a hospital? He lived only a mile from Alistair's apartment.

Today Joe is genuinely regretful he didn't help Alistair, talking of "my own guilt that I hadn't gone out with [Bon] that night and tried to keep an eye on things . . . this is where you take a lot of 'if only.' If only I'd gone to help Alistair try and get [Bon] into his own flat."

He thinks that if Alistair had in fact lost Bon's keys, he was concerned at the time with the question of "Where will I take him back to if I can't get into his flat?" This is perhaps understandable, if Joe was with Silver in a tiny apartment containing one bed and not much else. But "after so many occasions [of seeing Bon passed out] you just sort of think, 'Oh, it's another night out. Sleep it off in the car.'"

Joe says his reaction that night to Alistair's call for help might have been different "if Bon had been in reasonable condition, [if] he hadn't been drunk all the time."

The guilt lingers to this day even if the memories of that fateful morning remain foggy.

"I felt indebted a bit to Bon because he'd always been very generous [to me]. Later I was thinking, 'Well, shit, he rang and said, "Do you want to go out?" I should have said, "Yep."' If I had gone out with him then I would have got him [inside], sorta got him home. When Alistair called, maybe I should have said, 'Okay stay there, I'll come down' or 'Bring him back here' or something like that, which makes me think I was probably at Silver's place."

Were Bon's story a TV whodunnit, a natural deduction to make at this point is that Bon was possibly already dead. Is that why Alistair was calling Silver in a blind panic? Had he told Silver and Joe the whole truth of what was going on? A man in such a predicament might have thought that leaving Bon's keys inside his flat would make it look like Bon had been there; that he'd stopped by to collect something and gone somewhere else.

We know from Walker's book that the caretaker at Ashley Court left a note behind for Bon on the 19th, saying a set of keys had been found on the mat inside the front door, the door of the flat was open, and all the lights and radios were left on.[64]

But why would they be left on? Turning on a radio is not the first thing you do in the early hours of the morning while attempting to carry a passed-out friend to their bedroom or bathroom, unless you're trying to wake them up.

⚡

> I then drove to my flat on Overhill Road and tried to lift him out of the car, but he was too heavy for me to carry in my intoxicated state, so I put the front passenger seat back so that he could lie flat, covered him with a blanket, left a note with my address and phone number on it, and staggered upstairs to bed.

I propose to Paul Chapman that Bon may have already been dead, Alistair panicked, and made the decision to leave Bon's body in the car to make it look like he died of natural causes during the night. At 67 Overhill Road, there were only six flats. It wasn't a large building. Alistair's one-bedroom flat was on the top floor, #6. It really wouldn't have taken a huge effort to get Bon up the stairs and inside.

"Surely somebody wouldn't just leave him there? *Wow*. I've never thought of that. Now that's just opened up a whole new thing in my head. Who would do *that*? Somebody must have been extremely out of it upstairs, wherever upstairs was, and forgotten Bon was in the car. I remember how cold it was at my flat when the Calor gas went out, let alone being in a car outside. Whoever was down there with Bon in [East] Dulwich must have been upstairs nodding out. That's the only thing I can think of. I cannot believe that somebody would not go out and check on him in that weather."

Chapman mentions the weather and it's worth elaborating upon. There are sundry misleading stories of Bon dying from hypothermia or freezing to death. In the 1991 film *Don't Blame Me*, Ozzy Osbourne boldly claimed, "In actual fact [Bon] died from hypothermia in his car . . . it was winter and he froze to death."

I checked with the Met Office. Temperatures that morning of 19 February 1980 didn't get colder than five degrees Celsius, according to Mark Beswick of the Met Office National Meteorological Archive. He sent me some figures.

18 February 1980
- Maximum Temperature: 10.4 deg C (slightly above average)
- Minimum Temperature: 3.9 deg C (slightly above average)
- Rainfall: 0.0 mm
- Sunshine: 3.4 hours (at Heathrow)
- A dry day with a few sunny intervals with a gentle to moderate SE'ly breeze.

19 February 1980
- Maximum Temperature: 10.6 deg C (slightly above average)

- Minimum Temperature: 5.0 deg C (above average)
- Rainfall: 0.0 mm
- Sunshine: 2.3 hours (at Heathrow)
- A dry day with a few sunny intervals with a gentle to moderate E'ly breeze.

So there was no frost. The figures are backed up by the Met Office's *Monthly Weather Report* of February 1980: "The month as a whole was very mild with mean temperatures above average everywhere."

The air temperature wasn't *that* cold, then, for Bon to freeze to death. He wasn't exposed to wind. It wasn't raining. Bon was clothed, dry and, according to Alistair, had a blanket, possibly two. Hypothermia typically occurs after exposure to a combination of wind, water and cold air, or at least two of those factors. And while alcohol and drugs can reduce body temperature and exposure to cold air can bring on an asthma attack, Bon would have had to be especially unlucky to perish from hypothermia when he was dry, protected from the wind in an airtight space, and the temperature was "above average."

On the balance of probabilities and with all the available evidence, there's very little to show that Bon died from hypothermia but plenty to suggest he perished from something else.

CHAPTER 31

WHAT DO YOU DO FOR MONEY HONEY

Now at this critical point in the story Alistair Kinnear is, by his own admission, "intoxicated." Yet despite his supposed drunkenness, he's just driven his Renault 5 for 11 miles across London from Kings Cross/Camden via Victoria/ Westminster to East Dulwich. According to Silver Smith he made a phone call at 1 a.m. from Victoria. Alistair doesn't mention another phone call to Silver in his statement to Maggie Montalbano, yet both Silver and Joe Fury previously claimed in interviews that there was a second phone call.

Silver denied there was ever any collusion between her and Joe in their accounts of the morning Alistair phoned. Joe certainly is adamant he was *not* with Paul Chapman in Fulham.

According to Silver, "By the time [Alistair] got [to East Dulwich] Bon had just completely passed out; [Alistair] couldn't even get him out [of] the car."

Joe estimated that the second phone call came at 3 a.m. That is a full *two hours* after Alistair's first phone call to Silver. A car journey of 11 miles at 1 a.m. across London shouldn't take very long. What was Alistair doing between Victoria/Westminster and East Dulwich that would take two hours? Attempting to resuscitate a dying or even dead Bon?

Recalled Silver for the ABC, "When [Alistair] got home he rang me again and said, '[Bon's] down in the car, I can't get him up here.' So I said [to Alistair], 'Well, take down some blankets.'"

Speaking to me, she rubbished the idea that she should have contacted the AC/DC camp immediately after Alistair got off the phone.

"People think, you know, it's like today where everyone's got Facebook, everyone's got their bloody mobile with them every minute of every day. It wasn't like that."

Even if she'd had their numbers, which she didn't, she thought she would have been ignored had she called the Youngs and told them Bon had passed out. As uncomfortable and provocative as that argument may be for some people, she might have had a very good point.

"If I'd rung Malcolm and Angus and said, 'Oh, listen, Bon's passed out in a car in South London at two o'clock [sic] in the morning, they would have just gone, 'What the *fuck* are you telling me for?' Do you know what I mean? It was like, well, what's *new*?"

Joe holds a similar view: "Four o'clock [sic] in the morning and someone's having to take care of Bon, *again*. When I first met Silver, and I'm talking about her in relation to Bon, there was a lot of that [with Bon]. It all sounds good. But he was hard, *very* hard work in terms of passing out on you somewhere, which is partly why the relationship between me and her sort of developed a bit. She [wanted] someone a bit more organised, a bit more together."

"The other thing," Silver continued, "is if everybody rang an ambulance and moved their friend to hospital, everyone that ever passed out on alcohol, we'd need a bloody big ambulance service and also an expansion of the hospital system. That's just stupid. That's the sort of thing, you think, 'Well, shit. Are you *kidding*?' I would have thought it would be logical.

"I mean, how many times have you had friends pass out on alcohol, especially when you were young? You don't ring an ambulance and get them to hospital. They wouldn't thank you for it in the morning. Bon did that all the time. *All the time.* He didn't *ever* think how it was going to be for the people around him. *Ever.* He just *did*."

However, despite Silver's legitimate protestations, it's concerning that by her own account she got two phone calls from Alistair, quite panicked ones, and never thought the entire day of the 19th to either call Alistair to see how Bon was or try to call Bon herself or send someone around to Alistair's flat to check on both of them.

Then there is the issue of the blanket or blankets. Silver told me Alistair "took down pillows and blankets."

"I don't think there was a blanket," says Chapman. "I don't think there was anything. Whoever left him in the car probably left him in there thinking that they weren't going to be very long."[65]

Were there no blankets at all, then hypothermia would be possible.

"You see what I mean? 'Oh, we'll be out in a minute. Oh, *look*, he's passed out. Leave him there for a minute.' Then next thing you know they go in, whoever they are . . . and they probably went, 'Oh, give us a bit of *that*.' And they do a bit of *that*. And the first thing that happens is you put your head [down], *bang*, and you go, 'Oh, that's *great*.' And then you nod off. I think whoever went with Bon to Dulwich [sic] sampled some of what it was they were getting, which is exactly what I would have done."

Chapman has been thinking about Bon's death for some time.

"I'm burned on this. When I say I'm burned on it, it's just that I can't dig in any more corners and nooks and crannies in my brain." He pauses for a moment. "After this happened [with Bon passing away], I went into my dealer's and there was someone there who shouldn't have been there." Chapman names that someone. It was another member of AC/DC and he was buying heroin.

"He went, '[*Expressing horror*] Herrrhhh, Tonka! Whhhsssshhh. I gotta go.' And he was out the door. I was like [to the dealer], 'I didn't know you *knew* . . .'"

Pete Way says the same band member later pulled a shotgun

on a former member of AC/DC who'd paid him an unexpected house visit.

"He was running off the rails. He was very wired and in a bit of a state and he had a shotgun . . . really, like, in a *condition*. The guy only came out to say hello and he didn't expect to be greeted by a shotgun. A lot of things were going on around then that should never have been going on."

⚡

According to Silver, Alistair left a note with his address inside the car for Bon, "thinking when Bon's come out of it he'll just come upstairs."[66] Said Alistair:

> It must have been 4 or 5 a.m. by that time, and I slept until about 11 when I was awakened by a friend, Leslie Loads. I was so hungover that I asked Leslie to do me a favour of checking on Bon. He did so, and returned to tell me my car was empty, so I went back to sleep, assuming that Bon had awoken and taken a taxi home.

This is the most perplexing part of Alistair's statement. Who on earth is "Leslie Loads"? No Loads has ever been interviewed or spoken publicly about the day Bon died, which surely would have happened by now — unless Loads, as I suspect, was a pseudonym.[67]

"Poor Alistair, not being used to drinking, woke up the next morning with a terrible hangover and decided not to go to work, went back to bed," Silver told the ABC in that same 2010 radio interview. "And when he got out later, which was like mid afternoon, there was poor Bon still in the car."

Alistair was working where exactly? Silver said "he was working a lot in Central London" but could not recall what he was doing at the time of Bon's death.

"He used to do a lot of repairs on mechanical things . . . he was very good at jewellery repair, so he did a lot of stuff for market people. Alistair fiddled with sound equipment, too. He was a whiz at installing small, personal, easy-to-get-at-but-invisible stashes in people's houses, usually in big large doors or mantelpieces: a noble and historically trusted profession. One day Ron Wood popped in [to my apartment] and was playing 'mum' all afternoon with my dragon teapot because I was busy repainting the door."

But Alistair's son Daniel Kinnear tells me he and his mother, Mo, "had zero financial support from my father," grew up in a "very deprived household" and "were supported by government benefits and from additional money that my mother earned via cleaning jobs in pubs or other people's houses."

Mo, he says, "was a single parent with no family. She herself was an orphan and therefore had no broader family support. Like Al she had her drug problems too and was mentally ill — in and out of institutions across my childhood."

So the idea of Alistair being gainfully employed in a day job sounds most unlikely, just as unlikely as mystery figure Loads going down to the car and seeing it empty. A comatose man in two blankets would surely be spotted even if he were stretched out asleep on the back seat or lying on a semi-flattened front seat. In their version of events, Way and Chapman were also informed Bon was dead well before Loads supposedly went down to Alistair's car and found nothing inside.

The introduction of Loads into Alistair's story just doesn't seem plausible on any level. Was Alistair trying to give himself some sort of alibi, to make it look like Bon had momentarily left the car to go somewhere else? Was Loads there all along but not wanting to be identified? Was he even a he? And if the claim of Loads being there is actually true, could Bon's dead body have been hidden under a blanket or other items in the boot of the car? It seems unlikely albeit possible so long as it was done before rigor mortis set in. The width of the Renault 5's boot is around four-feet-one-inch or 1.24 metres, with a minimum storage capacity of nine-and-a-half cubic feet. But this increases to 32 cubic feet (or just over 900 litres) when the back seats are folded away.

For the first time, I can reveal the identity of a third person that was with Bon and Alistair in East Dulwich on the morning of 19 February 1980. The admission came during an exchange of online messages in late 2015.

"I was there when he died, as I spent the night at Alistair's flat," says Zena Kakoulli, Peter Perrett's wife and the manager of The Only Ones. "I don't know why [I stayed there], as I lived not far from him. Alistair had met Bon before that night; it wasn't the first time they met."

This totally corroborates what Alistair and Silver said about Alistair's friendship with Bon: they weren't strangers.

You were asleep in Alistair's flat when Bon was in the car?

"Yes."

Did you go back with Bon and Alistair in Alistair's car to East Dulwich? Or did you arrive later? Was Peter Perrett with you?

"I went back with Alistair and [Bon] to Alistair's flat. It was very late when we got back and I remember it being very cold. Peter did not go with us that night . . . Alistair was a close friend; the last time I saw Alistair was a few days before he went to sea [in 2006] and unfortunately disappeared . . . I met Bon Scott that night as Alistair was friends with Silver and I think knew Bon through her. It is a sad memory that still haunts me."

So was Bon left in the car because you couldn't both carry him? Was he still alive when you went inside? Do you know if he took heroin? I'm only interested in establishing the truth.

She's selective in her answer, ignoring my first two questions, but reveals more than I was expecting.

"I didn't see him taking heroin, but both Alistair and Silver were users at the time. I would think it probable that [Bon] did take heroin as I would not have thought somebody that was used to drinking would have been sick. It's well known that if you take heroin when you have been drinking, especially if you don't normally, it could lead to you vomiting, plus cause you to pass out.

But I can only presume that's what caused him to fall asleep and later vomit. He didn't seem unreasonably intoxicated.

"If he had taken heroin it was with Silver and Alistair at the venue; I didn't see him [take heroin]. Unfortunately the only persons that can know for sure are Silver and Alistair. I know how devastated Alistair was, and how it affected him for years afterwards. It is so bad that we will never know what happened to Alistair. He was such a lovely guy, and his disappearance has left an unsettling feeling. I miss him."

It's a mind-blowing admission after nearly 40 years of silence for a multitude of reasons. Zena was with Bon and Alistair in East Dulwich all along, rendering illogical the explanations proffered by Alistair, Silver and Joe about why Bon was left in the car, though there is no evidence Silver or Joe knew she was with Alistair.

According to Zena's account, two able-bodied people were in the car with Bon — herself and Alistair. They could have carried him inside to either Silver's flat (with Silver's and Joe's assistance, were he there, as he claims) or Alistair's flat (on their own).

Why didn't Zena offer to help Alistair? Did she offer to help? Why didn't Alistair take Bon to the hospital when Zena described him as being "sick" and having vomited, surely a possible sign of a heroin overdose, especially so given the company he was in at The Music Machine? If Alistair truly thought he was just dealing with a case of drunkenness, then why bother to phone Silver? Who calls and wakes up someone at both 1 a.m. and 3 a.m. if it's not an emergency? The conventional telling of Bon's demise — Silver's, Joe's and Alistair's — just gets completely blown to smithereens.

I attempted to contact Zena for a series of follow-up questions to clarify some of the things she said, but my messages went unanswered. Yet she left me with enough information to convince me Bon had succumbed to a fatal heroin overdose and it had effectively been covered up.

A former heroin user now afflicted with chronic obstructive pulmonary disease (COPD), a condition that has been widely linked in scientific literature to heroin inhalation, Zena thinks it was "probable" that Bon took heroin. She was there when Bon passed out and believes he hadn't consumed enough alcohol to become unconscious. She confirms there was vomit, though whether she witnessed that herself or is basing her statement on media reports is unclear. Sensationally, she also suggests that Silver was actually at the venue with Alistair and Bon, which again fatally undermines the commonly accepted story as put forward in the Walker biography. But, again, there is no evidence Silver was at The Music Machine. If she was, she never admitted it while she was alive.

Zena's sister Koulla Kakoulli of Lonesome No More also saw Bon in the last hours of his life: "[Bon] had so much to live for. Yes, he did come to our gig. If I remember right he was found in his car the next morning. Alistair was with him most of the night."

So you knew Alistair? Were they drinking, doing drugs?

"I don't think I should say. All I can say is Alistair was heavily into heroin at the time of Bon's death. I know [Bon] was dead in the car outside."

Heavily. An individual who was at The Music Machine that night and performed onstage doesn't want to be quoted publicly but drops another bombshell: "Bon had a lot to drink that night. And I would be very surprised if he too [like Alistair] didn't take a lot of drugs that evening, mainly heroin. I don't wanna upset anybody this late in the game. End of the day it was a tragic accident. But [speaking] as an ex-junkie, Bon looked *stoned*."

To be clear, the inference being made isn't to getting high on marijuana.

The inference is to heroin.

At about 7.30 that evening I went down to my car intending to pay a visit to my girlfriend who was in hospital . . .

Wait, Alistair discovered Bon at 7:30 p.m.? But Silver Smith had said it was "mid afternoon." The announcer for VH1's *Behind the Music*, meanwhile, made a right royal blunder (or quite possibly got it completely right): "In the morning [Bon] was found dead."

And who was Alistair's girlfriend? Says Daniel Kinnear: "The only girlfriend I recall was a lady called Janice . . . I remember being taken [in 1982] to the Liverpool versus Tottenham Milk Cup final; my first football game. I think Janice's mother (or father) was one of the directors of Tottenham Hotspur F.C. I was nine at the time."

Silver independently told me of Janice, so that part of the story is substantiated.

"The reason why [Alistair] was at a loose end or wanted to catch up [with me the night Bon died] was that Janice was

CHAPTER 32

ROCK AND ROLL AIN'T NOISE POLLUTION

in hospital. She'd had an accident a few years before and kept having to have corrective surgery. It was spinal. She had to walk with a stick. He was visiting her in hospital, so it was like, 'Well, [we] might as well catch up.' So it was just sheer luck, just weird twist of fate, that it happened to be him, poor guy, that had to deal with it all."

Why wouldn't anyone walking down Overhill Road knock on the window of the car when the lead singer of AC/DC was out of it in the car for practically an *entire* day? There is an enormous, 13.8-acre, 296-home housing estate called Dawson's Heights directly opposite 67 Overhill Road. It was completed in 1972. The idea that no one saw and recognised Bon, who'd only been on BBC-1's *Top of the Pops* less than two weeks earlier, seems a little far-fetched.

Was Bon even in the car at all? Where is the proof he was left there other than the testimony of Alistair and now Zena Kakoulli? A dead Bon conceivably could have been carried to and from Alistair's car under the cover of darkness so as not to arouse suspicion from neighbours (the sun began setting that day at around 5:20 p.m. and it would have been dark by 6 p.m.). Was the visit to the hospital delayed for as long as possible in the hope that no traces of heroin would be found in Bon's body?

> . . . and was shocked to find Bon still lying flat in the front seat, obviously in a very bad way, and not breathing. I immediately drove him to King's College Hospital, where Bon was pronounced dead on arrival. The Lambeth coroner's report cited acute alcohol poisoning, and death by misadventure.

Why didn't Alistair call an ambulance when he allegedly discovered Bon's lifeless body? Instead Bon was apparently taken to the hospital in an important piece of evidence: the car in which he reportedly died. When Alistair got to the hospital in Denmark Hill, Camberwell, a 10-minute drive, he says he gave Silver's name as a contact and left in the same car.[68] It might suggest he didn't want ambulance officers or police examining Bon's corpse where it lay in situ.

The hospital called Silver but didn't tell her that Bon, who'd already been identified, was dead; only that his condition was serious.[69] Silver and Joe Fury allegedly went to the hospital together, but if Chapman's version of events is to be believed, Joe already knew Bon was dead over 12 hours earlier.

When I spoke to Joe, even more confoundingly he told me at one point he and Silver "found out Bon was dead . . . late that afternoon, I imagine late that afternoon, because I can remember going to the hospital of the night, the evening or something."

But later he contradicted himself by saying they'd got a phone call from Alistair and "he said, 'They've taken [Bon] to hospital. I think he *could* be dead.' We then went straight to the hospital. At the hospital we were informed that he was in fact dead."

So, if Alistair hadn't taken Bon to the hospital, then who? Ambulance officers? Joe believed Alistair had called Silver after "he'd found in him in the car, rang an ambulance, did all that sort of stuff."

Unfortunately all ambulance clinical records are destroyed after a minimum of 10 years. The London Ambulance Service confirmed as much: "We do not have records from 1980." If there was any documentation, it no longer exists.

Hospital records also proved impossible to obtain. I made a Freedom of Information request to King's College Hospital regarding Bon's medical files and was informed that because I was neither a member of his family nor had a claim arising out of his death, I could not obtain access: "Our duty of confidentiality still continues after a patient's death. The Health Records Act 1990 provides certain individuals with a right of access to a deceased individual's notes."

I kept pestering them. The hospital tried to help me but couldn't locate anything.

"Unfortunately I can find no trace of Mr. Ronald Belford Scott on our database with the information provided . . . the Department of Health guidance requires Trusts to retain records for eight years following death; therefore we can only assume that any documentation has been confidentially destroyed. Although had there been any records remaining we would still be unable to release any information pertaining to a patient to a third party."

Angus Young confirmed that "the hospital wouldn't say anything until the police contacted the parents. We got our manager [Peter Mensch] and tour manager [Ian Jeffery] to go down to the hospital and check out the news . . . as soon as we found out, we were terribly upset."

Said Mensch: "I get a phone call that Bon Scott has died and I have to come and identify the body. I say to the rest of AC/DC, 'Couldn't you guys go?' And they go, 'No, you should go, you're the manager.' So I went and there he was, *death by misadventure*. That was the first time I heard that classic British phrase for dying by drinking yourself to death."[70]

$$\text{\textit{\textbf{\Lightning}}}$$

It has since been speculated that Bon choked on his own vomit, but I can neither confirm nor deny this, and his death certificate says nothing about it. There was no vomit in the car and contrary to other reports I've read, he was not wrapped around the gearstick when I found him. I made a statement to the police at the hospital, and later spoke to the *Evening Standard*, relating everything I knew at the time.

Alistair not being able to confirm or deny whether Bon vomited is strange. He either did or he didn't, in his mouth or outside of it. He'd know if Bon had puked, even if there was no vomit in the *car* (as opposed to on himself). A simple examination of his mouth would have settled it; something a person might typically do if they found a friend "not breathing."

Joe Fury told me he was informed at the time that Bon had vomited: "The fact is that Bon, I gather from what I heard, this is the information I heard, died because he choked or something on his own vomit in the car."

So why would Alistair be reluctant to admit Bon vomited unless he thought it pointed to drugs?

The *Evening Standard*'s reporter was John Stevens, who quotes a "distraught" Alistair meeting up with Bon to go to Camden "but he was pretty drunk when I picked him up. When we got there, he was drinking four whiskies straight in a glass at a time. I just could not move him so I covered him with a blanket and left him a note to tell him how to get up to my flat in case he woke up. I went to sleep then and it was later in the evening when I went out to the car and I knew something was wrong, immediately."

Angus's view was that Bon "more or less, you know, asphyxiated." Malcolm Young thought Bon "choked through the night, the position he was sleeping in, you know." Bon's successor, Brian Johnson, toed the Young family line: "The truth of the matter was that Bon died because he vomited when his neck was twisted and he choked. Had somebody been there in the car with him then it might have been a different story. It's the kind of freak accident that happens to people every day but because he was a star the story becomes inflated."[71]

Bon's family believed no one was at fault.

Said Graeme Scott: "It wasn't Alistair's fault. He just took Ron [sic] out for a few drinks in a Kings Cross bar. It was just an accident. He fell asleep and put his head on the wrong angle. It happens to people all the time. He always drank from the time he was 15. It was nothing unusual."

Derek Scott agreed: "On the night he died he'd been writing song lyrics all day and he'd gotten bored, and when his mate rang up and said, 'Why don't we go out for a beer?' Bon was up for it, just to have a break."

Yet Silver said Bon wasn't that close to his family and had very little in common with his two brothers.

"Bon didn't talk about Derek a lot. I don't think they were close but I don't think there was a problem either. I think they probably just were very different from very early on in life. He talked of him in a positive way but I never got the impression they really were close or anything; just very different. I think Derek got married young as well and had children pretty much straight away.

"Graeme wasn't into music. He didn't read. Well, he read a little bit. He wasn't interested in literature. He wasn't interested in *anything*. He was probably one of the most boring people I've ever met in my life. In Bangkok, he just stayed in his room. He didn't even eat Asian food. He'd been living there for a few years at that point. And back then it was very difficult to get Western food. He only ate meat and potatoes. That was it. His room didn't have any pictures up or anything. It was just very bland. I didn't particularly like Graeme. I found him to be a really difficult person. I didn't like his attitude to Bon, his lack of respect. He didn't get on well in London; he didn't understand how things worked there."

As I had with King's College Hospital, I made a Freedom of Information Request to the Metropolitan Police Service to access files on Bon and was informed "searches were conducted at MPS Performance Risk & Assurance (Records Management)" but "failed to locate any information relevant to your request; therefore, the information you have requested is not held by the MPS.

"Despite reasonable searches no information has been located for this matter over 35 years ago and that in line with MPS retention procedures, records are reviewed after a period of seven years and either retained or destroyed. There appears to be nothing in wider records to indicate that there was anything suspicious or criminal about Mr. Scott's death."

Pattee Bishop, for one, isn't convinced. She says there are too many inconsistencies and jarring details in the accepted, AC/DC-approved explanation for how Bon died.

"The many calls back and forth to Silver, the note in the car, the blanket, the vomit, the whole thing . . . I think Silver knew almost everything that was going on with Bon that night; that guy [Alistair] was her friend. She said Alistair wasn't a big drinker. She told him to leave Bon in the car with a note. My *God*, who does that unless it was more than drinking? Silver was a mess herself, with that heroin stuff. Why not take him to the hospital?

"I've seen Bon out of it, but never to the point where I didn't know if he was okay. I'm sure because he was hanging with Silver, that's why he ODed. He wasn't used to it. I bet that happened when he died. I was 25 when Bon died. Blew me away. So how from 1977 to '79 did he become a junkie and Malcolm let that go on? That's what I mean with Silver. His life ended because of her in some form."

Are you saying you think Bon died because of her?

"I really think so."

It's a harsh assessment, one I personally don't share, but typical of many AC/DC fans who have cast Silver as Bon's destroyer or, as she put it herself before her own death, "the dreaded dark queen."

Roy Allen, his drinking partner, agrees there might be more to the story: "I just can't believe someone left him out in the car like that. And although the [death certificate] says he died of alcohol poisoning I ain't buying that all the way. I think because Bon could drink so much and had such a tolerance, it would have taken a hell of a lot of alcohol to kill him, but he and I were drinking a hell of a lot back then. I don't see any way that Bon could have died from alcohol poisoning. It wasn't just alcohol, I can just about guarantee that."

⚡

One person who saw Bon's corpse, Ian Jeffery, was, according to Walker, "struck by the fact Bon's neck was twisted, and showed bruising . . . it was accepted then — with an autopsy yet to be performed — that Bon had choked on his own vomit."

This is possibly an important clue. How to explain the bruising Jeffery allegedly saw on Bon's neck? The bruising cannot be explained by choking, unless Bon was trying desperately not to suffocate and grabbing his own neck to try to clear a constricted airway. Roy Allen came very close himself to choking on his own vomit. He thinks it's important to understand how easily it can happen and it could have happened to Bon.

"I felt this burning battery acid in my throat. It felt like I could not breathe; like I was about to go out from lack of oxygen, so I took a big gasp of air. This all happened in what felt like a split second and the next thing I knew I have this battery acid–like substance in my lungs and they were on *fire*. I was trying desperately to cough it out and get air as I jumped out of bed to get water, only to stumble back down. I was gasping loudly through my restricted throat and finally, after a few long minutes, things got to where I could breathe a little.

"Not something I got over quickly. It was horrible and it scared the shit out of me because it felt like a little too close of a call. I remember feeling I was really lucky and it felt like I had survived something. If I had not woken up at that moment to breathe, all of that would have happened while I was still passed out or unconscious from lack of air. I figure something similar happened to Bon. Did he wake up and it was too late or did he just stay [passed] out and drown in stomach acid?"

The way Roy, an alcoholic who'd been to the brink, could describe such an event so vividly it seems very possible that Bon had died in a similar fashion. What it doesn't explain is what caused him to vomit. Further, had Bon been startled into consciousness from choking, enough to desperately clutch at his own mouth or throat, he surely would have had the presence of mind to open a door from inside the car to try to get help. That didn't happen.

What is more plausible is that the bruising was caused by mouth-to-mouth resuscitation, which in forensic pathology parlance is a category of "damage." According to the forensic science manual *Knight's Forensic Pathology*, "bruising of the face and neck, finger marks and nail marks on the face and neck, and damage to the lips and inner gums" are markers of "mouth-to-mouth resuscitation, when the face and neck have been gripped by hands." In that case, if there were neck bruising and twisting it would suggest Alistair or someone else — possibly Zena — attempted to resuscitate Bon and later move him, which might support the notion he was already dead when he got to Alistair's flat in East Dulwich. Alternatively, he was found the next day, his neck already twisted, and resuscitation was attempted then — only to fail. Bon had sustained a neck injury from his 1974 motorcycle accident. Injury to neck muscles can cause twisting or locking (torticollis) during sleep.

"No way could you miss Bon in the front seat, *dead*," says Pattee. "I think this guy [Alistair] knew he was dead and didn't know what to do, so left him there until he had to do *something*. It was like, all hush hush. Nothing makes sense."

Could that explain why no one — not *one* person — saw Bon in the car the next day until Alistair left his flat to check on him? Could Bon have been *under* a blanket? There were press reports, unsubstantiated, that Bon's body "was still wrapped in the blanket" when it was found. Or was he dead inside Alistair's apartment for the better part of 19 February? Deliberately leaving a body for over half a day in a car on a busy street would be awfully risky.

"It's all a bunch of crap," alleges Pattee. "I think he didn't need to die. I helped Bon walk drunk; I could handle him. Something happened. He died or needed help and [whoever was with him] panicked. To be stuck with a dead Bon would have been hell."

And hell it was, even after his death had been reported in the media.

"To be honest both [Alistair and I] really just hid from the press at the time, because it was just too difficult," admitted Silver. "Some press can be pretty intrusive at a time like that."

Or they're just doing what they're paid to do: try to uncover the truth.

⚡

The next day Silver came around to see me. She told me for the first time that Bon had been receiving treatment for liver damage, but had missed several doctor's appointments. I wish that I had known this at the time. I truly regret Bon's death. Hindsight being 20/20, I would've driven him to the hospital when he first passed out, but in those days of excess, unconsciousness was commonplace and seemed no cause for real alarm.

Silver said of Alistair's statement: "I don't recall ever saying that Bon had liver damage, but I presumed he would have."[72] And if unconsciousness were "no cause for real alarm," why did Alistair ring Silver not once but *twice* in the early hours of 19 February? It just doesn't make any sense. What's more troubling than all these holes in Alistair's testimony is that in 1981 he was directly quoted in a Liechtenstein publication, *AC/DC: Aktuelle Dokumentation Nr. 5*, contradicting almost everything he said in his statement to Maggie Montalbano. The article's byline is Tenner & Co, Berlin. Its veracity cannot be vouched for, but its content is intriguing.

Paraphrasing from the original German, it puts Alistair's arrival at The Music Machine at 1:30 a.m. and says he and Bon were there for two hours, during which time Bon was talking to some girls at the bar and cracking jokes. He had drunk half a bottle of bourbon before arriving at the club. Alistair put a legless Bon in his car at 3:45 a.m. No mention is made in the 1981 story of going back to Bon's flat and Alistair locking himself out. Alistair and Bon got to East Dulwich at 4 a.m.: in just 15 minutes.

There is no mention either of Leslie Loads going down to the car and not seeing Bon. In fact, Alistair says he woke up in the "afternoon," looked out the window and saw Bon was still where he'd left him. It's a very interesting detail because it raises the question of why Loads — whoever that may be, if Loads even existed at all — would be needed to go down to check if Bon was in the car if Alistair could see the vehicle from his bedroom window. It was only a short distance, the front of the building being very close to the street and a side driveway leading to a stable yard.

When Alistair went out to his car, he found Bon in the back seat, not the front passenger seat, his head was bent over the back seat and there was vomit everywhere. He was dead and Alistair was later informed (by unknown authorities) that Bon had died eight hours before his discovery, which would place Bon's death at around 11 a.m. that morning. In the same story, Alistair says Bon died from "death by suffocation" and his liver was ravaged from alcohol consumption.

Angus Young, however, was prepared to give Alistair the benefit of the doubt over his actions on that dark day: "I suppose he would feel worse about it, but possibly he thought he was doing the right thing at the time 'cause he'd been out with Bon a few times and Bon had done the same thing before."

Similarly, Joe absolves Alistair of blame but alludes to something other than alcohol being possibly involved: "Alistair wasn't the guy's keeper. Bon hammered himself obviously one way or the other, whether he got into some dope that night or whatever. He'd drink or take or whatever himself into a situation where other people would have to carry him home . . . Bon gave up what he had. No one took it off him."

Joe even raises Bon's "long run" on the road in North America as a possible factor in his demise.

"He may well have not quite been the same person he was before he left. I don't know how hard that run was in the States, whether it took its toll on him, whether he started to be a more heavy drug user than just a drinker. You might have evidence to say, 'Well, yeah he did,' and I would understand that. Maybe that happened . . . [but] if he took drugs or he drank or whatever, it was a part of trying to fire himself up so his performance would be as he knew everybody expected."

Bon had been putting on a show for everyone, right to the end.

⚡

It has been implied that I mysteriously "disappeared," but in fact I have been living on the Costa del Sol for 22 years, still working as a musician, and am in touch with most of my old friends in England and in other parts of the world, so I am not hiding from anyone.

PART FIVE
AFTERMATH

CHAPTER 33

ROCKER

On Wednesday, 20 February 1980, Scotland Yard issued a statement saying there "were no suspicious circumstances" in Bon's death, which, given he'd only died the day before, was rather hasty and presumptuous. How thorough could the police investigation have been? Far from being a cold case, Bon's death was never much of a case at all.

An unknown bobby quoted in one newspaper story said, "Scott was taken to hospital at about 7:45 last night. We do not suspect foul play but we are waiting for a post-mortem examination." The next day, Thursday, 21 February, the results were announced. By Friday the 22nd, the inquest was underway, with Alistair Kinnear in attendance before the faintly Rumpolish figure of Sir Montague Bernard "Monty" Levine, assistant deputy coroner at Southwark. From the discovery of Bon's body to the conclusion of Levine's inquest, it was all dealt with and wrapped up in less than 72 hours.

Why so quickly? There are a number of possible reasons, which can only be speculated upon, but one important point

missed in virtually everything ever written about Bon's death —
apart from the notable exceptions of Paul Stenning's and Mick
Wall's biographies of the band — is that the standard of autopsies in
England is not uniformly excellent and, as a national inquiry found,
the "level of diagnostic accuracy" is only required to be "probably
true" not "accurate beyond reasonable doubt." Additionally, toxicology tests are prohibitive because they're expensive and time consuming, so not every case of a drug overdose actually has toxicology
tests ordered by the coroner. It appears Bon's death was one of them.

Grahame Harrison says a toxicology report would have
"stunned the doctors a bit," had one been taken.

"'How did he manage to take *that that that that that that
that*, smoke *that*, snort *that*, inject *that*, all in the space of 12
hours? Was this guy a fucking Superman or something? How'd he
survive that?' And I'd also say because of his enormous alcohol
and drug habit over the years, I wouldn't be surprised if parts of
Bon's internal anatomy were wearing out as well. Fuck, his liver
must have been a mess. Who knows what state his lungs were in,
because he smoked [pot] like a chimney."

Procedurally, inquests are held, among many other reasons,
when "the cause of death remains unknown" and have the remit
to determine "how, when and where the death occurred." They
are not permitted to make determinations of criminal or civil liability. Once the inquest is over and the coroner is satisfied that the
cause of death has been established, he or she notifies the registrar of deaths, who issues a death certificate. There is nothing to
stop an inquiry dragging on over months to collect the necessary
information on how someone died, but in Bon's case it was dealt
with quickly, and without any fuss, even when it should have been
obvious there was more involved than simple "acute alcoholic
[sic] poisoning" and "death by misadventure."

The pathologist investigating Bon's death was the late Dr. Arthur
Keith Mant, best known for heading up the special medical section of the British Army war crimes group investigating Nazi war-
time atrocities. According to his obituary in the *Guardian*, he was
an honorary senior lecturer in forensic medicine at two medical

schools in London, including King's College Hospital. So he was well credentialled for the task he'd been entrusted with by Levine.

Forensic science in 1980 was advanced enough to be capable of finding traces of drugs in a corpse. Drugs and poisons could be detected in low concentrations. But how hard did Mant really *look* for them? There was no autopsy report publicly released, only a death certificate. There was no toxicology report or one ever made available. A proper toxicology report would have taken days, weeks, even months. There was no histopathology report (microscopic examination of samples of removed organs and whole tissues). Were comprehensive blood and urine tests for drugs conducted? Was it a basic autopsy (involving an internal and external examination of the body) rather than the more thorough forensic autopsy undertaken when investigating a suspicious death? What biographical background on Bon was given to Mant other than the fact he was a rock 'n' roller and a prodigious drinker? Who provided the information? Was Bon's history with cocaine, Quaaludes and heroin mentioned at all? Did Mant inspect the location — Alistair's car — where Bon's body was found?

Vince Lovegrove claimed in a 2006 piece for the *West Australian* that a blood test had been taken: "According to the coroner's report, there were no traces of drug substances in his blood stream." However, he did not provide evidence for this and, in any case, only a toxicology report would be able to determine the presence of a variety of drugs.[73] Blood tests are at the discretion of the pathologist.

But if true, there is a very good chance the test simply didn't catch what it should have. As Paul Stenning rightly pointed out in *Two Sides to Every Glory*, "If an excessive amount of alcohol were found in the bloodstream of a victim, it was then customary to presume that that was the cause of death, rather than looking for other 'clues.'"

Heroin can also be undetectable in the blood from about six to 12 hours since last use. Twelve hours was roughly the time that elapsed from when Bon was left in the car to when he was taken dead to the hospital, which to suspicious minds might appear awfully convenient but could be a complete coincidence.

In his book *Michael Hutchence: A Tragic Rock 'N' Roll Story — A Definitive Biography*, Lovegrove questioned an Australian coroner's findings in the death of the INXS frontman: it was ruled suicide. Lovegrove believed autoerotic asphyxia might have contributed to Hutchence's death. He stated publicly in 1999: "There are many questions about the death and the coroner's report that have remained unanswered. Why wasn't the autopsy report made public?" Why not then the same scepticism from Lovegrove about the far more mysterious death of his mate, Bon? Why didn't he call for Bon's autopsy to be made public?[74]

Were any tests done on the synergistic reactions of combining substances? In Bon's case, this could have involved alcohol with cocaine, Quaaludes and heroin, or any combination of those things. Standard autopsies involve physical inspection of things that can be *seen*, such as organs. Bon's autopsy had shown "the singer's liver, kidneys and general health had been excellent considering his reputation for going over the top" and "the equivalent of half a bottle of whisky" was found in his stomach. All of these comments relate to Bon's internal organs, suggesting the autopsy was rudimentary rather than exhaustive.

But what tests were done on the things that can't be seen? Heroin is metabolised fast into 6-monoacetylmorphine (6-MAM), then morphine. Tests on blood, saliva, hair, liver, urine and bile can detect morphine. Was there a nasal swab and was it analysed?

Isn't it slightly odd that there was no officially released calculation of Bon's blood alcohol level? Led Zeppelin drummer John Bonham died from 40 vodka shots later the same year, but he consumed that alcohol over 12 hours. Country musician Keith Whitley died aged 34 in 1989 with a fatal blood alcohol reading of .477: the equivalent of 20 whisky shots. Amy Winehouse clocked .416, also a "death by misadventure." According to Alistair's account, Bon drank seven double whiskies (roughly half a bottle of whisky) at The Music Machine, which advertised "Live Groups, Food, Bars, Dancing 8 p.m. – 2 a.m." on its ticket stubs in 1980, so it's safe to assume that he left the club sometime between 1 a.m. and 2 a.m., possibly as late as 3 a.m. It was hardly enough alcohol to put him in the ground, even if he had been drinking at home in Victoria prior to Alistair picking him up.

For too long, Mant's seemingly cursory examination of Bon's cadaver has been treated as the last word on the matter. But an autopsy is only one part of the process.

As American forensic pathologist Judy Melinek, M.D., argued in a story for *Forensic* magazine: "The autopsy pathologist can only tell so much from a dead body. Trying to figure out the cause of death from a dead body alone without knowing anything about the scene, circumstances, or medical history of the decedent would be like a surgeon coming in to perform surgery on an unconscious patient without the benefit of a physical exam, medical records or X-rays."

The coroner, Sir Montague Levine, would have had no eyewitness testimony whatsoever other than Alistair Kinnear's, which told only his side of the story. It was a flawed process.

⚡

There are conflicting accounts of what transpired at the inquest. Sir Montague Levine unhelpfully declared at its conclusion, "Scott was a man of considerable talent who was the captain of his own destiny."

Silver, however, defended him: "[Levine] was a decent guy, very sympathetic and gentle with poor Alistair."

But like all records pertaining to Bon's death, the inquest papers seem to have been expunged from the face of the earth. After a formal request to obtain the papers was made on my behalf by the Inner South London Coroner's Court to the London Metropolitan Archives, I was informed that "Mr. Scott's file was not kept after their recent review."

"He died of what is called 'misadventure,'" said Angus Young, clearly ignorant of the fact that the term is used to describe the manner of death (in Bon's case, an accident arising from a wilful action) rather than the cause. "He didn't die of alcoholic [sic] poisoning. The coroner said that Bon's kidney was in good condition and so was his liver. He was a perfectly healthy guy."

Ian Jeffery held the same view: "If Bon had been seeing a doctor, I would have known about it, and I never saw any notes, any prescriptions, never took him to any appointments."

Silver claimed that Levine "questioned the medical guy [Mant] giving evidence who said the poisoning had caused major organ failure leading to death. So the cause of death would have been listed as 'acute alcohol poisoning.'" She thought it was Mant who said Bon's organs were "like a 60-year-old's."[75]

"Joe and I met Alistair [at the inquest]. I can't remember if [Alistair's father] Dr. [Angus] Kinnear was there or not and whether he gave evidence. It's probable. The coroner also said some kind remarks about Bon as well in his closing. There weren't a lot of press there, they had lost interest, so we weren't bothered by anyone."

Phil Carson, who'd flown in from New York, went to King's College Hospital himself and has a "vague memory of speaking to someone who said a lot of people died the same night the same way, across the world: they drink too much, their head is in the wrong place, they throw up and they can't evacuate the vomit. And that's how people die. I remember him telling me that. I think it must have been a doctor."

Silver even proposed Bon was a kind of innocent when it came to narcotics: "Bon sort of pushed the physical bounds beyond anything most of us had ever come across when it came to alcohol and people were very loath to give him drugs, although drugs were very rife at that time, for that reason."

Again, this is demonstrably untrue. Carson had a copy of Bon's autopsy report but threw out most of his papers after they were damaged in Hurricane Sandy in 2012.

"I don't even know why I had the autopsy report. I just know it was sitting gathering dust on a shelf in my office for years."

Do you remember anything of what was in it? Was there any mention of drugs?

"I don't recall seeing anything about drugs in there."

The report, he says, only contained reference to "an overdose of alcohol and Bon threw up. That's all I know."

How do you think Bon died?

"As per the coroner's report. I was told [Alistair and Bon] didn't have enough money for a curry."

A *curry*? Carson explains he was told Alistair and Bon had been drinking at several establishments, not just The Music Machine, and stopped by Alistair's, where Alistair went inside to get money and fell asleep or passed out, unintentionally leaving Bon in the car.

"That's what I was told had happened. I could have heard that from Peter Mensch or Ian Jeffery."

Paul Chapman is sceptical: "I never heard that before. Why would he go all the way down there [to East Dulwich] for *that*?"

However, in one respect Carson's story does tally with what Clive Edwards of Wild Horses and Herman Rarebell of Scorpions heard on the grapevine: that Bon was *accidentally* left out in the car. Where their stories differ from Carson's is that they heard other people were also at Alistair's flat. But if Carson is right, Chapman's theory about people "nodding out" upstairs at 67 Overhill Road is very shrewd. Certainly no one was going outside to hand Bon a blanket if they nipped inside to get money for a curry or snort heroin or whatever else they were doing and passed out.

Alistair, who was "cleared of any wrongdoing," testified at the inquest that Bon had been drinking before he was picked up in Victoria and consumed seven double whiskies at The Music Machine. He said he and Bon left the club at 3 a.m. (not 1 a.m., as he told Maggie Montalbano) and made no mention of the phantom "Leslie Loads."

The *Guardian* reported: "Mr. Kennear [sic] said that when he woke up at about 5 p.m. the next day, he went to the car. 'When I got to it Bon was still there.' He thought he was dead and drove to King's College Hospital where Mr. Scott was pronounced dead on arrival."

Now it's *5 p.m.*? Not 7:30, as he told Maggie Montalbano in 2005? Alistair's timekeeping is all over the place. His account of that day can only be treated as highly unreliable.

In 2016, Joe Fury was still confused when he recalled for me the moment Alistair discovered Bon's body: "Obviously he'd got up in the morning . . . he probably got up at lunchtime and realised that, you know, Bon was still in the car. He had a big night out. He wouldn't have been up bright and early checking the car. So it may have been . . . I imagine it was sort of late that afternoon, it was early that evening."

As for AC/DC's view of how their lead singer died, Peter Mensch "told the court that Scott, who joined the band in Australia after being their roadie, drank a lot before and after gigs 'but he was always able to perform' . . . members of the band can only recall Scott missing one gig with them — when he inadvertently got off an aeroplane at the wrong city."

Bon's own coronial inquest shouldn't have been treated as just another chance for the band to tell a funny story. Mensch singularly failed to mention what Ross Halfin alleged to me: that Mensch blamed Pete Way for giving Bon drugs. In fact, Way, Paul Chapman and the rest of UFO weren't mentioned at all. Yet in later years various insinuations were made by members of AC/DC itself of more being involved in Bon's death than simple alcohol poisoning.

"We weren't there but we knew exactly what went on there," was one reported quote from Malcolm Young. "We still haven't told what we know because it's more of a personal thing for Bon . . . Bon was really low and Bon was a big drinker, so that night he went a little bit further. But he didn't drink himself to death; that was for sure. He had too much to live for."

It was a collective dereliction of duty of care to Bon. If AC/DC and its then manager, Mensch, had been able to give Levine's inquest a full history of Bon's drug taking at the time, the course of the inquest might have changed completely. It was a chance to help Levine and it wasn't taken. But it's far preferable for an ambitious band and its equally ambitious manager to ride the legend of a lead singer who loved to drink Jack Daniel's than it is to admit that he used smack.[76]

CHAPTER 34

AIN'T NO FUN (WAITING 'ROUND TO BE A MILLIONAIRE)

Bon's death reverberated around the world but it was anything but headline news.

"Scots-born rock singer Bon Scott, of the AC-DC rock band, drank himself to death, a coroner said yesterday at Southwark," wrote the *Glasgow Herald*. "An inquest heard that 33-year-old Scott, of Ashley Court, Westminster, was found dead in a car in East Dulwich, London. A verdict of death by misadventure was recorded." The *Daily Mail*, under the heading "Killer Spree," said he'd died "in a friend's car after a late-night drinking spree." The *Montreal Gazette* reported "Don Scott [sic] was found dead." The *Australian* put Bon's age at 35 and said "in the six years since they were formed, [AC/DC] have revelled in and promoted an image as marathon drinkers, love-'em-and-leave-'em woman-isers, and performers who flirt with danger and the law at every turn." Bon's death was "a typical scene, simply part of Scott's lifestyle."

Nothing suspicious here, move along.

In England, the *Times* didn't print the band's name, referring to Bon as "a rock singer" who had "died from acute alcoholic [sic] poisoning after consuming a large quantity of alcohol." *New Musical Express* said "his death comes at a time when AC/DC have reached a peak of popularity in this country, where their name is paid silent embroidered tribute on the back of countless denim jackets." The BBC quoted an unnamed woman: "[AC/DC] were in pre-production in London at the time for their forthcoming Atlantic album so things have been put on hold for a while; everybody's really shocked. The band will continue, there's no doubt about that."

Smash Hits, whose teenage readers were hardly AC/DC's core market, was moved enough to write something more meaningful: "Although we could hardly pretend that 'Smash Hits' has ever been particularly enthusiastic about AC/DC, it's impossible to deny that they were enormously popular and, more important, never forgot their British fans when they were doing extremely well in America. They toured constantly and gave pleasure to a lot of people, and it's unlikely that even a tragedy like this will mean the end of the band."

Back in Australia, Sydney radio station 2SM reported that Bon's parents "learned of their son's death late this afternoon. AC/DC members have been called together by recording company officials to discuss the future of the group. Just repeating, Bon Scott, lead singer of AC/DC, has been found dead in London."

Malcolm Young delivered the information to Chick and Isa: "Someone had to tell them, you know. It [was] better coming from one of the band than from a newspaper. The most difficult thing I've ever had to do; God knows how they felt. I hope I never have to do anything like that again."

Yet Australia's *Rolling Stone* was informed differently in 1980 — "Bon's parents first heard of their son's death on the radio" — and Isa herself had a different story. She'd celebrated her 61st birthday the day before Bon died.

"I can remember like it was yesterday when I heard Ron had died," she said in 2006. "I'd just come in from the bowling club, and the phone was ringing. So I ran for the phone, and I said, 'Ron?' But it was Angus Young. I'll never forget that day. I thought

I was talking to Ron. Angus just told me right out, 'Ron has died.' I couldn't talk so I handed the phone to my husband. Angus has since told me it was the worst day of his life, too. It was all over the radio, and the police came, and you just didn't get a chance to come to your senses."

A reporter from Dublin's *Sunday Independent*, Mark Smith, called Alberts in Sydney. He would recall for a 1994 piece: "I phoned the Australian studio where the band had made their first recordings to break the news and get reaction. It was midnight their time, and a sleepy producer answered the phone. 'Bon Scott's dead,' I told him. From 10,000 miles away came the reply: 'I'm not fucking surprised, mate.'"

Bon's musician friends were processing what had happened.

"I was very shocked when he died," says Herman Rarebell. "I'm so sad about it until this day; he was such a great guy and a great singer, for me the best singer AC/DC ever had, in my opinion . . . Bon is Bon."

Like the unnamed producer at Alberts in Sydney, Ted Nugent vocalist and rhythm guitarist Derek St. Holmes had seen it coming.

"I was not surprised, sad to say. We all did a lot of things back then in excess . . . [Bon] was drinking from the word go, you know. I never saw him [taking drugs], I didn't, but I know he did [drugs] . . . we did a lot of cocaine and a lot of drinking."

Quaaludes?

"Yep, we were doing all that stuff, yeah . . . the rigours of the road. You were trying to come way down from that big high every night and then trying to hide the stress from being away from your home as long as we were."

It was up to six months at a time, sometimes eight. But it was worse, says St. Holmes, for Bon and AC/DC.

"I know it was hard for them because they were completely out of their country all the way over here [in North America]. It took its toll on all of us. But that's what we signed up for when we wanted to be rock 'n' rollers, right? I just thought to myself, 'I can't imagine how they're going to find *anybody* to replace him.' Nothing would have been like Bon at all. And it turns out they never did find anybody that was just like him. Just found a completely different kind of situation. Don't get me wrong, I like the other guy [Brian Johnson], he's great, but it's a totally different thing.

"I think that when Bon was [in AC/DC] it was a real garage-based, sexy, rock 'n' roll band. You could tell they were all from the same street, you know what I mean? There was just a bond there; it just seemed like that was the real deal. Then when he passed, it was devastating. I just thought, 'Boy, how is it going to go forward?' I didn't know how the band was going to go, truly. But I guess it worked out fine for them. They certainly went much more commercial."

Mick Jones agrees: "I think Bon's probably been more of an influence than we even know. His phrasing was great, his expression, he was the real thing. There always was tongue in cheek in their songs. So Australian, the way I've learned to love and appreciate it over the years, but with this tinge of dark humour in there. It's a big attitude, AC/DC. Bon set the stage for what was to come, too. Who knows what would have happened? He's definitely in the top-five rock vocalists in my book, maybe top three."

"Bon took AC/DC to another level and Bon was almost like a god to people," says Pete Way. "He sang the words and lived the words. I think there was so much expectation. And you can't take it away from AC/DC. *Back In Black* was a very, very good album. They were waiting to have their number-one album. It was all there. They'd built their fan base. They'd worked very hard."

Says David Krebs, the man who changed the destiny of AC/DC by putting them on tour with Aerosmith: "Don't get me wrong. Is Angus fabulous? Yes. But Bon Scott was magical on the level of any singer I worked with from Steven Tyler to [Scorpions'] Klaus Meine to [Humble Pie's] Steve Marriott and others. This guy was amazing. There was magic. He had the sexuality in the band. He was the sex symbol. What sexuality did the Young brothers have? *Zero.* Everybody really liked Bon. I don't remember ever hearing a bad word about him and that was my experience with him. But if you want to talk about personality [*laughs*], he had all the personality between the three of them."

The job of embalming Bon was left to the late Desmond C. Henley OBE of funeral directors J.H. Kenyon Ltd, Paddington. He had embalmed Jimi Hendrix, Winston Churchill, Earl Mountbatten, King George VI, Queen Mary and Judy Garland, among others. Bon's casket was loaded onto a plane for Perth, the same one carrying the band and its entourage as passengers. He was cremated on 29 February 1980, a leap year, and a public funeral took place the next day in a chapel at Fremantle Cemetery. It was a Uniting Church service. His ashes were interred in the ground niche of the cemetery's frontage memorial gardens. Silver, Pattee and Holly did not attend.[77]

According to Joe, the Young brothers had prevented Silver from meeting Bon when he was on the road, "banned her from being anywhere near him," and it had caused Bon immense anguish. Unsurprisingly, there was "no contact" at all from the band following Bon's death, and Silver "was cut out totally," including plans for the funeral.

"For them to be so vindictive that even after he died to not acknowledge that there was something there [in her relationship with Bon], I often wondered whether that was the management side of things or those two guys personally. If it personally came from Malcolm and Angus then all I can say is, well, Malcolm's probably feeling it and maybe Angus will feel it soon.

"They justified [the funeral shutout] by saying, 'We took care of his immediate family back home,' or his parents and family back home in Western Australia. But there was no recognition that [Silver] was around with Bon when they were just a little fucking pub band, basically. She wasn't there to be with a famous rock star. She was attractive enough and in the scene enough that if she wanted a particular rock star to be hanging out with, it could have been Ron Wood. It certainly didn't have to be some guy with tattoos screaming and shouting out front of a rock band.

"The way [Bon] kept coming back [to England], keeping in contact with her and visiting her despite maybe having an American girlfriend or a Japanese girlfriend, [the Youngs] had to be aware that she was the major relationship of his life. And then just to not even let her into that whole process of grieving . . . it was obviously deliberate from someone. Somebody said, 'Nope, she's not party to anything,' and that was it.

"I think Bon would have found that pretty fucking cruel. If he was ever going to leave [AC/DC], I think he would have left this time. He probably often felt a bit embarrassed that he didn't tell [the Youngs] to stuff it when they first started laying down decrees for him but he'd always wanted to be the rock star and he was so close [to making it big]. This was obviously going to be the one shot at it. Maybe that torment tore at him a bit too."

The day he was laid to rest, Bon's death notice appeared in *Billboard*. It was manifestly inadequate for a man who'd achieved so much in such a short space of time: "Bon Scott, 30 [sic], singer with the AC-DC rock group, in London Feb. 19. A Scot, he became prominent in 1976. He also was a successful songwriter. An autopsy is scheduled."

Bon's parents placed a more emotive notice in the *West Australian* newspaper.

IN MEMORIAM

SCOTT Ronald (Bon): 19.2.80

*In loving memory of our son, time is quietly passing
but time is everlasting.*

Mum and Dad.

Bon did not leave behind a last will and testament. Despite being effectively excommunicated from his affairs after his death, Silver corresponded with Isa Scott for years.

"His parents were really happy in their own new unit. They didn't want a big house, or money. They were happy and proud of what they'd achieved for their family. I could relate to that . . .

they were good but naive people, Bon's parents. I felt protective of Isa."

She recalled an exchange of letters in 1982.

"Isa was thrilled that Alberts paid for her and Chick to have a week's holiday in Singapore," she said. "That would have cost peanuts from Perth. She was sad that Bon didn't get to make the big money he was expecting. I wrote back explaining the copyright/royalties stuff and that with no will it should go to his family. I told her to get a list of copyright lawyers from the Perth Law Society and get a lawyer straight away and not sign anything sent by Alberts."

⚡

So did heroin kill Bon? Was it Quaaludes? Or was it simply just a lifetime of too much alcohol finally catching up with him? AC/DC would have you believe he died of none of those things. It was just the way his body was positioned in the car: he choked on his own vomit. My view is it was likely a combination of factors, but heroin was involved. This is *not* a new opinion. There have been other writers before me — notably Mark Putterford and Mick Wall — who have pursued the same line of thinking but I believe I have gathered enough new information to now make it irrefutable.[78]

Bon was an alcoholic who used and abused drugs: marijuana, cocaine, Quaaludes, heroin and more. Suggestions he was not an alcoholic have been made and continue being made. Mark Evans: "Bon certainly wasn't an alcoholic." Pete Way: "Bon wasn't an alcoholic. . . . an alcoholic is someone who lets drink interfere with their work. Bon never let alcohol interfere with his work." Angus Young: "He wasn't an alcoholic. He liked a drink but he saw drinking as a pleasure, not a vice."

"I've seen Bon on many occasions drink three bottles of bourbon straight off and he could drink like that constantly," the same Angus told *Sounds* in 1980, a month after Bon's death. This, remember, was the same guy who said Bon wasn't a heavy drinker.

"He was basically healthy; it was just the position he was in in the car that did it. Maybe if he'd been in a bed he would've been okay, but you can't really say 'cause he could just as easily have laid on his back or something and would still have choked. It's a thing that could happen to anyone who drinks a bit or is sick for whatever reason.

"He used to get into a lot of mischief and things when he had a bit of time off . . . but nothing ever *that* serious. I remember he was somewhere one night and the people he was with filled him full of dope and he was really drunk then too. But fortunately they took him straight to hospital and they kept him in for the day and he was alright then."

This has all been disproven. Bon's drinking did get in the way of his work. There was the train wreck of a concert at Warwick, Rhode Island, on 25 August 1978. Many other shows were affected by Bon's drinking. He might have liked a drink, as Angus says, but it didn't preclude him from also depending on it. He wasn't the archetypal drunk in a gutter with a bottle in a brown paper bag — he was a rock star with a backstage bar — but alcoholics come in all shapes, sizes and forms.

There is also strong resistance, so strong it is almost wilful denial, to the fact he was a heroin user. In 1994 Clinton Walker stated, "Scott didn't use heroin." Walker said the same thing in a 2006 piece: "Bon was an alcoholic, not a junkie, and the coroner found only the best part of a bottle of Scotch in his system. Ultimately, it was just that he'd lived too hard for too long that killed him."

This is utterly false.

"No one gave Bon drugs," Silver told Walker. "He could have used any time he wanted, but the thing was, we just wouldn't let him . . . he would have ended up blue on the floor."

It's an eerie statement given what I came to learn about his death from the testimonies of Zena and other people who saw Bon "stoned" from a substance almost certain to be brown heroin at The Music Machine. As much as Quaaludes could have been involved in Bon's death, on the balance of probabilities and given what we now know about the night he died, heroin would have been the cause of an old-fashioned overdose or deadly reaction with alcohol.

The idea that Bon didn't use heroin is wishful thinking. All the people who figure directly or indirectly in the final night and morning of his life were alleged heroin users at the time: Alistair Kinnear, Zena Kakoulli, Peter Perrett, Silver Smith, Joe Fury, Paul Chapman, Pete Way. Bon's friend from Australia, Mick Cocks, was a heroin user. As Chapman said, even another member of AC/DC was buying and using heroin.

London was oversupplied with brown heroin after the Iranian Revolution, and Bon was firmly in the drug-taking scene. He would have to have had Buddhist mind training to resist snorting a line in the kind of company he kept — and Ronnie Roadtest wasn't that sort of person. He wasn't a classic junkie of the needle-in-the-arm variety but he used heroin. It's already well established Bon had possibly two known heroin overdoses from which he survived: the first in 1975, the second in 1976. I believe the third, in 1980, was fatal.[79]

Said Brian Johnson: "[Bon] had a terrible thing happen to him when he passed on. He wasn't a wild, wild, wild man — he was just as wild as the other boys were. He was just unlucky. We've all done stupid, dumb things where we're young, but we got away with it. He didn't. It was just one of them stupid things that shouldn't have happened, and it was accidental and it was stupid."

He used the word "stupid" three times.

CHAPTER 35

HIGH VOLTAGE

Sometime after the discovery of Bon's body, Paul Chapman spoke to Joe Fury again. He's not sure of the time of that second phone call but says it was "within a day" of the first phone call he got from Joe. Bon's expensive newfangled VCR was missing, among other things.[80]

"Joe was complaining about, somehow or other, the flat [having been broken into], the VCR and the TV's gone, and he was going on about Peter Mensch: 'I can't believe I've called [him] and he just came and gutted this place.' Joe said, 'Everything's gone. The flat is empty.'"

Chapman claims Joe also told him about Bon's missing notebooks of lyrics and notes.

"Joe told me that on the phone. That was *definite*. That wasn't a hallucination, right there."

Says Joe today: "As soon as Bon died, AC/DC's machine just sorta shut Silver and anybody else out of it. It was just like the wall went up straight away . . . I remember Mick [Cocks] and I were like, 'Well, whatever happened to all the songs that were sitting in his flat that he was writing?'"

He denies he spoke to Mensch afterwards, as Chapman claims, or indeed anyone in AC/DC. AC/DC's manager, a New Yorker from a middle-class background, rubbed him up the wrong way.

"He would have been the sort of guy who would have gone into Bon's flat if there was anything there. But maybe not . . . I think I earned the disdain of the Young camp because I was fairly outspoken in London at the time, saying, 'Fuck, you know, well if you're going to use these songs, why don't you publish his songbook that he would have written as poems?' But you don't know; you're making claims without any evidence.

"It was Mensch I remember I just really took a dislike to . . . I had a feeling he was pushing Bon around prior to [his death]. I had a feeling that he wasn't showing Bon the respect [he deserved]. I had that feeling that he'd gotten the green light from the Youngs, [that] 'No, he does what you tell him' sort of thing. Pushing Bon down on the chain below the Youngs was inevitable. But then pushing him down below an accountant from fucking *New York*, and saying that that guy could say what he liked to you because basically he had the Youngs at his back, not *your* back, I hate that sort of thing.

"At that level, Bon should have had a paid-for minder . . . a 'percy' assigned to him. Someone to drive him so he never did anything stupid driving, someone to get him to the clubs, someone to have an excuse why they're to leave the club and, if Bon insisted on staying till he drank himself senseless, that person would be the person who physically picked him up, drove him back home and put him to bed. They wouldn't be drinking. They wouldn't be partying with him. That was their *job*. Artists at that level knew that. It was just accepted. The [management] companies would invest in that."

Not in every case, evidently. AC/DC were about to record the most important album of their career. What would any self-respecting band do if your troubled but inordinately gifted singer and lyricist had just died, leaving you without the songs he was writing? What would a normal reaction be? You'd try to find his notebooks.

Pete Way, meanwhile, had spoken to Angus Young, who had revealed something unusual.

"I had a conversation with Angus. I called him the following day [after learning of Bon's death] and I said to him, 'I'm really sorry about Bon.' Which, of course, you would be. And Angus said, '[Adopting Angus's accent] Yeah. It's really hard for me, you know. I've got a load of his stuff in the flat.' So whether or not or why they would take stuff out, I don't know, but I know Angus had some [of Bon's things] . . . unless he was keeping it for him and he was in-between looking for flats, so I don't know."[81]

So you're saying Angus had Bon's things in his flat?

"Yeah, he just said it was harder for him because he'd got some of Bon's stuff in his flat."

When you spoke to Angus did he tell you what those possessions were?

"No, no. It was just casual, really, because obviously I felt pretty bad about [having to call Angus]. It upset me; I was shocked. To be asked [by Paul Chapman] if I had a number for the band made it even worse because I had to sort of think to myself, 'I'll give out the number but I'll give Malcolm's number.' Malcolm behind the scenes was always in charge . . . it could have been like [Bon's stuff was] *moved* into [Angus's] flat. They were making the album, you see? So consequently I guess if you've just moved into a flat from being on the road for a year probably there's always bits and pieces. I know myself from moving, you don't always get everything in the place at the same time, you know."

Bon's family never got the personal effects the band said would be sent to them. Silver said she phoned Mensch and was told, "The flat's all cleared out."

I asked her: Who cleared it out, Ian Jeffery?

"Yeah, that's what I was told."

In fact, some years ago Jeffery admitted to me he still had a collection of Bon's lyrics, rumoured to be 15 songs. I confronted him on their whereabouts and he replied, cryptically: "I think I still have them somewhere." He also said that Bon "would quite often leave stuff at my place." So rather than being stolen after Bon's death, Jeffery was implying the lyrics had been left behind at his flat. That was about as much as Jeffery was prepared to disclose, though in Mick Wall's AC/DC biography he claimed the posthumous cleanout of Bon's apartment was a "quick sweep." He and Jake Berry had gone around "just to put his things in a plastic bag."

Why would Angus have Bon's things in his flat if he'd already moved into his own? If Bon's notebooks weren't returned, was that the action of band members and band employees that have been described as brothers and best friends to Bon?[82]

Again, Joe believes Mensch was behind the alleged "break-in," even if his fingerprints weren't on the door.

"If anybody went to his flat and got anything, Mensch would have been the guy that authorised it. I can't imagine why a guy working at that level would break into [Bon's] flat and do that. It's not the sort of thing you'd do if you're working at that level. Because what are you planning to steal? I could imagine [a roadie might] do it if you were told to 'Go over there and pick up anything that was there and never say that I told you to go and do it and bring it back here.' I could imagine that that would be very much on the cards: get someone further down the ladder to put their fingerprints on the door. But I can't imagine why anybody who was working in a road crew would just go and break into someone's flat after they'd died like that."

The publicity-shy Mensch, who was later sacked by AC/DC, was contacted for this book via his third wife, Louise Mensch, but he chose not to reply or even comment.

Why his famous silence about AC/DC?

Says David Krebs, his former boss: "I think he feels [AC/DC] fucked him; and I agree with him by the way."[83]

Pattee Bishop says Bon kept pictures and magazine articles about himself, along with backstage passes to shows.

"He had all his clippings and articles. Pictures and passes he kept; little stuff from his travels. I would cut them out for him, the ones in the Florida newspapers, and keep them in an envelope until I saw him. Or he took coasters from bars that had the bars' names on them; those cardboard things."

Another item that went missing was lyrics Bon was preparing

to give to his friends in French band Trust, with whom he collab-
orated on the last song he'd ever record, a jam of "Ride On" at
Scorpio Sound, Camden, on 13 February 1980. These were his
English adaptations of songs from Trust's album *Repression*. A
cassette on which Bon had recorded the words also disappeared.[84]

"His then manager Peter Mensch, an asshole, never wanted to
give me the eight songs that Bon Scott translated into English for
me," complained lead singer Bernie Bonvoisin. "I did not even
read them."

CHAPTER 36

IT'S A LONG WAY TO THE TOP (IF YOU WANNA ROCK 'N' ROLL)

It is to Bon's old friend Vince Lovegrove that we owe one of the most revealing and damning newspaper stories about AC/DC. From 2006 in the *West Australian,* it was written to commemorate what would have been Bon's 60th birthday. In it, Lovegrove all but confirmed the widespread rumours that the Bon Scott Estate gets publishing or songwriting royalties from the album he supposedly had nothing to do with: *Back In Black.*[85]

"The [Scott] family share the wealth, including a small share of royalties from *Back In Black*, which comes in the form of half-yearly payments. There are many unanswered questions about the death of Ronald Belford Scott, but they have more to do with his uncredited but royalty-paid contribution to the monumental *Back In Black* album, and the disappearance of his personal belongings after he died, rather than the manner in which he died."

Yet Phil Carson, the only man from Atlantic thanked on *Back In Black*, doesn't back away from his conviction that Brian Johnson wrote the lyrics for the album.

"He wrote all the lyrics," he says. "It's fucking stupid to say anything else."

Are you saying anyone who has theories otherwise is fucking stupid?

"Unless someone can prove otherwise it's inflammatory and I think it's stupid, yes. Because I know Brian is a very good lyric writer. Why would he need Bon Scott's lyrics? Bon Scott was a very interesting and cheeky lyric writer, too, a bit of tongue in cheek . . . I think it is stupid to continue this conspiracy. Anyone who wants to do that should join the Kennedy conspiracy theorists."

Do you have knowledge of who ended up with Bon's notebooks?

"No. It certainly wasn't Brian Johnson. Brian wrote the lyrics. It's absolutely what happened."

Are you aware of the Scott family getting royalties for *Back In Black*?

"I have no knowledge of that whatsoever. I don't see why they would. Never heard that before."

Carson said it himself: Why would they be getting royalties? His defence of Brian might be convincing — and certainly Carson, a friendly, generous, helpful guy, is not a man to be doubted — were it not for the fact that Angus Young put his foot in it. First, he has stated Bon was working on lyrics when he died: "He had this pile of lyrics he'd been kicking about." Second, he actually admitted not once but *twice* that Bon's lyrics appeared on *Back In Black*. In 1991 he did an interview with Paul Elliott of *Kerrang!*:

> ELLIOTT: Who wrote the lyrics on ['Given The Dog A Bone'] and the others on *Back In Black*? Bon, or Brian, or both?
>
> ANGUS: Bon wrote a little of the stuff.

Then in 1998 Elissa Blake of Australian *Rolling Stone* caught him napping.

BLAKE: Have you ever thought about quitting?

ANGUS: The only time was when Bon died. We were in doubt about what to do but we had songs that he had written and wanted to finish the songs. We thought it would be our tribute to Bon and that album became *Back In Black*. We didn't even know if people would even accept it. But it was probably one of our biggest albums and the success of that kept it going. We were on the road with that album for about two years so it was like therapy for the band after Bon's death.

Bizarrely, before and since, Angus went with an altogether different story.

1981: "Some things we can't do, you know, that was strictly Bon's songs, and things."

1996: "No, we were gonna start working on the lyrics with him the next week [after he died]."

1998: "The week he died, we had just worked out the music and he was going to come in and start writing lyrics."

2000: "Bon was just about to come and start working with us writing lyrics just before he died."

2005: "There was nothing [on *Back In Black*] from Bon's notebook."

It's a line the band now doggedly sticks to despite mounting evidence that Bon's lyrics were used. As Ian Jeffery admitted to me, cagily: "Not totally certain about *Back In Black* but I seem to remember a couple of words, lines [of Bon's being on there]. Maybe not."

On *Behind the Music: AC/DC*, a program made with the cooperation of AC/DC, Malcolm Young sets out the official band narrative.

"We said, 'We're just about ready for you [to come in], Bon, you know, so maybe next week some time, you know. And, of course, it never, it *never*, happened . . . he went out just for a drink, [for] relaxation, you know. Maybe to clear the head, you know. And then look forward to getting into his writing, coming up with some ideas, you know. He had it all in front of him.'"

Says VH1's narrator, underlining the point: "Bon would *never* put lyrics to the music Malcolm and Angus had written."

But did the Young family put *music* to the lyrics Bon had written? They had mined Bon's notebook before. In John Tait's *Vanda & Young: Inside Australia's Hit Factory*, a book notable for the rare cooperation of Harry Vanda, the author wrote, "Vanda has always raved about Bon Scott the lyricist . . . Bon had an exercise book where he would jot down ideas as they came to him. George [Young] would go through his book looking for ideas."

Angus also said as much: "George would look through [Bon's] book. One day George spied the line 'a long way to the top if you wanna rock 'n' roll.' It was just sitting there. He hadn't written any lyric for it, just the title."

The Youngs' friend Fifa Riccobono of Alberts told *Classic Rock* in 2015 that Bon had telephoned her in the days before he died.

"He said that he'd just been with Malcolm and Angus, and he'd been listening to some of the things they'd been writing for the new album, some of the riffs. He said, 'Fifa, wait until you hear this, it's going to be brilliant, a fantastic album.' In my mind, he was going in the studio three or four days later."

Isn't it a funny thing for Bon to be saying to an employee of AC/DC's Australian record company when he supposedly had nothing prepared? Surely this prodigious note-taker had some lyrical ideas he was working on, days out from going into the studio? Alberts' documentary *Blood + Thunder* repeated the

Angus-and-Malcolm-did-everything version of events. But this time Riccobono was on camera.

"[Bon] just said, 'This is going to be a big one. Some of their ideas are amazing.'"

Is it sinking in yet? *Their* ideas.

Lest there be any doubt what AC/DC and their record companies want you to think, Brian Johnson told *VH1 Ultimate Albums*: "It made us a little angry later on when people were saying the songs had already been written by Bon, which was ludicrous. Bon hadn't got together with the boys yet. The night he died he was just getting ready to get together with the boys."

But Joe Fury remembers February 1980 very differently: "I was at Bon's flat one night — it wasn't like a big drinking night or anything like that — with Mick Cocks [and Bon]. Mick was trying to break into the music business. And it was a bit like, 'Okay, Bon, you've done it.' That's where I got [it] into my head that Bon was talking about having written or substantially written the next album."

Silver Smith wouldn't have a bar of Riccobono's and AC/DC's stories either. What she told me challenges everything the band has ever said about Bon's preparations for the album.

"I've never sat down and listened to [*Back In Black*] but the night that he died that was why he wanted to go out. He'd *finished*. I'd been around for the writing of a few albums by then so he knew that I knew what his pattern was. He would write *away* from the band. If they were in the studio he'd be up in the kitchen, a couple of floors away or something; pretty much just stay there by himself.

"So the boys wrote the music and Bon would come up with the lyrics and then it would get censored. They'd cut out anything that was too sloppy or too political or too clever because you don't mess with the formula. It makes sense. I mean, you can't blame them for that. So yeah, it would go through the 'censorship run.' I'm presuming he actually hadn't done that because he was at home and had been spending a couple of days at home, writing, so it wasn't the final draft. But yeah, he'd finished all the songs for the album."

That's what Bon said to you?

"Yeah. That's why he wanted to go out. 'I've finally bloody finished it. It's *done*. I've still got to get censored, though.' [The Youngs] got the final [say]. Anything that they didn't understand had to go out; anything that was obviously too clever. Bon liked quirky things.[86] He really liked Steely Dan. [Walter] Becker's and [Donald] Fagen's lyrics. Clever stuff. But I think most people know that [Bon wrote *Back In Black*] now.

"The Youngs and Alberts aren't ever going to comment on it. I have always believed that Bon wrote most if not all of *Back In Black*, because he told me the night he died that it was finished. They may have changed things, of course, because he still had to hand it in for Malcolm's and Angus's editing process."

CHAPTER 37

DIRTY DEEDS DONE DIRT CHEAP

Just as the manner in which Bon died has been covered up too long, so, possibly, has his involvement in the creation of songs on *Back In Black*.

Why would royalties be going to the Bon Scott Estate if he had nothing to do with the lyrics? Charity? It's possible though extremely unlikely, because that historically is not like the Young brothers. They ferociously protect their financial interests. Ask Mark Evans, who had to sue them to get album royalties; Tony Currenti, the drummer on *High Voltage* and '74 *Jailbreak*, who can't even get to meet them to say hello, despite approaching the band multiple times; or Brian Johnson, who after 36 years out front as the band's singer was replaced by Axl Rose on the pretext that he was going deaf. Well before then, there'd been financial disputes between Johnson and the Youngs.

As for Bon, *Back In Black* is by far and away AC/DC's biggest selling album. Why hand over millions to the family estate of a band member who, by Silver's account, wasn't that close to his brothers, was in conflict with Malcolm, and potentially on his way out of the band before he died? Angus and Malcolm have never been that sentimental. Bon was as expendable as any other member of AC/DC who didn't have Young as a surname.

Or did they, as so many people have grounds to suspect, use some of Bon's titles or lyrics after all? There would have been ample motivation behind such a decision: they couldn't afford to risk *Back In Black* being a failure after the breakthrough of *Highway To Hell*. Are regular payments to the Scott family a gesture of goodwill or a means of assuaging guilt? Was a deal done with the estate before the album was released to use Bon's songs but credit Brian?[87] Having Bon credited on the album would certainly have undermined what AC/DC rightly wanted: to have fans accept and embrace their new singer. Did Isa Scott, as Silver urged her to do, engage a copyright lawyer and nut out a deal on royalties with Alberts? Were they threatened with legal action?

One Australian rock journalist surmised: "A few of the *Back In Black* album's tracks had been demoed before Bon's death, though apparently no lyrics were written or vocals were added, with Bon reverting to his original musical forays and playing drums only on the demo tracks. Nevertheless, a percentage of royalties from this mega-selling album continue to this day to go to Bon's family, in recognition of his invaluable contribution to the band."

It's a generous assessment. Joe Fury thinks guilt may have been a factor: "I'm sure Bon, if he'd been around to see the way Silver was treated after he died, would have been fucking pissed as. Just because it was *his* business what he and Silver [wanted to do together]. He contributed to the money that AC/DC made. It was just as much his right to have his share go [to where he wanted]. I didn't know about the family getting [money], what happened there. I wouldn't be surprised if there's a lot of guilt. I know there was a lot of guilt with the way Alberts did some dealings . . . they played pretty hardball."

If there were any doubt what Vince Lovegrove himself thought about the issue, he dispelled it on his personal blog on 12 October 2011 just before his death: "Although Scott did not receive songwriting credits on [*Back In Black*], his older [sic] brother, Derek, told me that the family has always received Scott's songwriting royalties for the album, strongly suggesting that Scott indeed wrote most [of the] lyrics for the album. One listen from devoted AC/DC/Scott fans, along with anecdotal evidence, seems to confirm this."

I'd argue that was the reason for Lovegrove's clear hostility to Brian, which he nakedly displayed in an online interview with AC/DC fan Dr. Volker Janssen in 2001. Brian is known for his likeability and amiability, so Lovegrove's comments were startling for their viciousness.

> JANSSEN: Have you seen AC/DC live with Brian Johnson singing? What did you think?

> LOVEGROVE: I saw and met Brian Johnson singing with AC/DC on their first ever tour after Bon died. I didn't like his singing in the band he was in pre-AC/DC (Geordie, I think), I didn't like his singing in AC/DC, I still don't like his singing, I don't like his lyrics, I don't like him as an entertainer, I don't like him as a person. I disliked him as much as he disliked me. But that was a long time ago. I'm sure he's such a fab guy now.

⚡

Pete Way has his own theory.

"There's some songs that I sort of think, 'That sounds exactly [like] what Bon would have written,'" he says. "But it's anybody's guess, really and truly. I think that Malcolm had quite a lot of influence over the words as well, because I know on certain albums Malcolm would write the words. But I think where Bon was concerned it would be Bon's words because they liked his words and he was an essential part [of the band] . . . Bon could write exactly what [the Youngs] wanted."

"You Shook Me All Night Long" sounds exactly like a song Bon would have written.

"Oh, very much so. I still prefer in many ways some of the lyrics that [were] obviously being written the way Bon would [write them]. Because he had a unique ability to have a tongue-in-cheek way of singing something. You weren't quite sure if he was having a bit of a laugh at the same time. There was never anything menacing. Even with "Highway To Hell"; it's still kind of poking fun."

A lyric like *She told me to come/But I was already there* is very Bon, isn't it?

"Oh, exactly. That's *absolutely* Bon. I've been listening to the words from the [post-Bon] albums. I wouldn't want to say Brian Johnson didn't write that many [songs] but it must have been a new experience to have to write in that style where, you know, it's right-on-the-edge type of writing. Like you said, *She told me to come/But I was already there*. It's tongue in cheek, isn't it? Double entendre. You can read whatever you like into it."

But that's what I always found intriguing about the title of the album itself. If you read the lyrics, "Back In Black" is really about coming into money as opposed to being a memorial song. It's a song about money.[88]

"Well it's quite possible [Bon] did write that like that and it fitted to show respect [to him] on the album; that's very true. I never thought of it like that."

Joe Fury says there's no question that Bon knew before he died that the band had made it and was about to cash in.

"Bon knew before his death that he'd achieved [his goal]. He'd done it . . . there was just that whole feeling that they had moved to that top level. I'm gratified to know that he knew he'd made it. I would have been more devastated if they'd went on and made it afterwards and he never realised how big they'd become. But he already knew they were big . . . he *knew* in himself. I remember having that conversation [with him] that 'We've cracked it. We're there.'"

He had also proved his mettle as a writer. Bon was so good, so adept at editing himself so that his words were distilled to their most potent deliverable form, that, according to Joe, any line from his lyrics "could have [been] turned into another song."

"In that late '70s period you were talking about Peter Gabriel being a songwriter. Jackson Browne was a songwriter. Bruce Springsteen was a songwriter. You never would have thought, even when [AC/DC] became successful, that Bon Scott was a song-writer . . . the way he could turn a phrase in those songs, I can't think of anybody else I've known — and I've met guys like Keith Richards and quite a few so-called stars — who would have the personality to write some of the lines that are in those songs.

"*The body of Venus with arms.* It was a few years before I realised what that line meant. How does a guy like Bon come up with a reference to the statue of Venus [de Milo], which doesn't have any arms [*laughs*]? There's little subtleties in his songs that you just don't associate with the simple image you have of the guy singing the song."

Joe characterises Bon's lyric-writing style as "Aussie larrikinism with sophistication without trying to be pompous . . . it was so Aussie, it was so *us*, so us on the street in Sydney, playing pubs."

It's an excellent description of one band's music that, decades on, still means so much to Australians from all walks of life. I believe it's because they recognise a little bit of their own life sto-ries in Bon's songs. So many of us have gone through, at one time or another, the kinds of challenges or situations he writes about. But Bon's great gift is that the everyday themes of his lyrics tran-scend Australian life and connect with people wherever they are.

David Krebs thinks Brian was credited on *Back In Black* instead of Bon for practical reasons: "I think [AC/DC] may have done that while giving the money to Bon Scott within the same theory of Phil Carson's that [Atlantic Records president] Doug Morris made a mistake by putting out [*Dirty Deeds Done Dirt Cheap*] after [*Back In Black*]; they did not want to have 'Brian Johnson' on an album that was written by Bon Scott. It would have been that simple a decision. That same kind of thinking may be why they gave him the writing credit. They would have seemed much weaker if [*Back In Black*] had said 'Bon Scott' and not 'Brian Johnson.' I was not involved in that decision."

Roy Allen has his own suspicions about *Back In Black*.

"I can't say that I've ever listened to that whole album. I had such hurt feelings associated with all that; I didn't listen to a lot of AC/DC after that. 'You Shook Me All Night Long' just sounds like something Bon would have sung, for sure . . . it's very possible [it's] a song that Bon would have maybe even wrote. Think about it. Put his voice in that song. It's just such a perfect fit. I don't see any way he could not have contributed to that album."

They started recording it less than two months after he died.

"Well, that answers the question right there. Whether the band admits it or not, it is fairly obvious to me that Bon contributed to at least some of the songs on *Back In Black*, especially since it was released so soon after his death. I always had the feeling when I was around those guys that music and friendship came before money. It makes sense to me that since Bon probably contributed to the album that they would respect what would have been coming to him or his family, even if they legally did not have to. They were all very close and I always had the feeling that they knew Bon was who made them what they were; at that time there were no illusions or egos in that regard. Bon *was* AC/DC, with Angus close behind.

"But, since he was gone and they had to move forward, they likely didn't credit him on the album because the band as a business had to attempt to reestablish itself without him. I'm sure it was a very difficult time for the band with many unknowns and fears and they wanted to do the right thing with their friend but still carry on. This is just my opinion but I think there is some truth in it."

Paul Chapman says he recognised Bon's lyrics the moment he heard the album.

"For some reason, I could kind of feel it. UFO was touring the UK when that came out and I got the cassette and put it on in the car. The bell [for the opening track, "Hells Bells"] went. And as soon as they started we all looked at each other and we went, 'They've done it this time.' You knew straight off . . . right from *I'm rolling thunder/Pouring rain/I'm comin' on* . . . that's [Bon's] way of putting two and two together. It suggests [Bon], those lyrics, right there, to me."

One of Chapman's close friends was the late Larry Dankert, who Chapman says worked with AC/DC in North America, "a backline guy, maybe Malcolm's tech."

"[Larry] said, 'Yeah, the fuckers. I knew they'd do it. Sooner or later they had to.' Larry and I were laughing about it. He said, 'It's funny, you know . . . I always knew they'd do it, but it sounds an awful lot like Bon to me.' And I said, 'Yeah, it does.' This whole thing reeks of it to me. Not the whole thing, but the money riffs. The ones that stand out to me . . . the choruses, certain things that stick out."

The first verse and chorus of "You Shook Me All Night Long"?

"Yeah, there's a lot of it that catches me like that too."

"Back In Black" being a song about coming into money rather than a memorial to Bon?

"Even the melody in it."

Do you think Bon is owed some recognition for his work on *Back In Black*, if it can be proven he did contribute lyrics to it?

"I think he already has it in a funny way. I don't think that album would have been as big if Bon hadn't died and Brian hadn't done it."

⚡

So what does Brian himself think of the suggestion Bon was involved in the writing of lyrics on *Back In Black*?

"Bollocks. That's a load of bollocks," he told British rock writer Philip Wilding in 2000. "Someone said to me the other day that Bon's bigger in death than he was in life, which I don't agree with. But legends do grow like years on the age of your birthday and those stories are great to tell to younger lads at the bar. Once I thought that the web would help clear all this shit up, but it's just added to it. I can tell you that Bon hadn't even gone into the studio to even rehearse with the lads; he was getting ready to work on the lyrics when he died."

All this *shit*. Getting *ready* to work on the lyrics. It would help if Brian and the Youngs got their story straight.

CHAPTER 38

ROCK 'N' ROLL SINGER

In March 1980, "Wild Bill" Scott, a DJ who'd been an early supporter of the band on North American FM radio and had backyard parties with Bon and Angus, named former Easybeats frontman Stevie Wright as the new singer of AC/DC.

"He will be the new lead singer for AC/DC," he said on the air for WABX Detroit. "But they will not be able to put out an album until they rework the lyrics that fit Bon Scott's life so well into what kind of meaning 'Little' Stevie Wright can make with them. And so it will be an interesting album, one way or another. I don't know what's going to happen on it. We'll have to wait and hear it."

Both Wild Bill and Stevie are now dead, Wild Bill passing away in 2014 and Stevie in 2015. Stevie told me before he died that the rumours were true: "They asked me to join AC/DC after Bon Scott died." Instead, Brian Johnson was announced as AC/DC's new singer that April.

So the well-known story has it, Bon saw Brian carry Geordie's guitarist Vic Malcolm on his shoulders in England in April 1973. At the time Bon was with Fraternity (then in their death throes and getting around under the name Fang). The location for this seismic rock event has variously been put at Plymouth Guild Hall and Torquay Town Hall late that month but Brian himself said, "I'd met Bon in Hull years before when he'd supported us."

Over the decades since he joined, rock fans have been fed the story that Bon practically gave Brian his blessing, letting the "boys" know if he were to leave this mortal coil he'd be an ideal replacement. As AC/DC engineer Mark Opitz writes in his autobiography: "Bon became a fan of Geordie's lead singer, Brian Johnson, and apparently later told his AC/DC bandmates, 'If I ever die, you should get that guy.'"

Said Brian: "That one day changed my life because he told the boys that he'd never heard anybody sing like me."

It's a story that's never been challenged. It should be. While Bon at least seemed to know who Brian was — Joe Fury told me, "I know Bon liked the guy that replaced him" — the mystery is how well Brian really knew Bon.

Brian told New York's *Village Voice* in 2014 that "I'd met Bon . . . when he was with a different band, and he was supporting Geordie, the band I was in, and we got to know each other then. He was the funniest man and we had a lovely time."

Yet in December 1983 he informed *Circus* otherwise: "I never really knew [Bon] . . . I didn't know it was him . . . I remember the band [Fraternity] but I can't honestly say that I singled him out."

Huh? What's it going to be?[89]

⚡

Buzz Shearman of Moxy, the Canadian band AC/DC had supported on their first four North American shows in Texas in 1977, was asked to audition to replace Bon. His wife, Valerie, was approached by Moxy's Canadian booking agency, Dixon-Propas, to ask Buzz if he was interested.

"The agency called me to see if I could possibly talk to Buzz about considering going to audition for the spot in L.A. for the

Back In Black album, which was written, all the songs were done, he didn't have to worry about anything."

I ask her to clarify. All the lyrics and music were *done*? It backs up what Silver said about Bon's phone call to her on the evening of 18 February 1980.

"Yeah, apparently. When I got the call from the agency they said this album *Back In Black* is already done, it's already been written, everything's finished, all you have to do is go sing the songs. So they were making it sound simple. Like, 'You don't have to worry.'"

Again, so that includes the lyrics?

"Yeah, I believe so." She wavers momentarily, perhaps realising the significance of the question. "Maybe they weren't *quite* finished yet; I don't know the facts of that. But they said the album is pretty well complete — from the information I got back then. And I remember it pretty clear. They're trying to make it sound simple, 'Don't worry about it, you don't have to worry about things, come on in and just do the singing part.'"

If this is accurate, that the album was "pretty well complete," then rumours that Bon had not only written lyrics but recorded vocals for the album may well have some substance.

"I was aware of it," says Moxy guitarist Earl Johnson of AC/DC's interest in his band's lead singer. "Buzz and Bon had a very similar stage presence. I would say Bon was the stronger singer, Buzz was the better frontman. Buzz really worked the stage . . . he had a very intense personality onstage."

But Buzz turned down the offer to audition.

"Bon had only been dead for [a matter of] weeks," says Valerie. "Buzz was still pretty sad about that. He felt kind of eerie . . . it just freaked him out; it gave him an eerie feeling to step into his shoes. I said, 'Well, you could honour him by doing that.' But I was 21 and he kind of said, 'Stay out of it.' And he eventually got me to back off."

The Shearmans were invited by AC/DC to Brian's debut in Toronto.

"Buzz wept the whole concert. With the big bell and the whole bit. And I didn't know if he was crying because 'I should have taken the gig' or it really made it hit home that he missed Bon. He was pretty heartbroken. It was hard for him. People say that he turned down the [singing] position in AC/DC because he was struggling with vocal issues. That wasn't true at all. He never had any vocal issues. That guy could sing like a bird, day in and day out. It had nothing to do with his voice."

Shearman died in 1983, aged 32, in a motorcycle accident. He'd had his own issues with alcohol and had been drinking tequila when he was killed.

"Buzz was coming home not too late, with another motorcycle rider, and they were riding side by side and talking on their motorcycles, going about 60 [miles per hour]. Buzz ran into the back of a transport truck and was killed instantly. Had he taken that [AC/DC] opportunity, things would have been a lot different. He could have been still alive now. It's funny how fate takes you down different roads."

Ain't that the truth.

CHAPTER 39

YOU SHOOK
ME ALL NIGHT
LONG

"You Shook Me All Night Long" is the first song Brian Johnson claims he ever wrote for AC/DC. Prior to joining the Australian band, he'd got shared songwriting credits on only a handful of tracks — none of them radio staples — over three of Geordie's four albums: "Goin' Down" off *Don't Be Fooled By The Name* (1974); "I Cried Today," "She's A Lady," "We're All Right Now" and "Light In My Window" off *Save The World* (1976); and "Going To The City" off *No Good Woman* (1978). Vic Malcolm was the principal songwriter for Geordie. But holed up in a cabin by a beach on the island of New Providence in The Bahamas in April 1980, under pressure to write something, Brian conjured the greatest melody of AC/DC's entire career, straight off the bat.

"I don't believe in spirits and that," he said. "But something happened to me that night in that room. Something passed through us and I felt great about it. I don't give a fuck if people believe me or not, but something washed through me and went, 'It's alright, son, it's alright,' this kind of calm. I'd like to think it was Bon but I can't because I'm too cynical and I don't want people getting carried away. But something happened and I just started writing the song."

It took him just 15 minutes.

"About three, four months [sic] after Bon's death, I'm in The Bahamas. It was nerve-racking. After about three days, [the Youngs] said, 'Brian, have a listen to this and see if you can write lyrics.' They had a very basic riff, and said, 'We were thinking of calling it, 'Shook Me All Night Long.' I sat down that night with this blank piece of paper and within about 15 minutes, I had this song written."

A remarkable achievement given that by Brian's own admission he "really didn't have much to say in the songs . . . Bon's songs were more documentative [sic]. They were very true to life. Mine were just instances of life put together."

Malcolm's "special" friend, Robin Jackson-Fragola, had holidayed in Nassau, the capital of The Bahamas, with Angus's and Bon's former lover Beth Quartiano and Cliff's former lover Maria DeLuise around the time *Back In Black* was recorded. Compass Point, where the band was staying, is only nine miles from Nassau.

"Beth, Maria and I stayed in a house, the second largest house on the island [of Grand Bahama], in Freeport," she remembers. "We island hopped all the time. We would rent scooters and go all about Nassau exploring . . . we had our favourite spot, an old little skiff on the beach right across from Compass Point. Certain people would come out of the studio and enquire why we were choosing to be there instead of inside. Better vibes."

She doesn't accept the band-approved, Brian Johnson–peddled version of how *Back In Black* was written.

"Just listen to the lyrics and think about the song titles. This was not from a man who'd just entered the realm of the band. I know for a fact about the songs on *Back In Black*. We used to joke about why and who it was written about. If [Angus and Malcolm] chose to credit Brian for these songs, so be it. I know better. Bon is gone, Mal is out of sorts right now. I am at a loss for words over this.

"They may have given Brian some of Bon's writings and asked

him to tweak it a bit, who knows? I simply know that Brian did not write them. I don't remember ever meeting the man; maybe I did. I know that for us to discuss the songs before him means that they were already written. If you truly listen to what is said in the [VH1] doco, things were already written before Bon died. Brian talking about how he couldn't come up with anything then — *presto* — a vision from Bon himself.[90] Writings were presented and he had to fit his style into it. Ang and Brian aren't going to retract what has already been said. That leaves the band to end on a real sour note with the fans."

"Bon was never really part of the *band*," argues Joe Fury. "He was never one of the Youngs . . . there was a bit of a [dividing] line between the Youngs and Bon."

It wasn't just age difference.

"I think they were so driven, those guys and their brother [George], that in a lot of ways they saw Bon as a liability to the firm, if you like . . . I could see AC/DC thinking, 'He's going to die halfway through the biggest tour of our life and we're going to be fucked,' the way he lived.

"They were just so driven for success, and Bon was out there [having fun]. But again they obviously appreciated that [Bon's] personality was what that band needed . . . the magic that was coming from those [film] clips, those little looks, and the lyrics . . . Bon gave AC/DC that *light*. That joker in front of this massive battleship slamming into you made it all balanced."

Joe even goes so far as to describe Bon as "a solo act when he was still onstage with them. I know [the Youngs] pressured him and they didn't like anybody having any influence [over him]. They would have liked to have put him in a roadcase at the end of every show and uncased him at the next, literally. He was in probably the most blistering rock 'n' roll band at that time and he wasn't *in* the band."

So what about his rumoured solo album?

"No, I never heard him say anything. I imagine there would have been suggestions like, 'If you don't like it, mate, you can fuck off.' So maybe that might have been put to him on a few occasions."

So aside from Silver's extraordinary claim that Bon told her he'd finished writing lyrics for the entire *Back In Black* album on the very evening he went to The Music Machine with Alistair Kinnear, textual analysis alone of "You Shook Me All Night Long" supports the proposition of his involvement.

We have the clean motor (Bon's love of clean vaginas — for a full explanation, see endnote 21); the sightless eyes ("chartreuse" eyes were perhaps *too* smart for AC/DC's "censorship" committee); a seduction line that took double time (there just happened to be a horse with the same name owned by Bon's girlfriend in Miami); she wouldn't commit, was taking more than her share (of men) and had Bon fighting for air (a possible third reference to Holly X); the Bon-esque double entendre *She told me to come/But I was already there* that Silver Smith said Bon wrote in a letter to a friend of his in 1976; and, most memorably of all, those famous American thighs (which might also have been written as a lyric by Bon as far back as 1976 or could have belonged to either Holly or Bon's other blonde bombshell girlfriend, Pattee Bishop. Both women had the sort of figures that wouldn't have been out of place on the cover of *Sports Illustrated*'s Swimsuit Edition).

All anecdotal, circumstantial and subjective but compelling enough, especially when Brian said himself that Bon, 'more than I ever did, took things from real life. I took things from real life, but then I let my imagination run a little wild. Bon was pretty much — his songs were almost documentary . . . he was living them."[91]

I ask former Van Halen bass player Michael Anthony what he thinks of the suggestion Bon's lyrics were on *Back In Black*. The Brian Johnson–fronted version of AC/DC headlined Van Halen at the Monsters of Rock festival in Donington, England, in 1984.

"*Oh*. Were they? [*Laughs*] It could have been because the lyrical content seems kinda similar, kinda parallel to what Bon would write, you know? I don't know." He smiles. "What do *you* think about that?"

Holly X says she never saw any lyrics but Bon was working on melodies.

"It was more singing: [Bon] humming and singing it. He was very excited about his music. I remember him bouncing around singing the lyrics, humming the music, all of that, so when that song came out, I was like, 'Oh my God, *that's* the song! And somebody else is singing it. How awful is this?' And when I looked [at the album sleeve], it said it was written by the new singer. I was like, 'How could Malcolm do that to him after he died?'"

Brian had never been to the United States. In fact in 1980 he admitted "the closest I got to America was when I was with Geordie. We stopped off in Alaska for a 20-minute refuel, coming back to London from Australia." But since then he has come up with different explanations for how he came up with that memorable line about American thighs.

2000: "Go to Texas. You've got some long legs in this country. God bless America."

2001: "We were in The Bahamas and I had seen a couple of American girls. They were just so beautiful. They were blond, bronzed, tall . . . so I was just using my imagination; what I would do if I could. But Bon had done it all."

2003: "I'd seen them [American women] on the TV. And I'd always wanted to fuck one! They just looked fab. Everything pointed north on them."

2014: "It was as quick as it had to be, which was that night. I guess I had to try to impress somebody . . . it was just a thing that came at the time; I still think it's one of the greatest rock and roll riffs I've ever heard in my life and it was kinda easy . . . the boys had a title. Malcolm and Angus said, 'Hey listen, we've got this song. It's called "Shook Me All Night Long." And that's what we want the song to be called.' And if you listen to the chords on there — it was [*sings*], you know, *You shook me all night long* — it just fell in anyway, so I can't claim anything, credit on that thing. But the rest was just the fill, you know, the verses and stuff. And it all worked out smashing."[92]

Barry Bergman, a committed AC/DC and Young family loyalist who still stays in touch with the band, is unsure whether Bon had a hand in the lyrics for *Back In Black*.

"I don't know," he says. There is a long pause. "He might have been [involved] . . . *might* have been."

So when you were touring around with the band in North America in the late 1970s did you see Bon writing in his notebook?

"I didn't really see any of these guys writing in any notebooks. And I'll tell you why: I think that the stuff was written right in the studio, truthfully. I don't know for a fact but I guess that all these songs were created right on site."

They wouldn't have had much time.

"They were very prolific. Super talented. *Naturals*. They remind me of The Rolling Stones where they would argue and fight with each other and they were the best of friends at the same time. Nothing shocked me [with *Back In Black*]. The magic songs were there. 'You Shook Me All Night Long' was magic. And I never thought that the band was going to go out of business after the death of Bon Scott. It was by fate that Brian was found. If I recall, it came through a fan letter to check him out . . . it all came through a fan letter. That band read fan mail."

Sure. But did they read Bon's notebooks?

CHAPTER 40

LIVE WIRE

The problem with Barry Bergman's theory about the writing of *Back In Black*, as sweet as it is, is that Angus Young, whose mouth has frequently got the band in trouble, admitted in an interview with Allan Handelman in 1983 that AC/DC's songwriting process was a little different.

"We were in Miami [in 1979]. Well, actually it started in Australia . . . [Bon] used to come in [the studio] with, like, poems and things, he used to write. And when me and Malcolm were fooling around with this riff for this [song], he said, 'I think I've got something [that] would fit in there quite nicely, and that was the title "Beating Around The Bush."'"

Even earlier, in 1975, Bon said pretty much the same thing about AC/DC's first Australian LP, *High Voltage*: "That album was recorded in a rush. Angus and Malcolm wrote the music and I dug into my book of poetry [*laughs*] and fitted some words to what they were playing."

Says Pattee Bishop: "The music was ready before Bon went in to do the lyrics. He wrote the lyrics; that was his part. The Youngs had no interest in the writing back then. The songs all had a story to them. Bon thought they were funny, because they all came from a real story."

So we're to believe that Bon changed the habit of years and had nothing doodled on paper, nothing prepared, nothing written down, no titles at *all*, when he was about to start recording *Back In Black*? Where exactly did the Youngs' working title "Shook Me All Night Long" come from? When Brian was asked to audition for the band, the title "Back In Black" was also already in place, as he said himself: "That's all they had; was just a title." But the mere suggestion that any of Bon's words are on *Back In Black* is "complete bollocks," according to Malcolm: "Poor old Brian's had to deal with that one for the past 20 years; it just won't go away."

If that is the case, then why would Angus admit some of Bon's lyrics were on there? These inconsistencies have been around for years, but all most music or celebrity journalists seem to care for is asking Angus where he got the idea for his schoolboy outfit or how AC/DC was named or how many records they've sold and isn't it great they continued on bravely without Bon. These inconsistencies should be noticed. Instead the world laps up the heroic narrative: two grieving brothers and a greenhorn with a Geordie accent and next-to-no experience in lyric writing who against all odds managed to write one of the biggest selling albums of all time in a matter of weeks after the death of the single greatest life-force in the band: Ronald Belford Scott.

Malcolm says Chick Scott told them at Bon's funeral: "You've got to find someone else. Whatever you do, don't stop."

"I know that [Bon] approves of what the new lineup is trying to do," said Brian. "He would have wanted us to build on the spirit he left behind."

Does that spirit include not returning things to his family? It's now well established and cannot be disputed that Bon was working on lyrics *before* he died. Wrote Clinton Walker in a 2006 article for Australian *Rolling Stone*: "Scott's mother Isa told me that the frontman had already written a lot of lyrics for the album."

If Bon's dear late mother can't be believed, who can? Bon also carried around not only notebooks but a cassette recorder. During the *Highway To Hell* tour, he lost it, according to Angus.

"One night Bon got drunk. Three months later he sobered up and it was gone . . . his method of songwriting is to sing ideas into the microphone when other than sober, play them back to his mother, and if she says they are 'not nice,' keep them in the act."

⚡

In a *Sounds* interview with Angus just weeks after Bon's death, written while AC/DC was still auditioning new singers, British journalist David Lewis made it plain nothing of Bon's would end up on *Back In Black*.

"Even though Bon left behind some unused lyrics and there are several rejected tracks from him on tape, none of them will be used on the band's next album," he wrote. "To Angus that would be nothing short of calculated grave-robbing and he wants nothing to do with it."

Said Angus: "A lot of people like to scrape barrels and take whatever they can when someone dies, but we don't want that. It would be like using his death as a means to gain something. If we'd done things in the studio with him we would possibly have used them; but it's probably best for him too that we won't. There's some stuff of his left, songs off other albums, but to use them wouldn't be the right thing 'cause we rejected them then and it would just be scraping the barrel. And that's possibly the worst thing that could happen."

Did AC/DC scrape the barrel? It's the question that won't go away.

"We can't really say anything, because it's between the Youngs and the Scotts, AC/DC and us," said Graeme Scott to Clinton Walker on the subject of royalty payments to the Bon Scott Estate for AC/DC's back catalogue.

Now why would Bon's younger brother say that, why would there be such secrecy, if the Bon Scott Estate were simply getting thè songwriting royalties to which it is entitled, being those songs Bon wrote for the band between *High Voltage* and *Highway To Hell*? It doesn't wash. But if the estate were getting money for lyrics on *Back In Black*, then naturally secrecy would be paramount. It would be a major news story. There has been nothing but a firewall of silence over this issue.

"As a family, we were all shocked when we found out how much money came in from his songwriting," admitted Graeme in another interview. Astonishingly, he received a letter from his late brother Bon in 1984, telling him he was writing lyrics for *Back In Black*. It had taken over three years to arrive in the post.

Said Derek: "Bon said if the next record didn't work out, he wanted to get out of the business. He said to me: 'I'm 33. What am I going to do to earn a living?' He was so much older than the others in AC/DC. And in those days, once you got to [the age of] 30 in a band it was all over. You were over the hill. [Bon] never had more than 100 bucks in his pocket. That was their allowance. He said to me he'd been working all this time and all he got was 100 bucks a week."[93]

⚡

Within a decade of *Back In Black* being released, Brian was asked to stop writing completely for AC/DC. For 27 years from 1989 to 2016, when he departed the band, he failed to secure a single songwriting credit: a strange way for the Youngs to treat a man who was supposed to have co-written one of the biggest selling albums of all time.

"I don't know if any reason was actually given," says Phil Carson. "This was a Youngs band and they could see that they would make more money if they didn't have to share the writing with Brian, and that was the way it worked. I have always felt it was a mistake because Brian's writing has an edge to it that really fitted the band. Malcolm and Angus never came up with better songs than Malcolm, Angus and Brian would have generated."

For his part, though, Brian, who's become a millionaire dozens of times over (his fortune was estimated to be £65 million [over U.S.$80 million] by the *Sunday Times* in 2016), remains proud of "You Shook Me All Night Long": "To me, it might be one of the best rock songs ever written — if I do say so myself."

CHAPTER 41

LET THERE
BE ROCK

When Bon left North America
for what would be the last time,
10 and *Apocalypse Now* were
the hit movies, *M*A*S*H*,
Dallas and *Mork & Mindy*
were the high-rating TV shows
and Herb Alpert's instru-
mental "Rise" was on top of
the album charts. Bon's cheeky
reference to Barry Manilow on
Highway To Hell hadn't quite
come true: Manilow was still
getting played with the truly
dirgy "Ships." But AC/DC had
a hit LP and *Highway To Hell*
was on its way to becoming the
band's first million seller anywhere in the world, going platinum in the United States on 18
March 1980, almost a month to
the day after Bon's death.

Albert Productions had
taken out an ad in the American
music-trade press three days
before, omitting to mention
Bon altogether: "Drive, determination, guts, energy, power,
consistency — it all pays off
in the end." That October, it
was announced in *Billboard*
magazine that *Highway To
Hell* was one of the top 300
LPs of the previous five years,
alongside albums from Atlantic
label mates ABBA, Chic, Sister

Sledge, Crosby Stills & Nash, Genesis, Roberta Flack, Firefall and Foreigner.

Roy Allen found out about his friend's passing over the radio in Vancouver, Washington, where he was living with his Aunt Wanda. He'd been sent there by his concerned father, Roy Leonard Allen Sr., to get his life sorted out, but it didn't go to plan. Roy was arrested for stealing a bottle of Visine — eye drops, of all things — from a grocery store. He was given an ultimatum by a judge to spend 30 days in jail or undergo 30 days of rehab. He chose rehab.

"AC/DC were supposed to play in Portland before long and I planned on seeing Bon then. I will always regret not being able to have been a better friend to Bon when he needed it and wished I had better listened to what he was saying. I have made peace with this but it still bothers me at times. A therapist once reminded me that I was a bad alcoholic at that time and was not capable of helping myself, let alone others, but that never helped much."

He nearly became the third member of the Allen family to suicide.

"I ended up in treatment a month or so [after Bon's death] and quit for a few months. Within a year I was drinking around the clock; such a horrible place to be. I felt so hopeless. Life's only meaning was alcohol. I bought a pistol, 50 [tablets of] two-milligram Valium, and a bottle of whisky. I learned I didn't have what it takes to shoot myself so over the course of a few hours I took all the pills and drank the whisky, but early the next morning I woke up. I ended up back in treatment and quit drinking again for five years. My dad died from a long bout with cancer and my divorce was final all in the same week. It took a while but a year or so later I started drinking again for a brief period. It didn't take long and I was getting really sick again. I went back to treatment in March '87 and have not drank since.

"Just about every time I talked about Bon, people either acted like they didn't believe me or didn't care so I just quit mentioning it at some point. I'm not going to claim Bon and I were best friends but we were what I consider good friends, and on some level we understood each other very well. I wish I could have shared more of life's journey with him, however small."

Roy confides in me that many years ago he'd begun writing a letter to Malcolm Young but abandoned it. He finds a copy of it on an old PC in his garage and, unsure how to save it — the computer is so old it has a floppy disc drive — emails me some pictures he took of the Microsoft Word document as it appeared on screen. In the letter, Roy writes Bon was going to take a "break" from AC/DC rather than leave the band but he chose that terminology because "I don't know if I wanted to tell Malcolm. I didn't want to freak him out or hurt his feelings or nothing."

Written after VH1's *Behind the Music: AC/DC* went to air in 2000, Roy said he wrote it because Malcolm had been in rehab too.

"It was important for me to let him know that Bon had got to the point of reaching out a little and that I was sure he would have succeeded in recovery if he just could have had an opportunity. I also wanted him to know about the rest of that last phone call from Bon."

The band was also saying good things about Bon in the program, which impressed him: "They just praised Bon throughout the whole thing; rightfully so."

Roy's letter has been edited for clarity but no words have been changed. It was never sent to Malcolm because Roy didn't know where to send it, until now. It was too late to save Bon when it was written. It is too late to get to an ailing Malcolm now. I wish I could have given it to him when he passed me on the street in Sydney back in 2014, but I didn't know about it then. It deserves to finally be read.

Hi Malcolm

This is Roy Allen writing; you may or may not remember me. I was a friend of Bon's and you during the late '70s. We first met in Austin, Texas, in 1977. I hung out with y'all whenever the band was near or in Texas during those years.

The reason I'm writing is to let you know about a phone call I received from Bon not long before his death. I know that was long ago but I have always felt the need to let one of you guys know what he said to me that day.

It was early in the morning in Texas and I was already stoned when the phone rang. To my surprise it was Bon and I got very excited. He was calling from somewhere in Europe and he didn't sound good but unfortunately I did not pick up on that at first. He told me that he just couldn't do it any more; it was killing him and he needed to take a break from alcohol, the road and the hectic lifestyle that he had been living. He said it was just getting too much. He asked if he could come to where I lived in Texas to quit drinking and even suggested that maybe we could do it together. Looking back, he had a "somebody help me" tone of voice.

This is the part that I have always regretted. He didn't actually say "quit drinking"; he used a term I can't recall but is equivalent to "dry out" or "get on the wagon." As you know, we both spoke English but there was a language barrier there as to the terms and slang we used. As a result, I did not pick up on the part about not drinking until we had hung up the phone. I was too wrapped up and excited in the thought of him coming to stay with me and all the fun we would have so that's what I talked about. He kept saying "no"; he was tired of that and wanted a place to come to quit.

We hung up and that's when it hit me about what he was trying to say. I tried calling him back by calling your record company and finding out where the band was staying but I did not have any luck. That turned out to be the last time I talked to Bon or any of you guys. I did receive a Snoopy Christmas card from him not long after that call; the card had Snoopy sitting on top of his doghouse with a French caption, signed by Bon.

I was driving down the road while in Portland, Oregon, when I heard the news about Bon's death on the radio. AC/DC was supposed to play in Portland sometime during the first part of 1980, I believe, and I was really looking forward to seeing all of you. Within three months of Bon's death I was arrested for being drunk and stupid and sentenced to alcohol treatment for 30 days; I was 24 years old. It took a few years to get to the point Bon was and I finally quit and have not had a drink since 1987. Somehow, the thought of the opportunity I got that Bon didn't has helped along the way.

One of the things that I remember about Bon was that he was one of the few people who drank like I did; he would ask for doubles and I would bring triples and he would smile with that special little grin he had.

Alcohol treatment was a new thing back in 1980 and I have always wished that it would have been better known because I believe that Bon was at the "had enough" spot that some of us alcoholics hit at some point. Given the chance, I believe in my heart that Bon would have successfully quit by using the program and be with us today. I'm sorry I could not have been a better friend or known more. Knowing Bon has influenced my life in a positive way. Bon was a gifted man with a kind spirit and I wish he was still with us.

Bon told me one time, "You got to give us one thing, Roy, we know how to rock and roll," and indeed you do.

I hope this letter finds you and finds you well and happy.

Kindest regards
Roy Allen

Bon changed Roy's life for the better, just as he has changed the lives of millions of people around the world.

"I used Bon's death as some kind of motivation during the time when I was struggling so much with not drinking. It was like I was going to quit for the both of us, although he was gone. I have even felt guilty about him dying on some level because if he hadn't died there is a good chance things would not have worked out for me like they did. I had been carrying it all inside for so long.

"Bon's story is of youth, life and adventure. He was not an introverted weirdo; not a heroin addict, not a Satan worshipper. He was not depressed. He was not conflicted. He was not complex on a personal level. He was rare. He was kind. He loved his job until he got too sick. His story is unique in many ways.

"I saw a regular Australian guy who was proud of his Scottish heritage. He was a person who was full of life and infected those around him with gusto. He was brilliantly talented and could work a crowd like few others. He was a person who was most pleased when he was pleasing others. He was also an alcoholic who loved to party and enjoy life to what we thought was the fullest: an alcoholic who never got a shot at rehab.

"His drinking did not get to an unmanageable level until the last year or so; that makes it a small but important part of the story. What he accomplished while being so sick is a testament to itself. He epitomised the lifestyle of the '70s in a lot of ways."

But unlike Roy, unlike Mick Jones, unlike Holly X and unlike Malcolm Young himself, Bon wasn't given the chance to go to AA. In 1977–80 AC/DC was at a critical point where it wouldn't stop for anyone. That Bon was even considering packing it all in, everything he had worked so hard for, right when the band was in sight of riches and glory demonstrates just how badly the man was struggling with his personal demons.

It's also a mark of his personal integrity that he was prepared to walk away from all of it for the sake of the one thing that really mattered: his health. The biggest tragedy of all is not that *Back In*

Black became so successful after Bon died, but that he didn't get the help he needed when he needed it most.

But Bon still visits Roy, in his own way.

"Within a year of me quitting drinking the second time, I had a vivid dream. The kind where you wake up and ask yourself did that really happen or was it just a dream: Bon and I were riding on surfboards, riding through outer space. We never said a word. Just flying through the solar system side by side, past Jupiter and through the rings of Saturn. Smiling, laughing, having fun. When I think of Bon, that's how I choose to remember him."

CLOSER

RIDE ON

Back In Black was released around the world on 25 July 1980. In less than three months, one million copies had been sold in the United States. By 1982, AC/DC was voted the number-one band in the land, according to a Gallup Youth Survey, ahead of Styx and The Rolling Stones.

Brian Johnson was asked in an interview with *Circus*: Do you think Bon Scott's death helped AC/DC in a twisted way?

"It's a hard question to answer," he replied. "But yes, with the publicity in front, plus the fact that we came out with an album, *Back In Black*; that, and the fact we actually went out on tour the same year, really ensured our success."

Two world tours in quick succession promoting *Back In Black* and *For Those About To Rock We Salute You* brought the band to Japan for the first time, a place Bon would never live to see. But North America had always been the end-game for the sedulous Young brothers. Watching them perform in Los Angeles in February 1982, Keith Dunstan of the *Sydney Morning Herald* was rapt at AC/DC's triumph: "I have watched American children in a state of total frenzy over, glory be, an Australian group . . . I guess the kids never think of the former lead singer Bon Scott, but the parents do."

Back In Black went on to become a platinum album 22 times over in the United States, outsold only by Michael Jackson's *Thriller*, Eagles' *Eagles: Their Greatest Hits, 1971–1975*, Billy Joel's *Greatest Hits, Volumes I & II*, Pink Floyd's *The Wall* and Led Zeppelin's *Led Zeppelin IV*.[94] Globally, it's the second biggest selling album in history, with certified sales of over 25 million and double that unofficially.

The first single, "You Shook Me All Night Long," reached an American chart position of #35 on 25 October 1980 and spent three weeks in the top 40. It was also re-released in 1985 as a "Limited Edition Gatefold Sleeve Package" with a live recording of Bon singing "She's Got Balls" as a B-side. In 2003, inducting AC/DC into the Rock & Roll Hall of Fame in Cleveland, Aerosmith's Steven Tyler said the song's "primal stink . . . lit a fire in the belly of every kid that grew up born to break the rules." In 2016, in the same city, it was played at the Republican National Convention that nominated Donald Trump as the party's candidate for President of the United States. He'd take Ohio and win the election later that year.

Today, hearing AC/DC on FM radio or over PAs in football stadiums is as much a fixture of life in the "heartland" of America as Applebee's, Walmart and the National Rifle Association: a supreme irony for a band that began its North American journey with Bon in 1977 dismissed by critics and all but ignored by program directors.

In the liner notes to its 2003 compact-disc reissue, David Fricke spells out why *Back In Black* had such an impact on the heartland: "The story of this album begins with the end of a life . . . *Back In Black* is really a silent tribute to Bon Scott: an all-black cover with raised tombstone-like lettering. There is no dedication, no mention of his name. But the Youngs' determination to rock, no matter what, was the supreme salute."

Money was flooding the Youngs' bank accounts.

"We didn't make any, really any money, if you're looking on it [as] a financial thing, until *Back In Black*," said Angus Young, "because before that we were always in the red . . . it cost a lot of money at the time to keep the thing on the road."

But Bon, AC/DC's charismatic frontman, the person who had made it all come together for the Youngs, was dead. Had the band done enough for him? I believe not. To some degree the band, its management and its record companies failed him. Vince Lovegrove thought similarly.

"Those of us in Australia who knew Bon well, those of us who had known him since the '60s, could not quite comprehend how, on the edge of international success, he could die alone in a car, parked in a lonely London street, in the middle of winter, with not a friend in sight."

Certainly "the thing" — AC/DC, the Young brothers' band and its unrelenting ambition — ultimately contributed to the death of Bon. But no one else other than Bon was responsible for throwing away the opportunity he had. Bon chose his path. He chose to use heroin. He chose to mix hard drugs with alcohol. He chose to play up to the role his fans and his bandmates expected of him when deep down he was someone very different who wanted a new life — a wife, kids, a place to call home — but didn't know how to break away. He'd never make a clean exit from the Young family, AC/DC, drugs or the bottle.

Everyone wants somebody to love. Everyone wants to be respected for their work. Everyone wants to become the best version of themselves they can be. At the end, Bon hadn't quite achieved any of those things. Fame and riches might have been coming, but they weren't ever going to make Bon truly happy when he remained so ripped up inside.

Like Lynn Lankford drag racing Roy Allen in their Mustangs on that dark, desolate stretch of Route 79, he took a chance that morning in London because that was the way Bon embraced life: in the moment. This was his "destructive side," as Silver put it; his predilection to do something completely inexplicable with no thought of the consequences for himself or those around him. Only this time he'd run out of luck.

Both men crashed from life. One man died gurgling on his own blood; the other on vomit. Bon made a poor decision, one from which there was no coming back, but he took the last highway of his own volition.

Wherever he was in his mind when he died, in a dream or some place else, one can only hope he was finally at peace with himself.

⚡

In November 2015, I went out to a three-quarter-full football stadium in Sydney to see the *Rock Or Bust* juggernaut, which to all intents and purposes was Angus Young doing a two-hour solo. A struggling Brian Johnson repeatedly failed to hit the right notes and clearly felt "C'mon" exhortations to the audience would cover up those parts of the concert where his voice was failing. Hearing him mangle "Sin City," a song that embodied the songwriting craft and life of Bon, a song Bon personally dedicated to Pattee Bishop onstage in a tiny club in Florida, was painful knowing how unforgettable this band had once been.

It's often said AC/DC went on to bigger things after Bon died. That cannot be denied. But with Bon they could have gone on to even greater things. Foreigner's Mick Jones believes AC/DC has benefited enormously from branding, describing them and Kiss as "the big logo bands. AC/DC have got a fantastic logo which everybody wants to be seen wearing . . . they've carved their space out as a live touring band or an event that you can go and see, especially as Led Zeppelin aren't really around anymore. AC/DC has almost benefited from that, probably; they've carved that area that's missing."

But the best brand of all, of course, was Bon. Now with no Malcolm Young, no Phil Rudd, no Brian Johnson and no Cliff Williams, AC/DC *is* The Angus Show. He's a unique musical force, a world star that deserves all the acclaim he gets for his musicianship and showmanship. In their excitement, fans snap up extortionately priced T-shirts not knowing that the guy who designed the logo they're about to wear makes exactly nothing from every item sold.

At the Sydney concert, the power of the brand overtaking the band was obvious. For all the pyrotechnics, fireworks, lighting, smoke machines, rising platforms, audiovisuals, animation, cannons, bells, cheesy karaoke graphics during "You Shook Me All Night Long" and even a giant Rosie in a top hat, there was not one image of Bon. He was later shown at the band's Perth show, in homage to his home state, but it wasn't nearly enough. It never is.

Angus jumps at the end of each song to signal its end. The lights get turned down every time. But there is no resonance because it is all so manufactured. Your skin doesn't feel goosebumps. You aren't buzzing. You are being sold a memory of a once-great band, certainly what used to be the most uncompromising rock 'n' roll band of all time. Bon was more than the lightning bolt in AC/DC. He was the spirit of rock.

Mark Evans once told me wistfully: "Sometimes, I think, 'Gee, boy, it would have been great if Bon had have been able to hang [on] for one more record.'"

Something, it has to be said, all AC/DC fans of that era have probably done at one point or another. So it was nice to hear it coming from someone who'd been inside AC/DC and shared a stage with Bon. They are a select and privileged bunch of men.

"But then it would have been a different record," continued Mark, "so would it have been as successful? I don't know. Everything reached that critical mass and it's just the way it's happened. You can't change things."

That's the trouble with death. It's the end of the road.

So just how did Bon die? What happened from the time he decided to leave his apartment on the evening of 18 February 1980 to Silver Smith's phone call made to AC/DC, informing them that he was dead, on the morning of the 20th?

Based on evidence gathered for *Bon: The Last Highway* as well as information already in the public domain, what follow are two theories for how the AC/DC legend perished on 19 February 1980. The first is almost completely new. The second is largely the one already well known by AC/DC fans but with a heroin overdose substituted for alcohol poisoning.

They are only theories — some will undoubtedly dismiss them as conjectural fantasies — but they incorporate the important parts of the version of events put forward by Paul Chapman and Pete Way of UFO and the well-travelled Silver Smith/Joe Fury/Alistair Kinnear account of what transpired before and after Bon's fateful visit to The Music Machine in Camden.

These are the two strands of Bon's story that have never been reconciled. They have not been perfectly matched

CARRY ME HOME

here by any means, but there is enough common information for a discerning reader (provided they don't subscribe to the coroner's finding of alcohol poisoning) to make up their own mind about what happened to Bon. In the interests of fairness, the first is predicated on the assumption that Chapman and Way are telling the truth and that Silver was — and Joe is — mistaken. The second is predicated on the reverse: Silver and Joe told me the truth, and Chapman's and Way's accounts aren't accurate. Occam's razor doesn't necessarily apply here. As for Alistair, it has been comprehensively established by this book that he didn't tell the whole story when he was alive. Doubt must be cast on his entire account.

I cannot say with any certainty who is right and who is wrong. Silver is no longer around to defend herself, in any case. My considered opinion is that both camps have told truths, but I cannot fathom why, as Silver and Joe came to allege, Chapman would completely fabricate a story. What purpose would it serve? Way, who is not exactly a close personal friend of Chapman, also vouches for its authenticity. He has no known reason to lie.

Equally, a cynic might propose that the two musicians from UFO, Chapman and Way, might have something to hide. But the reality is this: apart from Ross Halfin's allegation that Peter Mensch blamed Way for giving Bon drugs, next to no information has come forward to suggest any nefarious conspiracy involving UFO. For the record, Way in his autobiography denies he had anything to do with Bon's death and says he didn't see Bon again after the last of UFO's Hammersmith shows on 7 February 1980.

Silver and Joe were adamant that they were the ones telling the truth and, if so, it would mean that Chapman's entire tale of spending the night of the 18th and early morning of the 19th with Joe waiting for Bon to come to his flat in Fulham is simply wrong. Under the Silver/Joe scenario, the crucial phone calls to Chapman and Way would have to have been made between midnight and 2 a.m. on the 20th, not sometime after dawn on the morning of the 19th.

Granted, it is worth bearing in mind the possibility that Chapman, a former heroin addict, has simply muddled up his story horribly, interpolating incidents that happened on separate dates, weeks apart. Way, also a former heroin addict, one given to an abundance of conversational fillers when speaking, is not entirely reliable either. But were Silver and Alistair before they died? Is Joe? Who are we to believe?

Of most significance to me is the fact Chapman says Bon — sometime in the month he died — was around heroin and actively involved in looking to procure heroin. For that reason alone, Chapman's story matters, *whenever* it happened. If it is also true that Mensch accused Way of giving Bon drugs (something not mentioned at all by Mensch at the coronial inquest), then I think it's fair to peg heroin as the most likely agent of Bon's demise.

I disagree with those people — like Bon's ex-wife Irene Thornton — who say that it's unimportant how Bon died. Irene wrote in her book: "It doesn't matter to me. Knowing the real story wouldn't change the way it ended." But Bon didn't set out on the evening of 18 February 1980 *intending* to die. He wouldn't have known he was having a fatal overdose the following morning as his eyes closed, he fell unconscious and began vomiting, never to wake up. Our memory of him deserves the truth. The real story deserves to be told and it deserves closure, not more perpetuation of a rampant myth.

What dramatically changed the course of my investigation was Zena Kakoulli's admission that she was with Bon and Alistair in East Dulwich, as well as the well-placed eyewitness at The Music Machine who saw Bon "stoned" on what this person clearly believed was heroin.

The fact that this person pointedly didn't "wanna upset anybody this late in the game" (and wanted to leave it at that) only convinced me heroin was involved in Bon's death, aside from all the other strong indicators that pointed to an overdose.

These two crucial eyewitness accounts combined with Clive Edwards's recollection that Silver was at Jimmy Bain's house snorting heroin and not at home when she got a phone call to tell her Bon was dead are, I believe, game-changers; certainly enough new information to up-end what we think we already know about Bon's death.

It's clear that both the police investigation and the coronial inquest were grossly inadequate, demonstrably deficient and potentially incompetent. It is worth considering the very real possibility that Bon may have already been dead when he was left in Alistair's car. It's horrifying to imagine but cannot be discounted.

I am making no judgements of or casting any aspersions on individuals interviewed for this book; most of all, Silver and Joe. I don't believe that either Silver or Joe had anything to do directly with Bon's death. There is no evidence of them supplying heroin to Bon or even being in his company when he died. I found both of them to be friendly, helpful, likeable and sincere. They had their own stories and they stuck to them. But inescapably they remain players in the *Fargo*-like mystery of Bon's last hours.

Whether certain people, dead or alive, have been less than forthright or others are still being protected is another question entirely. In time, I hope, new information about Bon's death may come to light. I am merely presenting here two theories involving heroin, using the only accounts likely to be available any time soon.

I welcome any readers with more information about Bon's death to contact me via the book's official Facebook page (facebook.com/acdcbooks) or my personal Facebook account. If you have your own theory, you're also more than welcome to get in touch with me.

THEORY ONE: *Alistair Hides the Body*

It was just another run-of-the-mill Monday night in London. Bon could have stayed in at his Victoria apartment and watched a BBC-2 marathon of Spyro Gyra live from Leeds University on *Rock Goes to College*, *The Goodies* and *Des O'Connor Tonight*, but he'd finished writing the lyrics for the album that would become *Back In Black*. He was in the mood to celebrate.

Bon met up with Paul Chapman and Joe Fury somewhere in inner London. He possibly met Pete Way, too, according to Ross Halfin, though that seems unlikely. Either way, he was out and about, mingling with friends in the rock scene. Bon said he'd get some heroin and hook up with them again later. Chapman and Joe went to Chapman's flat in Fulham. Bon phoned Silver, to tell her he'd finished writing lyrics and ask what she was doing. Was she interested in coming out with him? It wasn't a call to buy heroin from Silver. Bon knew this was not something to broach with the woman he'd bitterly disappointed with his behaviour so many times.

Silver suggested he meet Alistair. Bon well knew Alistair was a heroin user, having known him for some time. The two made contact and agreed to go together to the Lonesome No More gig at The Music Machine, where heroin and free booze would be in abundance. Alistair's friends Peter Perrett and Zena Kakoulli, smack users both, would be there. So Bon went to Camden, drank his usual amount of whisky but also snorted heroin backstage in the company of unknown persons at the gig. Alistair was among them.

Early on the morning of the 19th, Bon, Zena and Alistair left the gig in Alistair's car to either party on at another location, get more heroin from a dealer or go to Chapman's in Fulham (as Bon had promised), but not long into the journey Bon began nodding off. He fell unconscious. He vomited. Alistair panicked and made his phone calls to Silver.

Not knowing Bon had snorted heroin, Silver reasonably presumed he'd passed out from drinking. He'd done it many times before. Alistair (who wasn't letting on at this stage what he'd witnessed backstage at The Music Machine: Bon snorting heroin) relaxed when told this. Maybe it was just alcoholic intoxication after all. But then Bon stopped breathing altogether. Alistair attempted to resuscitate him but failed, in the process leaving marks on Bon's neck. AC/DC's lead singer was dead and dawn hadn't even broken in London.

By now Alistair was in a state — the lead singer of AC/DC was stone cold dead in his tiny Renault 5 — and he didn't know what to do. He was reluctant to call Silver again, especially with this news. But what was he supposed to do with the body? If he took Bon to the hospital, heroin would be detected instantly. Zena would be little help carrying his dead weight into Alistair's apartment.

In Fulham, Paul and Joe were still waiting for Bon to arrive. Joe had had enough of hanging around and left for Silver's flat in South Kensington. When he got back, he was informed about Bon's overdose by Silver, who'd got another phone call from Alistair, this time telling her Bon was dead.

Alistair needed help.

Joe then made his early-morning phone call to Chapman. Chapman made his phone call to Way. Way gave Chapman a number for AC/DC. Chapman told Way he and Joe would handle delivering the news. Chapman duly gave Joe the number with which to call AC/DC.

But Alistair was very cognisant that he — and potentially one of Alistair's higher profile friends, such as Zena and Peter — could be in serious trouble if pathology tests showed that Bon had snorted heroin supplied by either him or one of his friends at The Music Machine. The tabloids would crucify them. The police would also ask questions about why Bon was out and about buying heroin and whom he was buying it for. The ramifications didn't bear thinking about.

So Alistair requested Silver and Joe delay the phone call.

The chances were slim that Chapman or Way would break the news of Bon's death to AC/DC before it came either from Silver or Joe. The priority for Alistair was ensuring the heroin was undetectable. So Bon's body was left not in the front passenger seat but under a blanket in the back seat of the car or even put in the boot with the back seat folded down. There is another possibility, worth considering, that Bon's body was left in another location altogether, such as Alistair's apartment.

This might explain why no passers-by saw Bon the entire daylight hours of the 19th and why Alistair's phantom friend "Leslie Loads," whomever that may be, if Loads existed at all, never saw Bon when asked to go down and check on the car by the supposedly soporific Alistair. Wherever Bon was, he was effectively hidden — concealed from view.

Half a day elapsed. Alistair spent it inside, pacing the room, half panicked, waiting for nightfall. When it got dark, he made his move. If Bon's body was left in the car, Alistair removed the blanket covering it and positioned it upright on one of the seats. If it was moved inside the apartment, he received assistance from an unknown person or persons taking it back down to the car.

Alistair then drove Bon's body directly to the hospital and left as soon as he could. Silver, at Jimmy Bain's home, received a phone call to go to the hospital. She went with Joe. Having obtained AC/DC's phone number from Paul Chapman via Pete Way earlier that morning, Joe gave Silver the number. She made the call.

THEORY TWO: *Alistair Gets a Big Fright*

It was around 7:30 p.m., Monday, 18 February 1980. Bon had completed the lyrics for *Back In Black*. Restless at home at his sparsely furnished apartment in Victoria, he called Silver, curious if she was doing anything that evening. He hadn't seen her for a while and was feeling nostalgic for her company.

Silver wasn't available but Alistair was. They arranged to meet and Alistair picked up Bon from Morpeth Terrace. He was well lubricated on Scotch when Alistair arrived and in the mood to party. Through his friendship with Peter Perrett and Zena Kakoulli, Alistair had got them both on the door for the Lonesome No More gig at The Music Machine. It might not have been his kind of music but a free backstage bar sounded good to Bon.

Bon and Alistair proceeded to Camden and met Peter and Zena. Heroin was being conspicuously consumed. Bon was particularly pleased with himself; he'd just finished writing an album of lyrics, some of his best work yet. He had a discreet toot (tonight he was Bon Scott, rock star on the town) and listened to a bit of the concert; but it wasn't his bag. He was itching to go somewhere else. Zena, who'd just met Bon and was keen to spend more time with him and Alistair, agreed to leave with them. They all piled into Alistair's Renault 5. The night wasn't over yet.

But they'd barely travelled a few miles when Bon started to pass out. He slumped in his seat. He was comatose. Alistair made his phone calls from Victoria and East Dulwich to Silver and she told him to put some blankets on Bon and let him sleep it off. Alistair didn't mention heroin to her and Silver didn't suspect an overdose.

Joe, lying next to Silver in her bed, not unreasonably thought this was just another occasion of Bon being Bon; nothing to worry about. So Alistair and Zena did what Silver recommended they do and left Bon in the car, wrapped in a blanket. They wrote him a note, snorted some heroin inside Alistair's apartment and then nodded out.

At around 11 a.m., a groggy Alistair briefly woke and asked Zena, who was up and about, to see if Bon was still in the car. Zena either peered through one of the flat's windows or stepped out in the cold for half a minute, but as she wasn't in the best condition herself, her inspection was halfhearted. She saw nothing.

Alistair slept the rest of the day, unaware that Bon, who had stopped breathing in his sleep and was now deceased, was still outside his apartment. When the sun went down, Alistair woke up, had a shower and got dressed. He had something to eat in his kitchen before he went to visit his girlfriend, Janice, in hospital. Zena had already left; there was no sign of her.

Early that evening, Alistair went down to his car and got the fright of his life. Bon had vomited on himself. He was still wrapped up in the blanket Alistair and Zena had covered him with but his skin was cold and lifeless. He was dead. There was no point calling an ambulance. There was no life to save.

So Alistair drove to King's College Hospital, alerted the medical staff that there was a dead man in the passenger seat of his car, watched on in great distress as Bon's body was removed, and left Silver's number as a contact.

Later that evening, Silver, having a quiet night at home with Joe in Emperor's Gate, got a phone call from the hospital. She was told that Bon's condition was serious and to come as soon as possible. She went with Joe. The doctor on duty told them both that Bon was dead. After midnight, Joe and Silver returned home, racking their brains to think of a way to contact AC/DC.

Joe knew Pete Way was a mate of Malcolm Young, and though he knew Way socially through his work with UFO, he wasn't close enough to have his personal phone number. So Joe called Paul Chapman, his friend, former employer and Way's bandmate. There was no daylight. It was the dead of night.

Chapman was stunned. He'd seen Bon only a couple of weeks earlier at the Hammersmith Odeon, when he'd gone off to buy heroin for him and Joe and never returned; it was the last time he'd seen Joe and the last he'd seen AC/DC's lead singer. Now Joe was calling to tell him *this*?

Chapman said he would call Way on Joe's behalf. Way, annoyed that he'd been woken up but naturally shocked by what he was hearing, happily obliged with a number for AC/DC. Chapman called Joe, gave him the number and tried to go back to sleep after hanging up but he too was deeply shaken by the news.

Joe handed over the number to the woman lying next to him. Silver, with dread but purpose, picked up the phone. She made the call.

DIRTY EYES

Ted Albert Founder of Albert Productions (Alberts). Died in 1990.

Roy Allen Friend of Bon Scott.

Joey Alves Guitarist of Yesterday & Today (Y&T). Died in 2017.

Joe Anthony Disc jockey at San Antonio radio station KMAC/KISS. Died in 1992.

Michael Anthony Bass player of Van Halen.

Jimmy Bain Bass player of Rainbow, Wild Horses and later Dio. Died in 2016.

Mike Barone Drummer of Critical Mass.

Barry Bergman Publisher at Edward B. Marks Music Corporation and "surrogate manager" of AC/DC.

Pattee Bishop Girlfriend of Cliff Williams and Bon Scott.

Albert Bouchard Drummer of Blue Öyster Cult.

Steve Brigida Drummer of Artful Dodger.

Michael Browning Manager of AC/DC.

Charlie Brusco Manager of Outlaws. Later manager of Lynyrd Skynyrd.

Bun E. Carlos Drummer of Cheap Trick.

Phil Carson Senior vice-president of Atlantic Records. Later manager of Foreigner.

Paul Chapman Guitarist of UFO.

Mick Cocks Guitarist of Rose Tattoo. Died in 2009.

Bob Defrin Art director of Atlantic Records.

Michael Dirse Friend of Pattee Bishop. Keyboardist of Tight Squeeze.

Billy Duffy Guitarist of Lonesome No More. Later guitarist of The Cult.

Sidney Drashin Concert promoter of Lynyrd Skynyrd and AC/DC.

Clive Edwards Drummer of Wild Horses. Later drummer of UFO.

Ahmet Ertegun Co-founder of Atlantic Records. Died in 2006.

Mark Evans Bass player of AC/DC.

Michael "Fazz" Fazzolare Lead singer and guitarist of Critical Mass.

Barry Freeman West Coast regional promotion director of Atlantic Records.

Joe Fury Friend of Bon Scott and Silver Smith. "Guitar tech" of UFO. Roadie of Little River Band.

Steve Gursky Engineer of Criteria Studios. Died in 2005.

Grahame "Yogi" Harrison Roadie of Rose Tattoo.

Paul Harwood Bass player of Mahogany Rush.

Robin Jackson-Fragola "Special" friend of Malcolm Young.

Mo Jasmin Mother of Daniel Kinnear. Died in 2006.

Ian Jeffery Tour manager of AC/DC.

Brian Johnson Lead singer of AC/DC. Replaced Bon Scott. Left the band in 2016.

Earl Johnson Guitarist of Moxy.

Mick Jones Guitarist of Foreigner.

Koulla Kakoulli Lead singer of Lonesome No More. Sister of Zena Kakoulli.

Xenoulla "Zena" Kakoulli Wife of Peter Perrett. Manager of The Only Ones and Lonesome No More. Sister of Koulla Kakoulli. Friend of Alistair Kinnear.

Scott Kempner Guitarist of The Dictators.

Alistair Kinnear Guitarist of Screw and England's Glory. Friend of Bon Scott and Silver Smith. Declared dead by a Spanish court in 2015.

Angus Kinnear Missionary, author and doctor. Father of Alistair Kinnear. Died in 2002.

Daniel Kinnear Banker. Son of Alistair Kinnear.

Liz Klein Friend of Holly X.

David Krebs Manager of AC/DC. Partner in management firm Leber-Krebs.

Robert John "Mutt" Lange Producer of Foreigner, Outlaws and AC/DC.

Lynn Lankford Friend of Roy Allen. Died in 1976.

Henry Laplume Bass player of Critical Mass.

Sir Montague Levine Coroner. Died in 1990.

Vince Lovegrove Lead singer of The Valentines. Friend of Bon Scott. Died in 2012.

Phil Lynott Lead singer and bassist of Thin Lizzy. Solo artist. Friend of Silver Smith. Died in 1986.

Keith Mant Forensic pathologist. Died in 2000.

Bill Martin Journalist and friend of Roy Allen.

Paul Matters Bass player of AC/DC.

Dave Meniketti Lead singer and guitarist of Yesterday & Today (Y&T).

Robin Mendelson Friend of Holly X and Pattee Bishop. Girlfriend of Cliff Williams.

Peter Mensch Manager of AC/DC. Employee of Leber-Krebs.

Neal Mirsky Disc jockey at WDIZ Orlando and program director at WSHE Miami.

Moses Mo Guitarist of Mother's Finest.

Maggie Montalbano Friend of Alistair Kinnear. Died in 2009.

Jon Newey Drummer of England's Glory. Friend of Alistair Kinnear. Editor of *Jazzwise*.

David Owen Guitarist of Critical Mass.

Candy Pedroza Friend of Pattee Bishop and Silver Smith. Girlfriend of Cliff Williams. Died in 2009.

Tony Platt Engineer of *Highway To Hell* and *Back In Black*.

Frank Prinzel Electronics maintenance engineer of Criteria Studios. Later sound engineer/guitarist of Critical Mass.

Mark Putterford Biographer of AC/DC. Died in 1994.

Beth Quartiano Girlfriend of Bon Scott and Angus Young. Friend of Robin Jackson-Fragola. Died in 2011.

Herman Rarebell Drummer of Scorpions.

Paul Raymond Keyboardist and guitarist of UFO.

Lou Roney Disc jockey at San Antonio radio station KMAC/KISS.

Teddy Rooney Bass player of Tight Squeeze. Died in 2016.

Phil Rudd Drummer of AC/DC.

Derek St. Holmes Lead singer and guitarist of Ted Nugent and St. Paradise.

Freddie Salem Guitarist of Outlaws.

Ken Schaffer Inventor of the Schaffer-Vega Diversity System. Friend of Angus Young.

Charles "Chick" Scott Father of Bon Scott. Died in 1999.

Derek Scott Brother of Bon Scott.

Graeme Scott Brother of Bon Scott.

Isabella "Isa" Scott Mother of Bon Scott. Died in 2011.

Ronald "Bon" Scott Lead singer of AC/DC. Died in 1980.

Douglas "Buzz" Shearman Lead singer of Moxy. Died in 1983.

Valerie Shearman Widow of Buzz Shearman.

Robert Shulman Music director at KRST Albuquerque. Later producer of Yesterday & Today (Y&T).

Darryl "Spyda" Smith Roadie of Rose Tattoo. Friend of Joe Fury and Bon Scott.

Margaret "Silver" Smith Girlfriend of Bon Scott and Joe Fury. Died in 2016.

Wade Smith Friend of Roy Allen.

Kenny Soule Drummer of Nantucket.

Doug Thaler Booking agent of AC/DC.

Irene Thornton Ex-wife of Bon Scott.

Harry Vanda Co-producer (with George Young) of AC/DC.

Larry Van Kriedt Bass player of AC/DC.

Clinton Walker Biographer of Bon Scott.

Pete Way Bass player of UFO.

Cliff Williams Bass player of AC/DC. Retired in 2016.

Holly X Girlfriend of Bon Scott.

Angus Young Lead guitarist of AC/DC.

George Young Co-producer (with Harry Vanda) of AC/DC.

Malcolm Young Guitarist of AC/DC. Retired due to dementia in 2014.

ACKNOWLEDGEMENTS
CRABSODY IN BLUE

While researching and writing this book was very much a solo passion project that took over my life for three years, I'd like to register my appreciation of some notable people, most of whom I am fortunate to be able to call friends, who contributed something substantial and meaningful to *Bon: The Last Highway*.

Firstly, Roy Allen, in Leander, Texas, for being so brave to tell not only his own story of recovery from alcohol addiction but his tale of unlikely mateship with Bon. It's worthy of a movie. Roy wrote me a letter to tell me that he wanted to know if it was possible to mention in the book that "Bon's death played a significant part in my recovery, especially early on," and that "all that hard drinking, partying and his death was not totally in vain." Roy remains devoted to his recovery. It's a lifelong commitment. Being part of this book, he says, has "improved my life in a big way." It has been my immense pleasure to tell your story, Roy.

Secondly, Holly X in Miami, Florida, for not just letting me in on her story that until now had been unknown, but generously opening up her home to me and letting me stay as a house guest. She allowed me to rifle through her old mementos from the '70s and fielded every difficult, sometimes indelicate, question of mine with patience and grace. She even packed me lunch for my return on the *Silver Star* to New York. Holly recently remarried and became a grandmother for the first time but Bon still has a special place in her heart. I hope I have done him justice, "Hol."

In California, thank you to Bon's old flame Pattee Bishop for her refreshing straight talk and fascinating insights into Bon between 1977 and '79. Former AC/DC and Aerosmith manager David Krebs indulged me on a number of occasions during the writing of the book. Former Van Halen bass player Michael Anthony was also exceedingly generous with his time.

In Florida, I'd like to express my sincere gratitude to Paul Chapman, Phil Carson, Michael Fazzolare, Robin Mendelson, Robin Jackson-Fragola, Neal Mirsky, David Owen, Frank Prinzel, Henry Laplume and Jackie Smith. UFO guitarist Paul's account of Bon's last night contained some revelations and, to his immense credit, he was refreshingly open about his own history with drug addiction. Thank you, Tonka. Phil opened up many doors for me during the writing of the book. Even when our opinions and conclusions about certain things differ — I'm sure this book won't be any different — he has been a supporter of my work. Neal and Michael proved the key to unlocking the secret of AC/DC's Miami interlude in 1979 and I cannot thank both of you enough: you really gifted me a great story. Jackie, Neal, Holly and Mick took the time to drive me around Miami, pointing out old AC/DC haunts from '79, and it was an experience that was incredibly useful and one I'll never forget.

In Texas, a special shoutout to the *Rockdale Reporter*'s Bill Martin, who crucially introduced me to Roy Allen; Roy's friend Wade Smith, for recreating so well the scene of AC/DC's first live show in the United States and sending me his perfectly preserved ticket; and former KMAC/KISS radio personality Lou Roney for going out of his way to connect me with people and gifting me memorabilia of the 1970s San Antonio hard-rock scene.

In New York, I am indebted to Foreigner guitarist Mick Jones for his honest reflections about the rock lifestyle that drove him to drink — and then seek help. Ken Schaffer, Carol Klenfner, Doug Thaler and Barry Bergman also took the time to meet me personally in Manhattan and share their memories of Bon, AC/DC and the glory days of the rock business.

In England, Rich Davenport went *waaaay* beyond the call of duty in connecting me with various musicians who knew Bon. Pete Way from UFO and Alistair Kinnear's son, Daniel Kinnear, were very helpful to me, and Daniel especially took me into his confidence, sending me unseen photos and documents. Once again, *Highway To Hell* and *Back In Black* engineer Tony Platt was conspicuous for his amiability. Zena and Koulla Kakoulli spoke to me with unexpected candour.

In Slovakia, Peter Píš, an unsung champion of Australian rock, kept me abreast of AC/DC or Bon Scott press mentions and interesting discussion on AC/DC fan sites, as well as being a sounding board for developments in my investigation into Bon's death. Almost every week for two years he sent me MP3s of audio recordings, PDFs of articles and huge files of photos on Dropbox, and I can't thank him enough. Peter, like many AC/DC fans around the world, just wants to know the real story about Bon. I hope I've delivered, Peter.

In Brazil, thank you to my Brazilian family — Massimo Carrara de Sambuy, Adriana Tommasini, Fabio Carrara, Marina Tommasini Carrara de Sambuy, Rita De Cássia Terrassan, Eduardo Finelli, Rosenildo Ferreira, Tatiana Flo Casenza, Angelo Carrara, Carolina Stanisci, Antonio "Stan" Stanisci — and all my São Paulo friends for their patience, hospitality and good-humoured tolerance of my non-existent Portuguese. Thanks also to Paula Carvalho, Tatiana Allegro, Thiago Reis and Rogério Alves at Editora Saraiva, my translator Marcelo Hauck (this is my second book with Marcelo), as well as Marco Bezzi for his crucial help in bringing the Brazilian edition to print. Brazil is now my second home, so it means so much to me to have it released there.

In Australia, I'm grateful to the late Silver Smith for the days, weeks and months we spent talking about her time with Bon. She endured many hardships in her life and died surrounded by her family. We argued quite a lot. She didn't appreciate some of my questions but answered them anyway.

As she wrote in one of her last emails to me: "Nothing really matters except the truth, which I promised to give you and to the best of my ability (as I remember it), I have. It's all we have at the end, isn't it? My 'word' was really important to me, and I've never broken it with anyone."

Silver was generous to me when she didn't need to be. While she could be erratic, shrill and unpredictable, she could just as quickly switch to being kind, sweet and cooperative. By the end, I considered her a friend. I hope she comes out of *Bon: The Last Highway* less demonised and more humanised. Silver was clearly a very special person to Bon and deserved better treatment from AC/DC and its fans while she was alive. She never got to write her own book — something she hoped to do — but I hope mine will serve in some way as a tribute to her memory. No one is perfect. Silver wasn't by any stretch but nor was Bon.

Silver's old boyfriend and Bon's friend Joe Fury was harder to track down than Osama bin Laden but when I did find him he was friendly, forthcoming, direct and keen to tell his side of the story. Thank you, Joe.

Former AC/DC bass player Paul Matters, a neglected figure in the history of the band, granted me his first ever interview since being heartlessly sacked by Bon in 1975. It took some courage, Paul. I hope AC/DC fans belatedly embrace you with open arms.

Thanks also to Jan Blum, Charlie Dreyer-Blum, Fred Fink, Rosie Hanly, Greg Stock and Tony Currenti, who, of course, was AC/DC's drummer on their very first album, *High Voltage*, but is much more important to me as a friend. It's a long way to the top being a writer and you need friends and family behind you.

I'm especially grateful to those musicians in the United States, Canada and Europe who helped me while writing the book. They were either from bands who played on the road with AC/DC between the years of 1977 and '80, knew Bon personally or would go on to be inspired by him in some way in later years. If the book were twice as big, I'd have fitted in all your stories. For mine, the late 1970s was the greatest era of music, the cradle of classic rock, and so many of you deserve far more acknowledgement than the Rock & Roll Hall of Fame will ever deign to give you.

A big thank you to the following people who helped me, tolerated me, encouraged me, or supported me while writing and researching *Bon: The Last Highway*: Scott Kempner, Stephen Ambrose, Sergio Marchi, Ronald Clayton, Janne Moller, Dion Simte, Marco Meierhöfer, Phil Thenstedt, Thang Luong, Daniel Feiler, John Fyfe, Bill Hale, Michael Dirse, Sidney Drashin, Liz Klein, Robert Shulman, David Gleason, Richard Potter, Dominique Giovanangeli, Prospector, Steven Jurgensmeyer, Anne-Maree Brown, Greg T. Walker, Joey Alves (RIP), Mantas Tamulevičius, Jan Nimmervoll, Jason Smart, Constance Carper, Walter Egan, Eoin Jordan, Neil Carter, Peter Head, Clive Edwards, Rob Grange, Frank Marino, Michael Clarkin, Robert Alford, Jenny Way, Brian Forsythe, Orville Davis, Steve Stokking, Patti Callahan, Rod Roddy, Rick Musselman, Beeb Birtles, Theresa Baxley Wilkeson Porter, Greg Myhra, Chris Hamall, Chris Bruce, Jack Orbin, Janet Macoska, Gino Zangari, Robby Gregory, Jim Arbogast, James Quinton, Ross Halfin, Les Gully, John Tait, Ed Fagnant, Mark Paton, Gary Granger, Rob Riley, Richard McCaffrey, KK Downing, Paul "Lobster" Wells, Ted Ferguson, Kevin Law, Richard Davies, Jeff Franklin, Sammy Hagar, Marian Pizzimenti, Bradley Starks, Ronald Paul, Renata Simões, Ross Ward, John Bisset, Curtis Frank Ingram Jr., Clint Weyrauch, Bob Defrin, Derek St. Holmes, Brent Alberts, Lisa Tanner, Earl Johnson, Barry Freeman, Paul Wozniak, Mike Kempf, Valerie Shearman, Larry Van Kriedt, Dave Tice, Herman Rarebell, Nate Althoff, Anthony Currenti, Jim Landry, Joe Matera, Shaun Harwood, B.J. Lisko, David Mitchell, Michelle Mulhall, Mike Fraser, Angela Morgan, Michael Browning, Thiago Waldhelm, Melinda Bolinger, Steve Scariano, Charlie Brusco, Nando Machado, Mark Carrillo, Rick Deyulio, Matthew Wilkening, Fernando Lima, Ricardo Artigas, Mark Naumann, Irene Thornton, Bobby Pickett, Bobby Baker, Lisa Walker, Paul Harwood, Steve Brigida, Jon Hyde, Harold Bronson,

John Cuthbertson, Don Keith, Kevin Elson, Kenny Soule, Gene Davis, Bob Ancheta, Tom Marker, Rick Tucker, Donna Kreiss, Joe Bouchard, Albert Bouchard, Lindsay Mitchell, Rusty Burns (RIP), John O'Daniel, Chet McCracken, Suzanne Allison Witkin, Moses Mo, Jonah Koslen, Mari Fong, Peter Spirer, Steve Sybesma, Jeff Carlisi, Freddie Salem, Hank Alrich, Rick Springfield, Grahame "Yogi" Harrison, Louis X. Erlanger, Joey Malone, Andrew Andreotti, Gordon Bass, David W. Larkin, Carter Alan, Monte Yoho, Drew Wills, Sandra Jackson, Jill Meniketti, Dave Meniketti, Marty Larkin, Mariusz Podkalicki, Geoff Chang, Ric Cacchione, Georg Dolivo, Simon Wright, Billy Duffy, Terry Slesser, Shane Stockton, Paul La Rosa, Tom Kovacevic, Mike Barone, Brian Carter, Earl Steinbicker, Louise Mensch, Oliver Fowler, Tony Berardini, Tom Hadfield, Redbeard, Craig Reed, Chuck Ingersoll, Paul Raymond, Jon Newey, Tami Danielson, Brad Sinsel, Jane Gazzo, Tim Smith, Bun E. Carlos, Charlie Starr, John Fannon, Fred Mandel, Mat Van Kriedt, Jason Woodman, Owen Orford, Jamie Feliciano, Marc Storace, Tristin Norwell, Ted Ruscitti, Loren Molinare, Helen Raymond, Jerry Goodwin, Ronnie Lightsey, Buster Bodine, James Del Balzo, Robert Valentine, Tom Donald, Phil Doherty, Linda Aizer, Ira Blacker, Koby Kruse, Adrian Lee, Juno Roxas, Rémi Cohen, Ben Upham, Tom Weschler, Sam Aizer, Matt Moore, Michael Cohen, Darryl "Spyda" Smith, Craig Tuck, Phil Rudd, Stefan Kaufmann, Paula Benstead at King's College Hospital Trust (London), Sue Carr at London Ambulance Service NHS Trust, Daisy Coleman, Maher Nizari and John Thompson at Inner South London Coroner's Court, Chris Read at State Library of South Australia, Maxine Cooper at Coroner's Office (London), Nikki Koehlert at Briscoe Center for American History (Austin), Siew Lee and Deanna Kronk at National Library of Australia (Canberra), Rachel Hollis at State Records Authority of New South Wales (Sydney), Judith Paterson and Loreta Tabellione at National Archives of Australia (Canberra), Shashikala Palagummi at the Supreme Court of New South Wales (Sydney), and Mark Beswick at the Met Office National Meteorological Archive (Exeter).

The research facilities provided by the National Library of Australia, National Archives of Australia, State Library of New South Wales, State Library of South Australia, National Film and Sound Archive of Australia, and New York Public Library for the Performing Arts were all beneficial to the writing of this book. Support your local library.

Penguin Random House Australia's Alison Urquhart, who I have known for nearly 20 years, was the Australian publisher both of *The Youngs* and *Bon: The Last Highway*. Nikki Christer was the original publisher of Clinton Walker's pioneering Bon Scott biography *Highway to Hell* in 1994, and in early 2014 as publishing director of Penguin Random House Australia, she gave the green light to *Bon: The Last Highway*, just as she did to *The Youngs* back in 2012. With such a combined pedigree between them, I couldn't ask for two better people to be behind this book. Alison and Nikki recognised that there was still a lot more to Bon's story that hadn't yet been told.

It was an easy decision to publish in North America with Michael Holmes at ECW Press. Michael was very enthusiastic about *Bon: The Last Highway* when he first read it and as fascinated by Bon's untold story as I was. My sincere thanks to my friend and *Van Halen Rising* author Greg Renoff in Tulsa, Oklahoma, for recommending Michael and all of the team at ECW who were involved in the preparation of the North American edition: Samantha Dobson, Crissy Calhoun, Susannah Ames, David Caron, Laura Pastore and Jessica Albert.

In Europe, Monika Koch at Hannibal Verlag was once again my German-language publisher and it has been a great pleasure to know and work with her over two books. Paul Fleischmann, Rainer Schoettle, Alan Tepper and Thomas Auer comprised the editorial and design team that pulled together the German edition. Campbell Brown and Janne Moller signed me up for another round with their excellent Scottish operation, Black & White. I am also very happy to be published for the first time in France with Le Castor Astral's music imprint, Castor Music. Thank you to Richard Begault, Marc Torralba, François Tétreau and

Jean-Yves Reuzeau. While in Japan, the gracious Makiko Nakai at DU Books published Japanese translations of both my AC/DC books, bringing them to a whole new readership.

Luke Causby was the book's designer and, like he did with *The Youngs*, he delivered big time with the cover. He also helps me out on social media promoting *Bon: The Last Highway*. It's what I'd expect from a good friend, and Luke has been just that for over 20 years.

Patrick Mangan, another old friend, was the book's editor. Having been at different times in my career both a book editor and an author, just like Patrick has, I know from personal experience how a good editor can make a huge difference to a project. Patrick is more than good; he's exceptional. He challenged me on facts, pointed out things I hadn't even considered and made suggestions that benefited the story. I couldn't ask for more than that. His shared love of Bon's music is reflected in the book you hold in your hands.

Scott Miller, my agent at Trident Media Group, and his foreign-rights colleagues Claire Roberts and Sylvie Rosokoff did the deals for *Bon: The Last Highway* and have been great supporters of my writing. Together with Nerrilee Weir and Vicki Grundy at Penguin Random House Australia they have brought my work to many countries around the world, for which I am happy and grateful.

To Billie Fink, you are the best daughter a dad could ever ask for. Thank you for putting up with my absences while writing this book. I love you.

And to the man this whole book is about, Bon Scott, thanks for the music and your flawed humanity. Because of your faults, not despite them, I admire you more than ever. You were one of the true greats but you were also just one of us.

Ride on.

BIBLIOGRAPHY

BEATING AROUND THE BUSH

Bon: The Last Highway *proved to be a detective exercise as much as a literary undertaking. Information was discovered in some unlikely places — from sheets of paper containing a few handwritten words to ticket stubs to newspaper clippings missing dates, publication titles and bylines. I found nuggets of important information in conventional places such as the New York Public Library of Performing Arts and unconventional ones such as eBay and the Supreme Court of New South Wales. I have endeavoured to reference sources, both for direct quotes and background information, with as much detail as is or was available. Quotes or statements referenced in the notes section refer to those contained in the main text and Endnotes. All reasonable efforts have been made to credit sources fully. Readers are welcome to point out any errors or omissions by contacting me through the book's Facebook page, facebook.com/acdcbooks, or my personal Facebook account. — JF*

OPENER

Shot Down In Flames

ANGUS YOUNG It's weird, because when he was alive *Kerrang!*,
September 1990; We were on the road for 10 or 11 months every
year *Rolling Stone* (Australia), May 2007; Over the years, there
have been numerous people *Record Collector*, January 1996; You'd
need several volumes just to chronicle what Bon got up to in one
day *Times*, 17 January 1998.

BON SCOTT Day-in, day-out, fly, drive, hotel-in, hotel-out
Leeuwarder Courant, 11 November 1978; It's sometimes a drag
Putterford, *Shock to the System*, 1992; Book of words, all my
poetry 2GZ Orange interview, circa 1975/76; I've got pages of stuff
Countdown, ABC Television, 1977.

MISCELLANEOUS Drunks and hookers acdccollector.com, 2007;
A dangerous individual who gave the impression he didn't know
who he was or where he belonged *Sydney Morning Herald*, 28
November 2008; Bon Scott succumbed to recreational substances
Sydney Morning Herald, 23 January 1984; A way of remembering
the real Bon *West Australian*, 18 October 2015; Bon's missing lyric
notebook "may" have been returned *Scottish Sun*, 4 December
2015; Ex *Scottish Sun*, ibid.; Literally the last story that we did on
AC/DC *Reading Eagle*, 8 November 2008; There were 10 shows
lined up for us and AC/DC *Billboard*, 18 July 1981; Kicked to the
kerb *Canton Repository*, 15 March 2016; Threw it in the rubbish
bin Renshaw, facebook.com, 20 July 2016.

PART ONE, 1977

1 | *Go Down*

MALCOLM YOUNG Started word of mouth *In the Studio with
Redbeard*, 1997; We played our first gig in front of a bunch of cowboys *Guitar One*, June 2000.

MISCELLANEOUS [Bon] wandered off . . . with all these Mexicans

Wall, *AC/DC: Hell Ain't a Bad Place to Be*, 2012; It's as unchanging a shtick as a Borscht Belt comic's *Daily News*, 28 August 2000.

2 | *Bad Boy Boogie*
BON SCOTT I've dropped a Quaalude Walker, *Highway to Hell*, 1994.

3 | *Whole Lotta Rosie*
MISCELLANEOUS Michael Klenfner, who headed up Atlantic's marketing and promotion, had gone down to AC/DC's first few gigs Browning, *Dog Eat Dog*, 2014.

4 | *Problem Child*
BON SCOTT It was amazing to see Putterford, ibid.
MISCELLANEOUS The most important figure in the record industry of the 20th century *Independent*, 16 December 2006; I'm not sure I would have signed them *Billboard*, 24 February 2007.

5 | *Dog Eat Dog*
MISCELLANEOUS Page Three–type blonde Putterford, ibid.; His arm wrapped around a buxom blonde *MOJO*, December 2000; In 1977, just six years after its birth, WEA felt flush George-Warren (ed.), *Rolling Stone: The Seventies*, 1998; I don't like the way people keep saying he died from drugs or heroin *Australian*, 1 July 2006.

6 | *Overdose*
BON SCOTT Dunno what I'd do without this band, y'know *Classic Rock*, February 2008.
MALCOLM YOUNG When we want to hear something we put on The Beatles *Cavalier Daily*, 19 September 1985.
MISCELLANEOUS Hooker *Rolling Stone* (Australia), January 2006; The meaning of the music isn't in the lyrics alone *Homebrewed Christianity*, 8 July 2012.

7 | *Hell Ain't A Bad Place To Be*
ANGUS YOUNG By the way he carried himself, you really thought that Bon Scott was immortal *Guitar World*, January 1998.

BON SCOTT My new schoolmates threatened to kick the shit out of me AC/DC, *Bonfire*, 1997; I was singing a couple of songs with a band at a dance *Advertiser*, 12 February 2000; To make housewives sort of cry into their tea towels 2SM, 1975; I heard the song 5KA, 1977; I was painting ships in Adelaide Harbour 2SM, ibid.; The band walks out in crimplene 5KA, ibid.; Knocked out . . . it was really good 5KA, ibid.; Got [AC/DC] on the road to check out what they were really like 5KA, ibid.; Gone home and thought, "No, I can't do it" 5KA, ibid.

MALCOLM YOUNG Tied him up and made him write some nice clean lyrics 2SM, 1975.

MISCELLANEOUS In a 1969 press release for The Valentines *Age*, 26 June 1987; Wasn't a trace of a Scottish accent on Bon Thornton, *My Bon Scott*, 2014; Committed to the Child Welfare Department for 12 months *Sunday Age*, 20 February 2000; Five trucks and 50 crew and we're off and we're running *Homebrewed Christianity*, ibid.

PART TWO, 1978

8 | *What's Next To The Moon*

ANGUS YOUNG He made a lot of friends everywhere *Sounds*, 29 March 1980; That's always been a bit of a myth *Island Ear*, April 2000; Bon was not a heavy drinker *Age*, 5 February 1988.

MISCELLANEOUS We were aware that he had a drinking problem *West Australian*, date unknown, 1981; I don't care who tells me anything different Fink, *The Youngs*, 2013.

9 | *Kicked In The Teeth*

MALCOLM YOUNG [Bon] was what he was . . . Bon never was on a deathwish, you know *In the Studio with Redbeard*, ibid.; I think Bon taught us in a way not to end up like him *Kerrang!*, September 1990.

10 | *Rock 'N' Roll Damnation*

ANGUS YOUNG Browning was always open to people's earholes, you know *Countdown*, Melbourne, 1986.

MALCOLM YOUNG A pretty rock bass player 2SM, 1975.

MARK EVANS **We were on tour with Black Sabbath** Fink, previously unpublished quote, 2013.

MISCELLANEOUS **Tired of touring** Larkin (ed.), *The Virgin Encyclopedia of Popular Music: Concise Fourth Edition*, 2002; **It had come down to musical differences** Unknown publication, 1977; **As always, everyone involved maintains there are no bad feelings** Unknown publication; ibid.

11 | *Gimme A Bullet*

MISCELLANEOUS **AC/DC have a calculated approach to whipping audiences into heat** Reproduced in the *Australian*, 22 February 1980; **Attempts to go sober — including hypnosis — had failed** Walker, ibid.; **They called me** 1Live, 3 July 2015; **A small guy's shoulder, the singer, who's just yelling into the microphone** Mensch, Royal Albert Hall interview, 2014; **AC/DC called me almost every day in my office just to give me news of them** *Metal Attack*, November 1985; **Was so incapacitated that he polished off an entire bottle of aftershave** Sellers, *An A–Z of Hellraisers: A Comprehensive Compendium of Outrageous Insobriety*, 2010; **Paul Chapman had also seen Bon drink aftershave** *Classic Rock*, February 2005.

12 | *Up To My Neck In You*

None.

13 | *Riff Raff*

BON SCOTT **I guess I have always had the idea of being rich and having a lifestyle to which I was suited** Ellis, typewritten story, 1978; **The more we work, the more we tour, we're getting more ideas** *Australian Music to the World*, 1978; **You've just got to have a break, you know** *Countdown*, ibid.; **I've been on the road 15 years** *Best*, December 1979.

MISCELLANEOUS **Dressed to the nines** Prism Archive, 2012; **Ragged around the edges** Prism Archive, ibid.; **He thought I got the best deal** Prism Archive, ibid.; **Live an ordinary life like anyone else and just play guitar** Prism Archive, ibid.; **There was a deep core of unhappiness** Prism Archive, ibid.; **An undertone of sadness** Prism

Archive, ibid.; **He had been touring non-stop on an upwardly mobile track** Prism Archive, ibid.; **Was something about Bon that was a touch effeminate** Prism Archive, ibid.; **Took away all the showbiz . . . something that wasn't slick** Prism Archive, ibid.; **He told me that he'd had enough** *No Nonsense*, 1999.

14 | *Down Payment Blues*
MISCELLANEOUS **[AC/DC] signed the worst record deal I have ever seen in my entire life** Mensch, ibid.; **We ended up signing [AC/DC] to a ridiculously long deal** Putterford, ibid.; **Solved that problem** Mensch, ibid.; **Bon received a royalty cheque from Ted Albert in the second half of 1976** Walker, ibid.; **A share in Albert Productions in lieu of cash** Milesago.com, "AC/DC," date unknown; **Partnership** Albert, *House of Hits: The Great Untold Story of Australia's First Family of Music*, 2010; **Three-way partnership** Tait, *Vanda & Young: Inside Australia's Hit Factory*, 2010; **Falling into a bloody goldmine** Wall, ibid.; **Its collective personal wealth was estimated to be $45 million as far back as 1992** *Sunday Age*, 14 February 1993; **They had a little savings account** Fink, *The Youngs*, ibid; **Bon died with just $31,162.52 in assets** "The Estate of Ronald Belford Scott, Late of Spearwood in the State of Western Australia," 9 July 1980.

15 | *Sin City*
None.

16 | *Cold Hearted Man*
ANGUS YOUNG **We just like being in the womb of the road** *Canberra Times*, 6 January 1982; **Earpiece** *In the Studio with Redbeard*, ibid.
BON SCOTT **Now that I'm in AC/DC I realise I'm not very musical** *Scream!*, Vol. 1 No. 11, 1975; **It's all so close to you, it's all right on top of you** KSJO, 21 July 1979; **Horrible place, Miami** *Record Mirror*, 18 August 1979.
CLIFF WILLIAMS **The stage around us was really dark** Johnson, *Get Your Jumbo Jet Out of My Airport: Random Notes for AC/DC Obsessives*, 1999.

MALCOLM YOUNG Jumped straight off the amps *Sounds*, 28 August 1976; Bon really delivered with his talkin' stuff *Family Jewels*, ibid.

MISCELLANEOUS You haven't got a commercial ear *In the Studio with Redbeard*, ibid.

PART THREE, 1979

17 | *Walk All Over You*

ANGUS YOUNG We'd $10 between us *In the Studio with Redbeard*, ibid.; Mal was banging on the drums *Guitar Player*, July 2003; We saw more of [Bon] than his family did Stenning, *Two Sides to Every Glory*, 2005.

BON SCOTT We did the album in a totally different way this time *Record Mirror*, ibid.

CLIFF WILLIAMS No, no, no . . . that was all, you know, lyrically, from Brian Johnson's influence GlamMetal.com, 2007.

MALCOLM YOUNG Bon always knew what he was doing, you know *In the Studio with Redbeard*, ibid.

MISCELLANEOUS Titled as far back as 1977 and recorded in four different versions *Australian Playboy*, May 1994.

18 | *Night Prowler*

MISCELLANEOUS As a non-addictive alternative to barbiturates PBS.org, 17 May 2011; In 1980 there were 66 deaths alone *Palm Beach Post*, 12 August 1981; Schoolchild *Miami News*, 16 January 1981.

19 | *Touch Too Much*

CLIFF WILLIAMS We were under a lot of time pressure on that one Johnson, ibid.

MISCELLANEOUS Bon Scott was having problems with the lyrics Engleheart, *AC/DC, Maximum Rock & Roll*, 2006; Obvious difficulty with the singer Wall, ibid.; Drinking like crazy and didn't have any lyrics Wall, ibid.

20 | *Love Hungry Man*
BON SCOTT About a guy who gets pissed around by chicks, and he heads for the horizon *Australian Playboy*, ibid.

21 | *If You Want Blood (You've Got It)*
BON SCOTT [Lange] really injected new life into us *Record Mirror*, ibid.

22 | *Girls Got Rhythm*
BON SCOTT Just . . . just . . . pure *pop*! *Record Mirror*, ibid.; We're beginning to make an impact [in North America] at last *Record Mirror*, ibid.; The change did us a power of good *Record Mirror*, ibid.
MISCELLANEOUS Blessing to some and frustrating to others *Morning Call*, June 1979.

23 | *Highway To Hell*
BON SCOTT I've become a bit of an alco Walker, ibid.

PART FOUR, 1980

24 | *Shoot To Thrill*
MISCELLANEOUS Another junkie acquaintance of Silver's Wall, ibid.; Allegedly a would-be musician; apparently a bass player *Classic Rock*, February 2005; A would-be musician, although he may have been nothing more than a ligger and a drug slut Walker, *Highway to Hell*, 2015; There is strong evidence to suggest that Alisdair [sic] Kinnear was, in fact, a false name Putterford, ibid.; Alistair Kinnear — who some claim was a rock journalist, not a musician — may have changed his identity *Classic Rock*, ibid.; When Alistair Kinnear . . . issued a very belated statement Walker, ibid.; [I] was quoted exasperatedly Walker, ibid.

25 | *Hells Bells*
MISCELLANEOUS Grieving fans had taken to affixing pictures of Bon to Alistair's front door *POP/Rocky*, 5 August 1981; A punk band, more than a decade before Malcolm McLaren got involved with the

Sex Pistols Cutler, *You Can't Always Get What You Want*, 2010; **May have experimented** Stenning, ibid.; **Wasn't a habitual user** Stenning, ibid; **Never spoke to Chapman, but in the interviews with him I've read he sheds no light** *Classic Rock*, ibid.

26 | *Shake A Leg*
MARK EVANS Bon Scott's personal assistant in London *No Nonsense*, 1999.

27 | *Let Me Put My Love Into You*
MISCELLANEOUS I've always felt like the guy who filled in for Mick Cocks Fink, previously unpublished quote, 2013; **However, Way is also previously on the record saying he didn't want to tell Angus that Bon was dead** *Classic Rock*, ibid.; **If you're not skilled at the art of heroin, then you do [a] dance with the devil** *Classic Rock*, ibid.

28 | *Given The Dog A Bone*
MISCELLANEOUS Chapman has previously stated in an interview with American radio host Eddie Trunk *Eddie Trunk Live*, 20 July 2015; **Some days after our Hammersmith gigs** *Classic Rock*, ibid.

29 | *Have A Drink On Me*
None.

30 | *Back In Black*
MISCELLANEOUS In late 1978 I met Silver Smith . . . err on the side of caution when we don't know all the facts *Metal Hammer & Classic Rock Present AC/DC*, 2005; **Mouth had turned blue. He was totally fucking completely gone** Antonia, *The One and Only: Peter Perrett — Homme Fatale*, 1996; **Bon wanted to go to the club Dingwalls** Walker, ibid.; **She had his number** Walker, ibid.; **When I saw him at the flat, [Bon] was already so drunk** Walker, ibid.; **I'm not sure** Jack Cool, 26 July 2016 **Bon was sober** Jack Cool, ibid.; **The keys got jammed inside the door** ABC Adelaide, ibid.; **A very distressed Alistair** ABC Adelaide, ibid.; **He's passed out. He's half

passed out. What do I do? ABC Adelaide, ibid.; I suggested he take him home ABC Adelaide, ibid.; I was up five flights, he was up three ABC Adelaide, ibid.

31 | *What Do You Do For Money Honey*
MISCELLANEOUS When [Alistair] got home he rang me again ABC Adelaide, ibid.; Thinking when Bon's come out of it he'll just come upstairs ABC Adelaide, ibid.; Poor Alistair, not being used to drinking ABC Adelaide, ibid.

32 | *Rock And Roll Ain't Noise Pollution*
ANGUS YOUNG The girl gave me the hospital number *Sounds*, ibid.; I had called the guy that was managing us *Behind the Music: AC/DC*, 2000; The hospital wouldn't say anything until the police contacted the parents *Rolling Stone* (Australia), ibid.; More or less, you know, asphyxiated *Behind the Music: AC/DC*, ibid.; I suppose he would feel worse about it *Sounds*, ibid.
BRIAN JOHNSON The truth of the matter was that Bon died because he vomited when his neck was twisted and he choked *Record Mirror*, 26 July 1980.
MALCOLM YOUNG Angus called me. I was just totally stunned *Behind the Music: AC/DC*, ibid.; Choked through the night, the position he was sleeping in, you know *Behind the Music: AC/DC*, ibid.
MISCELLANEOUS The hospital called Silver but didn't tell her that Bon, who'd already been identified, was dead *Wall*, ibid.; For his part, tour manager Ian Jeffery has said he got a call from Malcolm at 2:30 a.m. *Wall*, ibid.; Or 3 a.m. *Engleheart*, ibid.; The phone call came at midnight *Walker*, ibid.; The Jefferys got a visit from production manager Jake Berry *Wall*, ibid.; Mensch called and said they should go and identify the body *Wall*, ibid.; Berry dropped off Jeffery at Mensch's *Wall*, ibid.; Mensch and Jeffery went to the morgue *Wall*, ibid.; I get a phone call that Bon Scott has died *Sunday Times*, 28 October 2012; Don't fucking joke! Don't fucking wake me up to tell me this fucking shit *Engleheart*, ibid.; It wasn't Alistair's fault *Advertiser*, 12 February 2000; On the night he died he'd been writing

song lyrics all day *West Australian*, 8 July 2006; **Struck by the fact Bon's neck was twisted** Walker, ibid.; **Category of "damage"** Saukko and Knight, *Knight's Forensic Pathology*, 2016; **Was still wrapped in the blanket** Unknown publication, 1980; **To be honest both [Alistair and I] really just hid from the press at the time** ABC Adelaide, ibid.

PART FIVE, AFTERMATH

33 | *Rocker*

ANGUS YOUNG **He died of what is called "misadventure"** *Rolling Stone* (Australia), ibid.

MALCOLM YOUNG **We weren't there but we knew exactly what went on there** Wall, ibid.

MISCELLANEOUS **Level of diagnostic accuracy** Treasure, "The Coroner's Autopsy: Do We Deserve Better?, A Report of the National Confidential Enquiry into Patient Outcome and Death," 2006; **Probably true** Treasure, ibid.; **Accurate beyond reasonable doubt** Treasure, ibid.; **The cause of death remains unknown** southlondoncoroner.org, 2016; **How, when and where the death occurred** southlondoncoroner.org, ibid.; **Drugs and poisons could be detected in low concentrations** Butterworth, *What Good Is a Coroner?: The Transformation of the Queensland Office of Coroner 1859–1959*, April 2012; **There are many questions about the death and the coroner's report that have remained unanswered** *Sun-Herald*, 11 April 1999; **The singer's liver, kidneys and general health had been excellent** *Sounds*, ibid.; **The equivalent of half a bottle of whisky** Putterford, ibid.; **Choked on his own vomit after one of many heavy drinking sessions** *Music Backtrack* (blog), 18 February 2012; **Scott was a man of considerable talent who was the captain of his own destiny** Unknown publication, 1980; **If Bon had been seeing a doctor, I would have known about it** Wall, ibid.; **Bon sort of pushed the physical bounds** ABC Adelaide, ibid.; **Cleared of any wrongdoing** Johnson, ibid.; **Mr. Kennear [sic] said that when he woke up** *Guardian*, 23 February 1980; **Told the court that Scott, who joined the band in Australia** Unknown publication, 1980.

34 | *Ain't No Fun (Waiting 'Round To Be A Millionaire)*
BRIAN JOHNSON [Bon] had a terrible thing happen to him when he
 passed on *USA Today*, 5 June 2011.
MALCOLM YOUNG Someone had to tell them, you know *Behind the
 Music: AC/DC*, ibid.
MARK EVANS Bon certainly wasn't an alcoholic Putterford, ibid.
MISCELLANEOUS Bon's parents first heard of their son's death on
 the radio *Rolling Stone* (Australia), ibid.; I can remember like it
 was yesterday when I heard Ron had died *West Australian*, ibid.; It
 was a Uniting Church service Walker, ibid.; Bon wasn't an alcoholic Putterford, ibid., 1992; He wasn't an alcoholic *Rolling Stone*
 (Australia), ibid.; Scott didn't use heroin *Rolling Stone* (Australia),
 January 2006; Bon was an alcoholic, not a junkie *Age*, 13 July
 1994; No one gave Bon drugs Walker, ibid.

35 | *High Voltage*
MISCELLANEOUS All Chick and Isa got was a suitcase Walker, ibid.;
 He always said he was going to be a millionaire *Australian*, 1 July
 2006; He was writing words for their *Back In Black* album when
 he died *West Australian*, ibid.; When [Bon] died we didn't get
 any of his belongings back *West Australian*, ibid.; Never saw any
 [note]books Fink, *The Youngs*, ibid.; A cassette on which Bon had
 recorded the words also disappeared *Sounds*, 14 February 1981; His
 then manager Peter Mensch, an asshole *Paris Match*, 27 July 2015.

36 | *It's A Long Way To The Top (If You Wanna Rock 'N' Roll)*
ANGUS YOUNG He had this pile of lyrics he'd been kicking about
 Guitar World, April 2003; Some things we can't do, you know, that
 was strictly Bon's songs, and things *Countdown*, 1981; No, we were
 gonna start working on the lyrics with him the next week [after he
 died] *Record Collector*, January 1996; The week he died, we had
 just worked out the music and he was going to come in and start
 writing lyrics *Guitar World*, January 1998; Bon was just about to
 come and start working with us writing lyrics just before he died
 Island Ear, ibid.; There was nothing [on *Back In Black*] from Bon's

notebook *Classic Rock*, August 2005; George would look through
[Bon's] book *West Australian*, 21 November 1997.
MISCELLANEOUS Not totally certain about *Back In Black* Fink, *The
Youngs*, ibid.

37 | *Dirty Deeds Done Dirt Cheap*
BRIAN JOHNSON Bollocks *Classic Rock*, 23 November 2000.
MISCELLANEOUS A few of the *Back In Black* album's tracks had
been demoed before Bon's death The Rockpit, date unknown.

38 | *Rock 'N' Roll Singer*
BRIAN JOHNSON I'd met Bon in Hull years before when he'd sup-
ported us *Classic Rock*, ibid.; That one day changed my life *Times
Leader*, 2000.
MISCELLANEOUS They asked me to join AC/DC after Bon Scott died
Fink, *The Youngs*, ibid.

39 | *You Shook Me All Night Long*
BRIAN JOHNSON I don't believe in spirits and that Wiederhorn and
Turman, *Louder Than Hell*, 2013; About three, four months [sic]
after Bon's death, I'm in The Bahamas *New York Post*, 12 June
2011; More than I ever did, took things from real life *No Nonsense*,
2001; The closest I got to America was when I was with Geordie
Record Mirror, 26 July 1980; Go to Texas *Rolling Stone*,
7 December 2000; We were in The Bahamas and I had seen
a couple of American girls *No Nonsense*, ibid.; I'd seen them
[American women] on the TV *VH1's Ultimate Albums: Back In
Black*, 2003; It was as quick as it had to be, which was that night
Absolute Radio, 2014; They played a couple of the riffs Absolute
Radio, 2010.

40 | *Live Wire*
ANGUS YOUNG One night Bon got drunk *Gazette*, 18 October 1979.
BRIAN JOHNSON I know that [Bon] approves of what the new lineup
is trying to do *Kerrang!*, February/March 1982; To me, it might be

one of the best rock songs ever written — if I do say so myself *New Musical Express*, 23 March 2009.

MALCOLM YOUNG **Complete bollocks** *Classic Rock*, September 2003.

MISCELLANEOUS **You've got to find someone else. Whatever you do, don't stop** *SPIN*, September 2009; **As a family, we were all shocked** *Australian*, ibid.; **Astonishingly, he received a letter from his late brother Bon in 1984** Renshaw, *Live Wire*, 2015; **Bon said if the next record didn't work out** *Australian*, ibid.

41 | *Let There Be Rock*
None.

CLOSER

Ride On
ANGUS YOUNG **We didn't make any, really any money** *Night Flight*, 1983.

BRIAN JOHNSON **It's a hard question to answer** *Circus*, December 1983.

MARK EVANS **Sometimes, I think, "Gee, boy, it would have been great if Bon had have been able to hang [on] for one more record"** Fink, previously unpublished quote, 2013.

MISCELLANEOUS **Those of us in Australia who knew Bon well** *Advertiser*, date unknown, 2008.

BOOKS

AC/DC: Hell Ain't a Bad Place to Be, Mick Wall, Orion Books, London, 2012

AC/DC, High-Voltage Rock 'N' Roll: The Ultimate Illustrated History, Phil Sutcliffe, Voyageur Press, Minneapolis, 2010

AC/DC in the Studio: The Stories Behind Every Album, Jake Brown, John Blake Publishing, London, 2010

AC/DC, Maximum Rock & Roll: The Ultimate Story of the World's Greatest Rock Band, Murray Engleheart with Arnaud Durieux, HarperCollins, Sydney, 2006; (revised ed.) HarperCollins, Sydney, 2015

AC/DC: Shock to the System, Mark Putterford, Omnibus Press, London, 1992

AC/DC: The Kerrang! Files!, The Definitive History, Malcolm Dome (ed.), Virgin Books, London, 1995

AC/DC: The World's Heaviest Rock, Martin Huxley, St. Martin's Griffin, New York, 1996

AC/DC: Tours de France 1976–2014, Philippe Lageat and Baptiste Brelet, Éditions Point Barre, Parmain, 2014

AC/DC, Two Sides to Every Glory: The Complete Biography, Paul Stenning, Chrome Dreams, New Malden, 2005

A Fast Ride Out of Here: Confessions of Rock's Most Dangerous Man, Pete Way with Paul Rees, Constable, London, 2017

Alcoholics Anonymous: The Story of How Many Thousands of Men and Women Have Recovered from Alcoholism (The Big Book), Bill Wilson, Works Publishing Company, New York, 1939

Alice Cooper: Golf Monster: How a Wild Rock 'N' Roll Life Led to a Serious Golf Addiction, Alice Cooper, Aurum Press, London, 2007

Almost a Celebrity: A Lifetime of Night-Time, James Whale, Michael O'Mara Books, London, 2007

An A–Z of Hellraisers: A Comprehensive Compendium of Outrageous Insobriety, Robert Sellers, Random House, London, 2010

The Billboard Book of Top 40 Hits, 9th Edition: Complete Chart Information about America's Most Popular Songs and Artists, 1955–2009, Joel Whitburn, Billboard Books, New York, 2010

Buzzed: The Straight Facts about the Most Used and Abused Drugs from Alcohol to Ecstasy (Fully Revised and Updated Fourth Edition), Cynthia Kuhn, Scott Swartzwelder and Wilkie Wilson, W.W. Norton & Company, New York, 2014

Dirty Deeds: My Life Inside and Outside of AC/DC, Mark Evans, Allen & Unwin, Sydney, 2011

Dog Eat Dog: A Story of Survival, Struggle and Triumph by the Man Who Put AC/DC on the World Stage, Michael Browning, Allen & Unwin, Sydney, 2014

Drugs, the Straight Facts: Quaaludes, Justin T. Gass, Ph.D., Chelsea House, New York, 2008

Encyclopedia of Television Series, Pilots and Specials 1974–1984,
 Volume II, Vincent Terrace, New York Zoetrope, New York, 1985

The First Rock & Roll Confidential Report: Inside the Real World
 of Rock & Roll, Dave Marsh and the editors of *Rock & Roll*
 Confidential: Lee Ballinger, Sandra Choron, Wendy Smith, Daniel
 Wolff, Pantheon Books, New York, 1985

FM Atlas and Station Directory: A Handy Reference to the FM Stations
 of the United States, Canada and Mexico, Bruce F. Elving, Ph.D.,
 FM Atlas Publishing Co., Adolph, 1976 and 1978 editions

Get the Led Out: How Led Zeppelin Became the Biggest Band in the
 World, Denny Somach, Sterling Publishing, New York, 2012

Get Your Jumbo Jet Out of My Airport: Random Notes for AC/DC
 Obsessives, Howard Johnson, The Black Book Company, Pewsey,
 1999

The Girl: A Life in the Shadow of Roman Polanski, Samantha Geimer,
 Atria Books, New York, 2013

The Grove Dictionary of American Music, Second Edition, Volume
 One, Charles Hiroshi Garrett (ed.), Oxford University Press, New
 York, 2013

Highway to Hell: The Life and Times of AC/DC Legend Bon Scott,
 Clinton Walker, Pan Macmillan, Sydney, 1994; (revised North
 American ed. retitled as *Highway to Hell: The Life and Death of*
 AC/DC Legend Bon Scott) Verse Chorus Press, Portland, 2007;
 (revised Australian ed. retitled as as *Highway to Hell: The Life and*
 Death of AC/DC Legend Bon Scott) Pan Macmillan, Sydney, 2015

House of Hits: The Great Untold Story of Australia's First Family
 of Music, Jane Albert, Hardie Grant Books, Melbourne, 2010

Knight's Forensic Pathology, Fourth Edition, Prof. Pekka Saukko
 and Prof. Bernard Knight, CRC Press, Boca Raton (FL), 2016

Live Wire: Bon Scott, a Memoir by Three of the People Who Knew
 Him Best, Mary Renshaw, John Darcy and Gabby Darcy, Allen
 & Unwin, Sydney, 2015

Louder Than Hell: The Definitive Oral History of Metal, Jon
 Wiederhorn & Katherine Turman, HarperCollins, New York, 2013

Miami, Joan Didion, Simon & Schuster, New York, 1987

Music, Money and Success: The Insider's Guide to Making Money

in the Music Business, Seventh Edition, Jeffrey Brabec and Todd
  Brabec, Schirmer Trade Books, New York, 2011
My Bon Scott, Irene Thornton with Simone Ubaldi, Pan Macmillan,
  Sydney, 2014
The New American Standard Bible, The Lockman Foundation,
  Foundation Publications, Anaheim, 1997
The One and Only: Peter Perrett — Homme Fatale, Nina Antonia, SAF
  Publishing, Wembley, 1996
The Pursuit of Oblivion: A Global History of Narcotics 1500–2000,
  Richard Davenport-Hines, Weidenfield & Nicolson, London, 2001
The Rock and Roll Hall of Fame: The First 25 Years, The Rock & Roll
  Hall of Fame Foundation, HarperCollins, New York, 2009
The Rock Who's Who, 2nd Edition, Brock Helander, Schirmer Books,
  New York, 1996
The Rolling Stone Album Guide, Anthony DeCurtis and James Henke
  with Holly George-Warren (eds), Random House, New York, 1992
Rolling Stone: The Seventies, Holly George-Warren (ed.), Simon &
  Schuster, London, 1998
Sophisto-Punk: The Story of Mark Opitz & Oz Rock, Mark Opitz (as
  told to Luke Wallis and Jeff Jenkins), Random House Australia,
  Sydney, 2012
Texas Music, Rick Koster, St. Martin's Press, New York, 1998
This Business of Music: The Definitive Guide to the Music Industry,
  New 8th Edition, M. William Krasilovsky and Sidney Shemel with
  contributions by John M. Gross, Billboard Books, New York, 2000
The Virgin Encyclopedia of Popular Music: Concise Fourth Edition,
  Colin Larkin (ed.), Virgin Books, London, 2002
Vanda & Young: Inside Australia's Hit Factory, John Tait, University of
  New South Wales Press, Sydney, 2010
You Can't Always Get What You Want: My Life with The Rolling
  Stones, The Grateful Dead and Other Wonderful Reprobates, Sam
  Cutler, ECW Press, Toronto, 2010
The Youngs: The Brothers Who Built AC/DC, Jesse Fink, Random
  House Australia, Sydney, 2013; (revised North American ed.) St.
  Martin's Press, New York, 2015

AC/DC, Back In Black: Classic Albums Under Review, Umbrella
  Entertainment, Melbourne, 2008

"AC/DC, *Back In Black* 35th Anniversary — Angus Young, Brian
  Johnson, Malcolm Young," Redbeard, *In the Studio with Redbeard*,
  Dallas, 2015. Original recordings made in Dallas, 1991 (Angus
  Young and Brian Johnson); New York City, 1992 (Angus Young
  and Brian Johnson); BBC, London, 1997 (Malcolm Young); and
  New York City, 1997 (Angus Young)

AC/DC, Highway To Hell: Classic Albums Under Review, Umbrella
  Entertainment, Melbourne, 2009

"AC/DC, *Highway To Hell* 35th Anniversary — Angus Young,
  Malcolm Young," Redbeard, *In the Studio with Redbeard*, Dallas,
  2014. Original recordings made in Dallas, 1991 (Angus Young and
  Brian Johnson); New York City, 1992 (Angus Young and Brian
  Johnson); BBC, London, 1997 (Malcolm Young); and New York
  City, 1997 (Angus Young)

AC/DC group interview (Bon Scott, Angus Young, Malcolm Young,
  Phil Rudd), Ron E. Sparks, 2SM, Sydney, February 1975

AC/DC group interview (Bon Scott, Angus Young, Malcolm Young),
  Ron E. Sparks, 2SM, Sydney, March 1976

AC/DC, Let There Be Rock: The Movie, Eric Dionysius and Eric
  Mistler (directors), High Speed Productions in association with
  Sebastian International, Paris, 1980

AC/DC: Live at The Palladium, New York City, August 24, 1977,
  Bruce Bernstein, Nuclear Magenta Films, New York, 2013

Angus Young interview, Molly Meldrum, *Countdown*, Melbourne,
  1986

Angus Young interview, Richard Wilkins, MTV, Sydney, 1988

Angus Young interview, unknown, MCM Euromusique, Paris, 1996

Angus Young and Bon Scott interview, unknown, 2GZ, Orange, circa
  1975/76

Angus Young and Bon Scott interview, Sheila Rene, KSJO, San Jose, 21
  July 1979

Angus Young and Bon Scott interview, Vince Lovegrove, Paul Drane
  (director), *Australian Music to the World*, Atlanta, 1978

Angus Young and Brian Johnson interview, Allan Handelman, *Night Flight* (unedited raw footage), Raleigh (NC), 1983

Angus Young and Brian Johnson interview, Christian O'Connell, Absolute Radio, London, 2014

Angus Young and Brian Johnson interview, Howard Stern, SiriusXM, New York, 2014

Angus Young and Brian Johnson interview, Molly Meldrum, *Countdown*, Melbourne, 1981

Angus Young and Cliff Williams interview, uncredited, Reddit, San Francisco, 15 November 2014

Behind the Music: AC/DC, VH1, Viacom International, New York, 2000

Blood + Thunder: The Sound of Alberts (released in the United Kingdom as *The Easybeats to AC/DC: The Story of Aussie Rock*), Paul Clarke (producer), Bombora Film & Music Co., Sydney, 2015

Bon Scott death report, unknown, BBC, London, 20 February 1980

Bon Scott death report, unknown, 2SM, Sydney, 21 February 1980

Bon Scott death report, unknown, 5AD, Adelaide, 21 February 1980

Bon Scott interview, Angela Morgan, Kent North Radio, Liverpool, 6 November 1979

Bon Scott interview, Jay Crawford, *Edinburgh Rock*, Radio Forth, Edinburgh, 31 October 1978

Bon Scott interview, Dennis Frawley, WABX, Detroit, 1979

Bon Scott interview, Molly Meldrum, *Countdown*, Melbourne, 1 November 1977

Bon Scott interview, Neal Mirsky, WDIZ, Orlando, 1979

Bon Scott interview, Vince Lovegrove, 5KA, Adelaide, 1977

Bon Scott profile, Naomi Robson (presenter), *Today Tonight*, Seven Network, Sydney, 1993

Bon Scott tribute, Ron E. Sparks, 2SM, Sydney, 1980

Brian Johnson interview, Alan K. Stout, *Times Leader*, Wilkes-Barre (PA), 2000

Brian Johnson interview, Leona Graham, Absolute Radio, London, 2010

Callifornia World Music Festival commercial, KMET 94.7 and Wolf-Rissmiller Concerts, Los Angeles, 1979

Cliff Williams interview, Thomas S. Orwat Jr., GlamMetal.com, Buffalo, 2007

Clinton Walker interview, Fionn Davenport, *Davenport After Dark*, Dublin, 2013

Colin Burgess interview, Jack Cool (Jimmie Macmullin Jr.), mixcloud.com, Nova Scotia, 26 July 2016

Dave Stevens post, Dave Stevens, facebook.com, Melbourne, 18 February 2016

John D'Arcy and Mary Renshaw interview, Sarah Harris, *Studio 10*, Sydney, 13 October 2015

Family Jewels, AC/DC, Epic Music Video, New York, 2005

"Hollywood Sportatorium Was a Place for Rock and Roll But Now You Find Roast Beef," *South Florida's Dubious History* (video series), Wayne K. Roustan, *Sun-Sentinel*, Fort Lauderdale (FL), 9 March 2015

Lemmy Kilmister interview, unknown, R3TV, Norwegian Broadcasting Corporation, Oslo, 2008

Mary Renshaw interview, Wendy Stapleton, *Wrokdown*, Channel 31, Melbourne, 11 July 2016

Mary Renshaw and Jeff Jenkins interview, Pauly P, Triple R, Melbourne, 25 October 2015

Mary Renshaw post, Mary Renshaw, facebook.com, Melbourne, 20 July 2016

Ozzy Osbourne: Don't Blame Me, Jeb Brian (director), Epic Music Video, New York, 1991

Margaret "Silver" Smith interview, Matthew Abraham, ABC Adelaide, Adelaide, 2 March 2010

Mark Evans interview, Jesse Fink, previously unpublished quotes, Sydney, 2013

Mark Evans interview, Dr. Volker Janssen, acdccollector.com, New York, 1998

Miami in the 1970s, Martha Sugalski and Ike Seamans (presenters), NBC 6 South Florida, Miami, 2000

Noel Taylor interview, Dr. Volker Janssen, acdccollector.com, New York, 2007

Paul Chapman interview, Eddie Trunk, *Eddie Trunk Live*, SiriusXM, New York, 20 July 2015

Peter Mensch interview, Bianca Hauda, 1Live, Köln, 3 July 2015

Peter Mensch interview, Louise Mensch, Royal Albert Hall, London, 2014

Phil Rudd interview, Brady Halls, *A Current Affair*, Channel Nine, Sydney, 5 May 2015

Rob Riley correspondence, Jesse Fink, previously unpublished quotes, Sydney, 2013

Rock and a Hard Place: Another Night at The Agora, Aaron T. Wells (director), Maxim Films, Fort Lauderdale (FL), 2008

Silver Smith correspondence, Jesse Fink, Sydney, 2016

Silver Smith unfinished manuscript, Silver Smith, Jamestown (Australia), 2016

Stevie Wright interview, unknown, *Beatbox*, ABC, Sydney, circa 1985

Ted Nugent interview, Layne "Doc" Roberts, Penn's Peak Radio, Jim Thorpe (PA), 2014

VH1's Ultimate Albums: Back In Black, AC/DC, VH1, Viacom International, New York, 2003

Vince Lovegrove interview, Dr. Volker Janssen, acdccollector.com, New York, 2001

Vince Lovegrove interviews, The Prism Archive, Prism Films, London, 2012

LETTERS/PRESS RELEASES/PRESS ADVERTISEMENTS/ HANDWRITTEN LYRICS/BOOKLETS/THESES/EMAILS/ REPORTS/OFFICIAL PAPERS/MAGAZINE SPECIALS/ OTHER DOCUMENTS

"AC/DC," typewritten story by Rennie Ellis, Atlanta, 1978

AC/DC, Aktuelle Dokumentation Nr. 5, uncredited, Drei Sterne Verlagsanstalt, Schaan (Liechtenstein), 1981

"AC/DC, Flash and the Pan, John Paul Young, Angel City (The Angels)," Albert Productions advertisement, Sydney, 15 March 1980

"AC/DC History," Sunshine Promotions spreadsheet, Steve Sybesma, Miami, 2015

"A Correctly Referenced Error," letter by David Zelcer, *Goldmine*, Iola (WI), 3 September 2004

"Aerosmith: America's Biggest Draw," Columbia Records advertisement, New York, 1978

"Aerosmith: The Chronology," press release, Geffen Records, Los Angeles, 1989

"Alistair Keith Kinnear," death certificate, Rosario María Acosta García (funcionario delegado), Registro Civile Central, Madrid, 30 December 2015

"Alistair Kinnear," Board of Trade: Commercial and Statistical Department and Successors, Inwards Passenger Lists, National Archives of the United Kingdom, Kew, 1959

The AOR Story, Mike Harrison (ed.), Radio & Records, Inc., Los Angeles, 1978

"Armadillo World Headquarters: 1977 Calendar," Micael Priest, Austin, 1976

"Artisan Recorders, Inc.," Artisan Recorders, Inc., Fort Lauderdale (FL), 1978

"A Survey of Forensic Pathology in England Since 1945," A. K. Mant, *Journal of the Forensic Science Society*, Vol. 13, Issue 1, Harrogate, January 1973

"ATI Artist's Statement," American Talent International, New York, 26 August 1977

"Atlantic Sets Records," uncredited, *Fred Magazine*, Monterey (CA), 12 November 1979

Bon Scott and the Blues Lyric Formula, J.P. Quinton, Amazon Kindle Direct Publishing, Fremantle, 2016

"Bon Scott's Memorial at Fremantle Cemetery," National Trust of Australia (Western Australia) Historic Places Assessment Form, Helena Waldmann, Perth, October 2004 (revised February 2005 and September 2005)

"Califfornia World Music Festival," Wolf & Rissmiller Concerts advertisements, Wolf & Rissmiller, Los Angeles, February and March 1979

"Certified Copy of an Entry, Death, Ronald Belford Scott," C.R. Harris (registrar), London, 22 February 1980

"Commonwealth of Australia Application for an Assisted Passage to Australia Under the United Kingdom and Australian Government

Agreement: Charles Belford Scott," Department of Immigration, Australia House, London, 27 September 1951

"Commonwealth of Australia Medical Examination: Charles Belford Scott," Department of Immigration, Australia House, London, 19 September 1951

"The Coroner's Autopsy: Do We Deserve Better?, A Report of the National Confidential Enquiry into Patient Outcome and Death," Prof. Tom Treasure (chairman), *The National Confidential Enquiry into Patient Outcome and Death (NCEPOD)*, London, 2006

Death certificates for Ella Joyce Allen, Carl Joseph Allen and Daniel Lynn Lankford, Texas Department of Health, Bureau of Vital Statistics, Austin, 1971, 1972 and 1976

"Early Bob Dylan Lyrics Highlight Christie's Pop Culture Sale on June 23," Sara Fox, Christie's, New York, 20 May 2009

"Ella V. Lochem," Marriage Index, *England and Wales Civil Registration Indexes*, General Register Office, London, 1980

"Ernest Leslie Loads," Birth Index, *England and Wales Civil Registration Indexes*, General Register Office, London, 1916

"Ernest Leslie Loads," Death Index, *England and Wales Civil Registration Indexes*, General Register Office, London, 1974

"Ernest Leslie Loads," Principal Probate Registry, *Calendar of the Grants of Probate and Letters of Administration Made in the Probate Registries of the High Court of Justice in England*, High Court of Justice, London, 1974

"The Estate of Ronald Belford Scott, Late of Spearwood in the State of Western Australia," *Government Gazette of Western Australia*, V. Scott (trustee), Perth, 17 September 1982

"The Estate of Ronald Belford Scott, Late of Spearwood in the State of Western Australia," Supreme Court of New South Wales Probate Division, John McEwen (attorney), Sydney, 9 July 1980

Fatal Intoxication as a Consequence of Intranasal Administration (Snorting) or Pulmonary Inhalation (Smoking) of Heroin, I. Thiblin, S. Eksborg, A. Petersson, A. Fugelstad and J. Rajs, Department of Forensic Medicine, Karolinska Institutet, Stockholm, 2003

"Hi Malcolm," letter from Roy Allen to Malcolm Young, Rockdale (TX), circa 2000

"If You Want Blood You've Got It," Atlantic Records advertisement, Atlantic Records, New York, 1978

"In Late 1978 I Met Silver Smith," statement from Alistair Kinnear to Maggie Montalbano, *Metal Hammer & Classic Rock Present AC/DC*, Future Publishing, London, 2005

"Master Ronald Belford Scott," *Inward Passenger Manifests for Ships and Aircraft Arriving at Fremantle, Perth Airport and Western Australian Outposts from 1897–1963*, National Archives of Australia, Canberra, 1952

The Monthly Weather Report: Compiled from Returns of Official and Voluntary Observers, Volume 97, Number 2, Meteorological Office, Exeter, February 1980

"Overdue about Sailing Ship *Danarah*," fax alert by Maritime Rescue Co-ordination Centre La Garde, Sainte Marguerite (France), 24 August 2006

"Renault 5," brochure, Renault Limited, London, 1973

"Rock 'N' Roll Blues," Bon Scott, unrecorded and unpublished handwritten lyrics, Sydney, 1976

"*Rock Or Bust* World Tour Continues with Axl Rose," AC/DC press release, New York, 16 April 2016

"Ronald Belford Scott," Death Index, *England and Wales Civil Registration Indexes*, General Register Office, London, 1980

"Silver Smith," *British Phone Books*, British Telecom Archives, London, 1976

"Summerfun Concerts at the Capital Centre," Capital Centre advertisement, Capital Centre, Largo (MD), 3 June 1979

"To All Music Freaks," letter to radio stations by Tunc Erim, Michael Klenfner and Perry Cooper, Atlantic Records, New York, 1978

"U.F.O," press release, Chrysalis Records, Los Angeles, 1976

"UFO: A Message from the Heavy Mob," Chrysalis advertisement, Chrysalis Records, London, 1977

"Universals," Jeff Green (ed.), *Fred Magazine*, Fear and Loathing, Monterey (CA), 15 October 1979

"Well I Headed Down Town," Bon Scott, unrecorded and unpublished handwritten lyrics, Sydney, 1976

What Good Is a Coroner?: The Transformation of the Queensland

Office of Coroner 1859–1959, Lee Karen Butterworth, Griffith
University, Brisbane, April 2012

"When Foreigner Hits a Town They're Not Strangers for Long,"
Atlantic Records advertisement, New York, 1977

"You Shook Me All Night Long," Atlantic Records advertisement,
Atlantic Records, New York, 1985

BOOTLEGS

AC/DC: Against The Current, Klub Musik, live in Cleveland and
Columbus, recorded 1977 and 1978, released 1989

AC/DC: Blues Booze N' Tattoos, Reef Raff Records, live in Nashville,
recorded 1978, release date unknown

*AC/DC: The Complete Soundboard Collection With Bon Scott 1976–
1979*, Wonderland Records, live in various locations 1976–79,
released 2011

AC/DC: Live At Cleveland Agora, Observation Records, live in
Cleveland, recorded 1977, released 1991

AC/DC: Living In The Hell, Flashback World Productions, live in
Towson, recorded 1979, released 1991

AC/DC: Nearing The End Of The Highway, Lost and Found, live in
Newcastle upon Tyne (England), recorded 1980, released 2009

Bon Scott Forever, Jack Records, live in various locations 1976–80,
released 2000

The Bon Scott Project 1979–1980, "Extraneous Material," Howling
Leg, interview collection, released 2013

Loose-Connection: Live At Fort Lauderdale, In Miami [sic], *On
02.August 77* [sic], AC/DC, unknown, live in Fort Lauderdale,
recorded 1977, release date unknown

Unreleased bootlegs: 10 September 1979, Long Beach, CA; 30 October
1979, Manchester, England; 7 December 1979, London, England

ALBUM SLEEVES / LINER NOTES

Back In Black, AC/DC, Columbia Records, New York, 2003 (original
release 1980)

"Banks Of The River" b/w "Devil's Hour," Screw, Shagrat Records, London, 2007

Bonfire, AC/DC, East West Records, New York, 1997

Captured, Journey, Columbia Records, New York, 1981

It's What Inside That Counts, Critical Mass, MCA Records, Los Angeles, 1980

Lights In The Night, Flash and the Pan, Albert Productions, Sydney, 1980

Lights Out, UFO, Chrysalis Records, London, 1999 (original release 1977)

Long Way To The Top, Nantucket, Epic Records, New York, 1980

Solo In Soho, Philip Lynott, Warner Bros Records, New York, 1980

PODCASTS

"Theology of Rock with Barry Taylor," Tripp Fuller, *Homebrewed Christianity*, Redondo Beach (CA), 8 July 2012

NEWSPAPERS/MAGAZINES/ ONLINE ARTICLES/MUSIC CHARTS

"The Accidental Superstar," Mark Binelli, *Rolling Stone*, New York, 18 March 2004

"AC/DC," Richard Harrington, *Washington Post*, Washington, D.C., 4 August 1980

"AC/DC," John Holmstrom, *Punk*, New York, May/June 1978

"AC/DC," Liz Lufkin, *Trouser Press*, New York, December 1980

"AC/DC," John Rapa, *Record Collector*, London, January 1996

"AC/DC," Steven Rosen, *Record Review*, Los Angeles, Vol. 5 No. 3, June 1981

"AC/DC: Always Current," Jim Farber, *Daily News*, New York, 28 August 2000

"AC/DC and Nothing Can Harm Them!", J. Kordosh, *CREEM*, Birmingham (MI), Vol 15. No. 11, April 1984

"AC/DC and the Gospel of Rock & Roll," David Fricke, *Rolling Stone*, New York, 13 November 2008

"AC/DC's Angus Young Discusses Bon Scott and the *Bonfire* Box Set,"
Tom Beaujour, *Guitar World*, New York, January 1998

"AC/DC Announce New Bass Player," unknown, 1977

"AC/DC Are Back in Black," Andy Secher, *Hit Parader*, Derby (CT),
May 1982

"AC/DC: Australia Has Punk Rock Bands Too Y'know," Anthony
O'Grady, *RAM*, Sydney, 19 April 1975

"AC/DC's Angus Young: 'I'd Put Eddie Van Halen in That Category
of Being an Innovator Like Hendrix,'" Neil Zlozower, *Van Halen
News Desk*, Phoenix, 31 August 2011

"AC/DC's Bon Scott Dies," unknown, 1980

"AC/DC's Brian Johnson Issues Statement on Departure from Group,"
Matthew Wilkening, ultimateclassicrock.com, Greenwich (CT), 19
April 2016

"AC/DC's Brian Johnson Pens Passionate Memoir," Matt Manochio,
USA Today, McLean (VA), 5 June 2011

"AC/DC, Band in a Filmed Concert," Stephen Holden, *New York
Times*, New York, 26 May 1982

"AC/DC Bon's Mum Dies at 92," uncredited, *Weekend Courier*, Perth,
9 September 2011

"AC/DC Can't Match Its Earlier Heights," Terry Higgins, *Milwaukee
Sentinel*, Milwaukee, 9 December 1983

"AC/DC Celebrate Their Quarter Century," Sylvie Simmons, *MOJO*,
London, December 2000

"AC/DC Charged with High Intensity," Lennox Samuels, *Milwaukee
Star*, Milwaukee, 16 April 1981

"AC/DC's EastWest Boxed Set Pays Tribute to Bon Scott," Mark
Marone, *Billboard*, New York, 15 November 1997

"AC/DC Equates Music with War," Stephen Holden, *New York Times*,
New York, 9 December 1981

"AC-DC Fails to Generate Variety," Richard Cromelin, *Los Angeles
Times*, Los Angeles, 31 August 1977

"AC/DC Fever," Shane Rockpit, therockpit.net, Perth, 23 February
2010

"AC/DC's Founding Music Label Alberts Has Sold to BMG," Jessica
Gardner, *Australian Financial Review*, Sydney, 5 July 2016

"AC/DC: Forever Young," Glenn A. Baker, *Age*, Melbourne, 5 February 1988

"AC/DC Gets the Sword on New Disc," Dave Dawson, unknown, 20 August 1980

"AC/DC Group to Pay Bond," uncredited, *Age*, Melbourne, 10 January 1977

"AC-DC Heeft met Elektriciteit te Maken," uncredited, *Leeuwarder Courant*, Leeuwarden (Netherlands), 11 November 1978

"AC/DC's High-Voltage Sonic Assault," Ira Kaplan, *Rolling Stone*, New York, 16 November 1978

"AC/DC, *Highway To Hell*," uncredited, *Billboard*, New York, 18 August 1979

"AC/DC in Dallas," uncredited, *Record World*, New York, 27 October 1979

"AC/DC in the Spotlight," Scott Tady, *Beaver County Times*, Beaver (PA), 29 June 2000

"AC/DC Offers Bone-Rattling Rock and Roll," Steve Dobranski, *Cavalier Daily*, Charlottesville (VA), 19 September 1985

"AC-DC Leader Found Dead," Reuters, *Montreal Gazette*, Montreal, 21 February 1980

"AC/DC Madness," uncredited, *Juke*, Melbourne, 14 October 1978

"AC/DC May Finally Get a Little Respect with New CD," Nekesa Mumbi Moody, *Reading Eagle*, Reading (PA), 8 November 2008

"AC/DC Moomba Rock Concert," Turlough O'Meachair, *RAM*, Sydney, 9 April 1976

"AC/DC on Sex Shops, Masturbation & Hating The Ramones," Dan Condon, doublej.net.au, Sydney, 1 May 2014

"AC/DC: The Plot to Conquer the UK," uncredited, *Goldmine*, Iola (WI), 17 April 2009

"AC/DC — Plug In," Tommy Marlin, *It's Only Rock 'N' Roll*, San Antonio, August 1978

"AC/DC Puts Rock Back in the Black," Patrick Goldstein, *Los Angeles Times*, Los Angeles, 18 January 1981

"AC/DC: Que Sea El Rock," uncredited, *Pelo*, Buenos Aires, February 1984

"AC/DC's Johnson 'Kicked to the Curb,'" B.J. Lisko, *Canton Repository*, Canton (OH), 15 March 2016

"AC-DC's 'Razors Edge' Keeps its Edge, Guitarist Young Says," Mary Campbell, *Moscow-Pullman Daily News*, Moscow (ID), 8 November 1990

"AC/DC Return to Glory: Rock Legends Rally with *Fly On The Wall*," Rob Andrews, *Hit Parader*, Derby (CT), November 1985

"AC/DC's 'Rock' Falls Down," Ed Naha, *New York Post*, New York, 25 May 1982

"AC/DC, Rock's First Family: The Thrilling Adventures of the Naughty But Nice Kings of The Hill," Andy Secher, *Hit Parader*, Derby (CT), May 1982

"AC/DC Salute the British Blues: AC/DC, *For Those About To Rock We Salute You* (review)," John Swenson, *Circus*, New York, February 1982

"AC/DC Score Heavy Overseas Workload," uncredited, *RAM*, Sydney, 9 April 1976

"AC/DC, The Biggest Seller," Steve Morse, *Canberra Times*, Canberra, 6 January 1982

"AC/DC: The Last Punk Rock Band," Chuck Eddy, *Village Voice*, New York, 15 March 1988

"AC/DC: The Shocking Truth," David J. Criblez, *Island Ear*, Syosset (NY), April 2000

"AC-DC Spreading Sparks," Sue Severson (Susan Masino), *Emerald City Chronicle*, Madison (WI), January 1978

"AC/DC: The Stories behind the Songs," uncredited, *New Musical Express*, London, 23 March 2009

"AC/DC: Time to Pull the Plug," Michael A. Capozzoli Jr., *Observer-Reporter*, Washington (PA), 22 March 1996

"AC/DC Tragedy as Scott Dies," uncredited, *New Musical Express*, London, date unknown

"AC/DC Turning On the Power in New Album," uncredited, *Sun-Herald*, Sydney, 18 June 1978

"AC/DC, UFO Masters of Sonic Overkill," Alan Niester, *Globe and Mail*, Toronto, 13 June 1979

"AC/DC's Vince Lovegrove [sic] Recalls How He Took on Bon Scott,"
Vince Lovegrove, *Advertiser*, Adelaide, 21 November 2008

"AC/DC: Wired for Success," David Fricke, *Circus*, New York, 16
January 1979

"AC/DC, With Skull-Crushing Finesse," John Leland, *Newsday*,
Melville (NY), 13 November 1990

"AC/DC: Young — Fast," Marc Mayco, *Trouser Press*, New York,
November 1977

"AC/DC: 'You Shook Me All Night Long,'" uncredited, *Rolling Stone*,
New York, 7 December 2000

"AC Does It," Robin Smith, *Record Mirror*, London, 26 July 1980

"A City for Musicians But Not Industry," Frank E. Griffis, *Tonawanda
News*, North Tonawanda (NY), 14 April 1978

"Acts Firmed for Coliseum," Cary Darling, *Billboard*, New York, 10
February 1979

"A Day in the Life of Nesuhi Ertegun: *Billboard* Travels with WEA
International Chief as He Brings a Product Show to 3 Countries,"
uncredited, *Billboard*, New York, 14 October 1978

"Adds & Hots," uncredited, *Radio & Records*, Hollywood (CA), 1
September 1978, 9 November 1978

"Aerosmith: A Study in Almost Overnight Success," Ed McCormack,
Ledger, Lakeland (FL), 2 September 1976

"Aerosmith Concert a Sell-Out," uncredited, *Spokesman-Review*,
Spokane (WA), 27 July 1978

"Aged Currencies," Chuck Eddy, *huH*, Santa Monica, November 1995

"Ag Hall Hot — And So Were AC/DC, UFO," Jack McGavin, *Morning
Call*, Allentown (PA), June 1979

"A Hair-Raising Peter Perrett Interview," unknown, *MOJO*, London,
February 2009

"Ahmet Ertegun," Pierre Perrone, *Independent*, London, 16 December
2006

"Alarming Rate of Death Certificate Errors," Claire McKim, deadline-
news.co.uk, Edinburgh, 30 April 2013

"Album Radio Action," Claude Hall (ed.), *Billboard*, New York, 22
January 1977, 16 July 1977, 23 July 1977, 30 July 1977, 6 August
1977, 27 August 1977; Doug Hall (ed.) 24 June 1978, 26 August

1978, 16 December 1978, 23 December 1978, 6 January 1979, 11
August 1979, 18 August 1979, 25 August 1979, 1 September 1979

"Alice Cooper's Circus Act Brings Rupp Fans to Feet," Barry Bronson, *Lexington Herald*, Lexington (KY), 26 June 1978

"Alice Cooper: It's Just Show These Days," Bill Gupton, *Kingsport Times-News*, Kingsport (TN), 8 July 1978

"A Long Drop from the Top: Secret Love Letters Reveal Tragic AC/DC's Singer's Torment," Nui Te Koha, *Herald Sun*, Melbourne, 16 February 2006

"The Ang-ry Brigade," Mark Putterford, *Kerrang!*, London, January 1986

"Angus and Malcolm Young Sound Off," Richard Hogan, *Circus*, New York, 31 January 1985

"Angus Young," Elissa Blake, *Rolling Stone*, Sydney, May 1998

"Angus Young: 'AC/DC Wordt Meer Gekraakt Dan Welke Band Ook,'" Jip Golsteijn, *De Telegraaf*, Amsterdam, 27 March 1982

"Angus Young Looks Forward," Bruce Elder, *Rolling Stone*, Sydney, May 2007

"AOR," Jeff Gelb (AOR ed.), *Radio & Records*, Hollywood (CA), 19 January 1979, 9 November 1979, 14 December 1979

"AOR Activity," Jeff Gelb (AOR ed.), *Radio & Records*, Hollywood (CA), 23 June 1978, 1 September 1978; Mike Harrison (AOR ed.), 5 August 1977, 9 September 1977

"Armadillo Auction Was a Walk Down Memory Lane," Bill Martin, *Rockdale Reporter*, Rockdale (TX), 22 January 2015

"As Record Costs Set Record, Some Artists Battle Back," John H. Fisher, *Beaver County Times*, Beaver (PA), 19 June 1981

"Atlantic Pushing," uncredited, *Billboard*, New York, 21 May 1977

"Atlantic Rocks," Craig Rosen, *Billboard*, New York, 17 January 1998

"Atlantic Weather — Noon Feb. 17," *Daily Telegraph*, London, 18 February 1980

"Atlantic Weather — Noon Feb. 18," *Daily Telegraph*, London, 19 February 1980

"Atlantic Weather — Noon Feb. 19," *Daily Telegraph*, London, 20 February 1980

"A–Z: Das Grosse AC/DC — ABC!," uncredited, *POP/Rocky*, Baar (Switzerland), 5 August 1981

"Audio-Music Men: These Musicians Are All Ears When Turning on Their Hi-Fis," Gary Graifman, *Circus*, New York, 24 November 1977

"Australian Rockers Tour U.S. with Wrecking-Crew Act," Knight Ridder Newspapers, *Gazette*, Montreal, 18 October 1979

"A Year of Pop: Above All, There Is Wonder," David Chartrand, *Lawrence Journal-World*, Lawrence (KS), 31 December 1977

"Back in Book," Larry Getlen, *New York Post*, New York, 2 June 2011

"Back in the Ring with a Nervous AC/DC," Richard Hogan, *Circus*, New York, December 1983

"Back with the Bully Boys," Phil Sutcliffe, *Sounds*, London, 26 July 1980

"Bad Seed," Kate Legge, *Australian*, Sydney, 19 February 2010

"Ballroom Blitz," Geoff Strong, *Sunday Age*, Melbourne, 14 February 1993

"Band Members Say It's All Fun," Associated Press, *Hour*, Norwalk (CT), 8 April 1982

"Basic Rock Makes a Comeback," Bruce Meyer, *Wilmington Morning Star*, Wilmington (NC), 16 December 1976

"Beneath the Faded Jeans There's Plenty of Green," Barbara Lewis, *Ledger*, Lakeland (FL), 4 January 1974

"*Billboard* Hot 100," uncredited, *Billboard*, New York, 13 October 1979, 20 October 1979, 27 October 1979, 3 November 1979, 10 November 1979, 17 November 1979, 24 November 1979, 1 December 1979, 8 December 1979, 15 December 1979

"*Billboard*'s Recommended LPs: Pop," uncredited, *Billboard*, New York, 9 July 1977, 10 June 1978, 9 December 1978, 18 August 1979

"*Billboard* Top Boxoffice," uncredited, *Billboard*, New York, 13 August 1977, 27 August 1977, 16 September 1978, 23 September 1978, 30 September 1978, 7 October 1978, 14 October 1978, 20 October 1979, 27 October 1979

"*Billboard* Top LPs & Tape," uncredited, *Billboard*, New York, 13 August 1977, 20 August 1977, 27 August 1977, 3 September 1977, 10 September 1977, 17 September 1977, 24 September 1977, 1 October 1977, 8 October 1977, 15 October 1977, 24 June 1978, 1 July 1978, 8 July 1978, 15 July 1978, 22 July 1978, 29 July 1978, 5 August 1978, 12 August 1978, 19 August 1978, 26 August 1978, 2 September 1978, 9 September 1978, 16 September 1978, 23

September 1978, 30 September 1978, 7 October 1978, 23 December
1978, 6 January 1979, 13 January 1979, 20 January 1979, 27
January 1979, 3 February 1979, 10 February 1979, 17 February
1979, 24 February 1979, 3 March 1979, 10 March 1979, 17 March
1979, 25 August 1979, 1 September 1979, 8 September 1979, 15
September 1979, 22 September 1979, 29 September 1979, 6 October
1979, 13 October 1979, 20 October 1979, 27 October 1979, 3
November 1979, 10 November 1979, 17 November 1979, 24
November 1979, 1 December 1979, 8 December 1979, 15 December
1979, 22 December 1979, 5 January 1980, 12 January 1980, 19
January 1980, 26 January 1980, 2 February 1980, 9 February 1980,
16 February 1980, 23 February 1980, 1 March 1980

"*Billboard*'s Top Singles: Pop, Recommended," uncredited, *Billboard*,
New York, 12 August 1978

"Bitz," uncredited, *Smash Hits*, London, Vol. 2 No. 5, 6–19 March 1980

"Bon and Me," Vince Lovegrove, *Advertiser*, Adelaide, 22 November
2008

"Bon Scott: A Wild Rocker with a Soft Centre," Tim Clarke, *West
Australian*, Perth, 18 October 2015

"Bon But Not Forgotten," Vince Lovegrove, *Australian Worker*,
Sydney, Summer 2005

"Bon Rocks On," Carmel Egan, *Advertiser*, Adelaide, 12 February 2000

"Bon Scott," uncredited, *Juke*, Sydney, 1 October 1975

"Bon Scott: A Touch Too Much," Geoff Barton, *Classic Rock*, London,
February 2005

"Bon Scott's Biggest Fan Will Miss AC/DC Show," uncredited, *Sunday
Territorian*, Darwin, 28 February 2010

"Bon Scott's Pre-AC/DC Bandmate Shares Vintage Letters from Late
Singer, Reflects on His Legacy," Steve Baltin, *Billboard*, New York,
23 December 2014

"Bon Scott Death: AC/DC Speak Out at Last," Paul Du Noyer, *New
Musical Express*, London, date unknown

"Bon Scott Dies on the Highway To Hell . . . ," uncredited, *Sounds*,
London, 1 March 1980

"Bon Scott's Rock 'N' Roll Voyage," Vince Lovegrove, *Sunday Age*,
Melbourne, 20 February 2000

"The Bon Scott Legend Long Outlives Rock 'N' Roll Death," Vince Lovegrove, *West Australian*, Perth, 8 July 2006

"Bon Scott Memorabilia Up for Bids," Tiffany Wertheimer, *3rd Degree*, Edith Cowan University, Joondalup, 7 April 2006

"Bon's Way to Top of Rock," Murray Engleheart, *West Australian*, Perth, 21 November 1997

"Book Raises Doubts Over Hutchence Suicide," Peter Lynch, *Sun-Herald*, Sydney, 11 April 1999

"Book Shatters Myths about AC/DC Legend Bon Scott," Chris Sweeney, *Scottish Sun*, Glasgow, 4 December 2015

"Books: *House of Hits*," John Bailey, *Sunday Age*, Melbourne, 7 March 2010

"The Bottom Line for Boomerang — Home Truths," Jonathan Chancellor, *Sun-Herald*, Sydney, 6 June 1993

"Boxoffice, Stadiums & Festivals (20,000 & Over)," *Billboard*, New York, 23 December 1978

"Brian Johnson Interview," Pekko Päivärinta and Jarmo Katila, *No Nonsense AC/DC Webzine*, Helsinki, 2001

"'Briefcase' Bulges with Blues," Marty Racine, *Milwaukee Sentinel*, Milwaukee, 26 January 1979

"Charges Unlikely in Rock Star's Death," John Huddy, *Miami Herald*, Miami, 10 December 1976

"Cliff Williams: AC/DC's Venerable Undercurrent on Four Decades of Rock," Freddy Villano, *Bass Player*, San Francisco, 11 August 2015

"Closer to the Edge," Sylvie Simmons, *RAW*, London, October 1990

"Collecting AC/DC's Bon Scott — Worldwide Releases Feature Color-Change Vinyl, Different Album Covers," Bill Voccia, *Goldmine*, Iola (WI), 28 May 2004

"Concert Star Loses Fans," Carol Wetzel, *Spokane Daily Chronicle*, Spokane (WA), 27 July 1978

"Concerts in the Area," uncredited, *Daily News*, Bowling Green (KY), 21 September 1979

"Critically Speaking, Mass Aims at the Secular," Paul Beeman, *Good Times*, Westbury (CT), 30 September–13 October 1980

"Current Affairs," Hugh Fielder, *Sounds*, London, 28 July 1984

"Dead Ringers," David Peisner, *SPIN*, New York, September 2009

"Def Leppard High 'N Dry," Steve Mascord, *Canberra Times*, Canberra, 4 June 1992

"Did AC/DC's Missing Mate Fall Victim to Bon Scott's Curse?," David Murray, *Daily Telegraph*, Sydney, 5 February 2010

"The Dirtiest Story Ever Told," Phil Sutcliffe, *Sounds*, London, 28 August 1976

"Dirty Deeds Redone," Richard Bienstock, *Guitar World*, New York, April 2003

"Disco Action," uncredited, *Billboard*, New York, 23 July 1977

"Donington Ain't a Bad Place to Be," Paul Elliott, *Kerrang!*, London, August 1991

"Double Decade of Dirty Deeds," Malcolm Young (in his own words), *Metal CD*, London, Vol. 1 No. 1, 1992

"Drink Killed Rock Singer," uncredited, *Times*, London, 23 February 1980

"Drug Quaalude Called Health Menace," *Washington Post* News Service (wire), *Nashua Telegraph*, Nashua (NH), 24 August 1981

"Early Promise Unfulfilled," Michael Symons, *Sydney Morning Herald*, Sydney, 11 September 1971

"Eagles Uncooperative," Charles M. Young, *St. Petersburg Times*, St. Petersburg (FL), 16 November 1976

"Electric Music," Mike Hochanadel, *Daily Gazette*, Schenectady (NY), 9 June 1979

"Electro Shock Blues," Sylvie Simmons, *MOJO*, London, December 2010

"Englishman for AC-DC," uncredited, *Canberra Times*, Canberra, 10 April 1980

"'Es ist Egal, Ob Du Drei Millionen Follower Hast,'" Martin Scholz, *Die Welt*, Berlin, 2015

"Executive Interview: Louis Messina, TMG/The Messina Group," Joe Reinartz, *Pollstar Talent Buyer Directory*, Fresno (CA), 2008/2009 Edition

"February 19, 1980," Vince Lovegrove, *Music Backtrack* (blog), Rosebank (Australia), 18 February 2012

"Fightin' Words, with or without Wit and Wisdom: Television," Doug Anderson, *Sydney Morning Herald*, Sydney, 28 November 2008

"Finally a Post-War Baby's Show," Jonathan Takiff, *Boca Raton News*, Boca Raton (FL), 11 February 1982

"Fiscale Thunderstruck: AC/DC Blijkt Net Als Rolling Stones 'Nederlands,'" Henk Willem Smits, *Quote*, Amsterdam, 5 March 2013

"Five-Year Hot Catalog Chart," uncredited, *Billboard*, New York, 25 October 1980

"Flying High on Air Freelandia," *Harvard Crimson*, Sarah K. Lynch, Cambridge (MA), 27 February 1974

"Foreigner's Shrewd Strategy," Dick Nusser, *Billboard*, New York, 24 December 1977

"Forever Young," Bob Gulla, *Guitar One*, New York, June 2000

"Former AC/DC Star Fined," uncredited, *Canberra Times*, Canberra, 3 February 1988

"Former O'Neill Team Is Reunited," Carol Lawson, *Day*, New London (CT), 17 January 1979

"For Whom the Bell Tolls," Clinton Walker, *Rolling Stone*, Sydney, January 2006

"For Whom the Bells Toll," Geoff Barton and Jens Jam Rasmussen, *Classic Rock*, London, August 2005

"The Fremantle Drummer Boy," Roy Gibson, *West Australian*, Perth, date unknown

"The Frenzy of Aerosmith," Daniel P. Kelly, *Milwaukee Journal*, Milwaukee, 4 August 1978

"From the Music Capitals of the World," Peter Jones, *Billboard*, New York, 8 January 1977; Leif Schulman, 8 October 1977; Kari Helopaltio, 3 December 1977; Glenn Baker, 14 October 1978; Henry Kahn, 2 December 1978

"Gallup Youth Survey: AC/DC Band Electrifies Teens," George Gallup, *Free Lance-Star*, Fredericksburg (VA), 20 January 1982

"Gamecock/WUSC Concert Calendar," uncredited, *Gamecock*, Columbia (SC), 22 June 1978

"Get Out the Earplugs for Kiss Concert," Ellen Aman, *Lexington Leader*, Lexington (KY), date unknown

"Great Scott!," uncredited, *Sydney Morning Herald*, Sydney, 2 August 1994

"Hall's Dirty Deeds Rock AC/DC Man," Peter Holmes, *Sun-Herald*, Sydney, 19 January 2003

"Hard As a Rock," Alan Di Perna, *Guitar World*, New York, January 1993

"Heart and the Canadian Rock Explosion: Making Music to the Northern Lights," Kurt Loder, *Circus*, New York, 24 November 1977

"Heaven-Sent Stardom or, How to Join the Dead Rock Stars' Club," Mark Smith, *Sunday Independent*, Dublin, 17 April 1994

"Heavy Metal and the Deep Purple Diaspora," Larry Rohter, *Washington Post*, Washington, D.C., 21 November 1976

"Heavy-Metal Singer Denies His Song Led to Suicide," Associated Press, *Ledger*, Lakeland (FL), 22 January 1986

"High Speed Race Ends in Death," *Cameron Herald*, Cameron (TX), 13 May 1976

"*High Voltage*: Album Review," Billy Altman, *Rolling Stone*, New York, 16 December 1976

"Highway to Hell," Peter Watts, *Uncut*, London, December 2013

"The Highway to Hell from Herne Hill," Andrew Neather, *Evening Standard*, London, 29 October 2014

"The Hits and The Missus," Krissi Murison, *Sunday Times*, London, 28 October 2012

"Hits of the World: Britain," uncredited, *Billboard*, New York, 12 November 1977, 10 December 1977, 17 December 1977, 27 May 1978, 3 June 1978, 10 June 1978, 17 June 1978, 4 November 1978, 11 November 1978, 18 November 1978, 25 November 1978, 2 December 1978, 9 December 1978, 16 December 1978, 23 December 1978, 3 March 1979

"Hits of the World: Holland," uncredited, *Billboard*, New York, 12 August 1978

"Hottest Teen Group on Earth: And They're Australian," Keith Dunstan, *Sydney Morning Herald*, Sydney, 7 March 1982

"The House Ahmet Built: The Highest-Charting Albums and Singles in Atlantic Records History," *Billboard*, New York, 24 February 2007

"Hush Money," Simon Witter, *Times*, London, 17 January 1998

"Indict Ex-Broker in Pop Star's Death," Theo Wilson, *Chicago Tribune*, Chicago, 22 February 1975

"Inside Track," uncredited, *Billboard*, New York, 16 April 1977, 8 September 1979

"Interview: AC/DC Are Enjoying Themselves Too Much to Retire,"
Katherine Turman, *Village Voice*, New York, 1 December 2014

"Interview: Former AC/DC Bassist Mark Evans on Life in the Band,"
Joe Bosso, *Music Radar*, Bath, 11 October 2011

"Interview with Mark Evans," Pekko Päivärinta and Jarmo Katila,
No Nonsense AC/DC Webzine, Helsinki, 1999

"In the Supreme Court of New South Wales, Probate Division,"
uncredited, *Sydney Morning Herald*, Sydney, 7 August 1982

"Isa, Mother of a Rock Hellraiser," Roy Gibson, *West Australian*,
Perth, date unknown

"I Sing for the Sex," Bon Scott (in his own words), *Scream!*, unknown,
Vol. 1 No. 11, 1975

"Is There Life After New Wave? What Really Matters and What
Doesn't in Power Pop, Sophisto-Pop and The New Wave," Alan
Niester, *Globe and Mail*, Toronto, 6 September 1978

"Jazz, Glitter Pop Headline Here," Jon East, *Ocala Star-Banner*, Ocala
(FL), 15 March 1979

"Joe 'The Godfather' Anthony Dies At 52," Robert Wynne, *San
Antonio Light*, San Antonio, date unknown

"Keith Mant," uncredited, *Guardian*, London, 16 November 2000

"Keith Richard [sic], Shanachie Settle Suit Out of Court," Roman
Kozak, *Billboard*, New York, 18 July 1981

"Keranng! [sic] Whang! Kerrunch! It's AC/DC!," Daniela Soave,
Record Mirror, London, 18 August 1979

"Killer Spree," uncredited, *Daily Mail*, London, 23 February 1980

"Kiss, Kiss, Bang, Bang, at Fairgrounds Concert," John Finley, *Courier-
Journal*, Louisville (KY), 11 December 1977

"Last Man to See Late AC/DC Frontman Missing at Sea for Three
Years," David Murray, *Herald Sun*, Melbourne, 5 February 2010

"Leas on Life," Greg Baker, *Miami New Times*, Miami, 2 June 1993

"Legal Notices: In the Supreme Court of New South Wales, Probate
Division," uncredited, *Sydney Morning Herald*, Sydney, 5 August 1980

"Le Jour Où Mon Ami Bon Scott Est Mort," Bernie Bonvoisin (to
Sophie De Villenoisy), *Paris Match*, Paris, 27 July 2015

"Let There Be Bass: Cliff Williams of AC/DC," Scott Malandrone, *Bass
Player*, San Francisco, May 1996

"Let There Be Rock," Ken Micallef, *Guitar One*, New York, August 2003

"Let There Be Rock: AC/DC @ the 'Dillo,'" Marky Billson, *Austin Chronicle*, Austin, 29 August 2008

"Lifelines: Deaths," uncredited, *Billboard*, New York, 1 March 1980

"'Lights Out' Lights Up UFO: The British Quintet Charts a Straight Ahead Course," Peter Crescenti, *Circus*, New York, 18 August 1977

"Lookin' for Stubble?," Howard Johnson, *Kerrang!*, London, September 1990

"The Lusts of AC/DC: Band Bids for Supreme Punkdom," Bob Granger, *RAM*, Sydney, date unknown

"Malcolm and Angus Young: Interview," Dave Ling, *Classic Rock*, London, September 2003

"Man Sentenced in Rock Star's Death," William Farr, *Los Angeles Times*, Los Angeles, 8 January 1976

"Many Top Rock Bands Plus Amateurs Will Appear at World Music Festival," uncredited, *Kingman Daily Miner*, Kingman (AZ), 16 March 1979

"Meadowlands Crowd Enjoys Wet Boogie," Bruce Nixon, *Trenton Times*, Trenton (NJ), 18 June 1979

"Michael Browning: Manager of AC/DC, 1974–79," Joe Matera, *Classic Rock*, London, February 2005

"Mick Jones Opens Up about His Battle with Addiction," Emily Smith and Mara Siegler, *New York Post*, New York, 18 May 2015

"Mini Reviews," uncredited, *Globe and Mail*, Toronto, 28 May 1982

"Mick Wall: 'If Rock Stars Are Superheroes, the Truth is Kryptonite,'" Alec Plowman, ultimate-guitar.com, San Francisco, 24 July 2015

"Mike Shaw's Austin Corner," Mike Shaw, *San Antonio's Rock N Roll Magazine*, San Antonio, April 1977

"Mobsters and Shady Securities," Jack Anderson, *Free Lance-Star*, Fredericksburg (VA), 20 March 1974

"Mondo Metal: Still Heavy After All These Years," David Fricke, *Circus*, New York, 15 April 1980

"Moore on Pop," Susan Moore, *Australian Women's Weekly*, Sydney, 11 June 1980

"More Depression or Doc Watson," Jon Marlowe, *Miami News*, Miami, 11 May 1976

"More Than a Little Sunburn," Luis Feliu, *Canberra Times*, Canberra, 1 December 1978

"Mosh Bros," Tony Power, *Guitar Magazine*, unknown, November 1995

"Moxy Comes Back for Another Shot," Kieran Grant, *Canoe*, Toronto, 30 November 2004

"Moxy's Metal May Upstage Styx," Ian Haysom, *Ottawa Journal*, Ottawa, 28 January 1977

"New Mac Album Out in Eight Days," Donnie Sutherland, *Sydney Morning Herald*, Sydney, 9 September 1979

"New South Wails, AC/DC Newcastle," Ian Ravendale, *New Musical Express*, London, date unknown

"NME Charts," uncredited, *New Musical Express*, London, (week ending) 16 February 1980

"1980: La Folie AC/DC Aux Arènes De Poitiers," Delphine Léger, *La Nouvelle République*, Tours (France), 2 December 2014

"No Cord Wonder," Phil Sutcliffe, *Sounds*, London, 12 November 1977

"Obituary: Bon Scott, AC/DC Death," uncredited, *New Musical Express*, London, 1 March 1980

"October 13 1979," Vince Lovegrove, *Music Backtrack* (blog), Rosebank (Australia), 12 October 2011

"Old Gold," Richard Guilliatt, *Sydney Morning Herald*, Sydney, 8 April 1995

"One Man's Least-Liked 81 Albums," Jeff Slatten, *Optimist*, Abilene (TX), 26 January 1982

"Peter Mensch: Interview," Frank Watt, *Metal Attack*, unknown, November 1985

"Peter Pan of Rock 'N' Roll — AC/DC Singer Immortalised," Vince Lovegrove, *Sunday Telegraph*, Sydney, 8 July 2001

"Phil Rudd Talks 'Crock of Sh-t' Arrest, Hopes to Return to AC/DC," Jason Newman, *Rolling Stone*, New York, 10 August 2015

"Plea to Remember the Wild One," Donnie Sutherland, *Sydney Morning Herald*, Sydney, 28 October 1979

"Pop: AC/DC and Def Leppard," Robert Palmer, *New York Times*, New York, 3 August 1980

"Pop Album Briefs: *High Voltage*," Lisa Fancher, *Los Angeles Times*, Los Angeles, 30 January 1977

"Pop Album Reviews in Brief: *Let There Be Rock*," Terry Atkinson, *Los Angeles Times*, Los Angeles, 31 July 1977

"Pop Notes," Eve Zibart, *Washington Post*, Washington, D.C., 23 August 1978

"*Powerage*, AC/DC," Luis Feliu, *Canberra Times*, Canberra, 1 December 1978

"Prof. Irwin Corey's Barbs Perk Parley," uncredited, *Billboard*, New York, 19 August 1978

"Pushing Vinyl or Finding Out What the Record Biz Is Up to These Days," Jon Marlowe, *Miami News*, Miami, 14 September 1977

"Q-Prime's Burnstein and Mensch on Managing Metallica and Jimmy Page, Playing the Label Game, and Staying on Top for 33 Years," Jem Aswad, *Billboard*, New York, 29 March 2016

"The Quaalude Lesson," uncredited, *Frontline*, pbs.org, Arlington (VA), 17 May 2011

"Radio: Pick of the Day," Doug Anderson, *Sydney Morning Herald*, Sydney, 23 January 1984

"Readers' Poll: The 10 Best AC/DC Songs," Andy Greene, *Rolling Stone*, New York, 15 October 2014

"Record Crowd Sees Zeppelin in Detroit," Stephen Ford, *Billboard*, New York, 14 May 1977

"Records Records Records," Magic Dave (ed.), *San Antonio's Rock N Roll Magazine*, San Antonio, November 1976

"Record 3 Million Quaaludes Seized in Miami Drug Raid," Bob Murphy, *Miami News*, Miami, 16 January 1981

"Recording Czar Made It in Miami," Anne S. Crowley, *Palm Beach Post*, West Palm Beach (FL), 16 March 1979

"Rediscovering Pop Culture's Waste Paper," Suzy Freeman-Greene, *Age*, Melbourne, 26 June 1987

"Regional AOR Activity," Jeff Gelb (AOR ed.), *Radio & Records*, Hollywood (CA), 8 December 1978, 15 December 1978

"REO's Seven Year Itch Means Gold," Liz Derringer, *Circus*, New York, 18 August 1977

"Return of a Bad, Old Schoolboy," Suzy Freeman-Greene, *Age*, Melbourne, 5 February 1988

"Revealed: Bon Scott, Man of Letters," Patrick Donovan, *Age*, Melbourne, 10 August 2006

"Reviews," Mike Floyd, *St. Louis Post-Dispatch*, St. Louis (MO), 13 October 1995

"Riff Raff," Harry Doherty, *Classic Rock*, London, February 2008

"Rock Amphitheatre Planned for N.J.," uncredited, *Billboard*, New York, 24 December 1977

"Rock Concerts," uncredited, *Northern Daily Leader*, Tamworth (Australia), 20 December 1976

"Rock's Deadly Grind Claims Another Victim," Karen Hughes, *Australian*, 22 February 1980

"Rock Drummer Died After Drinking 40 Measures of Vodka," uncredited, *Guardian*, London, 8 October 1980

"Rock 'N' Roll Animal," Clinton Walker, *Age*, Melbourne, 13 July 1994

"Rock Roundup in Texas: Texxas Jam Corralled the World's Top Acts for a Weekend of Raunch & Roll," Cat Sundeen, *Circus*, New York, 31 August 1978

"Rock Singer Found Dead," Australian Associated Press, *Canberra Times*, Canberra, 21 February 1980

"Rock Singer Dies," uncredited, *Times*, London, 21 February 1980

"Rock Singer Verdict," uncredited, *Glasgow Herald*, Glasgow, 23 February 1980

"Rock Star Bon Dies After a Booze-Up," unknown, 1980

"Rock Star Dies After Drinking Bout," John Stevens, *Evening Standard*, London, 20 February 1980

"Rock Star Drank Himself to Death," uncredited, *Guardian*, London, 23 February 1980

"Rock: The Punk Circuit," John Rockwell, *New York Times*, New York, 26 August 1977

"The 'Rolling Stone' Hall of Fame: AC/DC — 'Back in Black,'" Barry Walters, *Rolling Stone*, New York, 30 October 2002

"The Rotgut Life," uncredited, *Time*, New York, 18 October 1976

"San Antonio Ladies Riot: Moxy Rox Texas," uncredited, *Record Month*, Toronto, Vol. 1 No. 3, 1976

"Scott's Gone But AC/DC Still Rocks," Steve Morse, *Boston Globe*, Boston, 28 July 1980

"7 Common Mistakes Regarding Autopsy Reports," Judy Melinek, *Forensic*, Rockaway (NJ), 9 September 2015

"'Sgt. Pepper': Greatest LP?," Robert Hilburn, *Los Angeles Times*, Los Angeles, 3 February 1979

"Setting the Record Straight," Patrick Donovan, *Age*, Melbourne, 8 April 2003

"The Show Must Go On," David Lewis, *Sounds*, London, 29 March 1980

"Skipping along the Golden Road of Rock," Dorothy Austin, *Milwaukee Sentinel*, Milwaukee, 21 April 1977

"Soldiers Attack City Marchers," uncredited, *Advertiser*, Adelaide, 9 May 1970

"Spirit of 76," Geoff Barton, *Classic Rock*, London, June 2009

"Statistics: Quaalude Deaths Rising in Dade County," Associated Press, *Palm Beach Post*, West Palm Beach (FL), 12 August 1981

"Still Rockin' in Southwest Florida," Jonathan Foerster, *Gulfshore Life*, Naples (FL), July 2016

"Sting, Brian Johnson and Mark Knopfler Represent North East in *Sunday Times* Music Millionaire Top 50," Debra Fox, *Sunderland Echo*, Sunderland, 21 April 2016

"Study: Nearly One-Third of All Death Certificates Are Wrong," Sarah Kliff, *Washington Post*, Washington, D.C., 12 May 2013

"Study Finds Miami Riot Was Unlike Those of 60's," Jo Thomas, *New York Times*, New York, 17 May 1981

"The Story Behind the Album: AC/DC's *Back In Black*," Philip Wilding, *Classic Rock*, London, 23 November 2000

"Subculture Misled on Drug's Safety," *Washington-Star News* (wire), *Milwaukee Journal*, Milwaukee, 25 March 1973

"Sunshine Concert Company Shaped Indiana Entertainment," David Lindquist, *Indianapolis Star*, Indianapolis (IN), 20 May 2013

"Sweet and Sour Notes," uncredited, *Australian Women's Weekly*, Sydney, 2 March 1977

"Taking the Rock Roll [sic]: A Guide to the Clubs," *Miami Herald*, Miami, 3 August 1979

"Talent in Action, AC/DC Def Leppard," Palladium, New York, Admission: $9.50," Mike London, *Billboard*, New York, 16 August 1980

"Talent Talk," uncredited, *Billboard*, New York, 6 August 1977, 9 September 1978, 30 June 1979

"Ted Nugent Is the Wild Man of Rock," Jim Sullivan, *Bangor Daily News*, Bangor (ME), 27 July 1979

"The Theenking [sic] Man's Heavy Metal Band," David Lewis, *Sounds*, London, 14 February 1981

"They've Still Got Juice: Angus Young on the Power of AC/DC," Dan Aquilante, *New York Post*, New York, 3 March 2000

"Thin Lizzy: The Boys Are Back in Town," Jon Marlowe, *Miami News*, Miami, 29 October 1976

"This 'N That in Entertainment," uncredited, *Observer-Reporter*, Washington (PA), 18 November 1977

"Thirty Years of Thunder," Jude Gold, *Guitar Player*, New York, July 2003

"Thomas Milner, 35, Longtime Disc Jockey," *Sun-Sentinel*, Fort Lauderdale (FL), 2 November 1985

"3 Martinis, 3 Margueritas [sic] . . . and Needlemarks: The Final Hours of a Rock Star," John Huddy, *Miami Herald*, Miami, 8 December 1976

"Thumping Drums, Searing Guitar and Maniacal Screaming," Mike Parker, *Sydney Morning Herald*, Sydney, 6 May 1977

"To Hell and Back," Joe Elliott (as told to Paul Elliott), *MOJO*, London, June 2010

"Tony Platt: 'I Was Continually Saying That Iron Maiden Need a Singer Like Bruce Dickinson, But Not Really Thinking They Would Take Me Completely at My Word,'" Steven Rosen, ultimate-guitar.com, San Francisco, 17 June 2015

"Top Box Office of the Year," uncredited, *Billboard*, New York, 22 December 1979

"Tower Ticker," Aaron Gold, *Chicago Tribune*, Chicago, 22 October 1976

"Tragedy Behind Them, AC/DC Unveils New Look," Andy Secher, *Daily News*, New York, 29 July 1980

"Trust Never Sleeps," Philip Bell, *Sounds*, London, 20 February 1982

"20 Questions: Bon Scott," Clinton Walker (reconstructed interview using archived interviews), *Australian Playboy*, May 1994

"The 25 Most Significant and/or Notorious Nights in Austin Music

History," Michael Corcoran, *Arts+Labor Magazine*, Austin, 19 September 2014

"25 Years On, AC/DC Fans Recall How Wild Rocker Met His End," Richard Jinman, *Guardian*, London, 19 February 2005

"Two Bands Add to the Heat," Dale Goodwin, *Spokesman-Review*, Spokane (WA), 28 July 1978

"UFO Do It on the Road: A New Live LP Puts These Britrockers in Their Place — On Stage," David Fricke, *Circus*, New York, 6 March 1979

"UFO Means Heavy Metal Savvy," Tom Hull, *Village Voice*, New York, 6 October 1975

"UFO — The Making of an Obsession," Dave Ling, *Classic Rock*, London, November 2003

"Vince Lovegrove Interview," Pekko Päivärinta, *No Nonsense AC/DC Webzine*, Helsinki, 1999

"Vox Jox," Doug Hall, *Billboard*, New York, 10 February 1979

"Voyage Au Bout De L'Enfer," Michel Embareck, *Best*, Paris, December 1979

"Waylon, Willie and the Boys: Country Music Fills Cotton Bowl," Newspaper Enterprise Association, *Florence Times*, Florence (AL), 22 July 1978

"Way Out Line-Up," uncredited, *Sydney Morning Herald*, Sydney, 5 June 1977

"WEA National Convention Photo Highlights," uncredited, *Billboard*, New York, 24 September 1977

"Wee Angus and the Machometer," Sheila Prophet, *Record Mirror*, London, 2 December 1978

"We Imitate What We're Supposed to Be: Jethro Tull On Tour," Bob Greene, *Audience*, Boston, May/June 1972

"We Partied Down," uncredited, *Classic Rock*, London, December 2013

"What? Do I Wanna Join AC/DC?," Paul Elliott, *Classic Rock*, London, February 2010

"When South Florida ROCKED!," Sean Piccoli, *Sun-Sentinel*, Fort Lauderdale (FL), 24 January 2007

"Whole Lotta Bon," uncredited, *Kerrang!*, London, 25 February–10 March 1982

"Will Streaming Music Kill Songwriting?," John Seabrook, *New Yorker*, New York, 8 February 2016

"Workin' on His Night Moves," uncredited, *Miami News*, Miami, 30 July 1978

"Working Stiffs," Alan Di Perna, *Guitar World*, New York, May 2000

"Wreck Claims Man, 18," uncredited, *Rockdale Reporter*, Rockdale (TX), 13 May 1976

"Young Lust," Alan Di Perna, *Guitar World*, New York, November 1995

"Young's Stage Antics Save AC/DC Concert," Brett Friedlander, *Gamecock*, Columbia (SC), 12 October 1979

aa.org

aa.usno.navy.mil

abr.business.gov.au

acdc.com

ac-dc.net

acdc-archives.fr

acdc-bootlegs.com

acdccollector.com

acdcfans.net

acdc-videos.com

albumlinernotes.com

allmusic.com

americanradio
   history.com

ancestry.com

archive.org

asic.gov.au

bethelga.org

billboard.com

bonscottblog.com

britishlivertrust
   .org.uk

canoe.ca

christies.com

copyright.gov

discogs.com

doublej.net.au

ebay.com

erenow.com

evidence.nhs.uk

findmypast.com

flickr.com

forcedexposure.com

forensicmag.com

4eigner.net

45cat.com

45worlds.com

44oint.com

grammy.com

highwaytoacdc.com

homebrewed
   christianity.com

imdb.com

intertrustgroup.com

julienslive.com

justcollecting.com

legendaryrock
   interviews.com

licensing.fcc.gov

limestonelounge
   .yuku.com

metoffice.gov.uk

milesago.com

mixcloud.com

municipaldreams
   .wordpress.com

musicradar.com

nhs.uk

nla.gov.au

pbs.org

qprime.com

rateyourmusic.com

reddit.com

riaa.com

sickthingsuk.co.uk

sl.nsw.gov.au

soundcloud.com

southlondoncoroner
   .org

stevehoffman.tv

stw.fr

teamrock.com

therockpit.net

tv.com

trademarkia.com

trust.connection.
   free.fr

ultimateclassicrock
   .com

ultimate-guitar.com

uncut.co.uk

vharchives.com

vhnd.com

welt.de

wisebuddah.com

wncx.cbslocal.com

wunderground.com

yosteelstrings
   .wordpress.com

youtube.com

GONE SHOOTIN'

Bon Scott's North American Shows 1977–79 (By Concert)

Special thanks to ACDC-Bootlegs.com's Nate Althoff of Fargo, North Dakota, for his help compiling this list. The following are confirmed gigs. Cancelled shows and dubious/ rumoured shows have been excluded. — JF

1977

AUSTIN, TX
27 July 1977, Armadillo World Headquarters
SAN ANTONIO, TX
28 July 1977, Municipal Auditorium
CORPUS CHRISTI, TX
29 July 1977, Ritz Music Hall
DALLAS, TX
30 July 1977, Electric Ballroom
WEST PALM BEACH, FL
5 August 1977, West Palm Beach Civic Auditorium
JACKSONVILLE, FL
6 August 1977, Veterans Memorial Coliseum

HOLLYWOOD, FL
7 August 1977, Hollywood
Sportatorium
ST. LOUIS, MO
9 August 1977, Mississippi Nights
KANSAS CITY, MO
10 August 1977, Memorial Hall
SCHAUMBURG, IL
11 August 1977, B'Ginnings
CLEVELAND, OH
12 August 1977, Cleveland
Convention Center
COLUMBUS, OH
13 and 14 August 1977, Agora
MADISON, WI
16 August 1977, Stone Hearth
MILWAUKEE, WI
17 August 1977, Riverside
Theater
INDIANAPOLIS, IN
18 August 1977, Circle Theater
DAYTON, OH
19 August 1977, Hara Arena
YOUNGSTOWN, OH
21 August 1977, Tomorrow Club
CLEVELAND, OH
22 August 1977, Agora
NEW YORK, NY
24 August 1977, Palladium and
CBGB *(Two venues)*
DETROIT, MI
27 August 1977, Masonic
Auditorium
LOS ANGELES, CA
29–31 August 1977, Whisky a
Go Go

SAN FRANCISCO, CA
2 and 3 September 1977, Old
Waldorf
FORT LAUDERDALE, FL
7 September 1977, 4 O'Clock
Club[95]
POUGHKEEPSIE, NY
16 November 1977, Mid-Hudson
Civic Center
ALBANY, NY
17 November 1977, Palace
Theatre
SYRACUSE, NY
18 November 1977, Onondaga
County War Memorial[96]
KNOXVILLE, TN
23 November 1977, Knoxville
Civic Coliseum
JOHNSON CITY, TN
24 November 1977, Freedom
Hall Civic Center
WHEELING, WV
25 November 1977, Capitol
Theatre
CHARLESTON, WV
26 November 1977, Charleston
Civic Center
ATLANTA, GA
27 November 1977, Capri
Theatre
NORTHAMPTON, PA
29 November 1977, Roxy
Theatre
CHICAGO, IL
1 December 1977, Riviera
Theatre

MILWAUKEE, WI
4 December 1977, Electric
    Ballroom
FLINT, MI
5 December 1977, Capitol
    Theatre
NEW YORK, NY
7 December 1977, Atlantic
    Studios
MEMPHIS, TN
9 December 1977, Mid-South
    Coliseum
INDIANAPOLIS, IN
11 December 1977, Market
    Square Arena
LOUISVILLE, KY
12 December 1977, Freedom
    Hall
FORT WAYNE, IN
15 December 1977, Allen County
    War Memorial Coliseum[97]
GREENSBORO, NC
18 December 1977, Greensboro
    Coliseum
LARGO, MD
19 December 1977, Capital
    Centre
PITTSBURGH, PA
21 December 1977, Stanley
    Theatre[98]

1978
NORFOLK, VA
24 June 1978, Norfolk Scope
    Arena

LEXINGTON, KY
25 June 1978, Rupp Arena
BIRMINGHAM, AL
26 June 1978, Birmingham-
    Jefferson Civic Centre
KNOXVILLE, TN
28 June 1978, Knoxville
    Civic Coliseum[99]
HOUSTON, TX
2 July 1978, Summit
DALLAS, TX
3 July 1978, Fair Park
    Arena
LUBBOCK, TX
4 July 1978, Lubbock Municipal
    Coliseum
AUSTIN, TX
6 July 1978, Opry House
CORPUS CHRISTI, TX
7 July 1978, Ritz Music Hall
SAN ANTONIO, TX
8 July 1978, Municipal
    Auditorium
SALT LAKE CITY, UT
10 July 1978, Salt Palace
LONG BEACH, CA
12 July 1978, Long Beach
    Arena
LOS ANGELES, CA
13 July 1978, Starwood
FRESNO, CA
15 July 1978, Selland Arena
SAN JOSE, CA
16 July 1978, San Jose
    Convention Center

PORTLAND, OR
21 July 1978, Veterans Memorial
   Coliseum
OAKLAND, CA
23 July 1978, Oakland Stadium[100]
VANCOUVER, BC (*Canada*)
25 July 1978, Pacific Coliseum
SPOKANE, WA
26 July 1978, Spokane
   Coliseum
BILLINGS, MT
28 July 1978, Montana
   Entertainment Trade and
   Recreation Arena
WINNIPEG, MB (*Canada*)
30 July 1978, Arena
RAPID CITY, SD
1 August 1978, Rushmore Plaza
   Civic Centre
EAST TROY, WI
3 August 1978, Alpine Valley
   Music Theatre
CHICAGO, IL
4 August 1978, International
   Amphitheatre
5 August 1978, Comiskey Park
NASHVILLE, TN
8 August 1978, Record Bar
   Convention
SALEM, VA
9 August 1978, Roanoke Civic
   Centre
FAYETTEVILLE, NC
10 August 1978, Cumberland
   County Memorial Arena

ATLANTA, GA
11 August 1978, Symphony
   Hall
JACKSONVILLE, FL
12 August 1978, Veterans
   Memorial Coliseum
MIAMI, FL
13 August 1978, Maurice
   Gusman Concert Hall
HEMPSTEAD, NY
18 August 1978, Calderone
   Concert Hall
WILKES-BARRE, PA
19 August 1978, Paramount
   Theatre
BOSTON, MA
21 August 1978, Paradise
   Theatre
MORRISTOWN, NJ
22 August 1978, Morris Stage
ALBANY, NY
23 August 1978, Palace
   Theatre[101]
NEW YORK, NY
24 August 1978, Palladium
WARWICK, RI
25 August 1978, Rocky Point
   Park
WILLIMANTIC, CT
26 August 1978, Shaboo Inn
OWINGS MILLS, MD
27 August 1978, Painters Mill
SEATTLE, WA
29 and 30 August 1978, Seattle
   Center Coliseum

PORTLAND, OR
31 August 1978, Paramount
    Theatre
OAKLAND, CA
2 September 1978, Oakland
    Stadium
DENVER, CO
4 September 1978, Red Rocks
    Amphitheatre
BURBANK, CA
6 September 1978, *Midnight
    Special*, NBC Studios
WHEELING, WV
8 September 1978, Wheeling
    Civic Center
JOHNSON CITY, TN
9 September 1978, Freedom Hall
    Civic Center
COLUMBUS, OH
10 September 1978, Veterans
    Memorial Auditorium
MILWAUKEE, WI
12 September 1978, Riverside
    Theater
ROYAL OAK, MI
13 September 1978, Royal Oak
    Theater
SCHAUMBURG, IL
14 September 1978, B'Ginnings
CLEVELAND, OH
16 September 1978, Palace Theater
ALLENTOWN, PA
17 September 1978, Schnecksville
    Lehigh County Community
    College

HUNTINGTON, WV
20 September 1978, Huntington
    Civic Center
CHICAGO, IL
22 September 1978, Aragon
    Ballroom
KANSAS CITY, MO
23 September 1978, Uptown
    Theatre
OMAHA, NE
24 September 1978, Omaha
    Civic Auditorium Music
    Hall
BUFFALO, NY
27 September 1978, Buffalo
    Memorial Auditorium
ROCHESTER, NY
28 September 1978, Rochester
    Community War Memorial
DETROIT, MI
29 September 1978, Cobo Hall
SOUTH BEND, IN
30 September 1978, Athletic &
    Convocation Center[102]
TOLEDO, OH
2 October 1978, Toledo Sports
    Arena
FORT WAYNE, IN
3 October 1978, Allen County
    War Memorial Coliseum

1979
MADISON, WI
8 May 1979, Dane County
    Coliseum

DES MOINES, IA
10 May 1979, Veterans
  Memorial Auditorium
DUBUQUE, IA
11 May 1979, Five Flags Arena
DAVENPORT, IA
12 May 1979, RKO Orpheum
  Theatre
TOLEDO, OH
13 May 1979, Toledo Sports
  Arena
COLUMBUS, OH
15 May 1979, Ohio Expo Hall
SOUTH BEND, IN
16 May 1979, Morris Civic
  Auditorium
LOUISVILLE, KY
17 May 1979, Commonwealth
  Convention Center
SPRINGFIELD, IL
18 May 1979, Illinois State
  Armory
DAYTON, OH
19 May 1979, Hara Arena
CLEVELAND, OH
20 May 1979, Cleveland Public
  Auditorium
NASHVILLE, TN
22 May 1979, Tennessee
  Theatre
MARTIN, TN
23 May 1979, University of
  Tennessee
ATLANTA, GA
24 and 25 May 1979, Agora

ORLANDO, FL
27 May 1979, Tangerine Bowl
BUFFALO, NY
31 May 1979, Shea's Buffalo
  Theatre
ROCHESTER, NY
1 June 1979, Rochester
  Auditorium Theatre
DAVENPORT, IA
3 June 1979, John O'Donnell
  Stadium
PEORIA, IL
4 June 1979, Bradley University
ERIE, PA
6 June 1979, Erie County
  Fieldhouse
ALLENTOWN, PA
7 June 1979, Agricultural Hall,
  Allentown Fairgrounds
LARGO, MD
8 June 1979, Capital Centre
NEW YORK, NY
9 June 1979, Palladium
ALBANY, NY
10 June 1979, Palace Theatre
TORONTO, ON (*Canada*)
12 June 1979, Massey Hall
PITTSBURGH, PA
13 June 1979, Stanley
  Theatre
POUGHKEEPSIE, NY
14 June 1979, Mid-Hudson
  Civic Center
PHILADELPHIA, PA
15 June 1979, Tower Theatre

FORT WORTH, TX
20 June 1979, Tarrant County
Convention Center
AUSTIN, TX
21 June 1979, Municipal
Auditorium
SAN ANTONIO, TX
22 June 1979, Convention
Center Arena
HOUSTON, TX
23 June 1979, Sam Houston
Coliseum
CORPUS CHRISTI, TX
24 June 1979, Memorial
Coliseum
ALBUQUERQUE, NM
26 June 1979, University of New
Mexico
PHOENIX, AZ
27 June 1979, Arizona Veterans
Memorial Coliseum
DENVER, CO
29 June 1979, Rainbow Music
Hall
ST. LOUIS, MO
1 July 1979, Kiel Auditorium
PECATONICA, IA
4 July 1979, Winnebago County
Fairgrounds
WICHITA, KS
6 July 1979, Century II
SIOUX FALLS, SD
7 July 1979, Sioux Falls Arena
DES MOINES, IA
8 July 1979, Veterans Memorial
Auditorium

OMAHA, NE
10 July 1979, Omaha Civic
Auditorium Arena
SAN DIEGO, CA
19 July 1979, San Diego Sports
Arena[103]
OAKLAND, CA
21 July 1979, Oakland
Stadium
CLEVELAND, OH
28 July 1979, Cleveland
Stadium
EVANSVILLE, IN
29 July 1979, Mesker
Amphitheater
FORT WAYNE, IN
31 July 1979, Allen County War
Memorial Coliseum
INDIANAPOLIS, IN
1 August 1979, Market Square
Arena
CINCINNATI, OH
2 August 1979, Riverfront
Coliseum
PITTSBURGH, PA
3 August 1979, Pittsburgh Civic
Arena
NEW YORK, NY
4 August 1979, Madison Square
Garden
PHILADELPHIA, PA
5 August 1979, Philadelphia
Spectrum
OAKLAND, CA
5 September 1979, Oakland
Civic Auditorium

RENO, NV
6 September 1979, University
of Nevada
SANTA CRUZ, CA
7 September 1979, Santa Cruz
Civic Auditorium
FRESNO, CA
8 September 1979, Warnors
Theatre
SAN DIEGO, CA
9 September 1979, San Diego
Sports Arena
LONG BEACH, CA
10 September 1979, Long Beach
Arena
AMARILLO, TX
13 September 1979, Amarillo
Civic Auditorium
LUBBOCK, TX
14 September 1979, Lubbock
Memorial Auditorium
MIDLAND, TX
15 September 1979, Chaparral
Center
EL PASO, TX
16 September 1979, El Paso
County Coliseum
MCALLEN, TX
18 September 1979, McAllen
Convention Center
CORPUS CHRISTI, TX
19 September 1979, Memorial
Coliseum
HOUSTON, TX
20 September 1979, Houston
Music Hall

DALLAS, TX
21 September 1979, Dallas
Convention Center
SAN ANTONIO, TX
22 September 1979, Convention
Center Arena
BEAUMONT, TX
24 September 1979, Beaumont
City Auditorium
MEMPHIS, TN
26 September 1979, Ellis
Auditorium North Hall
NASHVILLE, TN
27 September 1979, Municipal
Auditorium
JOHNSON CITY, TN
28 September 1979, Freedom
Hall Civic Center
CHARLOTTE, NC
29 September 1979, Charlotte
Coliseum
GREENVILLE, SC
30 September 1979, Greenville
Memorial Auditorium
KNOXVILLE, TN
2 October 1979, Knoxville Civic
Coliseum
GREENSBORO, NC
3 October 1979, Greensboro
Coliseum
JACKSONVILLE, FL
5 October 1979, Veterans
Memorial Coliseum
BIRMINGHAM, AL
6 October 1979, Boutwell
Auditorium

DOTHAN, AL
7 October 1979, Dothan Civic
 Center

ATLANTA, GA
8 October 1979, Fox
 Theatre

COLUMBIA, SC
10 October 1979, Carolina
 Coliseum

NORFOLK, VA
12 October 1979, Norfolk
 Municipal Auditorium

WHEELING, WV
13 October 1979, Wheeling Civic
 Center

CHARLESTON, WV
14 October 1979, Charleston
 Civic Center

TOWSON, MD
16 October 1979, Towson Center

BUFFALO, NY
17 October 1979, Shea's Buffalo
 Theatre

CLEVELAND, OH
18 October 1979, Cleveland
 Public Auditorium

CHICAGO, IL
19 October 1979, Aragon
 Ballroom

TOLEDO, OH
20 October 1979, Toledo Sports
 Arena

COLUMBUS, OH
21 October 1979, St. John Arena
 (*Bon's last North American
 show*)

WITH BON SCOTT

Let There Be Rock (1977)
ATCO Records, United States, SD 36-151
Released in United States: 25 July 1977
"Go Down"
"Dog Eat Dog"
"Let There Be Rock"
"Bad Boy Boogie"
"Problem Child"[104]
"Overdose"
"Hell Ain't A Bad Place To Be"
"Whole Lotta Rosie"
All songs written by Angus Young, Malcolm Young & Bon Scott
Producers: Harry Vanda & George Young

Powerage (1978)
Atlantic Records, United States, SD 19180/KSD 19180
Released in United States: 25 May 1978
"Rock 'N' Roll Damnation"[105]
"Down Payment Blues"
"Gimme A Bullet"
"Riff Raff"
"Sin City"
"What's Next To The Moon"
"Gone Shootin'"
"Up To My Neck In You"
"Kicked In The Teeth"
All songs written by Angus Young, Malcolm Young & Bon Scott
Producers: Harry Vanda & George Young

Highway To Hell (1979)
Atlantic Records, United States, SD 19244/QSD 19244
Released in United States: 27 July 1979

"Highway To Hell"
"Girls Got Rhythm"
"Walk All Over You"
"Touch Too Much"
"Beating Around The Bush"
"Shot Down In Flames"
"Get It Hot"
"If You Want Blood (You've Got It)"[106]
"Love Hungry Man"
"Night Prowler"
All songs written by Angus Young, Malcolm Young & Bon Scott
Producer: Robert John "Mutt" Lange

WITH BRIAN JOHNSON

Back In Black (1980)
Atlantic Records, United States, SD 16018/XSD 16018
Released in United States: 21 July 1980
"Hells Bells"
"Shoot To Thrill"
"What Do You Do For Money Honey"
"Given The Dog A Bone"[107]
"Let Me Put My Love Into You"
"Back In Black"
"You Shook Me All Night Long"
"Have A Drink On Me"
"Shake A Leg"
"Rock And Roll Ain't Noise Pollution"
All songs written by Angus Young, Malcolm Young & Brian Johnson
Producer: Robert John "Mutt" Lange

AC/DC-RELATED OTHER RECORDINGS 1977–80

WITH BON SCOTT

Manque De Trop, Trust (2000)
XIII Bis Records, France, TBR000201
"Ride On"
Written by Angus Young, Malcolm Young & Bon Scott. Jam recorded
  in the studio with Trust on 13 February 1980 at Scorpio Sound,
  Camden, London. It is Bon's last-known recording and was
  included as a bonus track on this four-track French promotional
  single release, which also features the songs "Manque De Trop,"
  "Môrice" and "Marechal."

AC/DC LIVE ALBUMS 1977–80 (NORTH AMERICA)

WITH BON SCOTT

If You Want Blood You've Got It (1978)
Atlantic Records, United States, SD 19212/KSD 19212
Released in United States: 21 November 1978
"Riff Raff"
"Hell Ain't A Bad Place To Be"
"Bad Boy Boogie"
"The Jack"
"Problem Child"
"Whole Lotta Rosie"
"Rock 'N' Roll Damnation"
"High Voltage"
"Let There Be Rock"
"Rocker"
All songs written by Angus Young, Malcolm Young & Bon Scott
Producers: Harry Vanda & George Young

AC/DC PROMO-ONLY LIVE ALBUMS 1977–80 (NORTH AMERICA)

WITH BON SCOTT

Live From The Atlantic Studios (1978)
Atlantic Records, United States, LAAS 001
Released in United States: 18 November 1997[108]
"Live Wire"
"Problem Child"
"High Voltage"
"Hell Ain't A Bad Place To Be"
"Dog Eat Dog"
"The Jack"
"Whole Lotta Rosie"
"Rocker"
All songs written by Angus Young, Malcolm Young & Bon Scott
Engineer: Jimmy Douglass

AC/DC UNRELEASED ALBUMS 1977–80 (AUSTRALIA)

WITH BON SCOTT

12 Of The Best (1978)
Albert Productions, Australia, APLP 029
"It's A Long Way To The Top (If You Wanna Rock 'N' Roll)"
"High Voltage"
"Problem Child"
"TNT"
"Whole Lotta Rosie"
"Let There Be Rock"
"Jailbreak"
"Dirty Deeds Done Dirt Cheap"
"The Jack"
"Dog Eat Dog"

"She's Got Balls"
"Baby Please Don't Go"
All songs written by Angus Young, Malcolm Young & Bon Scott except
    "Baby Please Don't Go," written by Big Joe Williams
Producers: Harry Vanda & George Young

AC/DC SINGLES 1976–80 (NORTH AMERICA)

WITH BON SCOTT

"It's A Long Way To The Top (If You Wanna Rock 'N' Roll)"/
    "High Voltage" (1976)
ATCO Records, 45-7068

"Problem Child"/"Let There Be Rock" (1977)
ATCO Records, 7086

"Rock 'N' Roll Damnation"/"Kicked In The Teeth" (1978)
Atlantic Records, 3499/AT 3499

"Whole Lotta Rosie"/"Hell Ain't A Bad Place To Be" (1979)
Atlantic Records, 3553

"Highway To Hell"/"Night Prowler" (1979)
Atlantic Records, 3617/AT-3617

"Touch Too Much"/"Walk All Over You" (1979)
Atlantic Records, 3664

WITH BRIAN JOHNSON

"You Shook Me All Night Long"/"Have A Drink On Me" (1980)
Atlantic Records, 3761/AT 3761

"Back In Black"/"What Do You Do For Money Honey" (1980)
Atlantic Records, 3787/AT 3787

AC/DC OTHER ALBUMS 1975–1984 (INTERNATIONAL)

WITH BON SCOTT

High Voltage (1975) Australia
"Baby Please Don't Go"
"She's Got Balls"
"Little Lover"
"Stick Around"
"Soul Stripper"
"You Ain't Got A Hold On Me"
"Love Song"
"Show Business"
All songs written by Angus Young, Malcolm Young & Bon Scott except
    "Baby Please Don't Go," written by Big Joe Williams, and "Soul
    Stripper," written by Angus Young & Malcolm Young
Producers: Harry Vanda & George Young

T.N.T. (1975) Australia and New Zealand
"It's A Long Way To The Top (If You Wanna Rock 'N' Roll)"
"Rock 'N' Roll Singer"
"The Jack"
"Live Wire"
"T.N.T."
"Rocker"
"Can I Sit Next To You Girl"
"High Voltage"
"School Days"
All songs written by Angus Young, Malcolm Young & Bon Scott except
    "School Days," written by Chuck Berry, and "Can I Sit Next To
    You Girl," written by Angus Young & Malcolm Young
Producers: Harry Vanda & George Young

High Voltage (1976) International
"It's A Long Way To The Top (If You Wanna Rock 'N' Roll)"
"Rock 'N' Roll Singer"
"The Jack"
"Live Wire"
"T.N.T."
"Can I Sit Next To You Girl"
"Little Lover"
"She's Got Balls"
"High Voltage"
All songs written by Angus Young, Malcolm Young & Bon Scott except
   "Can I Sit Next To You Girl," written by Angus Young & Malcolm
   Young
Producers: Harry Vanda & George Young

Dirty Deeds Done Dirt Cheap (1976) Australia and New Zealand
"Dirty Deeds Done Dirt Cheap"
"Ain't No Fun (Waiting 'Round To Be A Millionaire)"
"There's Gonna Be Some Rockin'"
"Problem Child"
"Squealer"
"Big Balls"
"R.I.P. (Rock In Peace)"
"Ride On"
"Jailbreak"
All songs written by Angus Young, Malcolm Young & Bon Scott
Producers: Harry Vanda & George Young

Dirty Deeds Done Dirt Cheap (1976) United Kingdom, Netherlands,
   France, Canada, Israel, Republic of Ireland, Yugoslavia, Greece,
   Portugal, Germany (1980) Spain, Italy and Argentina (1981) United
   States, Thailand, Venezuela, Brazil, Colombia, Peru, Mexico and
   Japan
"Dirty Deeds Done Dirt Cheap"
"Love At First Feel"
"Big Balls"

"Rocker"

"Problem Child"

"There's Gonna Be Some Rockin'"

"Ain't No Fun (Waiting 'Round To Be A Millionaire)"

"Ride On"

"Squealer"

All songs written by Angus Young, Malcolm Young & Bon Scott

Producers: Harry Vanda & George Young

'74 Jailbreak (1984)

"Jailbreak"

"You Ain't Got A Hold On Me"

"Show Business"

· "Soul Stripper"

"Baby Please Don't Go"

All songs written by Angus Young, Malcolm Young & Bon Scott except "Baby Please Don't Go," written by Big Joe Williams, and "Soul Stripper," written by Angus Young & Malcolm Young

Producers: Harry Vanda & George Young

AC/DC ALBUMS OR BOX SETS (INDIVIDUAL TRACKS) 1986–2010

WITH BON SCOTT

Bonfire (1997) All tracks from Live From The Atlantic Studios *and the motion picture* AC/DC: Let There Be Rock, *plus a bonus live performance of "T.N.T." in Paris, 1979, and a new compilation of rarities, live cuts and works in progress: Volts. Tracks are "Dirty Eyes," "Touch Too Much," "If You Want Blood (You've Got It), "Back Seat Confidential," "Get It Hot," "Sin City," "She's Got Balls," "School Days," "It's A Long Way To The Top (If You Wanna Rock*

'N' Roll)," "Ride On." A remastered edition of Back In Black *was also included.*

Who Made Who (1986) "Ride On"

Backtracks (2009) "Stick Around," "Love Song," "Fling Thing" (instrumental), "R.I.P. (Rock In Peace)," "Carry Me Home," "Crabsody In Blue," "Cold Hearted Man," "Dirty Deeds Done Dirt Cheap" (live), "Dog Eat Dog" (live), "Live Wire" (live), "Shot Down In Flames" (live)

Backtracks: Deluxe Collector's Edition (2009) "High Voltage," "Stick Around," "Love Song," "It's A Long Way To The Top (If You Wanna Rock 'N' Roll)," "Rocker," "Fling Thing" (instrumental), "Dirty Deeds Done Dirt Cheap," "Ain't No Fun Waiting 'Round To Be A Millionaire," "R.I.P. (Rock In Peace)," "Carry Me Home," "Crabsody In Blue," "Cold Hearted Man," "Dirty Deeds Done Dirt Cheap" (live), "Dog Eat Dog" (live), "Live Wire" (live), "Shot Down In Flames" (live)

Iron Man 2 (2010) "Rock 'N' Roll Damnation," "Cold Hearted Man," "If You Want Blood (You've Got It)," "T.N.T.," "Hell Ain't A Bad Place To Be," "Let There Be Rock," "Highway To Hell"

YOUNG/YOUNG/SCOTT-CREDITED, PLATINUM-CERTIFIED STUDIO ALBUMS, LIVE ALBUMS AND EPS/COMPILATIONS BY UNITS SOLD (MILLIONS) IN THE UNITED STATES AND CERTIFICATION DATE

Bonfire (1997)	1	24 January 2001
'74 Jailbreak (1984)	1	22 January 2001
Dirty Deeds Done Dirt Cheap (1981)	6	22 January 2001
Highway To Hell (1979)	7	25 May 2006
If You Want Blood You've Got It (1978)	1	4 October 1990

Powerage (1978)	1	4 October 1990
Let There Be Rock (1977)	2	12 December 1997
High Voltage (1976)	3	25 May 2005

TOTAL: 22

YOUNG/YOUNG/SCOTT–CREDITED, PLATINUM-CERTIFIED STUDIO ALBUMS, LIVE ALBUMS AND EPS/COMPILATIONS BY UNITS SOLD (MILLIONS) IN THE UNITED STATES AND CERTIFICATION DATE, WERE BACK IN BLACK INCLUDED

Bonfire (1997)	1	24 January 2001
'74 Jailbreak (1984)	1	22 January 2001
Dirty Deeds Done		
Dirt Cheap (1981)	6	22 January 2001
Back In Black (1980)	22	13 December 2007
Highway To Hell (1979)	7	25 May 2006
If You Want Blood		
You've Got It (1978)	1	4 October 1990
Powerage (1978)	1	4 October 1990
Let There Be Rock (1977)	2	12 December 1997
High Voltage (1976)	3	25 May 2005

TOTAL: 44

Source: Recording Industry Association of America. Note: titles are U.S. releases only. The Australian LP Dirty Deeds Done Dirt Cheap *(1976) was belatedly released (with track changes) in the United States in 1981.* High Voltage *(1976) was a compilation of the Australian-issued* High Voltage *(1975) and* T.N.T. *(1975). '74* Jailbreak *(1984) was a compilation of additional tracks from the Australian-issued* High Voltage *(1975) and "Jailbreak" from* Dirty Deeds Done Dirt Cheap *(1976). The Iron Man 2 soundtrack album/compilation (2010), featuring seven Bon tracks out of 15, went gold.* Who Made Who *(1986), the nine-song soundtrack album for the film* Maximum Overdrive, *which featured Bon's "Ride On" from* Dirty Deeds Done Dirt Cheap, *as well as songs from* Back In Black, For Those About To Rock We Salute You *and* Fly On The Wall, *went five-times platinum. The band's second live album,* Live *(1992), featuring five Bon songs* in concert, went three-times platinum. A collectors' edition of Live featuring nine Bon songs went two-times platinum. The box set Backtracks (2009) failed to achieve gold certification. Bonfire (1997), a five-disc box set of Bon tracks and rarities put out by East West Records, intriguingly contains the full Back In Black album, credited to Young/ Young/Johnson. At the time of its release A&R executive Bruce Harris from East West's parent company Elektra told Billboard: "[Back In Black] was all about the shadow of Bon, in a good way. There's a real sentimental quality here . . . Bon loomed very large in [the band's] lives, and they've never had a chance as a band to reflect on him in a public way. That's the guiding force to the box, and that's also the guiding force to putting Back In Black on it." Back In Black is AC/DC's only diamond-certified (10 million) seller, two-times diamond.

LOCATIONS OF OFFICIAL MEMORIALS TO BON SCOTT

Fremantle, Australia
Kirriemuir, Scotland

LOCATIONS OF UNOFFICIAL MEMORIALS TO BON SCOTT

Šamorín, Slovakia
East Dulwich, England

POSTHUMOUS HONOURS OF BON SCOTT

Australian Recording Industry Association Hall of Fame,
Sydney, Australia
Rock & Roll Hall of Fame, Cleveland, United States

ANNUAL CELEBRATIONS OF BON SCOTT

Bonfest, Kirriemuir, Scotland
Internationales AC/DC-Fantreffen, Geiselwind, Germany

BACK SEAT CONFIDENTIAL

1   Mary and co-author John D'Arcy were interviewed on Australian Channel Ten's *Studio 10* in October 2015 while promoting *Live Wire*. At one point D'Arcy said, "I'd say a lot of those songs [on *Back In Black*] were written by Bon as well because he told us that it was all happening [before he died]," with a visibly uncomfortable Mary sitting next to him and nudging him. "No, we're not going there," she said. Why not? Mary admits she hasn't listened to *Back In Black*. But in an interview with Melbourne's Triple R, she revealed: "Without what happened [in East Dulwich], Bon would have been singing it . . . there's a lot of really [*pauses*] good words that Bon wrote in that album."

   Despite owning letters Bon wrote to her, Mary was also denied permission by the Bon Scott Estate to reproduce them in her book. She told Wendy Stapleton of Melbourne's Channel 31: "We weren't allowed to actually put the letters in the book. I really wanted to. But one of Bon's f — [*stops mid-sentence*] and even though they're my letters they apparently belong to the Bon estate, so I was not allowed to put them in the book. He wouldn't let me sort of put them in the book." She doesn't reveal who "he" is.

   Bon's family and its lawyers, fiercely protective of Bon's image and reputation, are notorious for trying to shut down anything unauthorised. I have a copy of a letter from a lawyer warning an individual who wanted to get the family's cooperation for a film project about Bon's life that "the Estate takes its rights in and to the name, image and reputation of Bon Scott very seriously" and "that if necessary the Estate will take legal steps to protect its rights in respect of any ongoing unauthorised use of the name 'Bon Scott.'"

2   "Before *Back In Black*, the band could never quite harness its sound and fury," *Rolling Stone* harrumphed in one of its album guides, rating the Bon suite of albums thus: *High Voltage* ★★, *Let There Be Rock* ★★½, *Powerage* ★★½, *If You Want Blood* ★★★ and *Highway To Hell* ★★★. It gave ★★★★ to *Back In Black* and, unbelievably, ★★★★ to *Who Made Who*. Today the previously maligned *Powerage*, containing Bon's best writing, is widely recognised the world over as AC/DC's masterpiece and one of the great records of the 1970s, as it should be. It's a flawless rock album.

3   Historical quotes from members of AC/DC have been used throughout *Bon: The Last Highway*.

Sources for these quotes (and selected other quotes used in the book without attribution in the main text) are listed in Bibliography, under "Notes."

4   Late Molly Hatchet bass player Banner Thomas told me the show was in Indiana, likely Evansville, not Tennessee.

5   Former Outlaws and Lynyrd Skynyrd manager Charlie Brusco says he got wind of Bon's mysterious solo plans: "Bon wanted to do a Southern rock record. I never heard of it being anything more than an idea that was being kicked around." Leon Wilkeson, the now-deceased bass player of Lynyrd Skynyrd, is one name that has come up frequently in connection to Bon's solo album. Jeff Carlisi, guitarist of .38 Special, believes the rumours may have substance: "Leon was a big fan [of AC/DC] and probably understood them and their music better than anyone." Outlaws drummer Monte Yoho tells a similar story about Wilkeson: "When we were touring a lot with Skynyrd, Leon came up to me one night with an AC/DC shirt on and asked me if I had ever heard this band. He told me how incredible they were and had been hanging out with some of the members. That might have been part of the connection to the Southern rock." But Outlaws guitarist Freddie Salem, who socialised with Bon, hadn't heard anything about it: "[Bon] did not mention a Southern rock album per se but professed his love for American roots music, like most British, Australian rock artists." Nor had Greg T. Walker, bassist of Blackfoot, formerly of Lynyrd Skynyrd: "We did a lot of shows with [AC/DC] back in the day. It was always a fun time with Bon, [late Blackfoot drummer] Jakson Spires and me doing a lot of drinking and living life to the fullest. It was a time before bands began to fragment because one member wanted to do a solo record. Neither of us had even thought of something this absurd, and Bon never hinted at such a notion. We spent a lot of time together in that period."

6   Four months later, Cliff Williams, who'd been with the band since 1977, announced he was retiring after the tour was over, saying the band had become a "changed animal." His last show with AC/DC was in Philadelphia, Pennsylvania, on 20 September 2016. His retirement party took place in Fort Myers, Florida, on 30 January 2017.

7   Not all the press was bad. In 1976, AC/DC got a plug in the *Chicago Tribune* entertainment column "Tower Ticker": "Atlantic Records is high on AC-DC, a punk-rock group from Australia." The *Washington Post* gave the band a reasonable review, praising Angus Young for his "great authority" and noting Bon Scott's appeal, saying he was "hard to ignore, playing the role of the sex-starved madman to such perfection that it's hard to see how these guys can miss." The *Los Angeles Times* astutely picked up on "a stunning sense of rock 'n' roll humour and heterosexual aggression like we haven't seen since the early Rolling Stones," while *Billboard* wrote, "This band is the Australian entry in the heavy metalspunk sweepstakes. Led by Malcolm and Angus Young on guitars, the band makes up in energy what it lacks in expertise." This, however, was about the sum of AC/DC's positive reviews.

8   AC/DC tour manager Ian Jeffery, watching all this happen, thought the single-cab pickup truck containing Bon, Roy, Roy's friend Byron Christian, and two women who'd tagged along were Mexicans, as he told AC/DC biographer Mick Wall in 2012: "[Bon] wandered off . . . with all these Mexicans he'd befriended at some bar somewhere . . . next thing this truck comes hurtling over the horizon, with AC/DC music blaring out of it. It's Bon with 10 of his new best friends all holding bottles of whisky and joints in their hands. It pulls up, Bon jumps out and says to me, 'Ian, this is Pedro and this is Poncho, et cetera; can you get them all on the guest list?'"

Roy laughs when I read him the quote: "I am absolutely positive there were no Mexicans. We may have had good tans but we definitely did not look like Mexicans — big difference. As far as listening to AC/DC, I don't see how that's possible since we didn't really know of the band. It could have been on the radio. Although Austin was a very permissive town back then, we still had to at least try and play it cool, so I don't see us riding through downtown smoking weed for all to see, either. We barrelled up to the band bus in the parking lot because we were cutting it close and there were a couple of guys standing outside anxiously awaiting Bon's return. Ian was one of them; they looked relieved and happy he was back. I am trying to be careful to only tell things as I remember them and to try to not fill in the gaps with stuff I think happened or even probably happened. All that being said, I like Ian's version much better [*laughs*] but I'd have to say he's exaggerating a bit."

9   Malcolm told New York's *Daily News* in 1980: "A lot of people just look at [Angus] in his uniform and they forget what a great musician he is. The 'schoolboy' thing started when he was 11. He was playing in a band with a lot of older guys, and they used to dress him up that way and advertise the show by saying, 'Come see the little guitar star.'" Which is curious, when the conventional version of the story is that the Youngs' sister Margaret "suggested that Angus wear his school uniform onstage, a gimmick that rapidly became their trademark." But that's the thing with AC/DC: they massage the story to suit the myth. In any case, the uniform has served AC/DC well. As rock critic Jim Farber once quipped, "It's as unchanging a shtick as a Borscht Belt comic's."

10   Ironically, "Carry Me Home" is the name of a track released in Australia in 1977 (AP-11403) as a B-side on the "Dog Eat Dog" single. It was re-released on AC/DC's *Backtracks* compilation in 2009. Lyrically, it's probably the closest Bon ever got to chronicling the depressing reality of his alcoholism.

11   In a 1975 profile for *Rock Australia Magazine* (better known as *RAM*), Bon's friend Anthony O'Grady cleverly broached the subject of heroin with him.

> I remark that Bon has both ears pierced and there are gold rings in them there lobes, giving him a distinctly piratical look. A few years ago, of course, it was the custom for heroin addicts to have the right ear pierced and to wear an earring there . . . is it at all possible that . . .
> "Nah," says Bon, "I'm not a druggie. What happened y'see, was a few years ago I was working on a cray fishing boat and there was this guy there I really respected and admired. And he had his ear pierced . . . so I got one of mine done then."

It was a story Irene Thornton rubbished in her memoir. Bon had had it pierced in a beauty salon in Adelaide.

12   It was eventually released in North America in 1981, albeit with an altered track listing.

13   Often seen spelled as Isabelle or Isobelle (Bon's birth certificate has it as Isabelle) though immigration and electoral records have it correctly recorded as Isabella, and her memorial plaque at Fremantle Cemetery also says Isabella. Ravenscraig is incorrectly called "Raymondscraig" in the Walker biography. Ravenscraig is a 15th-century castle in Isa's hometown of Kirkcaldy.

14   John Fyfe, an AC/DC fan from Forfar, told me: "Bon's celebrity in Forfar has mostly been overlooked in Forfar and 'stolen' by Kirriemuir; while he was born in Forfar he was a Kirrie lad and that's where his parents lived, so he is seen as a son of Kirriemuir. The memorial plaque to Bon is in Kirriemuir and it goes as far as saying he was born in Kirriemuir rather than Forfar — so the theft of Bon now also stretches as far as his birth. Me and a few mates keep reminding them that he was born in Forfar but it falls on deaf ears." He points out there is a massive difference between the Youngs and Bon. "I don't buy the 'Glasgow' shite. Well, I do in part as Glaswegians can have a huge chip on their shoulders — and their knees. But *fuck me*. There is a difference — a *huge* one — between East and West Coast Scots, Bon and the Youngs. Bon is what I would expect from someone born in Forfar and brought up by people fae Kirrie: easygoing, not too worried about what people thought, but knowing he'd do fine, and his family seeing a new country as an opportunity to have a 'better life' without too many pretensions. There are some

aspects of the 'Glasgow' mentality in the Youngs. But they have issues beyond that. And if there was something of an issue to be made I reckon someone fae a rural Scottish community could show someone fae a city what being 'pissed off' was all about. We choose not to. But as Bon showed, we can — when we feel it is 'appropriate.' Just not all the fucking time."

A statue of Bon was erected in Kirriemuir on 30 April 2016. It was funded entirely by fans. An inscription at its base calls him "the young lad from Kirriemuir."

15   "He printed everything, like a kid," says Pattee Bishop. "His writing was big letters only. He would sit at the pool and write lists. He didn't like stuff; his suitcase was packed so neat. He was a clean freak. He also had a notepad with names of girlfriends in it. I didn't know what he was writing; he had tour dates and pictures in it. I just saw the big block letters he used."

16   Photos exist of Bon on the band's tour bus, torpor and boredom etched on his face. It's easy to understand what he was feeling. AC/DC's other members wouldn't have been the most illuminating conversationalists for a man who liked to read Anaïs Nin. Mark Evans described AC/DC in his autobiography as "very insular" and having "no real camaraderie."

17   Vince Lovegrove didn't help dispel this fantastical notion by ridiculously comparing Bon to Peter Pan in print. "Bon has achieved that same never-grow-old immortality," he wrote in Sydney's *Sunday Telegraph* in 2001. "Some fans would even argue that [he] was the real Peter Pan personified."

18   When Malcolm had his alcohol problems, he just stepped away from the band between 1988–90 and slotted right back in, no questions asked. "I'd just fucked myself up so much and it got to the point where it became, 'Look, guys, I'd love to but I can't,'" he told Sylvie Simmons in *RAW* magazine. "The guys knew it. They knew it was best for me as well. I had to stop drinking and that was tough; it took a long time." It wasn't a luxury that was going to be extended to Bon — or anyone else in the band other than Angus. Case in point: Phil Rudd.

By 1983, Rudd had been ejected from the band for reasons never properly explained. The strong rumour was that he had been fired but the Youngs made out he had left of his own volition, explaining the departure in variously baroque ways. He returned to the band in the 1990s, then was removed again before the start of the *Rock Or Bust* world tour in 2015.

"Phil Rudd isn't the guy that's the 'hitman' guy today," says Barry Bergman. "I mean, I never knew *that* guy . . . something snapped. Phil was a nervous guy. He was a nervous young man when we originally met. He had nervous attacks and things, panic attacks and all kinds of things . . . he went through things, emotional stuff."

How did Phil manage his fragile emotional state?

"He snapped back. He always rose to the occasion. He always did what he had to do and it wasn't a problem. He really always rose to the occasion."

But not so, according to Pete Way: "I daresay he probably was fired from the band going back to when Simon Wright took over . . . I think [Phil] was kind of asked to leave to get himself organised or break whatever it was that he was doing. They don't take prisoners, the Youngs."

Pattee Bishop says AC/DC's drummer wasn't the most amenable individual: "Phil was an asshole. Phil was a prick. Phil was always high and would call people nasty names. I saw him get punched in the face; a real good one too [*laughs*]. Little shit."

Who hit him?

"At the hotel, that first gig I saw them [in Hollywood, Florida, in 1977], he was at the door pushing someone out, and the guy let him have it. I liked Phil. He was just not very nice to the girls I would see backstage or at the hotels. He would call them names and laugh at them. I never got close to him but he asked if I had a sister for him [*laughs*]. He just would slam doors and kick things and get mean-drunk. He liked to be naked and stand in the doorway. Too funny [*laughs*]."

Clearly, Phil was no saint. But in 2014 he had to deal with the sight of Bob Richards performing in the videos for "Play Ball" and "Rock Or Bust" and then Chris Slade taking his place on tour. AC/DC gave a disgraceful interview to Howard Stern while promoting *Rock Or Bust* where they essentially tore into Phil, Angus Young calling him "Tony Montana, Scarface." Brian Johnson joked of Rudd's arrest that he saw "this guy getting led out of a car with no shoes on looking like he'd been fucking dragged through a hedge backwards." No matter what happened with the court case, "We're all going to go on tour and nothing's going to stop us."

AC/DC had such short memories. In 1996 Angus praised Phil on returning for the *Ballbreaker* album to a French interviewer from MCM Euromusique: "When we had other drummers, like Chris Slade's a great drummer, they had to copy that [original AC/DC] style . . . it's a very natural style, what [Phil] plays . . . you can play a song and . . . it's like he's reading your mind, you don't have to arrange it or direct it." The interviewer asks Angus if he can feel the difference onstage. "Very much so, yes . . . with [some people] there's communication, and they pick up straight away . . . you don't have to direct it or anything, you don't have to look [at them]. They just do it."

19   Angus Young, in jest, once told the *Emerald City Chronicle* of Madison, Wisconsin: "I love young women. Ten, 11 years old."

20   Lovegrove's program was essentially a puff piece about Australian bands making it big overseas. Others were less enthused about the rise of Aussie rock, evidenced by this excoriating 1978 article from Alan Niester in Toronto's *Globe and Mail*: "The Aussies have chipped into the [punk] movement with a trio of bands. In descending order of merit, they are AC/DC with *Powerage* (they're a D), Radio Birdman with *Radios Appear* (terrible; an E) and The Saints with *(I'm) Stranded* (also an E)."

21   Pattee Bishop read Renshaw's *Live Wire*: "The one secret that was in the book was his love of pretty feet. My size 5, always-red toes he loved." What Bon hated most, she says, was girls who "didn't keep themselves clean enough down there for him; he told me that. Bon was so funny."
      Vaginally?
      "Yep, he hated nasty smells and ugly panties. He would kick or use a stick to move panties off the floor. I always had on beautiful bra and panty sets; white silk and lace, no cheap crap. Girls with hair on their toes turned him off."
      It makes *She kept her motor clean* in "You Shook Me All Night Long" suddenly very intriguing. Bon liked clean, sweet-smelling vaginas, then. What hot-blooded heterosexual man doesn't? Bon would have had the skill to disguise such a meaning in a rock lyric. Did Brian Johnson?

22   In Mark Putterford's biography of the band, Michael Browning is quoted as saying Atlantic was going to drop AC/DC after *High Voltage* but they accepted a $5000 reduction in their advance to stay on. In recent times, including in my book *The Youngs*, Jerry Greenberg has claimed some credit for signing AC/DC, which amuses David Krebs: "There is no fucking way that Jerry Greenberg is the number-one guy in this band's career; that is so far from the truth, that is sad. I don't care if he signed the cheques, but it's just not true." I ask Bergman whether it was Atlantic A&R executive Jim Delehant or Greenberg who wanted to dump AC/DC. "Both," he says, immediately. "No matter what they say." Greenberg, for his part, told me in 2013: "I never, *ever* was thinking about dropping the band."

23   In August 1980, a notice of intended distribution appeared in the *Sydney Morning Herald*: "Any person having any claim upon the Estate of RONALD BELFORD SCOTT late of Spearwood, in the State of Western Australia, Musician, who died on 19th February, 1980 must send particulars of his claim to John McEwen, the Attorney of Charles Belford Scott and Isabella Cunningham Scott, the parents at c/o ALLEN ALLEN & HEMSLEY, Solicitors, G.P.O. Box 50, Sydney, N.S.W. 2001, on or before 23rd October, 1980. The Administrators will distribute the assets of her [sic] Estate having regard only to the claims at that date they have notice. Letters of Administration were granted in New South Wales on 11th July, 1980." Curiously, the same listing, almost word for word, appeared again nearly two years later, in both the *Herald* and

Western Australia's *Government Gazette*. In the latter listing, "V. Scott" (presumably sister-in-law Valarie Scott) of "3 Chesterton Street, Spearwood" is given as the trustee.

24 Irene Thornton even wrote about Bon's haircut for the *Midnight Special* performance in her book, but she saw it very differently: "His hair was awful; he had curled bangs and a perm, both growing out awkwardly."

25 Why, then, wouldn't Bon work on the lyrics for *Back In Black* in the same way? *Highway To Hell* and *Back In Black* engineer Tony Platt said in an interview with *Ultimate Guitar*: "Angus and Malcolm would always have got the riffs together. It's pretty well documented that when Bon [Scott] was alive that they would come in with the riffs and he would get the lyrics together as the songs went down. It was kind of in that situation. There were lyrics written but not all of them. They were doing pre-production rehearsals in London whilst Mutt and I were doing this other album. So we heard little bits and pieces and Mutt had obviously heard a lot more of it than I had. I think if I remember rightly he probably spent a few days with them or maybe a week or so fine-tuning the songs and arrangements before we went out to The Bahamas."

26 "Back Seat Confidential," an early version of "Beating Around The Bush," appeared on 1997's *Bonfire* box set.

27 The dark themes and dubious lyrics of "Night Prowler," a song Bon claimed was titled as far back as 1977 and recorded in four different versions, were presaged in a 1976 *RAM* article about AC/DC playing Melbourne's Moomba Festival: "The climax of the evening for the girls with the *We do it for AC/DC* banner was a mock rape staged by Angus and Bon." In London the same year, Bon would tell rock journalist Phil Sutcliffe "15 to 17" was the "fuckable age" back home. "I just love getting round the law."

28 "The other guys [in AC/DC] weren't around much," says Holly. "They really didn't hang out with Bon at all. I'm assuming they were probably sick and tired of his behaviour and didn't want anything to do with him. Angus, the few times I did meet with him, he was very polite and very nice. It was very clear to me that Malcolm was in control, the sort of head of the band. Bon was afraid of disappointing him. I think he knew that he had disappointed him thoroughly through his uncontrollable alcohol and drug use. He felt really badly about those. I don't think Malcolm would let him off the hook. Everyone else let Bon off the hook."

Which suggests Angus's claim — "We saw more of [Bon] than his family did, especially us three. It was always me, Bon and Malcolm. We hung out together. Go to clubs together, get thrown outta clubs together" — is not so accurate.

"Angus wasn't normal," says Larry Van Kriedt, AC/DC's first bass player and a childhood friend of the Young brothers. Van Kriedt describes the teenage Angus as being "very outgoing. Not shy. He was leader of the pack. Even though he was little. Always surrounded by a gang. He adopted me as some kind of special friend and even acted as my bodyguard, me having just come from San Francisco, where everything was pretty mellow, to Burwood in Sydney where the teens were into roughing each other up a bit. The Youngs were to be feared. I could play the blues and some hot lead licks. I was more advanced than they were as far as guitar chops went. And they valued that a lot. At the time, I mean . . . I've known a lot of weirdos in my life. He's just another one."

Van Kriedt says claims he returned briefly to AC/DC in 1975 to fill in for Rob Bailey are wrong: "I have no idea where it comes from. Try taking it off Wikipedia and it goes back up again. It must have been published in some book so is regarded as 'fact.'"

29 It's listed with the United States Copyright Office as *Power Age*. Bon also referred to it in a 1978 concert in Columbus, Ohio, as *Power-age*. An early version of "Whole Lotta Rosie" appears on 1997's *Bonfire*: "Dirty Eyes."

30   Said PBS's *Frontline* in its program "The Quaalude Lesson": "The drug supply came from legitimately manufactured pills diverted into the illegal drug trade and from counterfeit pills coming from South America and illegal labs within the United States. By 1981, the DEA ranked Quaalude use second only to marijuana and estimated that 80 to 90 per cent of world production went into the illegal drug trade. Stress clinics, where customers paid about $100 cash for a Quaalude prescription from a licensed physician, became popular in urban areas. The DEA estimated that the 20 million pills on the street in 1980 would double in just a year and match heroin's popularity . . . yet within just a few years, the DEA got the problem of Quaalude abuse under control. By 1984, Quaaludes had all but disappeared from the U.S. marketplace."

According to Justin T. Gass: "In 1974, Quaalude overdose was responsible for 88 deaths in the United States. In 1976 and 1977 in the United States, an estimated 5500 emergency-room visits were associated with Quaalude use and its withdrawal symptoms . . . Quaaludes became one of the most abused drugs in the United States in the early 1970s."

31   "Shoot To Thrill" off *Back In Black* contains the line *Too many women with too many pills.* Bon was doing Quaaludes regularly, so why is Brian Johnson writing about pills? *Too many women with too many pills* is exactly the kind of Bon lyric the rest of the song might have been constructed around with its gun and phallus imagery: standard fare in the late-period AC/DC catalogue. The *VH1 Ultimate Albums* documentary on AC/DC claims that "Shoot To Thrill" "took its name from a phrase jotted down in Angus Young's notepad." Why would Angus be writing about women and pills when he was married and didn't touch drugs? Malcolm was married and drank. Brian was married and fixed vinyl roofs on sports cars. The Bon connection is very clear.

32   AC/DC's lyrics from 1980 onwards did become more obvious and obnoxious. Malcolm Young, interviewed by *Guitar World* in 1995, summed it up better than anyone: "People can go out and hear R.E.M. if they want deep lyrics. But at the end of the night, they want to go home and get fucked. And that's where AC/DC comes into it. I think that's what's kept us around so long. Because people want more fuckin'." Double entendres are their go-to formula. "A lot of our songs have double meanings," Malcolm told Mark Putterford in 1986, "because you can't just say, 'I'm gonna stick my dick right up your cunt.' You've got to cover up the filth somehow."

In a thesis called *Bon Scott and the Blues Lyric Formula*, author J.P. Quinton tabulated that the predominant themes in Bon's published songs were love (including sex) and being a musician. Authority, mortality, booze, drugs and money (or lack of it) were less important preoccupations.

33   An inaccuracy from Bon: Phil Rudd was the only Australian-born member of the band. Rudd has claimed German and Irish ancestry. His stepfather was Lithuanian.

34   Another of Bon's girlfriends during this time was Marilyn Ford, who worked as a coordinating assistant at AC/DC's booking agency American Talent International (ATI) and had been set up with Bon in New York City in 1979 by Doug Thaler, who worked for ATI.

35   Of Lynyrd Skynyrd's 1977 lineup, Ronnie Van Zant, Allen Collins, Leon Wilkeson, Steve Gaines and Billy Powell are all dead. The only original member still touring with Skynyrd, Gary Rossington, suffered a major heart attack in October 2015. Tales abound of AC/DC and Skynyrd jamming together on "Sweet Home Alabama" at a makeshift studio in Jacksonville, just months before the 20 October 1977 plane crash in Gillsburg, Mississippi, that claimed the lives of Van Zant, Gaines, his sister and back-up singer Cassie Gaines, the band's assistant road manager and two pilots. Rossington told *Classic Rock* magazine in 2013 that the meeting of the two bands actually took place: "Jamming with them was so cool. Both bands had really just made it and we were celebrating all that hard work . . . Kevin Elson, our mixing guy, recorded it. I don't know what happened to that tape, but I'd love to hear it now." *Both bands had really just made it?* It's an odd quote. AC/DC hadn't done anything in America at that point. Rossington also claims the jam happened the day after the Jacksonville show, but AC/DC was playing a concert

in Hollywood, Florida, 333 miles south of Jacksonville. The story, as good as it is, seems highly dubious. Journey producer Elson, who was Skynyrd's sound engineer at the time, was mystified when I asked him if it was true and whether tapes existed: "Unfortunately I don't have anything on the two groups getting together. Wish I did. I never got to know the guys." The only other living member of Skynyrd from the 1977 lineup, drummer Artimus Pyle, is estranged from the band.

Most likely, given Bon's social circles in 1979, the Southern rock record Bon wanted to cut was with Outlaws, not Lynyrd Skynyrd — or what was left of them. AC/DC and Outlaws were both booked by Doug Thaler and they were both produced by Mutt Lange. (*Playin' To Win* was released in October 1978 through Arista Records, with a cover by Gerard Huerta, AC/DC's logo designer.)

Arista boss Clive Davis wanted the band to use an English producer. As Brusco describes it, "He wanted somebody who could mix rock stuff with vocals because we had the big Eagles kind of vocals but we played much harder than they did." Lange, an Eagles fan, did the same thing with AC/DC on *Highway To Hell*.

36   Over the years a number of individuals have claimed to be or have been alleged to be Bon's son, yet no DNA tests have been conducted. A Melbourne man, Dave Stevens, claims that he is the child of Bon and a woman called Diane Ellis. She died on 18 February 2016. Ellis was 15 when she fell pregnant and Stevens was adopted out. Stevens said as much in a series of public posts on his Facebook page on the occasion of Ellis's passing, and with some rancour, stating Bon "impregnated" the "15-year-old Diane Ellis," which "led her to a life which she would not have experienced otherwise." He later deleted the posts. Stevens never met Bon and is not known to be a beneficiary of the Bon Scott Estate.

37   According to the book *Buzzed: The Straight Facts About the Most Used and Abused Drugs from Alcohol to Ecstasy*, the liver metabolises alcohol, "where an enzyme called alcohol dehydrogenase, or ADH, breaks ethanol down into acetaldehyde, which in turn is broken down by another enzyme called acetaldehyde dehydrogenase into acetate, which then becomes part of the energy cycle of the cell . . . in general, an adult metabolises the alcohol from one ounce of whisky (which is 40 per cent alcohol) in about one hour. The liver handles this rate of metabolism efficiently. If the drinker consumes more than this amount, the system becomes saturated and the additional alcohol simply accumulates in the blood and body tissues and waits its turn for metabolism. The results are higher blood alcohol concentrations and more intoxication." All of which means if Bon's liver was badly damaged, his body couldn't break down the grog he was chugging.

38   AC/DC was finally getting love where it mattered most: on FM radio. Stations playing *Highway To Hell* included WQXM Tampa, WBAB Babylon, KZEL Eugene, WYDD Pittsburgh, ZETA-7 Orlando, WMMR Philadelphia, WDVE Pittsburgh, WBCN Boston, KSAN San Francisco, KOME San Jose, KZAP Sacramento, KLOL Houston, WRAS Atlanta, WLVQ Columbus, KZEW Dallas, WNEW New York, CHOM Montreal, KMEL San Francisco, KROQ Los Angeles, KRSI Minneapolis, KEZY-AM Anaheim, KWST Los Angeles, WLPL Baltimore, KPAS El Paso, KREM Spokane, WSHE Miami, KRBE Houston, WIFU Philadelphia, WOLF Syracuse, WRJZ Knoxville, KFXD Boise, KLUC Las Vegas, KTIM San Rafael, KGON Portland, KSJO San Jose, KNAC Long Beach, WTIC Hartford, KTFX Tulsa, WEAM Washington, KUPD Phoenix, KBOS Fresno, WFLI Chattanooga, KCBN Reno, Y103 Decatur, WQLK Richmond, WZDQ Chattanooga, WJZQ Milwaukee, WYSP Philadelphia, WZOK Rockford, WABX Detroit, WZZO Allentown, 96KX Pittsburgh, WKXX Birmingham, WVIC Lansing, WGRQ Buffalo, WIYY Baltimore, WKLS Atlanta, KQFM Portland, M-105 Cleveland, WLRS Louisville, WCPI Wheeling, KSHE St. Louis, T-95 Wichita, KBPI Denver and WTIX New Orleans. They'd made it.

39   Jeffery told a completely different story to AC/DC biographer Mark Putterford: "All that stuff about drinking was a myth. Bon liked a drink, sure, but only socially. Okay, so he'd go on binges, but he'd also go two or three months without a drink — he wasn't a habitual drinker

at all, and he wouldn't drink before going onstage. The only time he was ever drunk was at the Southampton Gaumont [Bon's last show on 27 January 1980]. We'd had a big party the night before and Bon was still going — but that was the only time he ever drank before a show."

40 Bon said the plan was to go to England in the second week of January 1980 and write and record till March, touring the new album in April: "Hopefully the band's still alive then. We might all die from malnutrition and exhaustion. The exercise is one thing. Burning out's another . . . Charlie, do me a favour, darling . . . [*Charlie, a woman, can be heard in the background saying, "Yes?"*] could you pour me a nice stiff whisky and Coke? Would you mind?"

41 On 23 February 2005, four days after the original story was published, the *Guardian*'s "Corrections and Clarifications" column issued a retraction: "In [Jinman's] story, it was suggested that the name Alasdair Kinnear [sic] may have been a pseudonym used by one of Scott's associates. That was incorrect. Alistair (not Alasdair) Kinnear is the name of Scott's former friend and neighbour [sic]. We have been asked to make it clear that Mr. Kinnear reported finding Bon Scott immediately on discovery. Scott was then taken to King's College Hospital in Camberwell, where he was declared dead."

42 It's an interesting response from Daniel. He took it that I was suggesting murder, rather than a heroin overdose. Curious, when he knew his father used hard drugs. There is a conspiracy theory, a rather wild one, that Bon was murdered (specifically, that he succumbed to carbon monoxide poisoning). It is not borne out by any evidence whatsoever.

43 Evidently he was still smarting from her decision earlier that year to go their separate ways. Silver said Bon "probably" wrote "Gone Shootin'" about her: "Some poetic licence. 'Gone Snortin'' doesn't quite have the same ring, does it?" The first verse appears to be about Silver, with its reference to a woman buying a ticket to some place unknown. This could refer to her decision to separate from Bon on the road in Indianapolis in 1977, not her departure to Asia from Sydney in 1978.

44 Admitted Rob Riley to me: "I've always felt like the guy who filled in for Mick Cocks, as I was always used when he fucked up. Never knew my standing. Funny that, as I was the guy who wrote the singles off the [1982] *Scarred For Life* album, and was the guy who did the only American tour with the Tatts some 30 years back."

45 The Odeon at 1 Loampit Vale was just a three-and-a-half-mile drive to Alistair Kinnear's flat at 67 Overhill Road. The Odeon was demolished in 1991.

46 They were most likely Joe and Mick, though Joe denies being there.

47 In Murray Engleheart's *AC/DC, Maximum Rock & Roll: The Ultimate Story of the World's Greatest Rock Band*, Ian Jeffery says Bon had drinks with UFO's Phil Mogg and Pete Way at The Music Machine on Sunday, 17 February 1980: "They went up the pub like they normally do and then they went on to the Camden Music Machine after that, which was a Sunday-night haunt. I spoke to Pete afterwards and he said, 'We got hammered and we were going home and Bon didn't want to go — he wanted to carry on drinking.'"
    But Way denies this: "No, as far as I know, I certainly didn't make any arrangements with Phil [Mogg]."
    There is also no evidence that Bon intended to meet Mogg and Way at The Music Machine the following night, as claimed in Paul Stenning's biography and various other reports. Mogg was contacted for this book but his manager advised he was undergoing surgery and unable to comment.

48 Chapman is utterly flabbergasted when I tell him that Way doesn't remember Joe working with him as a guitar tech.

"He can't remember *that*?"

He says Joe supplied you with coke and smack.

"Oh, he did that, *yep*."

For his part, Joe denies he was a dealer for UFO — "I wasn't supplying my own drugs to 'em" — and denies dealing at all: "*Nooo*, I wouldn't have had the resources to be dealing drugs at the time." He says his stint with UFO ended after a falling out with the band's manager, whose name he can't recall but was presumably Wilf Wright, who didn't respond to my interview request. Joe ended up working for Chapman "on a personal basis, like housesitting with his wife."

49 Pete Way told Mark Putterford a different story: "I think I gave him Angus's number." AC/DC tour manager Ian Jeffery, very close to the Youngs at the time, informed AC/DC biographer Murray Engleheart that he received a phone call from Malcolm, who'd first heard from Angus that Bon had died. However, Way is also previously on the record saying he didn't want to tell Angus that Bon was dead, so instead he gave Malcolm's number to Chapman so he could break the news. In his 2017 autobiography, he says it was Malcolm. Which of the pair of Angus and Malcolm Young was first informed about Bon's death has not been conclusively established. Whether there was more than one person involved in delivering the news, and when that news was delivered, also remains in dispute. There are various conflicting accounts.

50 Again, Way is telling a different story to the one he told Putterford: "[Chapman] said he'd just had a call from [Joe's] girlfriend [Silver], and that Bon was dead." There are many inconsistencies in Way's recollections of that day. A friend of Way's, freelance audio engineer Chris LaMarca, who has worked with Way as a guitar tech, posted about Bon on Facebook in 2013 that heroin "was the cause of his demise . . . we are not supposed to know that, are we?" When I asked LaMarca what his insight was on the subject three years later, he wouldn't be drawn on it: "I wasn't there and have no further comment on the subject." To say the least, it was an intriguing reaction coming from someone connected to UFO and especially Way. "Bon wasn't a regular user of hard drugs," Way maintained in his book, but it was "at least probable that he sniffed some heroin that night and then passed out."

51 Joe claims he later met up with UFO in Los Angeles.

52 "Nodding out" "or "nodding off" is lingo for passing out from drugs.

53 When talking to Eddie Trunk about the same event, Chapman said Angus's number not Malcolm's. Joe, oddly, says he never received a call back from Chapman: "I don't recall Paul Chapman getting back to me and saying, 'I've got on to Angus Young,' or anything like that. I don't know who actually contacted the Young guys; I just assume somebody did . . . there certainly wasn't ever any follow-up with Paul Chapman about our conversation [regarding Bon's death]." When I recounted the Way/Chapman chronology of events around the phone call, though, he conceded: "Yeah, that sounds pretty much like it would have gone that way, I guess."

54 Joe and I spoke on a number of occasions. He later contradicted himself on this point when I specifically asked him if he went to The Music Machine that evening: "No, I didn't go out that night."

55 Again, Joe later contradicted himself on the timing of the phone call: "It would have been either that night after Silver and I went to the hospital or the next day."

56 How did AC/DC come to find out about their lead singer's death? The commonly accepted version of events (and likely the correct one) is that Angus Young first got the news, either from one individual or two (for the record, he's claimed both). According to Mick Wall's biography, Silver gave the hospital Peter Mensch's number and she phoned Angus when she got back from the hospital. Angus then called Malcolm. In a *Sounds* interview of March 1980 she's presumably

described as "the frantic friend's lady" who calls Angus. "The girl gave me the hospital number . . . I immediately phoned Malcolm 'cause at the time I thought maybe she'd got the wrong idea."

The *girl*? It doesn't sound like someone Angus knew — and he well knew Silver, though it may just be a case of Angus being Angus: as vague as possible.

Malcolm's version corroborates his brother's — "Angus called me. I was just totally stunned" — but makes out that Silver wasn't actually at the hospital.

"Angus got a phone call" from a "mutual girlfriend" of Alistair and Bon, wrote Sylvie Simmons in *MOJO* in 2010. "It was one of Scott's ex-girlfriends, 'hysterical,' he said, 'and trying to get some information.' She told him she'd heard that Bon had been taken to hospital, dead. Angus hung up and called Malcolm . . . the woman had given him the number of the hospital and Angus had called, but they wouldn't give him any information . . . Peter Mensch called from a South London hospital. He had identified the body."

VH1's *Behind the Music* also says Angus was the first to be informed in the band: "Angus was the first band member to get the sad news." He'd had it confirmed by Mensch: "I had called the guy that was managing us [Mensch] and he told me, that it was true that he had died."

The alternative version of events is that Malcolm Young was first informed about Bon's death. This is essentially the story told by Paul Chapman and Pete Way, though both have contradicted themselves on this point by also saying Angus was the first to get the call.

For his part, tour manager Ian Jeffery has said he got a call from Malcolm at 2:30 a.m. or 3 a.m. on 20 February, informing him of Bon's death. Anna Baba contradicts this. She was staying with the Jefferys and says the phone call came at midnight. Curiously, in the Walker account Anna picked up the phone and handed it to Jeffery's wife and Anna's friend, Suzucho; in Wall's account, she was "woken by screaming from the next room."

The Jefferys got a visit from AC/DC production manager Jake Berry, Mensch called and said they should go and identify the body, Berry dropped off Jeffery at Mensch's, and Mensch and Jeffery went to the morgue.

All this might seem like trivial detail, but it's not. It reveals the many inconsistencies in people's memories of the events — the *Rashomon* effect — that took place immediately after Bon's death and should raise doubts about the conventional story that has been told to the world since 1980. None of the accounts from members of AC/DC or from the management or employees of AC/DC mention the sequence of events of the early morning of 19 February 1980 linking Bon and Joe to Chapman and Way.

57   In Walker's book Silver said she gave the hospital Peter Mensch's number, yet she told me she met Mensch purely by accident in the days *after* Bon's death when she recognised him on the street: "He lived two doors down from me, how's that for irony?" Atlantic senior vice-president Phil Carson says he was at the Air India check-in desk with Mensch in New York when they got the news of Bon's death.

58   Joe's private arrangement as a housesitter for Chapman was independently corroborated by another source: "Joe looked after Linda while Paul was away on tour a couple of times."

59   Lady Sophia Crichton-Stuart was Silver's best friend at the time, according to Silver. Crichton-Stuart married Bain in 1979 and they divorced in 1988.

60   Curiously, Herman Rarebell from Scorpions heard a similar story: "Bon stayed in the car, this is what I understand, the others went upstairs with some chicks to party and forgot him in the car and he was completely drunk and that's the way he died."

61   Said Silver: "Joe saw a bit of her. She was a bit other-worldly and she was very, *very* young. She spoke very little English. She was in a completely different culture and she was quite devastated by it all. We both spent a lot of time with her on the phone in the days afterwards . . . she's

one of those people that you come across that are really lovely but they're not on planet Earth. You've got to accept that they're in a slightly different dimension to the rest of us.

"To do [Clinton] Walker credit, how she appears in his book . . . that's how she was. I think he read her pretty well. She was a sweet girl. There was nothing negative about her but there was no sense for Bon of it being permanent . . . she idolised him and she did everything for him and he quite liked it but he got *really* bored. When he was trying to work on the [*Back In Black*] album he found her presence just really distracting so he'd sent her back [to stay with the Jefferys] to get some work done."

Joe denies he ever met Anna.

62   Silver: "I had already arranged with Joe and a bass player he knew whose name I've forgotten to work out some songs for electric piano, guitar, bass and vocals, as we'd been given leftover studio time." She thought the artist who donated the studio time may have been either Phil Lynott or a member of Wild Horses. Joe made no mention of this to me at all. This obviously put her account at odds with Paul Chapman, who says Joe was with him that evening. She also added: "We never used the studio time . . . I was home both nights. The night Bon rang and the night the hospital rang." This contradicted what Clive Edwards said: that she was at Jimmy Bain's on the 19th. Joe also told me it was Alistair who informed Silver, not the hospital: "Alistair notified Silver." Though he admits, "I didn't hear that call directly."

63   Does Bon's certificate look like a thorough document when the address is wrong? Scotland Yard should at the very least reopen their investigation into Bon's death to see if nothing in the original investigation (if it can be called that) was missed.

64   Walker wrote that "Anna [Baba] went around to Ashley Court on the weekend" and picked up the note, where she was told by the caretaker that the flat had been rifled through on Wednesday, 20 February, the day after Bon's body was found by Alistair Kinnear. This is notable for two reasons. First, Anna has said she was denied access to Bon's flat after his death, which would suggest that she was no longer Bon's "current live-in girlfriend," as Alistair put it. She would have had a key if she were. Joe told me that only Bon had a key to the flat in Victoria. Silver believes that the two AC/DC crew members who gained entry to Bon's apartment, Jake Berry and Ian Jeffery, got access "through the management company" (i.e., Mensch).

65   AC/DC biographer Mark Putterford claimed Alistair made the point of "locking the car doors for safety" but provides no basis for the statement.

66   Was the note Alistair left for Bon admitted into police evidence or did it too disappear?

67   There has only been one Leslie Loads on the UK electoral roll, in 2011, with a Jack Boddy Way, Swaffham, Norfolk address, where Iceni House, a dementia and residential care home, is situated. Enquiries to the facility about the existence of Loads were not answered. Unusually, the only record of a Leslie Loads being born in Great Britain is an Ernest Leslie Loads, also of Norfolk, born in 1916 but who died in 1974. He lived at 4 Garden Bungalows, Swafield, Norfolk. Swafield is just over 40 miles from Swaffham.

In the few interviews she gave before her death, Silver never mentioned Loads at all and didn't know anything about him when I asked her: "I don't know him. I've never heard of him. But then I didn't know anyone in [Alistair's] scene down in South London."

68   The Renault 5 was made between 1972 and 1985. Whatever happened to Alistair's vehicle is a mystery (it would be a collector's piece now, albeit a macabre one). Was the car ever examined forensically for traces of drugs by a crime-scene examiner? Presumably not.

69   Or was it Alistair who made the call, as Joe claims?

70 Ian Jeffery said he called Mensch to give *him* the news after he spoke to Malcolm. Mensch was shocked, incredulous: "Don't fucking joke! Don't fucking wake me up to tell me this fucking shit."

71 The twisted-neck story first popped up in Walker's 1994 biography — "His body was curled around the gearstick, his neck twisted, his dental plate dislodged" — as well as a 2000 piece by Carmel Egan in Adelaide's *Advertiser*: "Bon had curled his 162 cm frame around the gearstick, crinking his neck so that vomit filled his windpipe as he slept." Silver claimed it's a furphy. Alistair, she said, "put Bon in a safe position. He hadn't moved." As for Bon's dental work: "Bon had a bridge fitted the day he left for Australia in 1976. It was the reason he didn't go to the airport with the band. It looked a lot better."

72 The common presumption is that if Bon did have liver damage it was caused by alcohol, though there is another possibility: hepatitis-C virus or HCV, transmitted by blood. Bon had used a needle when he'd overdosed on heroin in Melbourne in 1975. Hepatitis-C causes inflammation, fibrosis and (when chronic) cirrhosis of the liver, which can lead to liver cancer and death. Alcohol only aggravates the symptoms. Many rock stars have succumbed to HCV-related conditions, including Lou Reed and Mick Cocks.

73 Lovegrove concludes in the same story: "For 26 years the rumour-mongers, self-appointed experts and sensation-seekers would have us believe he died of a drug overdose, to the chagrin of his closest friends and family. The truth of his bewitching character, though, is a long way from this drug-addled conjectural hyperbole." But Lovegrove, like many in Scott's orbit, including his family, didn't have enough knowledge of the players from the evening and morning of 18–19 February 1980 to say whether Bon did or didn't die of an overdose.

74 Lovegrove also claimed on his own website, wrongly, that Bon "choked on his own vomit after one of many heavy drinking sessions; he also had a badly affected liver; he was an asthmatic, and it was bitterly cold that night in London, below zero temperatures."

75 Joe independently remembers the same thing: "It sticks in my mind of him saying [Bon] had the veins or the insides of a 60-year-old."

76 There's a curious, unattributed quote in the Murray Engleheart biography of the band: "During a 1980 interview for a U.S. magazine, a band member was quoted as saying that the coroner found Bon's death had resulted from choking; the band member added that the violent reaction had been triggered 'by certain things they didn't release.'"

77 It only took eight years for Bon's memorial plaque to be stolen. In 2006, Bon's gravesite was given national heritage status by the National Trust of Australia. It is reputedly the most visited gravesite in Australia.

78 Wall, a former heroin user who claims he had personally seen Bon do a line of either heroin or coke (but most likely heroin) in Silver's apartment in Gloucester Road, Kensington, made great hay about his heroin theory in his 2012 biography of the band, but then in 2015 appeared in the Alberts-vetted propaganda film *Blood + Thunder*, nabbing a researcher credit for his grovelling performance. If that weren't bad enough, soon after he penned a story about Bon for *Classic Rock* in which he wrote, "It hardly matters [how he died]. It's really not Bon Scott's death we should be remembering him for, but his extraordinary life."
    It hardly matters? Wall's shameless *volte face* was perplexing because while promoting his book, he was singing a very different tune. He even claimed in a 2015 interview with ultimate-guitar.com that "Bon actually died of a fucking heroin overdose from his junkie girlfriend."
    For the record, Silver denied Wall ever visited her apartment, for one very good reason: "Wall

has never been to my place . . . I left Gloucester Road in mid-December 1976. In 1979 I was living alone in Emperor's Gate and Bon never visited me there."

She did, however, cross paths with Wall while they were both on the road with Wild Horses.

"I only met him once. He was trying to get a [writing] gig with the rock rags, was only a kid really, and he did something really stupid in a hotel in the Midlands somewhere; it would have been 1978 or '79. *Sounds* told him to get an interview with Wild Horses and [the editors] would look at it. I tore a strip off him, and felt bad afterwards as I'm not like that, although no one else was there except Joe. Wall was crushed."

79   In his 1995 book *AC/DC: The Kerrang! Files!,The Definitive History*, Malcolm Dome speculated that Bon met up with Joe and "possibly" went to Silver's flat where he "injected himself with supplied heroin" and then went on to The Music Machine "where he met the innocent Kinnear." None of this has been substantiated with any eyewitness testimony or evidence.

80   If this statement is to be taken literally, the second phone call must have happened on Wednesday 20 February 1980 for Chapman's story to check out, the same day Ian Jeffery and Peter Mensch went to the morgue and the same day the first news of Bon's death appeared in the *Evening Standard*. Scotland Yard and the BBC also made public announcements of Bon's death on the 20th. As reported in Clinton Walker's *Highway to Hell*, the caretaker at Bon's building informed Anna Baba that "two big men,"who we now know were Ian Jeffery and Jake Berry, had gained access to the apartment that Wednesday. In Mick Wall's *AC/DC: Hell Ain't a Bad Place to Be*, Jeffery claims he went to Bon's flat, among other things, to "get his [white] T-shirt and some jeans" so that Bon would be dressed in them for when he was taken to the funeral home. Jeffery took the clothes back to the morgue and "I said, 'Please, can you put these on him?'" It would make perfect sense for Jeffery and Berry to have gained access to Bon's flat before Bon's death became public knowledge. But if the second phone call between Chapman and Joe took place on Thursday the 21st, then it would go some way to support Silver Smith's claim that Chapman has his dates mixed up between the 19th and the 20th. Either way, it still doesn't explain Chapman's and Way's assertion that it was after dawn and not after midnight when they first found out Bon had died.

81   Way said something similar to Mark Putterford in 1992: "[Angus] said he still had a lot of Bon's stuff at his flat and he couldn't look at it." But Pattee Bishop says Bon lived very frugally: "Bon didn't leave things thrown around. He had very little. If he had it he was using it or wearing it. So I bet he didn't have a lot of stuff in his place. Bon travelled light; he didn't like clutter." Silver even says she had to lend him things: "I lent him a lot of stuff . . . he borrowed a lot of things. That all disappeared . . . everything just disappeared within two days. He had a full suitcase. That's it."

Curiously, in his autobiography, Way changes his story about the timing of the call, saying he telephoned Angus "later the same day" he learned of Bon's death.

82   Clinton Walker spoke to both of Bon's parents before they died and was able to report: "All Chick and Isa got was a suitcase containing a few items of clothing and a couple of personal effects. Nothing else. No papers. Or musical instruments, records, photo albums — nothing." Isa told Vince Lovegrove in 2006: "He always said he was going to be a millionaire. I just wish he'd been alive to see it and enjoy it, you know? Almost every Christmas, Ron came home to visit. The last time we saw him was Christmas '79, two months before he died. Ron told me he was working on the *Back In Black* album and that that was going to be it; that he was going to be a millionaire. I said, 'Yeah, sure, Ron.'"

Isa had much more to say: "He was writing words for their *Back In Black* album when he died. He was going with a Japanese girl at the time and they wouldn't let her get into the room to get her clothes and things, or Bon's notebooks with the words for the album. Ron was a devil, a lovable devil."

Derek Scott, Bon's brother, told Lovegrove: "When [Bon] died we didn't get any of his belongings back. He'd only been in his room for a couple of days, and the only thing that was returned [to Australia] was his overnight bag he left home with. All his record collection went and everything, really. I don't know what happened over there in London after Bon died."

The band maintains everything is above board. Angus Young told Geoff Barton of *Classic Rock* in August 2005: "All [Bon's] stuff went direct to his mother and his family. It was personal material — letters and things. It wouldn't have been right to hang on to it. It wasn't ours to keep." He said it again in an interview with Reddit's "Ask Me Anything" in 2014: "Anything he left went back to his family. Any notes he had ever left, or messages. Because Bon was always a big writer, besides writing, you know, lyrics for the songs and ideas, he was also a big letter writer . . . one of the most prolific letter writers I ever met. Anything that was there that was his all went to his family."

Malcolm Young told Philip Wilding of *Classic Rock* in 2000: "The only thing [Ian Jeffery] ever gave me was a note with some scribblings of Bon's and that was within a few days of his death. It was something quite personal, and he didn't want to hand it to Bon's parents at the time. There were a couple of little lyrics on there but there was nothing with a title or that would give you any idea of where his head was at the time. But I kept that and I often wonder if I should send them back to Bon's mum . . . there wasn't even enough to build up into something that would stand up to Bon's reputation."

Jake Berry, the other man who went to Bon's flat, told me in 2013 he "never saw any [note]books."

83 Why was Mensch sacked? Mensch himself has said nothing, telling *Billboard* in 2016, "Who knows? They never told me."

Krebs has a theory; it involves Mensch's then-girlfriend and first wife Susan "Su" Wathan, a one-time "heavy girlfriend of David Coverdale." Krebs says AC/DC objected to Mensch bringing Wathan on tour to Australia.

"They felt she was working for the merchandising company. I got the call from [AC/DC's] lawyer. I was astounded . . . they thought [Mensch] had sold them out to the merchandise company by getting the merchandise company to pay for her to come over there to work the tour. That's absolutely why they fired him and I thought it was absurd. And I said that to them."

I ask Krebs to explain exactly what he means.

"[Wathan] sold merchandising and was flown from England to Australia at the merchandising company's expense. And [AC/DC] freaked out over that because I think they thought he was being disloyal. And to me it was like, 'What?'"

But being disloyal in which sense?

"They probably undersold [AC/DC] the merchandising deal to get them to pay for [Mensch's] girlfriend. Who knows what goes on in their minds? Look, you wrote in many pages [in *The Youngs*] how paranoid they are. That's true . . . I'm sure [Mensch] still doesn't really understand why they fired him. There's a guy named Greg Lewerke, who used to work for me. We managed Walter Egan. He told me Mensch was talking to him about getting him to leave [Leber-Krebs] with Mensch and [Cliff] Burnstein. It may be that AC/DC got upset if Mensch was approaching them about leaving us because we had all of the power, I don't know.

"As to whether Mensch made a direct approach to the members of AC/DC to leave Leber-Krebs and go with him because that's where he was moving, maybe their reaction was to blow him out. Because to fire him over his girlfriend, I never thought was enough reason. I didn't go after AC/DC [after Leber-Krebs was fired] because of all the artists I worked with my least happy relationship was with Malcolm. And I never got into the band through him. I got in through Bon, who I thought was the star, and I know you agree with me, so I know I'm talking to [*laughs*] people with conviction."

84 *Repression*'s artwork contained a handwritten homage to Bon when it was released but Trust got the date of his death wrong (22 February). When they fixed it for the English version of the album, they got it wrong again (18 February). The song "Passe" is a virtual mash-up of "Live Wire" and "Rock 'N' Roll Damnation." "Ton Dernier Acte" ("Your Final Gig") on the Tony

Platt–produced follow-up, *Marche Ou Crève*, is also a tribute to Bon. Other albums dedicated to Bon include Journey's 1981 live album *Captured* ("dedicated to the memory" of Bon, "a friend from the highway"), Flash and the Pan's *Lights In The Night* (1980) and Nantucket's *Long Way To The Top* (1980).

85   Daniel and Paul Scott, the two representatives of the Scott family that appeared at Bon's induction at the Rock & Roll Hall of Fame in 2003, were approached for this book to comment but did not respond.

86   Anyone whose musical tastes were as wide-ranging as Bon's warrants being called "quirky." He was into all kinds of music: ZZ Top, Bad Company, Flash and the Pan, Al Jolson, Kenneth McKellar ("I like Kenneth for the beautiful ballads he sings and the way he sings them," he told *Juke* magazine in 1975), Randy Newman, Roxy Music, The Rolling Stones, swing, blues, jazz, even gospel. Says Pattee Bishop: "We went to church once, and he cried; Bon wanted to go in, and we got caught up in the service [*laughs*]. I haven't been to church since, but he liked the music of the singers."

87   If Brian duly received a full one-third share of publishing royalties in perpetuity for *Back In Black*, it stands to reason he would have little reason to engage attorney George Fearon to secure him a better financial outcome in his employment by the Youngs. *Back In Black* alone would have made him a very rich man for the rest of his life. Brian *is* rich but not in the Youngs' league.

88   Malcolm Young told *VH1 Ultimate Albums*: "We didn't want to make [*Back In Black*] the story of Bon but at the same time we thought about 'He'll never die.' We wrote it around that vibe. And the good times that were involved as well, you know, in the back of a Cadillac, number one with a bullet, power pack."
        Curiously, there is supposedly a famous "mispress" of *Back In Black* with Bon inadvertently credited in a way because it contains tracks from *If You Want Blood You've Got It* (being Bon tracks). Said collector Jack Dawson to *Goldmine* magazine: "The *Back In Black* mispress: the only official *Back In Black* that actually features Bon Scott. Regarding *Back In Black*, it's my belief that Bon did actually write most of the lyrics for this one. I don't have proof of this, but the double-entendre lyrics were Bon's trademark."
        Malcolm and Bon once spoke about the similarly titled "Black Is Black" by Los Bravos in a radio interview with Sydney's 2SM in 1976. Could it have inspired the title?

89   The story of his audition and going on to replace Bon is another case where fiction seemingly has supplanted fact. In 1980, Johnson told *Trouser Press* magazine: "It's scary having to stand in the shoes of somebody who I admired a lot." Yet the man who loaned Johnson the money to go from Newcastle to London to audition for AC/DC, radio announcer James Whale, wrote of Johnson in his 2007 autobiography that "he'd never really heard of the band and wasn't very enthusiastic."

90   *VH1 Ultimate Albums* calls Brian's epiphany with the lyrics for "You Shook Me All Night Long" a "supernatural conference" with Bon: "Brian Johnson bore the burden of penning lyrics worthy of AC/DC. Inspiration came one muggy evening when the spirit of Bon Scott paid the new kid an unexpected visit — a supernatural conference he's reluctant to discuss 23 years later."
        Brian's own explanation in the documentary?
        "Something happened to me and I don't like to talk about it. But something definitely happened to me and that's all I'm going to say about it. And, uh . . . er . . . it was good. It was a good thing that happened."

91   Tony Platt told me in 2013: "Lots of lines used to get put forward. They just came from *everybody*." He told Mick Wall that "there were always a few lyrics that were missing or something that didn't quite work with the rhythm or the metre, so things got changed," which well sounds like the band was piecing lyrics around existing words or lines that were already in place. He

admitted, "It may have been that there were some lyrics lying around." Ian Jeffery also confessed to Wall: "A few of [Bon's] lines are in there [on *Back In Black*]. But not titles or anything like that. It hadn't got that far."

So if Brian wrote "You Shook Me All Night Long" in 15 minutes, as he says, why were some lyrics written by committee in the studio? Because there were snippets of lyrics from another source being used? It seems plausible, so I ask Platt to clarify how he came to be involved in the lyric writing for the song.

Regarding your involvement in the lyrics for "You Shook Me All Night Long," you've said you came up with *Working double time/On the seduction line* and that there were a number of people involved in contributing lines for that song; they were coming from everywhere. I'm interested in how that worked. Why was it collaborative for that song? Were any words from that line you came up with already in place; specifically, were you asked to come up with a complete line around a phrase like "seduction line" or "double time"?

"The context of this is *very* important. We were doing vocals at Compass Point Studios and Brian needed to pull the lyrics together for the songs. It is not unusual for lyric discussion to take place during a vocal session and everyone was involved. The key factor was interesting plays on words and I just happened to come up with that one and it stuck. There was no formal collaboration — it doesn't work like that. I contributed to the lyric in the same way as I contributed to the sound: they played, I tweaked. I think you have to get away from the concept that the sessions were especially choreographed — a great deal had to be spontaneous and perhaps that contributed to the 'spark' the album has."

So you came up with *Working double time/On the seduction line* completely from scratch, or AC/DC were already playing around with the words "double time"?

"I'm afraid I can't really remember — it's a long time ago . . . Brian certainly had the bulk of the lyrics written and he probably did do that quite quickly — it's a great riff/melody to work with. Somewhere in some vault will be the multitrack tapes and probably in the box will be my track sheets and notes, which will include the compilation sheet for the vocals.

"I think you may be digging for something that is not there. Bon was ever present during the making of that album but that was because he was there in our hearts and minds — everything else had to move on in order for the band to survive."

For what it's worth, Doubletime, Holly's horse from circa 1973/74 to 1979, was sold because she didn't have enough time to devote to it. Scrapbooks from her childhood contain drawings and jottings about horses; I've seen them for myself. She was *obsessed* with horses. How did Doubletime get the name? She was working with a horse trainer who was giving horses names containing the word "time": Overtime, Halftime, Time and Again. Coincidence? An amazing one, if that's all it is.

As for *She told me to come/But I was already there*, Brian claims it as his own handiwork. In an interview with Paul Elliott of *Classic Rock* in 2010, he said: "I thought I'd gone too far with that, I must admit, but nobody seemed to mind. There's a lot of lovely ways you can do things."

92   Brian was also presented by the two Young brothers with the title "Back In Black," as he admitted in a 2010 interview with Leona Graham of London's Absolute Radio: "They played a couple of the riffs that they had already written for *Back In Black*, just some rough riffs and they just said, 'See if you can sing,' and one of them was 'Back In Black' and that's all they had was just a title. And that's all I sang. It was [*mimics the riff*] and I'd just go, 'Back in blaaack, back in blaaack.'"

93   The themes of one of Bon's greatest songs, "Down Payment Blues" off 1978's *Powerage*, appeared earlier in a song that has never seen the light of day, "Rock 'N' Roll Blues," written during the *Dirty Deeds* sessions in 1976. The handwritten lyrics were auctioned in 2013 along with pages of untitled, barely formed ideas that contained echoes of "Kicked In The Teeth" on *Powerage* (*Two face woman why'd you put me down*), "Shot Down In Flames" on *Highway To Hell* (*Well I headed on down/To an all night bar/Where the ladies are*), and "What Do You Do For Money Honey" on *Back In Black* (*Before they let you drink/They wanna see your money first*). Ladies of the night abound in Bon's lyrics. Sold in two lots, they went for U.S.$4480 apiece.

94   Young/Young/Scott-credited albums collectively sold the same amount between 1976 and 1997.

95   Two Miamians I spoke to for *Bon: The Last Highway*, unknown to each other, claimed AC/DC played more than one show in the summer of 1977 at the 4 O'Clock Club. The claim could not be verified from documentary sources.

96   There have been persistent rumours of a show in Allentown, Pennsylvania, on 20 November 1977, but there is no hard evidence for it. Eagle-eyed fans will notice a T-shirt on AC/DC drummer Phil Rudd emblazoned with the letters "WSAN" in Jon O'Rourke's photographs of the *Powerage* sessions in early 1978, published in *The Youngs*, which suggests AC/DC went to Allentown. WSAN was the local radio station.

97   There are no reliable records of Aerosmith headlining AC/DC in Charleston, West Virginia, on 17 December 1977 despite claims in some AC/DC biographies that they did. I have not found a single reference to a 17 December concert on Aerosmith's "Draw The Line" tour. For the record, Aerosmith played shows in Quebec on the 12th and Philadelphia on the 19th. Aerosmith's first show with AC/DC appears to have taken place in 1978.

98   On 24 December 1977, *Billboard* reported that Bullwinkles, a club in New Jersey, had booked AC/DC for a gig at a newly built 3000-seat amphitheatre, but it never happened.

99   An Alice Cooper support slot with Rainbow on 29 June 1978 at the University of South Carolina Coliseum, Columbia, never happened. It was advertised in the university's *Gamecock* newspaper of 22 June 1978. The listing was likely a printing error: Cooper played Vancouver the same day.

100 AC/DC's name has cropped up in posters advertising an appearance the same day at Louisville's Summer Jam. Ted Nugent headlined Journey, Eddie Money, Starcastle and Frank Marino.

101 On 23 August 1978 the *Washington Post*'s Eve Zibart ran an item saying AC/DC was playing at Bailey's Crossroads (VA) club "Louie's Rock City, Monday and Tuesday," appearances which have never been recorded in the history books.

102 An ad was printed for a 1 October 1978 show at Waverly Beach Ballroom in Beloit, Wisconsin, but never happened. AC/DC were billed, amusingly, "From England."

103 AC/DC flew to the Netherlands for a 13 July appearance on then-public broadcaster Veronica's *Countdown* TV program in Rijnhallen, Arnhem. It was here that Angus Young met his future wife, Ellen van Lochem, who at the time was the girlfriend of Bennie Jolink, lead singer of the band Normaal. They married in London before Bon died in 1980. She's registered under the name "Ella V. Lochem."

104 Replaced "Crabsody In Blue" from the original Australian LP release (APLP.022 or APLP-022) and UK LP release (K 50366).

105 Missing from some issues of the UK LP release (SD 19180), which included "Cold Hearted Man," not contained on the American LP.

106 Parentheses were used in the title for the song, not the album of the same name.

107 Spelled as it appeared on the original album sleeve. Later corrected to "Givin'."

108 Recorded on 7 December 1977 and issued to American radio stations in 1978, it was officially released by AC/DC on the *Bonfire* box set.

GET IT HOT

Brian Johnson and, 104, 343–344, 348